SAP BusinessObjects Reporting Cookbook

Over 80 recipes to help you build, customize, and distribute reports using SAP BusinessObjects

Yoav Yahav

[PACKT] enterprise
PUBLISHING
professional expertise distilled

BIRMINGHAM - MUMBAI

SAP BusinessObjects Reporting Cookbook

First published: August 2014

Production reference: 1190814

Published by Packt Publishing Ltd.
Livery Place
35 Livery Street
Birmingham B3 2PB, UK.

ISBN 978-1-78217-243-7

www.packtpub.com

Cover image by Tony Shi (shihe99@hotmail.com)

Credits

Author
Yoav Yahav

Reviewers
Dmitry Anoshin
Charles Davies
Atul Bhimrao Divekar

Commissioning Editor
Antony Lowe

Acquisition Editor
Joanne Fitzpatrick

Content Development Editor
Nadeem Bagban

Technical Editors
Manan Badani
Menza Mathew

Copy Editors
Sarang Chari
Janbal Dharmaraj
Mradula Hegde
Insiya Morbiwala
Sayanee Mukherjee
Aditya Nair

Project Coordinator
Swati Kumari

Proofreaders
Simran Bhogal
Maria Gould
Ameesha Green
Paul Hindle

Indexer
Hemangini Bari

Graphics
Valentina D'silva
Abhinash Sahu

Production Coordinators
Arvindkumar Gupta
Alwin Roy

Cover Work
Arvindkumar Gupta
Alwin Roy

About the Author

Yoav Yahav is a BI consultant and a SAP BI expert with more than 13 years of experience in data warehouse projects and SAP BI consulting and training.

He has led numerous projects of SAP BusinessObjects implementation, from the server-side architecture through developing universes, reports, dashboards, and security.

In his projects, he implements the best practices approach while focusing on several main objectives: short time to delivery, self-service BI community, and following the most updated and advanced BI trends.

He also has rich international experience in SAP BusinessObjects training, specializing in the core SAP BusinessObjects modules. You can find his BI blog at `https://thebobaba.blogspot.com`.

About the Reviewers

Dmitry Anoshin is a self-motivated, client-focused, result-oriented certified Senior BI/DWH Consultant with more than 7 years of experience, including solid knowledge of BI tools, such as SAP BusinessObjects, SAS BI, Microstrategy, Tableau, and Microsoft BI as well as BI tools implementations in multiple business areas. He has experience in the data integration process and proficient use of various data warehousing methodologies. He constantly goes beyond project expectations while working for financial, machine tool, and retail industries.

He has completed and met deadlines for a number of multinational full BI/DWH solution life cycle implementation projects based on Teradata and Oracle databases. He has expertise in modeling (*Ralph Kimball* and *Bill Inmon*), and a background in multiple relational databases and OLAP systems along with business experience.

Charles Davies started his career in accountancy, gaining qualifications as a Chartered Management Accountant but always sat between the Accountancy and IT departments, when building systems and reports.

He has programmed old SuperCalc spreadsheets for product costing purposes. He has built statistical packages in MS Excel. He has also designed, built, and programmed SAP BusinessObjects solutions. In doing this, he has been challenging the reporting needs of businesses to ensure that the reporting and dashboarding solutions meet those requirements in a timely and cost-effective manner.

He has worked for large corporations in various industry sectors and is currently Director and Consultant of his own company Reportex Ltd., which provides SAP BusinessObjects and Xcelsius Dashboard solutions to large clients in the United Kingdom and Europe.

Atul Bhimrao Divekar has more than 5 years of rich experience in the SAP BO domain. He is currently working with Nomura Services India Pvt. Ltd. as a Senior Analyst for the BI Database and Middleware Technology group. Before joining Nomura, he was associated with Mphasis, L&T Infotech, and Angel Broking. He is a SAP BO, SAP HANA 1.0, ITIL 2011, and Linux administrator certified consultant.

He holds a BSc degree in Computer Science from Mumbai University. Apart from being a SAP BO and SAP HANA mentor, he is an ardent follower of recent technologies. So, if he is not working, then you are sure to find him on the Web learning and getting updated about the recent gadgets, mobile applications, and four wheelers in the international market.

www.PacktPub.com

Support files, eBooks, discount offers, and more

You might want to visit www.PacktPub.com for support files and downloads related to your book.

Did you know that Packt offers eBook versions of every book published, with PDF and ePub files available? You can upgrade to the eBook version at www.PacktPub.com and as a print book customer, you are entitled to a discount on the eBook copy. Get in touch with us at service@packtpub.com for more details.

At www.PacktPub.com, you can also read a collection of free technical articles, sign up for a range of free newsletters and receive exclusive discounts and offers on Packt books and eBooks.

http://PacktLib.PacktPub.com

Do you need instant solutions to your IT questions? PacktLib is Packt's online digital book library. Here, you can access, read and search across Packt's entire library of books.

Why subscribe?

- Fully searchable across every book published by Packt
- Copy and paste, print and bookmark content
- On demand and accessible via web browser

Free access for Packt account holders

If you have an account with Packt at www.PacktPub.com, you can use this to access PacktLib today and view nine entirely free books. Simply use your login credentials for immediate access.

Instant updates on new Packt books

Get notified! Find out when new books are published by following @PacktEnterprise on Twitter, or the *Packt Enterprise* Facebook page.

Table of Contents

Preface

BI launch pad (formerly known as Infoview) is the BI web portal of the SAP BusinessObjects Business Intelligence (BI) platform.

As a web portal, it provides access to the reports for business users, data consumers, and report developers, which are deployed into business folder structures that contain the BI content that is mainly reports from different kinds and types.

Through BI launch pad, we can open, refresh, manage, and schedule reports in ways similar to how we interact with familiar applications such as Office.

Through BI launch pad, we can run various BI applications that can access various databases and data sources, such as Excel and text files.

The main BI application is Web Intelligence, which is aimed at reporting and analyzing, and by using it, we can accomplish the following:

- Create simple and complex reports by using drag-and-drop, ease-of-use techniques
- Unify multiple data sources into one report
- Format the results with rich capabilities
- Perform drills and analyze the data from various angles
- Share, schedule and export the report results to various formats, such as Excel, PDF, Word, HTML, and more

What this book covers

Chapter 1, *Working with the BI Launch Pad*, provides information about the BI launch pad environment, how to work with reports and other types of applications, and how to adjust the BI launch pad preferences to match our requirements.

Chapter 2, *Creating New Queries*, provides all-round recipes to build simple and advanced queries, create complex filters, and get acquainted with fundamental terms in query building while also using best practices.

Chapter 3, *Working Inside the Report*, shows the report structure, how to use the various toolbars and functional panes of the report, and how to work with the different application modes and report properties.

Chapter 4, *Working with Tables*, provides recipes to create tables, explains which type of table is suited for which type of data, and demonstrates how to work with crosstab tables and how to adjust the table properties.

Chapter 5, *Working with Charts*, teaches you to use the different chart types and helps you understand which chart is suitable for the right type of data.

Chapter 6, *Formatting Reports*, explains in depth how to work with each toolbar and apply simple and advanced functionality to the report data, such as sorting, calculations, and ranking.

Chapter 7, *Filtering the Report Data*, explains and provides filtering techniques we can apply to the report tables and charts.

Chapter 8, *Merging Data*, shows us how to combine and synchronize data from several queries, universes, and data sources as well as using Excel as the data provider.

Chapter 9, *Using Formulas and Variables*, explains how to use the formula libraries, demonstrates how to build new calculations, and how to use variables in our reports.

Chapter 10, *Using Hyperlinks*, teaches us how to connect reports, how to pass parameters between them, and how to connect to external websites directly from our reports.

Chapter 11, *Using Drill*, teaches you how to use the drill, understand the hierarchy structure, and perform drill up, down, and through the data.

Chapter, 12, *Scheduling Reports*, provides recipes to create scheduled jobs and publications that will run and distribute our reports to various destinations and formats.

Chapter 13, *Working with BI Workspaces*, shows you how to create workspaces that will centralize our most important content and reports' data on one screen.

Chapter 14, *Web Intelligence Rich Client*, teaches you about the Web Rich Client application, its capabilities, differences, advantages, and disadvantages compared with Web Intelligence.

Appendix, Applying Best Practices, QA, and Tips and Tricks to Our Reports, provides numerous ways to apply best practices, how to perform QA, and provides tips and tricks and useful formulas. You can find this appendix online from: `https://www.packtpub.com/sites/default/files/downloads/2437EN_Appendix.pdf`

What you need for this book

In order to use this book, you will require access to:

- SAP BI4 server, SP2 and above
- Java Runtime Oracle JRE 6(*5)
- A Web browser—Internet Explorer 8 and above, Google Chrome, Mozilla, or Safari

You will be required to obtain rights to create Web Intelligence reports and have access to demo universes, such as Island resort marketing, eFashion, Motors, and Warehouse universes.

For the exact supported platforms (PAM) you can refer to the SAP official document at:
`http://www.sdn.sap.com/irj/scn/go/portal/prtroot/docs/library/`
`uuid/507d3365-009b-3010-04b0-e5abc8f00c91?QuickLink=index&overridelay`
`out=true&59407987714033`.

The data in the examples is quite basic and similar, any one of the universes mentioned can be used to create the reports across the book's chapters.

For *Chapter 14*, *Web Intelligence Rich Client*, you will require a local installation of Web Rich Client.

Who this book is for

This book is for Web Intelligence developers who are mainly beginners—users that want to extend their knowledge and get a set of tools of analysis and reporting. The book is also for analysts and data workers who require a better and deeper understanding in the ways they can extract, analyze, and display data. Besides this, the book caters to BI developers that want to get familiar with Web Intelligence and IT staff. Finally, it is also for managers that need to estimate and adopt a new BI technology.

This book provides hands-on and numerous practical examples, concepts, and real-life scenarios based on practical experience.

Conventions

In this book, you will find a number of styles of text that distinguish between different kinds of information. Here are some examples of these styles and an explanation of their meaning.

Code words in text, database table names, folder names, filenames, file extensions, pathnames, dummy URLs, user input, and Twitter handles are shown as follows: "The behind-the-scenes workflow can be thought of as the detailed query running on the `States with sales revenue greater than 7 million` table."

New terms and **important words** are shown in bold. Words that you see on the screen, in menus or dialog boxes for example, appear in the text like this: "Variables in the BEx query can be selected or ignored in the **Query Panel**."

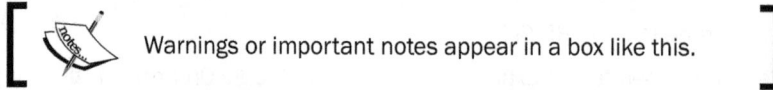

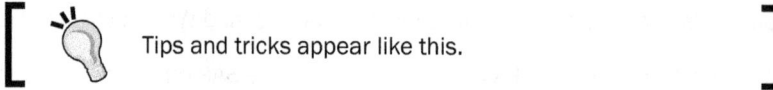

> Warnings or important notes appear in a box like this.

> Tips and tricks appear like this.

Reader feedback

Feedback from our readers is always welcome. Let us know what you think about this book—what you liked or may have disliked. Reader feedback is important for us to develop titles that you really get the most out of.

To send us general feedback, simply send an e-mail to feedback@packtpub.com, and mention the book title via the subject of your message.

If there is a topic that you have expertise in and you are interested in either writing or contributing to a book, see our author guide on www.packtpub.com/authors.

Customer support

Now that you are the proud owner of a Packt book, we have a number of things to help you to get the most from your purchase.

Errata

Although we have taken every care to ensure the accuracy of our content, mistakes do happen. If you find a mistake in one of our books—maybe a mistake in the text or the code—we would be grateful if you would report this to us. By doing so, you can save other readers from frustration and help us improve subsequent versions of this book. If you find any errata, please report them by visiting http://www.packtpub.com/submit-errata, selecting your book, clicking on the **errata submission form** link, and entering the details of your errata. Once your errata are verified, your submission will be accepted and the errata will be uploaded on our website, or added to any list of existing errata, under the Errata section of that title. Any existing errata can be viewed by selecting your title from http://www.packtpub.com/support.

Piracy

Piracy of copyright material on the Internet is an ongoing problem across all media. At Packt, we take the protection of our copyright and licenses very seriously. If you come across any illegal copies of our works, in any form, on the Internet, please provide us with the location address or website name immediately so that we can pursue a remedy.

Please contact us at copyright@packtpub.com with a link to the suspected pirated material.

We appreciate your help in protecting our authors, and our ability to bring you valuable content.

Questions

You can contact us at questions@packtpub.com if you are having a problem with any aspect of the book, and we will do our best to address it.

1
Working with the BI Launch Pad

In this chapter, we will cover the following recipes:

- ▶ Connecting to the BI launch pad
- ▶ Navigating within the BI launch pad
- ▶ Using the BI launch pad toolbars
- ▶ Adjusting the preferences
- ▶ Searching documents
- ▶ Launching applications
- ▶ The report menu functionality
- ▶ Working with different objects of the BI launch pad

Introduction

SAP BusinessObjects BI Platform is a worldwide leading BI platform that enables organizations and enterprises to improve their entire way of working by getting better business decisions and insights about each and every aspect of the organization's business processes, whether it's sales goals that require tracking, chain management, billing, revenue from sales of products, amount that the organization spends on salaries, measuring net profit, and so on.

In the 21st century—an era of mass data explosion and information that can be pulled from an endless list of data sources, which can be found in social networks, files, multiple databases, and unstructured data—we can say for sure that an organization without a solid BI platform will find it very hard to manage its resources, respond to the rapidly changing financial reality, or even fail to perform common and simple tasks such as reporting to its customers.

The BI launch pad (formerly known as **InfoView**) is the BI web portal of the SAP BusinessObjects Business Intelligence (BI) platform.

The BI launch pad is the core of the entire SAP BusinessObjects platform since it unifies the following two main aspects of the organizational BI layer:

> ▸ The BI content is stored here. The content includes reports that are created by the different types of SAP BusinessObjects applications and are published to the BI launch pad environment.

> ▸ Through the BI launch pad, we can launch various types of SAP BusinessObjects BI applications that are suited for the different tasks of data manipulation, whether it's a simple reporting and analysis report, a fancy dashboard, or a pivot table slicing an OLAP cube.

As a web environment, the BI launch pad can be accessed using a web browser such as Internet Explorer or Google Chrome through a local site that can also be accessed from outside the organization like any other website.

The BI content can also be easily accessed from mobile devices and tablets.

The BI launch pad environment supports various login methods such as Windows Active directory, SAP login, LDAP, and SAP BusinessObjects enterprise, which enables organizations to integrate their existing login method with the BI portal and client applications as well. The entire BI content is secured. Only users with the appropriate rights can access reports; this is one of the most important aspects of the BI environment as reports may display sensitive data such as sales figures, salaries, and data that should be secured like credit card numbers.

The data in the database can be secured as well by what is known as **row level security**, enabling common data security scenarios such as region managers viewing the sales per region report to retrieve only the relevant data for the region manager.

The rights for the BusinessObjects applications are secured as well, and we will usefully come across the following two main user types:

> ▸ **Report builders**: Users who can create new reports and use most of the report functionality such as slice and dice, sorting, and performing calculations and drilling

> ▸ **Report viewers**: Business users who mainly refresh exiting reports and use thin report functionality, mainly focusing on getting the most updated results and analyzing the data

The main and core functionalities of the BI launch pad are:

- ► Creating and modifying reports
- ► Rich report functionality
- ► Analysis and drill tools
- ► Sharing corporate and personal reports such as documents, dashboards, and exploration views
- ► Scheduling reports to e-mail, inbox, file folders, and FTP
- ► Reports that can be saved to Excel, PDF, CSV, Word, and HTML formats

Since data can be defined and analyzed in many different ways and there are different requirements on how to pull and display the data, the SAP BusinessObjects BI platform supplies various different BI tools that are categorized according to the following data requirements:

- ► **Reporting**: This is the main BI tool in almost every enterprise aiming to establish a self service BI approach. It enables non-IT users to build their own reports, ad hoc querying, and reporting based on various data sources. Under the SAP BI suite, we can find **Web Intelligence**, which is the core BI product and our book reporting tool, and also **Crystal Reports**, which enables you to create highly formatted reports.

- ► **Dashboards**: This is for creating beautiful and visualized interactive dashboards that can display monitored data, KPIs, and mainly aggregative data for the executive board and top managers. Here, we can find the **Dashboard Design** and **Design Studio** dashboarding tools; both are covered in separate books.

- ► **Analytics**: Although there are many tools that can be found under this category, I will focus on two of them that can also be launched from the BI launch pad: **SAP BusinessObjects Explorer** and **SAP BusinessObjects Analysis**. While the second tool mainly focuses on analyzing OLAP cubes such as BW, HANA, Essbase, Analysis Services, and other OLAP sources, by using traditional OLAP mutlidimensional slicing and dicing, the first tool enables data exploration by using simple search engines and getting highly visualized answers that also support geographical presentations (maps).

Almost every enterprise is combined with different audiences and different data structures that need to be analyzed in different ways supported by a specific functionality; this answers why we will usually come across at least one BI tool, either web-based or a client one.

This book focuses on the Web Intelligence BI tool, which I call the bread and butter of every BI environment.

Connecting to the BI launch pad

Our first practical step will be to log in to the BI launch pad environment using the common Internet Explorer web browser.

Getting ready

We want to access the BI launch pad and view which reports are displayed in our main home screen window.

How to do it...

Open a web browser that is installed on your computer and type the SAP BI4 server URL in the address bar.

Usually, the server URL is `http://ServerName:8080/BOE/BI`.

On the login page that will appear, we will choose the authentication type **Enterprise**, as shown in the following screenshot, and enter our username and password that are usually supplied by the SAP BI4 administrator:

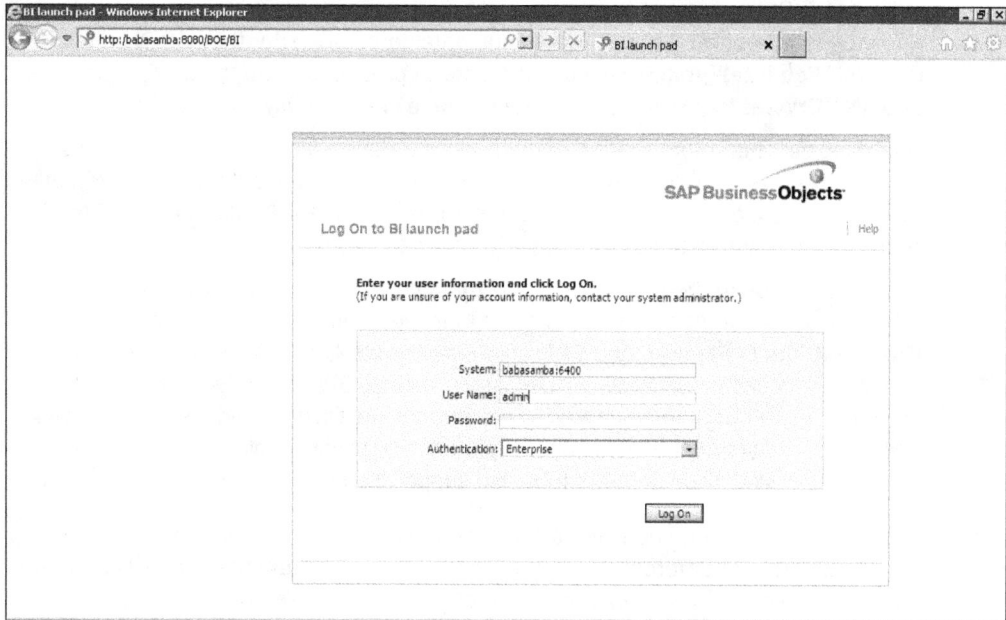

After successful login, we will reach the main home screen, which by default displays four main report areas, an application launch bar, and a main home tab.

There is also a general top-right toolbar that enables options such as **Log Off**, **Preferences**, search, and running applications, as shown in the following screenshot:

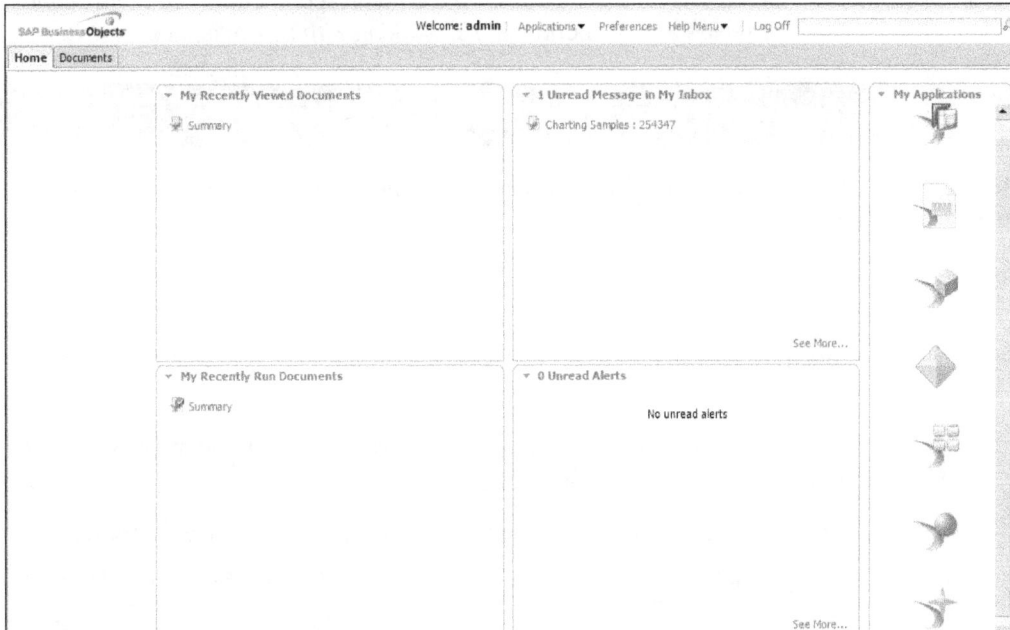

How it works...

The BI launch pad is a web application being run and hosted on the SAP BI4 server, and it functions as a website that can be accessed through a web browser, allowing the users and the organization to access their BI content using the Internet.

This setup requires configuration at the server side, IT, and security within the organization, but is considered a basic practice that leverages the launch pad accessibility and usability.

> You can bookmark the BI launch pad web address in your browser favorites.

There's more...

The login screen and the home screen can be customized and can be changed so that the look and feel will fit the organizational format and logo as well as the user requirements by using the customization kit.

See also

▸   For further information on how to customize the home screen, refer to the *Adjusting the preferences* recipe and also *Chapter 13, Working with BI Workspaces*

Navigating within the BI launch pad

The BI launch pad main screen is tab-oriented just like in any Internet browser. The main screen centralizes the most important and relevant views for the user.

Getting ready

We want to navigate from the main home screen and explore the other options as well as understand the main screen options.

The **Home** tab is the default tab. This screen is divided into the following five major parts and another report navigation tab:

▸   **My Recently Viewed Documents**: This shows the user their last viewed reports

▸   **Messages In My Inbox**: This shows the reports that have been sent to the user by other users or by scheduling jobs

▸   **My Recently Run Documents**: This shows which reports were last run by the user, as shown in the following screenshot:

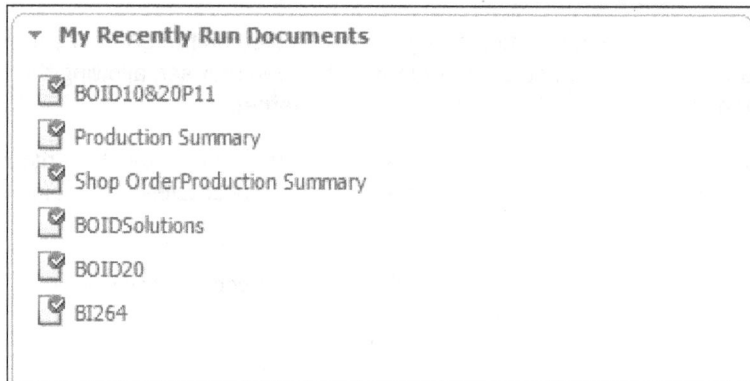

▾ **My Recently Run Documents**

    ☑ BOID10&20P11

    ☑ Production Summary

    ☑ Shop OrderProduction Summary

    ☑ BOIDSolutions

    ☑ BOID20

    ☑ BI264

▸   **Unread Alerts**: This shows alerts relating to specific trigger results in Crystal Reports

- **My Applications**: This is located at the right-hand side of the main screen, as shown in the following screenshot, and can launch various types of BI tools and special launch pad objects:

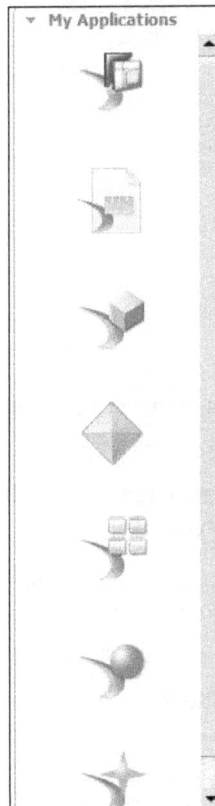

How to do it...

By clicking on any report name in any one of the report subareas, the relevant report will open and display its data. The relevancy of the data in the report is dependent on the date and time the report was refreshed and saved. For example, we can open a report that ran on yesterday's data three days ago.

The **Documents** tab presents the user-personal folder, inbox, and other personal objects such as alerts and subscribed alerts, as shown in the following screenshot.

The main folder is the personal folder where the user can watch all their private reports.

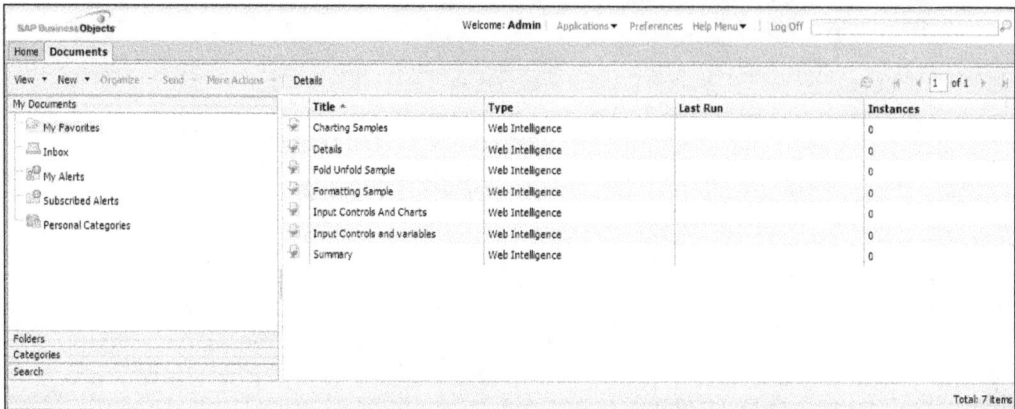

Under the user-private objects, there is an accordion menu that can direct us to the public folder view.

In **Public Folders**, we will be able to view, depending on the user's security, the organizational/company report tree structure.

In the public folder, all kinds of reports are kept and are ready to be used by the various types of users. This folder also has a structure that corresponds to the departmental divisions of the organization.

Here, the user can simply navigate to the relevant folders that they use, as shown in the following screenshot:

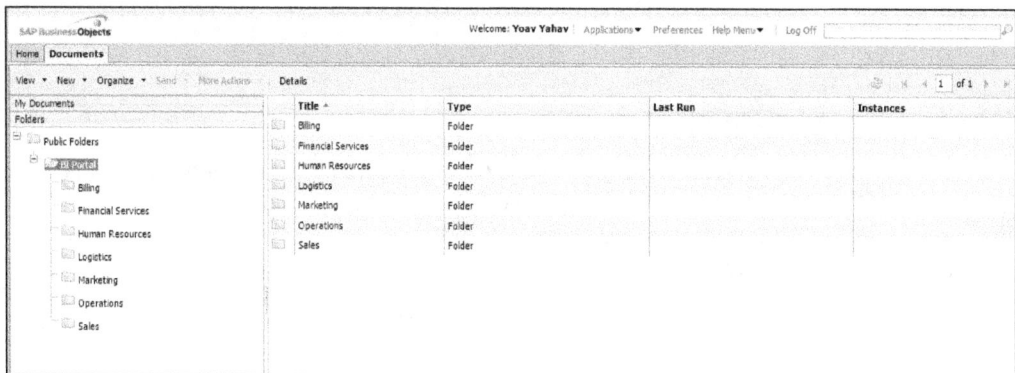

How it works...

The BI launch pad also enables simple file-folder navigation, allowing the user to switch between their personal data and views and the public and corporate reports, which are organized in a folder structure.

> The public folder structure is organized by data areas, the organizational department structure, the type of data, or any other logical grouping that makes sense.

See also

- ▸ For information on searching, refer to the *Searching documents* recipe
- ▸ For information on how to work with different applications, refer to the *Launching applications* recipe and *Chapter 2, Creating New Queries*

Using the BI launch pad toolbars

When we switch to the **Documents** tab, we will be able to see a toolbar located at the top-left of the screen. This toolbar is used for general functionality that can be applied to the reports and objects hosted in the BI launch pad, as shown in the following screenshot:

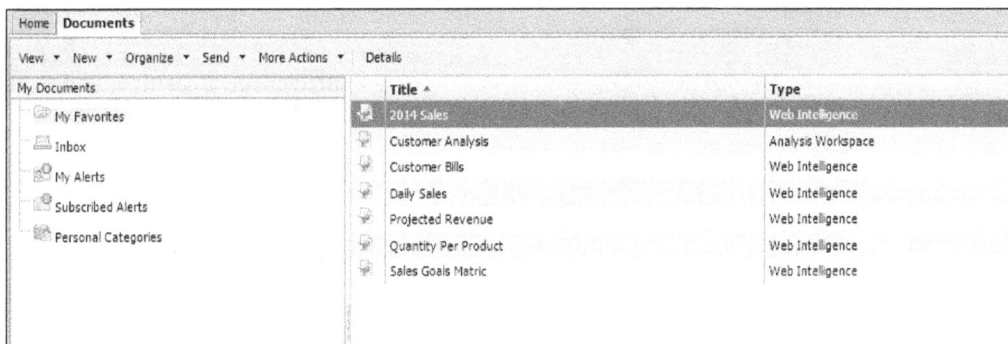

Home	Documents		
View ▾ New ▾ Organize ▾ Send ▾ More Actions ▾ Details			
My Documents	**Title** ▴	**Type**	
My Favorites	2014 Sales	Web Intelligence	
Inbox	Customer Analysis	Analysis Workspace	
My Alerts	Customer Bills	Web Intelligence	
Subscribed Alerts	Daily Sales	Web Intelligence	
Personal Categories	Projected Revenue	Web Intelligence	
	Quantity Per Product	Web Intelligence	
	Sales Goals Matric	Web Intelligence	

This toolbar enables us to perform basic functionalities that will help us to easily manage the reports by using the following options:

- ▸ **View**: This enables the user to view a marked report and get the report properties (location, report description, and created and last modified dates)
- ▸ **New**: This enables the user to build a new folder under the private folder or under the public folder tree, adding a local Crystal Report and office files and building a new publication (a scheduled report job) and a hyperlink.

The following options are available from the toolbar only if a report is marked:

- ▸ **Organize**: This cuts, copies, creates shortcuts, and deletes the report
- ▸ **Send**: This sends the report to another user or group inbox
- ▸ **More Actions**: This modifies the report, schedules the report, creates a link to the report, and also adds the report to a category

How to do it...

We can use the BI launch pad toolbars by performing the following steps:

1. We will mark a specific report in one of the public folders. Click on the **Organize** button and choose **Copy**, as shown in the following screenshot:

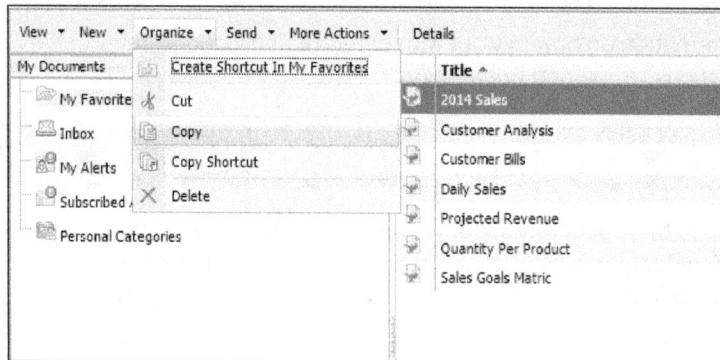

2. Go to your private folder and click on it. Go to the toolbar, click on **Organize**, and choose **Paste**, as shown in the following screenshot:

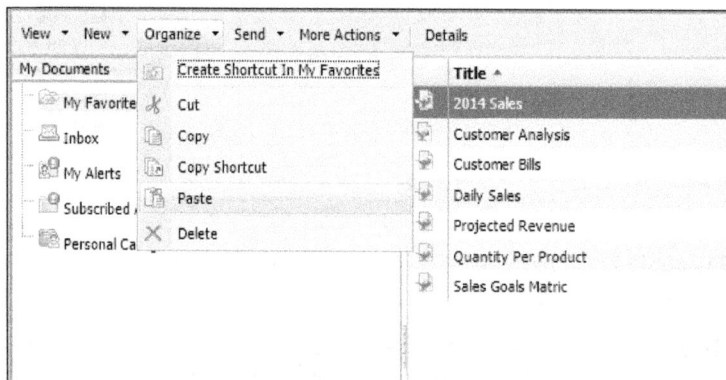

The report has been copied.

> Copy is probably the most common action ever in any application we have worked with, but on the other hand, a quite painful one as business users can copy and paste reports to multiple destinations, sometimes for the wrong reasons, causing report inflation and multiple copies of the report. Is it because of a slight change in the report or because you require another version for scheduling? It's best to consult your SAP BI administrator.

How it works...

The availability of the toolbar is based on marking the relevant object; once we do that and mark, for example, a report, the main toolbar becomes fully available.

See also

- For information on working with scheduled jobs, hyperlinks, and other options, refer to the *Working with different objects of the BI launch pad* recipe

Adjusting the preferences

The preferences are a set of options that can adjust and configure the BI launch pad default environment's behavior. We can find among the preferences options that can change the user password, define a new look and feel for the Home tab, or even create shortcuts for a preferred public or private folder.

How to do it...

The **Preferences** button is located in the BI launch pad main bar, as shown in the following screenshot:

SAP BusinessObjects

Welcome: **Yoav.Yahav** | Applications ▼ Preferences Help Menu ▼ | Log Off

Home | Documents

By clicking on the **Preferences** button, a new screen will appear, structured from the following seven main categories:

► **General**: In this tab, the user can adjust the look and feel of the **Home** and **Document** tabs, for example, the **Document** tab can be adjusted in a way that every time the user switches to this tab, a specific public folder that they mainly work with will immediately show its content, as shown in the following screenshot:

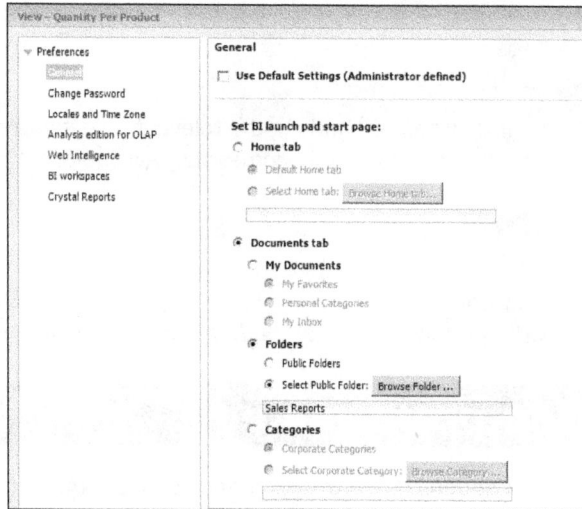

In the next frame, the user can adjust the columns that will appear in the Report list view:

The last option in the general category is adjusting the working mode of the Internet browser with the reports. Another option is fixing the number of reports per page, as shown in the following screenshot:

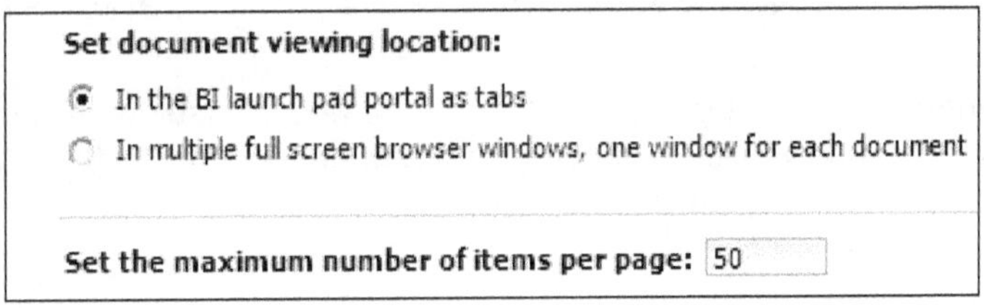

Set document viewing location:

⦿ In the BI launch pad portal as tabs

○ In multiple full screen browser windows, one window for each document

Set the maximum number of items per page: 50

▸ **Change Password**: In this category, the user can change their password:

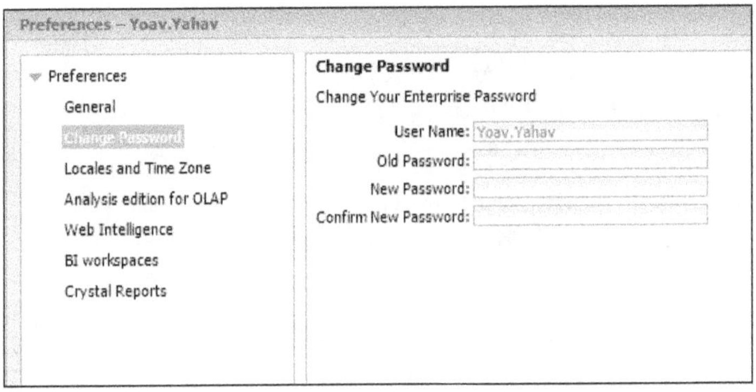

Preferences – Yoav.Yahav

▾ Preferences

  General

  Change Password

  Locales and Time Zone

  Analysis edition for OLAP

  Web Intelligence

  BI workspaces

  Crystal Reports

Change Password

Change Your Enterprise Password

          User Name: Yoav.Yahav

      Old Password:

     New Password:

Confirm New Password:

▸ **Locales and Time Zone**: In this category, the user can adjust the product, language, and time zone locales. These definitions are mainly important to maintain the local conventions of date, numbers, and time that will be applied on the viewed objects such as reports, object names, and descriptions, as shown:

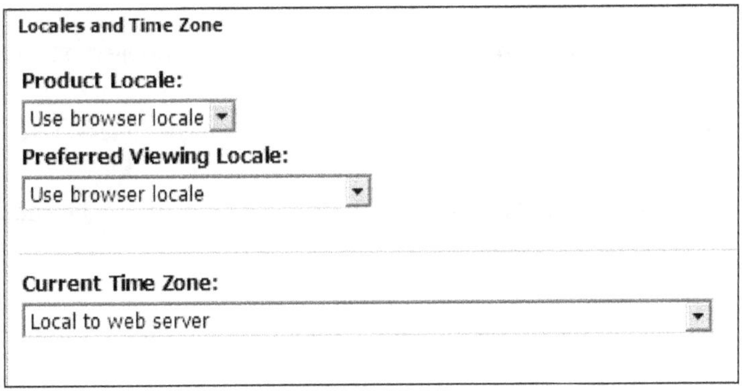

Locales and Time Zone

Product Locale:

Use browser locale ▾

Preferred Viewing Locale:

Use browser locale ▾

Current Time Zone:

Local to web server ▾

▶ **Analysis edition for OLAP**: This defines the connections to OLAP analysis that will be used to create new workspaces.

▶ **Web Intelligence**: This category sets several important options. The **View** and **Modify** options can be adjusted to thin or rich functionality, but are also fitted to non-Java environments.

If Java runtime is installed and ran through the web browser, then choosing **Rich Client Application** would be the preferred view and will modify the options to enhance the Web Intelligence functionality.

Web Intelligence

View

          ○ Web (no download required)

          ◉ Rich Internet Application (download required)

          ○ Desktop (Windows only) (installation required)

          ○ PDF

Modify (creating, editing and analyzing documents):

This is also the interface launched from the Go To list or My Applications shortcut.

          ○ Web (no download required)

          ◉ Rich Internet Application (download required)

          ○ Desktop (installation required)

The **Select a default Universe** option enables the user to set a default universe for new report creation.

Drill Options control which drill options will take effect:

❑ **Prompt when drill requires additional data**: In case the drill results in fetching another query, the user will get a prompt notification before the query will run again

❑ **Synchronize drill on report blocks**: Drill will be applied on all report blocks (tables, charts, and so on)

❑ **Hide Drill toolbar on startup**: The drill bar will be hidden when starting a new drill

❑ **Start a drill session**: This will start the drill on a current or new report

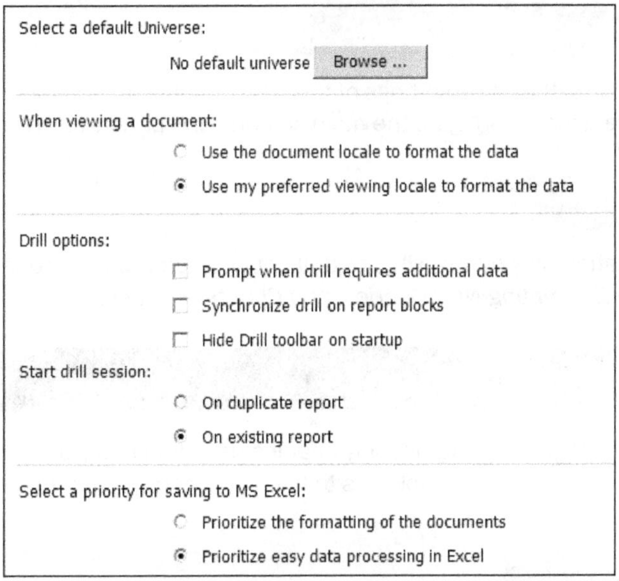

Select a default Universe:

No default universe | Browse ...

When viewing a document:
○ Use the document locale to format the data
◉ Use my preferred viewing locale to format the data

Drill options:
☐ Prompt when drill requires additional data
☐ Synchronize drill on report blocks
☐ Hide Drill toolbar on startup

Start drill session:
○ On duplicate report
◉ On existing report

Select a priority for saving to MS Excel:
○ Prioritize the formatting of the documents
◉ Prioritize easy data processing in Excel

> ❑ **Select a priority for saving to MS Excel**: This sets the format options of a Web Intelligence document when scheduled and the report output is saved as an Excel file:

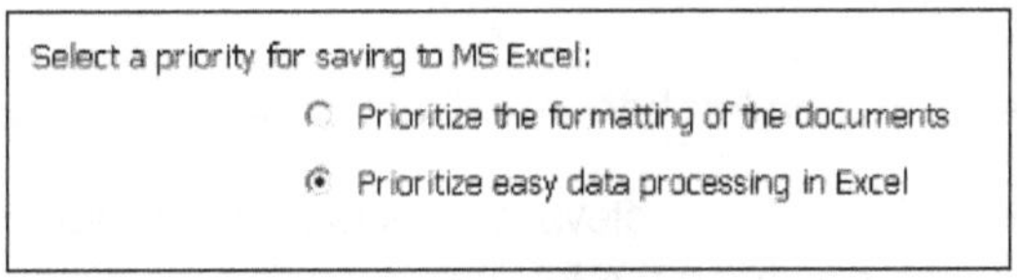

Select a priority for saving to MS Excel:
○ Prioritize the formatting of the documents
◉ Prioritize easy data processing in Excel

> ▶ **BI workspaces**: In this category, a workspace's style and grid can be adjusted, as shown in the following screenshot:

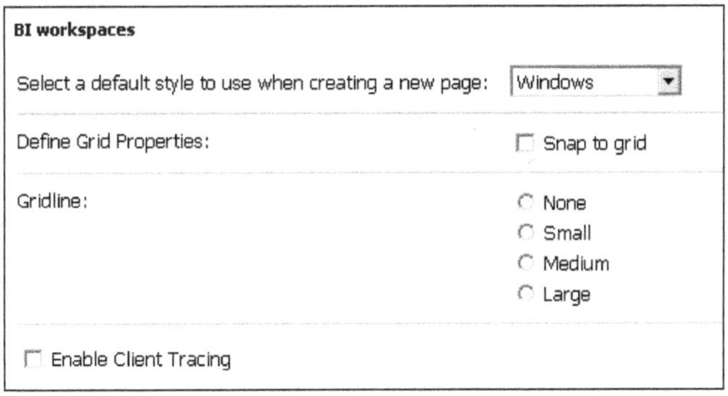

BI workspaces

Select a default style to use when creating a new page: | Windows ▼

Define Grid Properties: | ☐ Snap to grid

Gridline:
○ None
○ Small
○ Medium
○ Large

☐ Enable Client Tracing

> ▶ **Crystal Reports**: This category sets the viewing options for crystal reports.

How it works...

The preferences control the basic settings of the view options, the BI launch pad's look and feel, and enable the user to configure the main screens and panels for their way of working.

See also

- ▶ For information on working with the drill options, refer to the *Scope of analysis* recipe of *Chapter 2, Creating New Queries*, and *Chapter 11, Using Drill*

Searching documents

Searching across the BI launch pad not only enables us to find reports without knowing their location or entire name, but also enables us to look for reports that are using a specific object or even specific data.

Getting ready

We are looking for a report that relates to the sales revenue.

How to do it...

Using the search engine on the top-left bar, we will enter the search words `sales revenue`.

The results will be presented in a list of relevant objects that correspond to the search results as well as categorized search results in the left panel, such as by type of the report, folder location, and objects, as shown in the following screenshot:

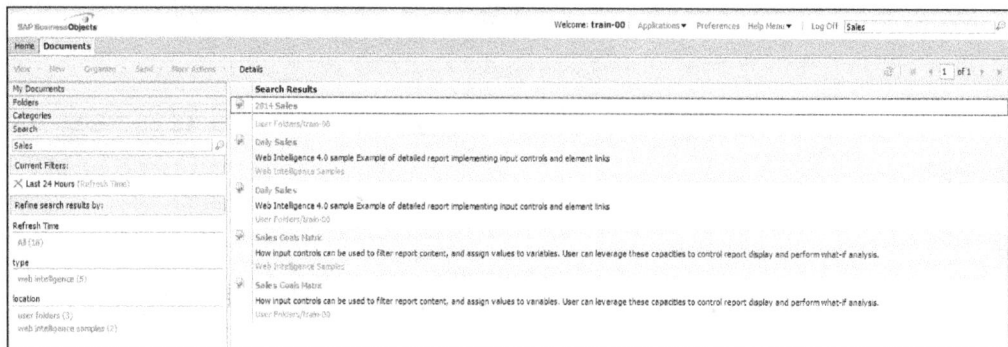

How it works...

All the objects in the BI launch pad are being indexed, and as a consequence, this allows the user to search reports not just by the report name, but also by the data inside the reports.

There's more...

The search results can be expanded by clicking on the bottom option **Show More Filters**.

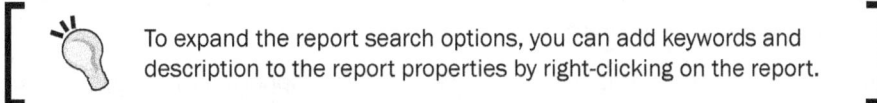

> To expand the report search options, you can add keywords and description to the report properties by right-clicking on the report.

Launching applications

The BI launch pad hosts various reporting and analysis tools, and each one serves a different purpose.

In the **Applications** launch bar, we can find six different applications. The following options are available from the toolbar only if a report is marked:

- ▸ **Module**: This is a module created to be used and embedded in **BI Workspaces**
- ▸ **Analysis edition for OLAP**: This can access OLAP cubes from SAP BW and non-SAP data sources such as MS Analysis
- ▸ **Crystal Reports**: This is a client reporting tool with enhanced formatting capabilities
- ▸ **BI Workspaces**: This creates a BI workspace and can present different reports and BI launch pad parts in one screen
- ▸ **Web Intelligence**: This is the main reporting and analysis tool
- ▸ **Explorer**: This is a search and navigation tool that can find answers to user business questions
- ▸ **BEx Web Applications**: These can be accessed from the BI launch pad once created in the BW environment

We distinguish between two types of applications by their way of launch:

- ▸ Applications that run through the BI launch pad environment tab and don't require any extra installation (BEx Web Applications, Module, BI Workspaces, Explorer, and Web Intelligence)

> ▸ Applications that require local client installation and only supply quick and centralized access to those applications that will be opened locally on the user's machine (currently only Crystal Reports)

As we discussed in the *Introduction* section, the set of different reporting tools handles different aspects of data as well as different functional requirements, for example, an interactive report versus a data presentation that doesn't require drilling or analysis.

As a prerequisite for the successful running of the different web applications, a Java runtime environment is required to be installed on the user's machine or terminal; the installation part of Java is usually done by IT, but can also be downloaded manually by the user the first time they launch an application that uses Java.

To get the exact information about which Java versions are supported by which web browser, you can refer to this official guide at *SAP BusinessObjects BI Platform 4.1 Supported Platforms (PAM)* at `http://www.sdn.sap.com/irj/scn/go/portal/prtroot/docs/library/uuid/507d3365-009b-3010-04b0-e5abc8f00c91?QuickLink=index&overridelayout=true&58879706677981.`

Getting ready

In order to create a report using Web Intelligence, we will launch the appropriate application from the home screen and the right-hand side application launch bar, as shown in the following screenshot:

How to do it...

By clicking on the Web Intelligence icon, the Java runtime message will pop up first asking us to enable this application to run.

Once this application is approved, the message won't reoccur and we will be able to launch Web Intelligence and other applications that are using the Java runtime without the following intermediate stage:

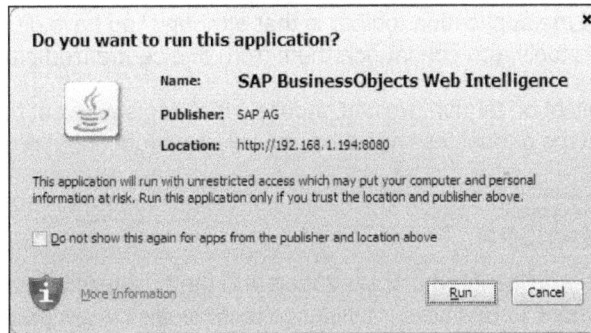

The Java runtime activates an applet that enables rich functionality while working with Web Intelligence reports. This option can be configured by changing it in the Web Intelligence category. In order to get a better understanding of what are the differences in terms of functionality between Java and the HTML panel, I suggest you to read: `http://scn.sap.com/community/businessobjects-web-intelligence/blog/2013/12/16/feature-differences-between-the-web-intelligence-clients-bi41-sp02`. Now, the report interface will be launched and will be ready for the next step of creating the Web Intelligence report, as shown in the following screenshot:

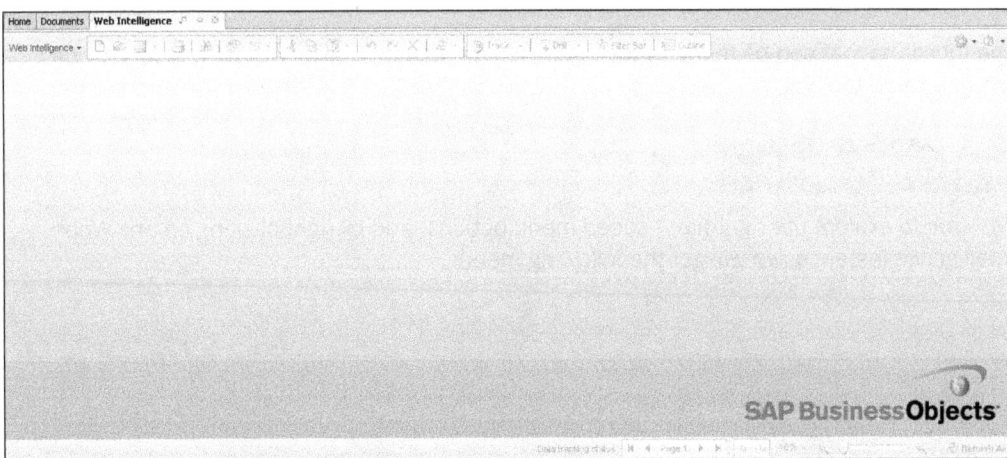

> You can also launch applications while viewing a report or from the **Documents** tab by using the **Applications** button on the top main toolbar.

How it works...

The BI launch pad can access all the report applications from one main toolbar.

The main idea behind the application toolbar is that although you have different types of reporting and analysis tools, you can launch them from one centralized place.

Working with the application launch, we can choose which tools we want to operate and address the relevant type of business question as well as its functional requirements.

There's more...

The question of which application the organization and the business users should adopt is one of the main questions in Business Intelligence technologies in general, and can easily fill an entire book.

For further reading on this matter, I recommend reading the official SAP article regarding choosing the right SAP BusinessObjects BI client at `http://scn.sap.com/docs/DOC-38981`, or just search `Which BI tool + SAP BI4` on Google.

The report menu functionality

Another way to interact with the report functionality and other different objects in the folders is by using the right-click menu.

The functions that can be found in the right-click menu are equivalent to the BI launch pad left-hand side toolbar.

Getting ready

We want to explore the right-hand speed menu options, and by right-clicking on any Web Intelligence instance, we will get the following menu:

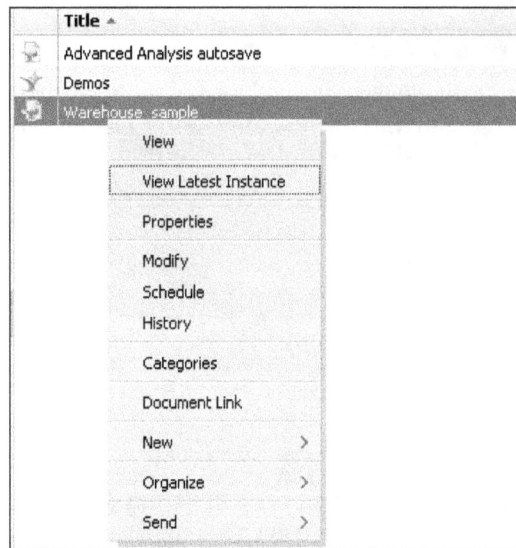

The report menu has the following options:

- ▶ **View**: This can be used to view the report results
- ▶ **View Last Instance**: This can be used to view the last report scheduled result
- ▶ **Properties**: This can be used to view and edit the report properties such as report name, keywords, and description
- ▶ **Modify**: This switches to edit mode of the report
- ▶ **Schedule**: This schedules the report by time and destination
- ▶ **History**: This is used for viewing the report schedule history
- ▶ **Categories**: This is used for attaching the report to a category
- ▶ **Document Link**: This creates a link to a specific report
- ▶ **New**: This is used for creating a new folder, publication (an advanced schedule), hyperlink, or a local file (crystal or office files upload)
- ▶ **Organize**: The following are the options available under **Organize**:
  - ❑ **Create Shortcut In My Favorites**: This creates a shortcut in the user's favorite folder
  - ❑ **Cut**: This cuts the report
  - ❑ **Copy**: This copies the report
  - ❑ **Copy Shortcut**: This copies the shortcut to a specific destination
  - ❑ **Delete**: This deletes the report
- ▶ **Send**: This sends the report to a user's inbox

How to do it...

In order to view a report's schedule history, right-click on the report name. Go to the **History** option. In the next screen, we can view the report's history data, as shown in the following screenshot:

Instance Time ▾	Title	Status	Created By	Type	Parameters
Nov 23, 2013 6:40 PM	Fold Unfold Sample	Success	admin	Web Intelligence	

History – Fold Unfold Sample

How it works...

As we have seen, the right-click menu simply enables us the same functionality as in the main toolbar by speeding up the basic functions that can be applied on a report.

See also

▸ For further information on how to schedule reports, refer to *Chapter 12, Scheduling Reports*

Working with different objects of the BI launch pad

Working with objects in the BI launch pad can be categorized into two main types:

▸ **Reports**: Working with the different types of reports created by the various BI applications such as Web Intelligence, Crystal Report, Analysis, and Explorer

▸ **Non-report objects or simply BI launch pad objects**: Publications (advanced schedule objects), hyperlinks, folders, categories, and local files are used mainly for organizing objects, scheduling, and adding external files such as office files

Getting ready

We want to understand the basic difference between folders and categories.

Folders and categories are both used for report organizing and grouping, while folders can be seen as the physical layer that actually contains the files, and categories are the logical layer enabling report navigation and can be seen as a pointer to a folder.

The basic idea behind categories is that this structure supports multiple locations by using one report file.

The system administrator can give permissions to a folder while organizing the reports in a totally different category structure.

How to do it...

We want to add one of the reports to a category. We will right-click on one of our reports and choose **Categories**, as shown in the following screenshot:

Title ⌃	
Fold Unfold Sample	
Formatting S	View
Input Contrc	View Latest Instance
Input Contrc	Properties
	Modify
	Schedule
	History
	Categories
	Document Link
	New >
	Organize >
	Send >

In the next screen, we will chose the category that we want to add the report to:

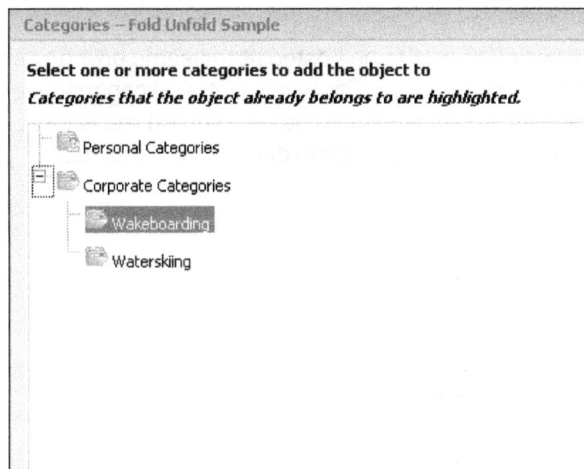

Categories – Fold Unfold Sample

Select one or more categories to add the object to
Categories that the object already belongs to are highlighted.

- Personal Categories
- Corporate Categories
  - Wakeboarding
  - Waterskiing

After adding the report to the category, we can navigate to the report and confirm that the report is there, as shown in the following screenshot:

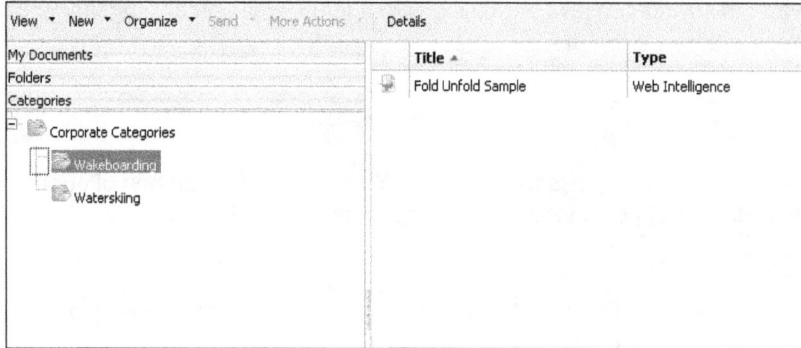

How it works...

As we have seen, the BI launch pad is the heart of the SAP BI environment that contains all kinds of different objects: report file types, scheduled objects, hyperlinks, and other type of objects.

All the objects can be organized in a folder structure and can be grouped in a category structure as well.

Once we have the basic structure of the report's folders, we can allow users from the entire organization to access, share, send, edit, and create reports in one secured and easily accessed environment.

By enabling different types of objects to be hosted at the same environment, the organization can adopt a centralized approach towards its BI content, and can manage and run the reports, automatic scheduled jobs, users, and other standard repository objects that can be accessed through workstations, laptops, mobile devices, and tablets.

2

Creating New Queries

In this chapter, we will cover the following recipes:

- ▶ The universe structure
- ▶ Creating a simple query
- ▶ Editing the query
- ▶ Filtering the query results
- ▶ Using prompts
- ▶ Using AND/OR logic in conditions
- ▶ Creating nested filters
- ▶ Using a subquery
- ▶ Using combined queries
- ▶ Adding another query
- ▶ Working with several queries
- ▶ Working with the query properties
- ▶ Using the data preview
- ▶ Viewing the SQL
- ▶ Using other query results
- ▶ Scope of analysis
- ▶ Using database ranking
- ▶ Using BEx queries

Introduction

Creating queries is considered in many ways the core functionality of the Web Intelligence application. The source for every report is a query that is based on a database (relational or operational), a data warehouse, an OLAP cube, a BEx query, a web service, or even an Excel or a text file.

The general idea and main theme when building a query is that we create a structure that can access our data sources and fetch relevant, meaningful, useful data to our report presentation layer, according to the user requirements.

Creating queries is the first step in creating a report and it is important because it defines the context of the data we are analyzing as a well as its accuracy.

A *good* query would be one that retrieves only the data slice that is relevant to the report consumer.

In terms of efficiency, query running time, and performance, we are more dependent on the way and type the database is structured. However, for the end user (the report builder), what matters is the fact that he or she can build the query by himself or herself, without being dependent on IT personnel or the Business Intelligence team.

Creating queries in Web Intelligence is aimed at self-service, as it is based on dragging-and-dropping and not on programming or advanced technological knowledge.

In this chapter, we will learn how to define a simple query from scratch, get familiar with key concepts such as a **universe** and **query panel**, and learn how to implement advanced query techniques such as **combined queries** and **subqueries**.

The universe structure

A **universe** is a semantic layer that maps a specific data area or several areas in the data warehouse or in any database such as SQL Server, DB2, Oracle, and many others. The universe uses a connection in order to connect to the database, and once it's set, users can navigate to the universe, build queries, and connect through the universe connection to the database, retrieving the most updated data according to the data update date in the database.

The universe represents the data in a lucid manner, so business users don't require database programming knowledge or an understanding of how the database is structured.

What the user does need to know is how the universe is structured: its main business purposes, what kind of queries can be built using it, and what kind of objects can be used to build his reports and where can he find them in the universe.

Traditionally, a universe maps a specific data subject such as Sales, Marketing, Human Resources, Logistics, Billing, and so on.

Each database can be mapped into a universe that we can also define as the business representation of the data in the tables.

It is possible to build a multisubject universe, but such a universe will usually create over-complexity and will lose the "specific subject" orientation as well as its audience. However, it is possible to combine queries from different universes, as we will learn in *Chapter 8, Merging Data*.

How to do it...

The basic universe structure is a set of objects that maps specific columns in the database. Each object is actually a mapped field in a database table.

The objects are grouped into logical folders and each folder corresponds to a specific data subject in the universe, such as time, sales figures, and products.

Every universe is based on the following four main types of objects:

- ▶ **Dimension objects**: These are used to present the basic type of data: customer name, city, employee number, and sales date. Dimension objects are also used to slice measure figures. Dimension objects can be numeric, character, or a date type. They are represented as a blue square.

- ▶ **Attribute objects**: These are used to present the same type of data as dimension objects but they are located as subobjects under dimension objects. Their primary function is to structure the universe, but they usually have a complementary meaning, for example, the code name of the product or the name of the dimension object. In other cases, we can say that when attribute objects are used for presenting data, they are not so meaningful without the dimension objects that are allocated above it; for example, the ZIP code as an attribute object won't tell us much unless we use the customer address as well. Attribute objects are represented as a blue rhombus with a green asterisk underneath.

- ▶ **Measure objects**: These are used for calculations. They are aggregative objects that represent facts: the number of products sold, revenue, income, tax, VAT, budget, and so on. Usually, a measure object will use an aggregation function such as sum, count average, maximum, and so on. Measure objects are represented as an orange line.

- ▶ **Filter objects**: These are predefined query conditions that are used for filtering the query results.

The following screenshot shows the structure of a universe:

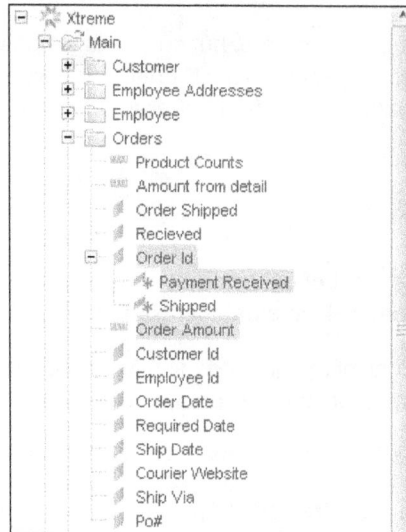

> By hovering over the object names, we can see the object description and type of data. This will help us get a better understanding of the object's purpose and reveal its type.

How it works...

The universe is simply a business map of the database. It can be described as the dictionary of a technical and complex structure that the business user or report builder can't navigate directly without technical knowledge.

When objects are created in the universe, they are named in widely used business lingo, which users already understand or will find easy to adapt to.

The universe reflects the structure of the tables and their relationships via joins and columns. The universe is created by an IT specialist, a Business Intelligence developer, or a person with the relevant development skills.

A universe is built for users because it enables them to create complex reports by themselves while keeping the data secure and the database protected from any changes and damage (the queries can be set to read-only mode).

There's more...

A universe is created as a result of a business request coming from one of the organization's departments or the business users' community, or as a part of the BI development plans.

The primary concerns that will define the scope of the universe will be:

- What kind of data is required?
- Which reports are required to be built?
- What business purposes will the universe serve?

The universe can evolve, be changed, and be adjusted over time so that it will keep up and correspond to the business user's requests.

See also

- For further information on how to use several queries and use Excel files as data providers, refer to *Chapter 8, Merging Data*

Creating a simple query

Our first step will be to create a simple query based on a universe called **motors**.

This universe is used for ad hoc reporting about a car rental and sales company.

The core data in this universe is the car rental and sales figures that can be sliced by customer, time, type of car, and geographical data.

Getting ready

We want to create a query that will display the sales revenue for each car category.

How to do it...

First of all, we will be required to access the motors universe.

We will launch the Web Intelligence application through the main launch panel in the home screen. In the empty tab that has opened, we will click on the **New** button that is located to the left of the **Open file** icon, as shown in the following screenshot:

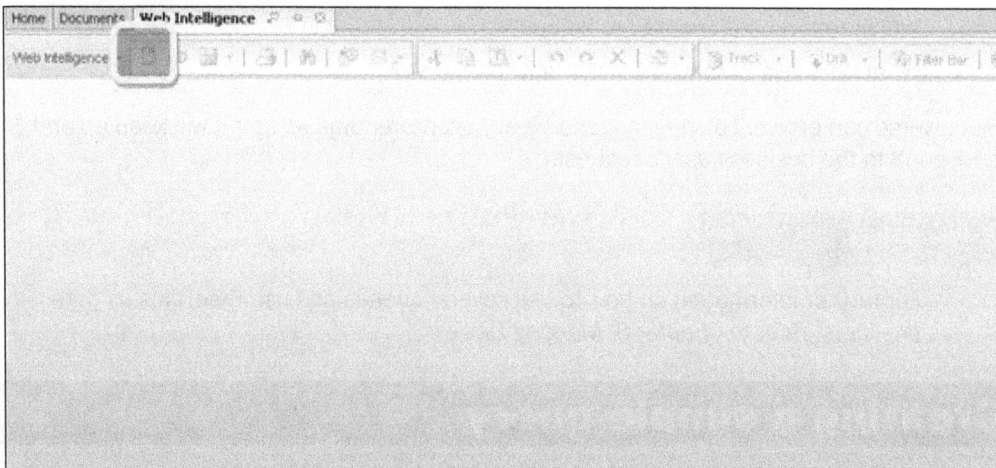

The next screen will prompt us to choose the data source we want to use in order to create our query. The options are as follows:

- **No data source**: This enables us to preformat the report without creating or running a query

- **Universe**: As discussed earlier, a universe can be based on a relational database, an OLAP cube, or even Excel files

- **Excel**: This uses an external Excel file as the data source

- **BEx**: This uses a BEx query or a BW OLAP cube

- **Analysis View**: Analysis workspaces can be exported in **Analysis View**; these workspaces are created by using the Analysis edition for OLAP

- **Web Services**: This uses a web service as data source that is based on an HTTP communication protocol

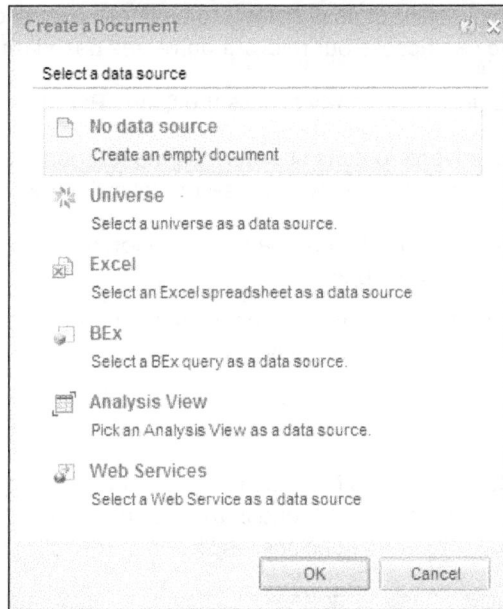

We will choose the second **Universe** option. The universe prompt list screen will promptly appear and we will be able to choose the **motors** universe from the list, as shown in the following screenshot:

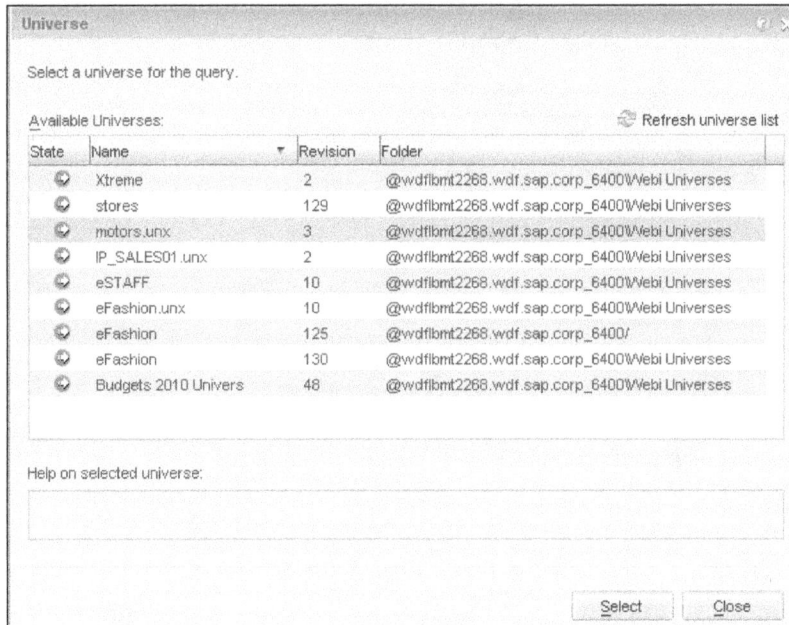

The universe list appearing in front of us is subject to business user security rights and business associations. We can access our relevant universes based on them.

After choosing the motors universe, we will access the **Query Panel**.

We will be able to see the universe outline structure on the left-hand side pane of the main screen, and on the right-hand side pane, we will see the following three panes:

> ▶ **Result Objects:** All the objects that the query will fetch as columns in the report layer via the presented data will appear here

> ▶ **Query Filters:** Here, the query conditions are set in order to restrict the fetched data to correspond to a specific set of rules

> ▶ **Data Preview:** This enables us to preview the row data returned before the data is presented in the report layer

We drag-and-drop the following objects from the left-hand side pane to the **Result Objects** pane: `Category of Car`, which can be found in the `Car` class, and `Sales Revenue`, which can be found in the `Sales Figures` subclass, as shown in the following screenshot:

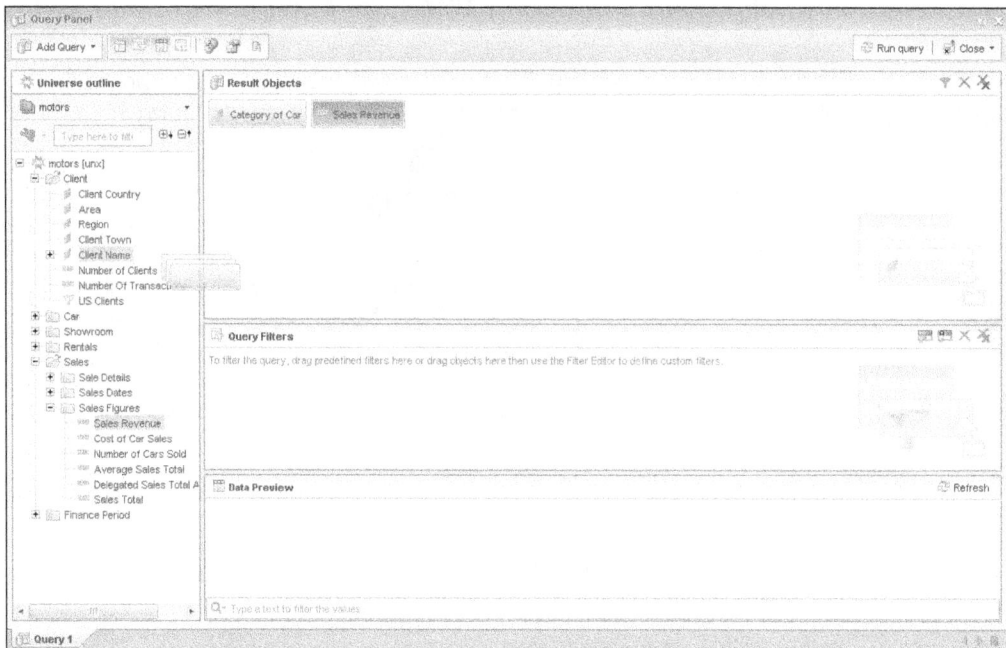

We will click on the **Run query** button on the top-right-hand side of the **Query Panel** window. The query will run and fetch the relevant data and display it in the report, as shown in the following screenshot:

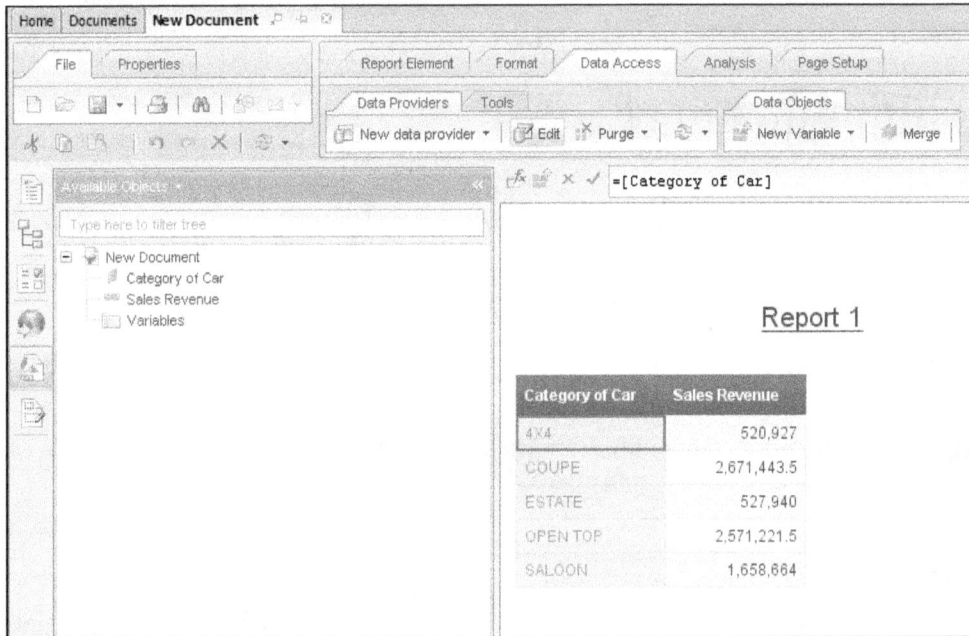

How it works...

When objects are being dragged-and-dropped into the **Result Objects** pane, the universe structure begins to be formed and SQL code is generated, which is the basic query language for databases.

This SQL code, generated according to the objects, is *thrown* to the database once we execute the query and retrieves all the relevant rows as the objects are mapped to the actual tables in the database.

The query panel can also be described as a SQL generator using drag-and-drop.

See also

▸   For further information on SQL code generation, see the *Viewing the SQL* recipe

There's more...

The order of the objects in the **Result Objects** pane will be the same as those of the objects displayed in the report. If a business user needs to change the order of the displayed columns, he or she can easily do so by dragging-and-dropping the table column.

Editing the query

Queries can be edited in order to adjust to the evolving requirements of the report. Through my work, I have come to know a simple fact: most reports are edited at one stage or another.

Editing is easy and is conducted in the same way a query is created, that is, by adding objects to the query or by removing some of them.

Getting ready

We want to extend the current query definition and add the model dimension to it so that we can analyze the sales data at a more detailed level.

How to do it...

On the report screen, we will click on the **Edit** button under the **Data Access** ribbon; this will open the **Query Panel**.

We will drag-and-drop the `Model` object and run the query.

The result table will remain the same. In order to present the additional object that we added to the query, we will drag `Model` from the **Available Objects** panel to the existing table, as shown in the following screenshot:

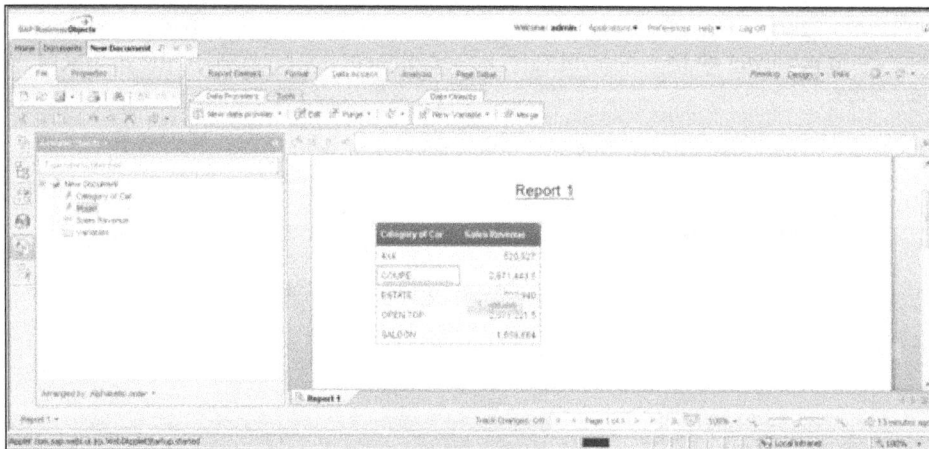

The final table will now display the new object as well, showing for each category the model and sales. Have a look at the following screenshot:

Report 1

Category of Car	Model	Sales Revenue
4X4	Cherokee Sport 2.5	236,925
4X4	Forrester S Turbo All Weather 2	188,512
4X4	Grand Cherokee Karedo 4	95,490
COUPE	911 Carrera Coupe 3.4	233,298
COUPE	Bentle Kontinental R 6.8	399,510
COUPE	DB5 Coupe 3.3	169,990
COUPE	E456 GT 5.5	670,876

How it works...

As we saw, the query can be easily edited, and once an object is added to or deleted from the query, a new query run is required in order to reflect the changes in the query structure.

> The nature of measures is dynamic. The display of aggregative-level measure objects is dependent on the dimensions and/or the attribute objects presented with them.

There's more...

You can also add objects to the query by double-clicking on an object name. Objects can be deleted from a query by dragging-and-dropping, using the **X** button, or simply pressing the *Delete* key on the keyboard.

It is also possible to run a search for object names in the universe outline. By typing in the object's first letter(s), we will be able to run a search and find objects whose names begin with those letters, as shown in the following screenshot:

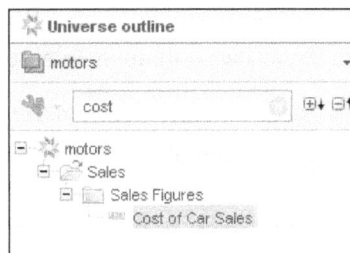

Universe outline

motors

cost

motors
  Sales
    Sales Figures
      Cost of Car Sales

> You can also find objects by marking one of them in the **Result Objects** pane. The class contacting that object will immediately open and show its exact location in the universe outline.

One last point to note is that you don't have to run the query if you just need to build the query structure (let's assume the database is currently unavailable, so we can't run the query). To do this, you have to click on the **Close** button located on the right-hand side of the **Run query** button and choose **Apply Changes and Close**, as shown in the following screenshot. This action will save the query structure, go to the report screen, and enable us to save the report without data.

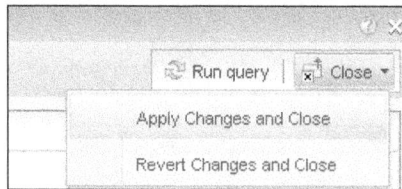

Filtering the query results

Every query is built to retrieve a specific set of results.

When we define a query, the data can be processed and analyzed in several possible contexts:

- **Time**: This gives information about when an event occurred; for example, the sales for the current week (a "when" business question)
- **Data type and specification**: This gives the model specifications of the cars that were rented or sold (a "which" business question)
- **Measure**: This gives a range or a value that is greater or less than (a "how much" business question)

Without a filtering context, a query is somewhere between serving a meaningless purpose and answering a very general question. The main idea when creating query filters is to fetch only the data that is relevant to the business question. The rule of "garbage in garbage out" applies here. By defining all the relevant conditions, we ensure that we will get accurate results as well as better performance.

Every condition is structured from the following three main parts:

- **Object**: Every condition is based on an object from the universe
- **Operator**: This is a logical operation that the condition uses, for example, equal to or greater than
- **Operand**: This part can contain a value, a constant, a prompt, or even use other query results

Getting ready

We want to add a filter to the query that will present *only* the sales for the United Kingdom clients.

How to do it...

Drag the **Client Country** to the **Query Filters** pane.

In the second part of the condition, click on the arrow. A drop-down list of operators will open. We will pick the **Equal to** operator, as shown in the following screenshot. This operator enables you to choose only one value.

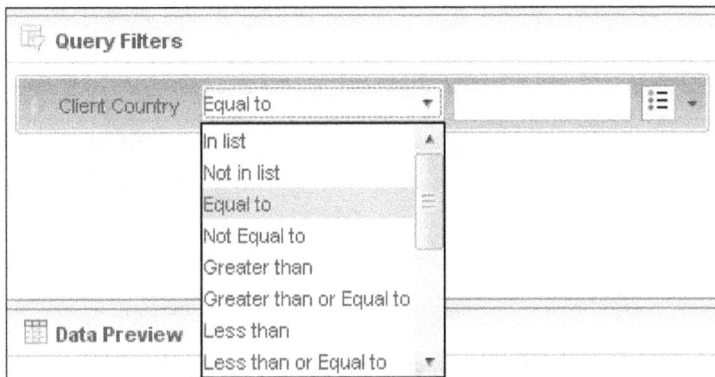

In the third and last part of the condition, we will pick the second option, **Value(s) from list**, as shown in the following screenshot:

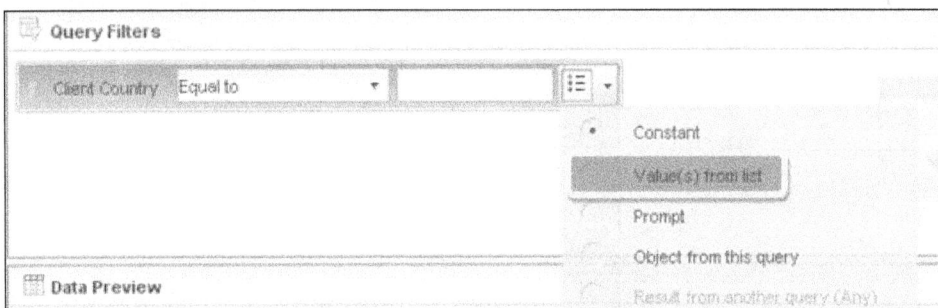

In the next window that will appear, we pick the value **United Kingdom** from the list and click on the **OK** button at the bottom-left side of the window, as shown in the following screenshot:

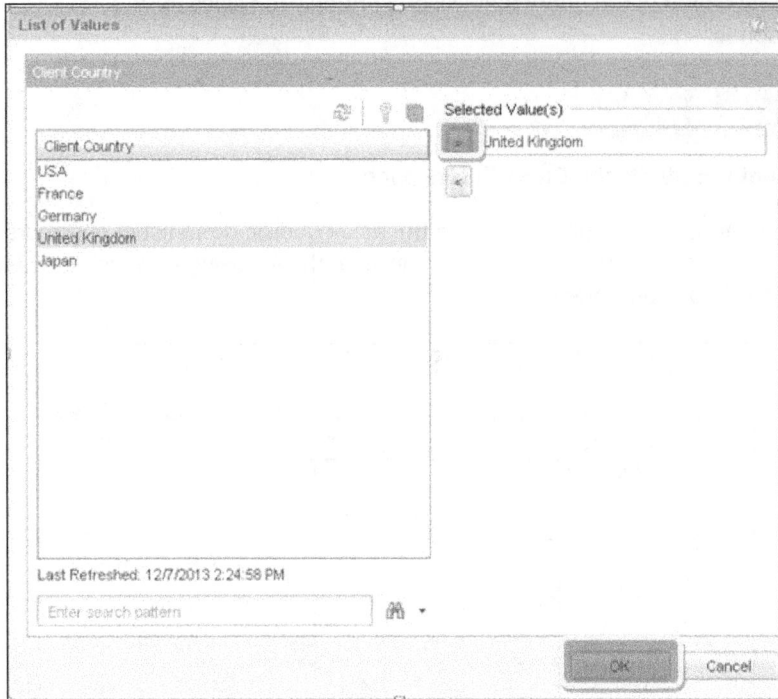

After filling the three parts of the condition, it will be set and the query is ready to retrieve the results based on this query filter, as shown in the following screenshot:

We will click on the **Run query** button and get the relevant results. There's a whole bunch of operators that can be used:

> ▶ **In list**: This enables you to pick more than one value of the object. This operator uses an OR operator on the values.

- ▶ **Not in list**: This enables you to retrieve data that doesn't correspond to more than one value.

- ▶ **Equal to**: This enables you to pick only one value.

- ▶ **Not equal to**: This enables you to pick a value that is different from to the **Equal to** operator.

- ▶ **Greater than**: This will retrieve data which is greater than a value. It is very useful for date, measure, age, and numeric data.

- ▶ **Greater than or equal to**: This retrieves data that is greater than or equal to a value (includes the value we are matching plus anything greater than it).

- ▶ **Less than**: This operator retrieves which is data lower than a value.

- ▶ **Less than or equal to**: This retrieves data that is less than or equal to a value.

- ▶ **Between**: This retrieves data between and including two values. It is very useful for date range and measure range filtering.

- ▶ **Not between**: This retrieves data that is outside the range of two values.

- ▶ **Is null**: This retrieves records that have a null value. A null value can signify an event that has not happened, for example, if there is a client in the database who hasn't paid, he will have a null pay date. We can use this to query which customers haven't paid yet.

- ▶ **Is not null**: This retrieves records that do not have a null value.

- ▶ **Matches pattern**: This operator retrieves data that includes a specific string or part of a string. This is a search operator that enables us to identify data by running a search for it. In order to identify strings that start with the X character, we will use the syntax X%. For strings that contain the X value, we will use the syntax %X%, and for strings that end with the X value, we will use the syntax %X.

- ▶ **Different from pattern**: This returns data that doesn't include a specific string.

- ▶ **Both**: This retrieves data that corresponds to two values by establishing an AND operator between them; for example, who bought products A and B?

- ▶ **Except**: This retrieves data that corresponds to one value and excludes another.

> You can pick more than one value from a list by using the **In list** operator. Holding the *Ctrl* or the *Shift* key and pressing the down arrow will enable you to mark several values at once.

How it works...

A query is simply a set of result objects combined with a set of conditions. A condition in the query runs a search for all the rows in the database tables that correspond to the value or values in the operand.

By choosing a specific value, we define which rows will be retrieved, and the result objects will display the data that corresponds to the filter.

> Note that we didn't use the **Client Country** in the result objects. This is the rule for single-value returned objects as they bring nothing new to the rows' display as they will repeat the same value in each row. If these types of objects are used to display informative titles, then they can be useful in the report.

There's more...

A simple condition can also be created by dragging an object from the **Result Objects** pane to the **Query Filters** pane.

Another practical operand type is **Object from this query**. This option enables us to compare objects of the same type, such as dates and just values.

Using this operand can help us answer business questions such as which products were shipped on the same day they were ordered and which customer with a current purchase purchased the same product the previous time they purchased a product? This is illustrated in the following screenshot:

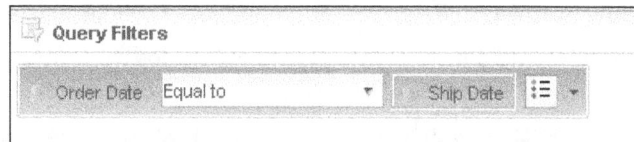

Using prompts

Prompt is an operand that enables a dynamic value insertion into the condition's last section. When we think about it, most reports use prompts as they require dynamic values in the conditions. The best example is a time-ranged report that requires the picking of different date values every day.

Getting ready

We need to edit our existing query filter so that business users will be able to choose country values dynamically.

How to do it...

First, we will change the operand type to **Prompt**, as shown in the following screenshot. Note that generic text is added to the prompt area that says **Enter values for Client**.

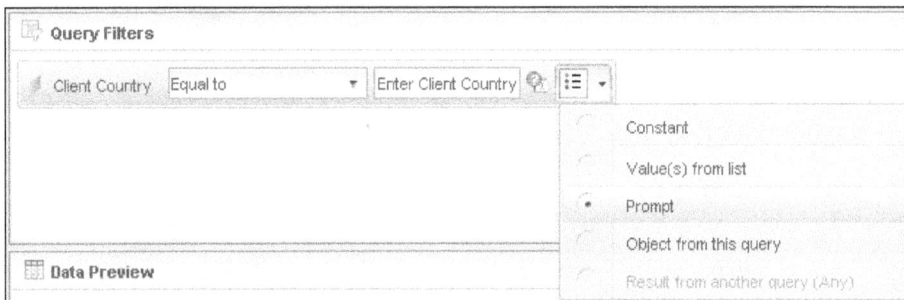

We will click on the **Run query** button. A prompt window will appear. In this prompt window, we will be asked to pick a value from the existing list of values, as shown in the following screenshot. As long as a value isn't picked, a red arrow will appear next to the prompt text.

We will pick the country **Japan**. The red arrow will change to green, confirming that the prompt has been answered.

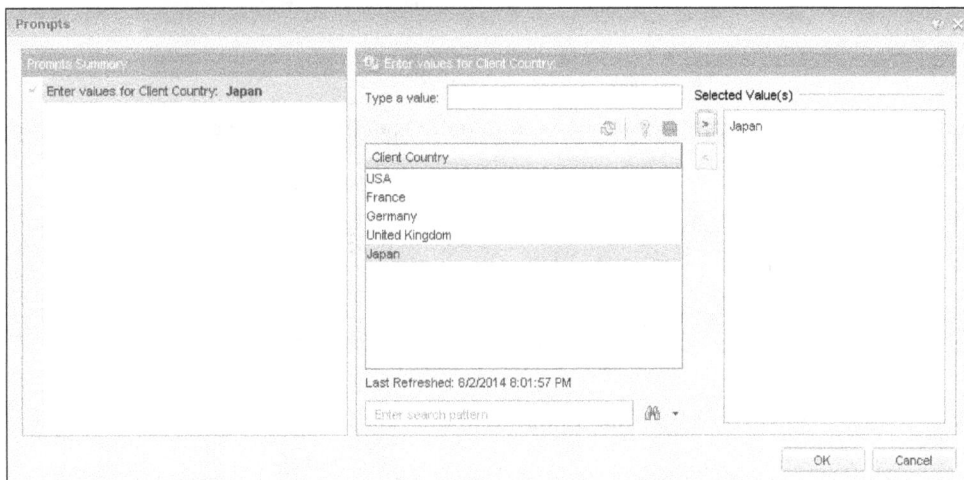

You can run a search in the list of values by using the binoculars icon located at the bottom-center part of the prompt screen.

By clicking on the **OK** button, the query will run based on the value we picked and retrieve data for **Japan**, as shown in the following screenshot:

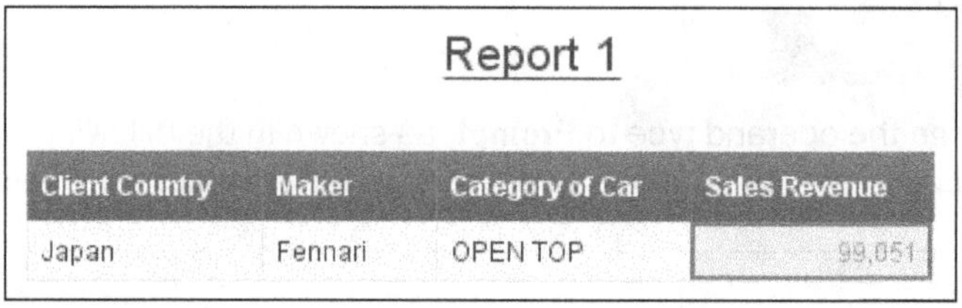

Report 1			
Client Country	**Maker**	**Category of Car**	**Sales Revenue**
Japan	Fennari	OPEN TOP	99,051

The next time we refresh the report, the prompt screen will launch again and enable us to change the value in the prompt.

How it works...

The prompt is an open question—a hardcoded condition always retrieves the same value. The prompt enables reports to be run according to parameters by creating the prompt window that enables users to pick a value dynamically.

Prompts are great for reports that are date-based, since potentially they need to run every day on a different range of dates. The same applies to regional sales reports—each regional manger requires the same report but different values in the conditions.

Prompts are probably the most common operands since they are so handy and, being dynamic, are in sync with most of the reports' nature.

There's more...

We can find the properties that enhance prompt options in the prompt condition.

Clicking on the question mark icon in the prompt condition makes the **Prompt Properties** window appear, as shown in the following screenshot:

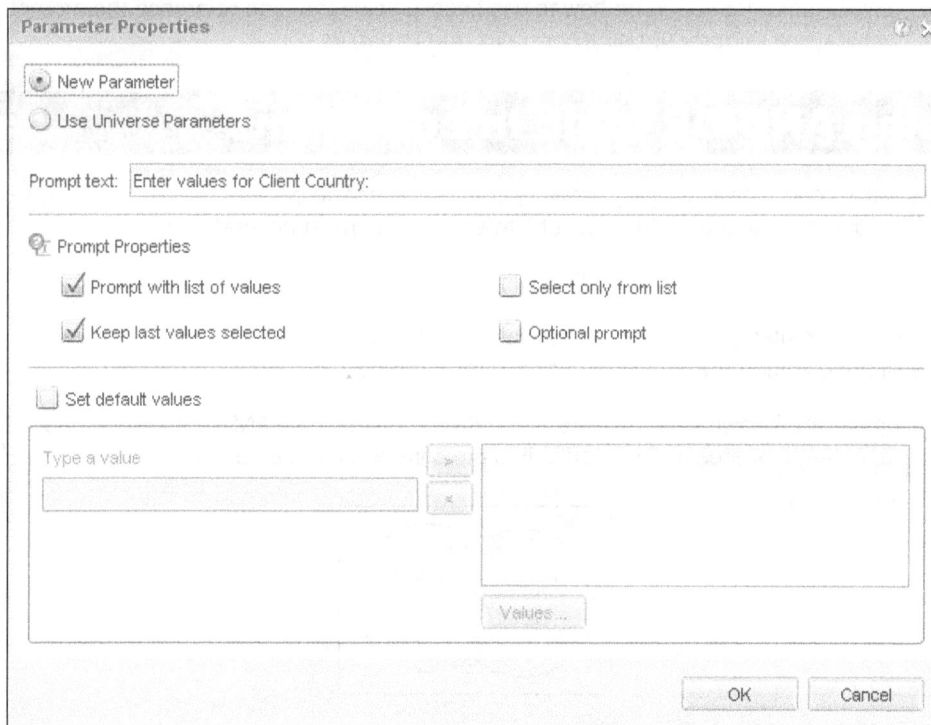

The **Prompt Properties** window has several configuration options:

- **Prompt with list of values**: This can use a list of values or enable free typing.
- **Keep last values selected**: This keeps the last value that was picked in the prompt.
- **Select default value**: This keeps a default value in the prompt.
- **Select only from list**: This disables the free typing option and enables us to pick the value only from a list of values.
- **Optional prompt**: This enables us to run the report without picking any value in the prompt. This is equivalent to ignoring the prompt if no value is picked but still enabling the user to pick a value, several values, or all the values in a single prompt.

The value or values returned by the prompt can also be displayed in a special predefined cell called **Prompt Summary** in the report, providing the right context of relevancy for the data in the report.

See also

▶ For further information on how to use special fields that can reference the prompt values, see *Chapter 9, Using Formulas and Variables*

Using AND/OR logic in conditions

Using several conditions in a query is a very common scenario because, in many cases, we are required to build a query with a set of filters to get the most accurate results.

Conditions in queries can use the AND or OR operators.

A relation that creates an intersection between conditions is called an AND relation. This means all the common rows for Filter A and Filter B will be retrieved.

Have a look at the following figure. Here, the data retrieved by the AND operator can be described as the dark area in the middle. It is the common intersected area.

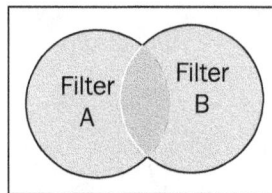

For instance, if our query has a set of two conditions: year equal to **2014** AND **product name** equal to **smart phones** and no smart phones were sold in 2014, the query won't return any results since the conditions didn't have common rows.

The relation between conditions using an OR operator is a relation that uses a union operator, meaning there is no need for the conditions to have common rows. If any one of the conditions is found valid, data will be retrieved. The data retrieved by the OR operator can be described as the entire area of the following figure:

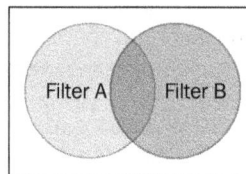

Getting ready

We are required to create a query that will present the number of cars sold per client country and maker.

The query should retrieve data only for **USA** and by the maker **Fennari**.

How to do it...

First, we will create the **Client Country** filters by dragging the **Client Country** object to the filter pane. Then, we will use the equal operator, and in the operand choose the value **USA**.

Once the second object has been dragged, an **And** operator will appear between the two filters, as shown in the following screenshot:

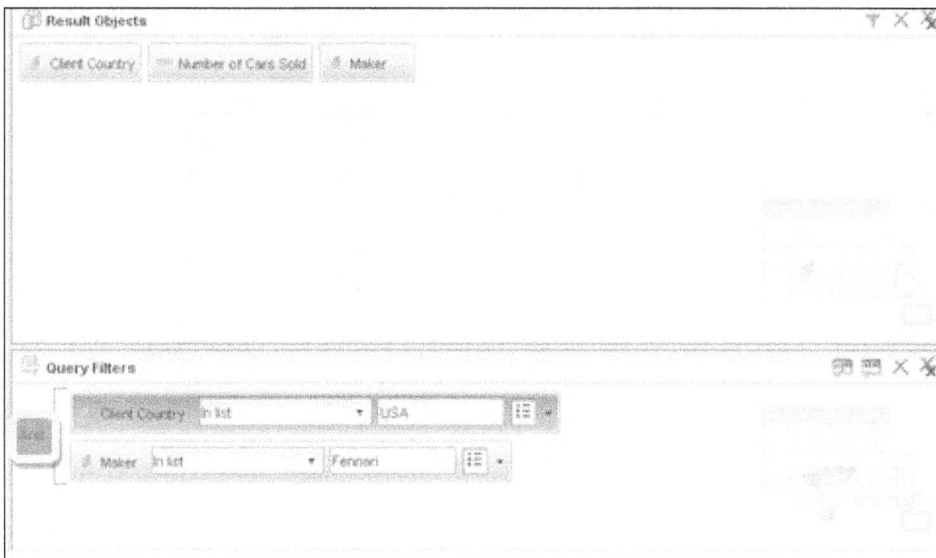

The relation that has been established between the two filters is an intersection relation, meaning only a common dataset that corresponds to both of the filters can be retrieved. If one of the filters is found to be false (for example, no such models were bought in USA), then the query will not retrieve any data.

We will now run the query. Surprisingly, we will get only one row, as shown in the following screenshot:

Client Country	Maker	Number of Cars Sold
USA	Fennari	19

We will now change the AND operation to OR in the **Query Panel** by clicking on the AND operation. By doing so, we will establish a union relationship between the two query filters, meaning if any one of the filters is found to be true, then the query will retrieve that data. Have a look at the following screenshot:

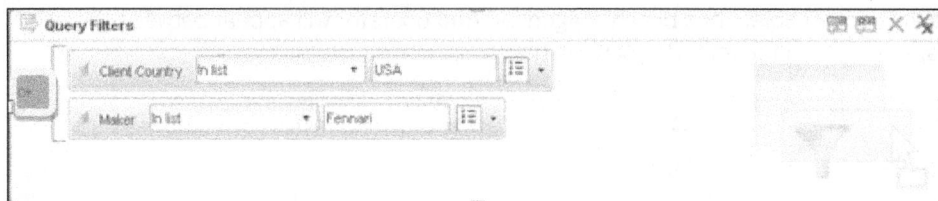

We will run the query. We will notice that there is an increase in the number of rows, as shown here:

Client Country	Maker	Number of Cars Sold
Japan	Fennari	1
USA	Austin Martini	6
USA	Fennari	19
USA	Forsche	14
USA	Jaggular	10
USA	Leep	18
USA	Lowtoos	14
USA	Rolls Choice	8
USA	Valdo	20

The reason for the increase in the number of rows is that we set the OR operator, which retrieves all the **Fennari** rows or all the **USA** rows.

Notice that the first row displays data for Japan as Fennari sold cars in Japan too.

How it works...

When creating a set of filters, we will always use an AND/OR operation. While the AND operation is more restrictive and requires that all the conditions be valid, the OR operation requires that at least one of the query filters be valid.

When the query is sent to the database in order to retrieve the relevant data, the filters are executed using the AND/OR operators.

The use of each type of operation depends on the purpose of the query and how the data can be identified. Both operators can be combined in a single set of conditions.

There's more...

A great way to understand how the AND operation works is by demonstrating what it can't do.

In the following screenshot, we have the **Client Country** condition used twice. The first condition is equal to **USA** and the second is equal to **Japan**.

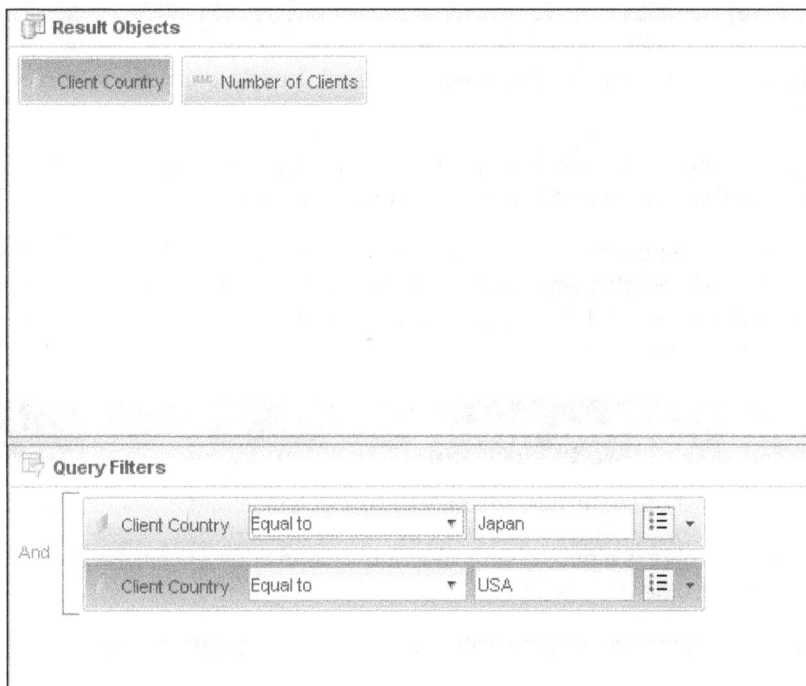

Running the query will result in the following informative message:

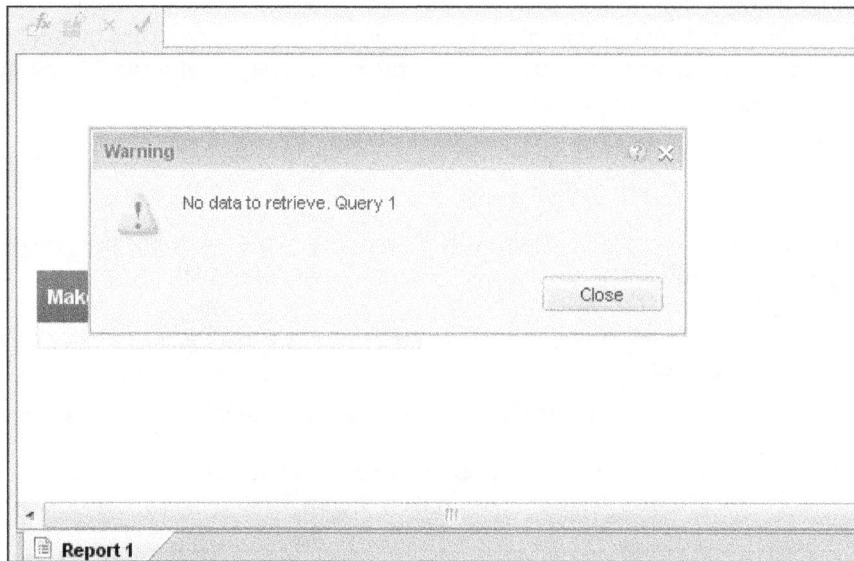

This message simply says that the data criteria we tried to retrieve doesn't exist in the database.

We can argue that there is data for both of the countries, but if we take a closer look at the equal operator, we will realize that it means only one value can be matched.

By creating two conditions of the same object, we are actually contradicting the arithmetic meaning of the equal operator, saying it can be equal to two different values. This set of conditions will not work in any kind of reporting tool or even simple Excel filters as the meaning of equal to is universal.

Creating nested filters

Nested filters are used when the query requires a more complex set of conditions.

Nested filters mean there is a priority set to a group of conditions while the other group or groups are set with a different priority.

The most basic rule is that the AND operation is prioritized *before* the OR operation.

Nesting filters allow us to ask more complex questions but implement them easily with the drag-and-drop method.

Getting ready

We are required to set these conditions in the query: retrieve the sales revenue for **USA** for the car maker **Leep** (there is an AND relation between the first two conditions) OR retrieve **Model Colours** that equal **BLACK**.

How to do it...

We will create the three conditions by dragging-and-dropping the relevant objects from the universe structure to the **Query Filters** pane:

1. In order to create a nested filter between the first and the second filter, we will drag-and-drop the **Country** filter on the **Maker** filter, as shown in the following screenshot:

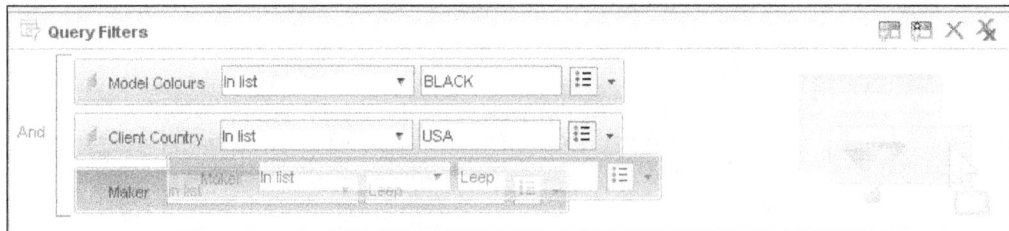

2. The result will be a nested filter that is bound with a bracket, as shown here:

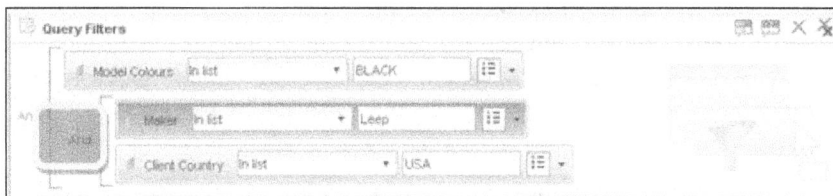

3. We click on the external **And** operation and turn it into the **Or** operation, as shown here:

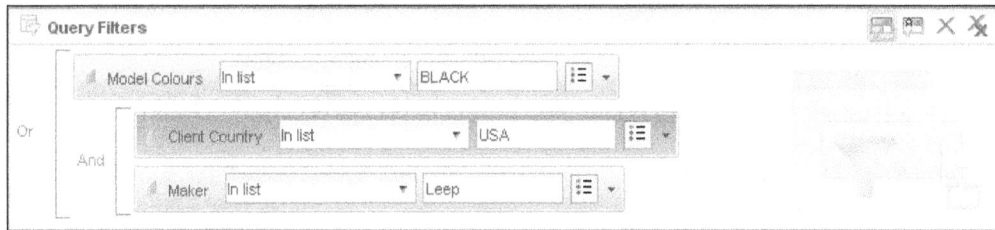

4. We will get the following results on clicking on the **Run query** button:

Client Country	Maker	Model Colours	Sales Revenue
United Kingdom	Lowtoos	BLACK	181,105
United Kingdom	Scoobaru	BLACK	59,184
USA	Forsche	BLACK	286,420
USA	Leep	BLACK	95,490
USA	Leep	BLUE	236,925
USA	Lowtoos	BLACK	249,800

Examining the results will show data for the car maker Leep in USA (the AND condition) as well as the countries and makers' sales revenue with black color models (the OR condition).

How it works...

Nested filters use brackets in order to prioritize filter groups. By using the simple drag-and-drop technique, we can establish a relatively complex statement of filters. This makes it a very flexible method of querying.

There's more...

Filters can be further nested into more complex subsets. There is no limit to the number of possible conditions that can be put in one query; however, we need to remember that the more conditions we create, theoretically, we are decreasing the number of rows that will be returned. On the other hand, the query is requested to execute more functions in order to retrieve the data.

Using a subquery

A subquery is a querying technique designed for more complex business questions that require us to analyze them further and additional information based on the data retrieved.

The subquery technique is used to return data that will be used by the main query. For example, we want to generate a better analysis for the sales team and understand which types of cars were bought by the same client.

The goal of this business question is to investigate whether a specific combination of car types are being bought by clients: did clients who bought Austin Martini cars buy other types of cars as well?

By analyzing this data, we will be able to make better marketing and sales offers to the customers as well as get some basic information about sales trends and customer behavior.

Getting ready

We want to analyze the client's car sales combinations; we will drag the **Client Name**, **Maker**, and **Sales Revenue** objects.

Here comes the catch. Creating a query filter based on the model object with the value Austin Martini can't solve this business question and nor can using an **in list** operator that will enable us to choose several values.

Using any one of these methods, we will only get half the answer: which client bought a specific model or several ones. However, if we necessarily need to retrieve all the clients who purchased Austin Martini cars and based on this population check which other car types they purchased as well, then that kind of business question will have to be split into two queries.

How to do it...

We will use the **Add a subquery** button located on the right-hand side of the **Query Filters** pane.

Since the focus of the query is finding clients who bought cars, the client object will be marked in the result objects. A subquery condition will be created by clicking on the **Add a sub query** button, as shown in the following screenshot:

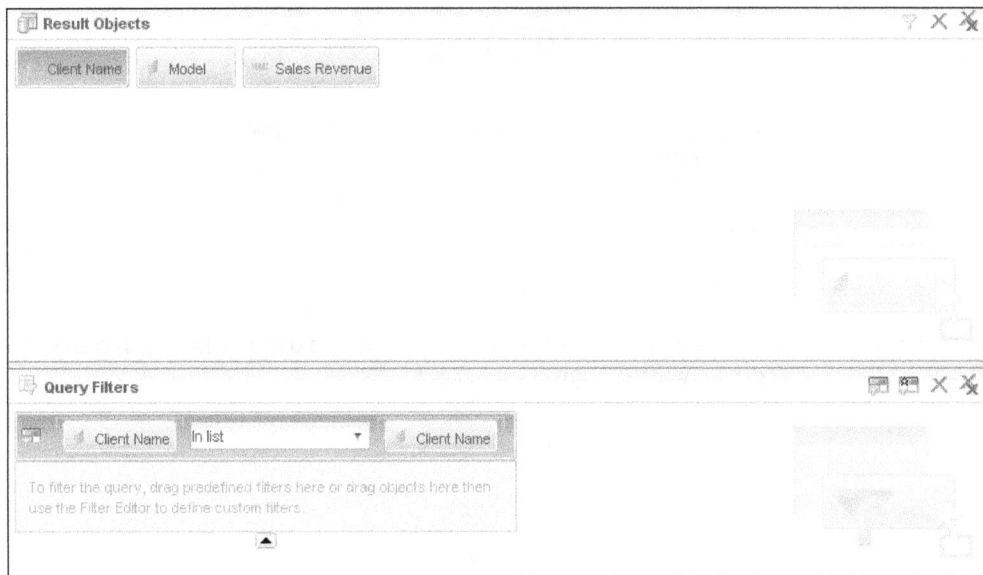

The operator that will be used in this query will be the **In list** operator since there is a very high probability to find more than one customer that have bought cars made by several car makers.

We will add another maker filter to the subquery area and choose the value **Austin Martini**, as shown in the following screenshot:

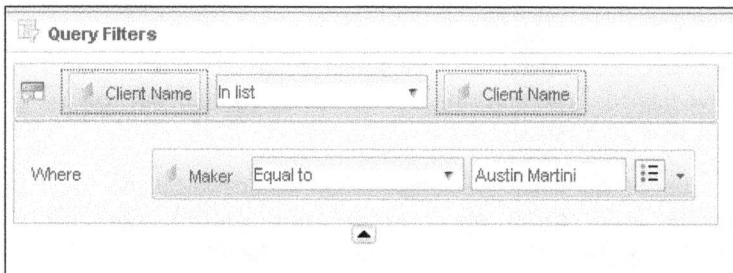

We will now click on the **Run query** button and get the following results:

Client Name	Maker	Sales Revenue
Brent, Paul	Austin Martini	170,959.5
Brent, Paul	Rolls Choice	145,005
Gustagini, Tony	Austin Martini	84,995
Gustagini, Tony	Rolls Choice	199,755
Hugheston, Howard	Austin Martini	84,995
Hugheston, Howard	Rolls Choice	199,755
Murphy, John	Austin Martini	189,955
Penn, Paul	Austin Martini	170,959.5
Penn, Paul	Rolls Choice	145,005
Travelto, John	Austin Martini	189,955

Note that several customers returned two rows.

The **Austin Martini** rows were retrieved by the subquery that was used by the main query to find which other makers' cars were bought by the client.

How it works...

A subquery is a query that serves only one purpose: *feeding* the main query with its results for further lookup.

A subquery has no meaning in a standalone query; it's a part of the main query.

In this example, the subquery retrieved a list of all the clients who bought a car made by Austin Martini. This list was the base for the main query to run and fetch the rest of the car makers' cars that were bought by those clients retrieved in the subquery.

Using a subquery does not ensure that all the clients owning cars from more than one maker will be fetched. If any one of the Austin Martini clients are found with other makers, those rows will be pulled too; if not, a single row will be presented for the client, as we can see in the query results.

In terms of dependencies, the subquery runs first and fetches the client list, then the main query uses that client list as its base for fetching data.

There's more...

Subqueries can use operators such as =, <, >, >=, <=, In list, and Between. Undoubtedly, the In list operator is one of the most useful ones as it deals with classic business questions such as:

- ▶ Which customers bought product x and bought other products as well?
- ▶ Which customers that weren't billed in the last month were not billed in the current month either?

As a basic rule, the subquery can only have one result object. This rule further emphasizes that the subquery is just a list that is retrieved and used by the main query.

The subquery can also be used to eliminate certain types of rows by using the operator Not in list; for example, to eliminate the customers who bought a specific product.

See also

- ▶ To know about more advanced query techniques, go through the next recipe, *Using combined queries*, and the *Using other query results* recipe

Using combined queries

Combined queries are a form of advanced querying technique that uses several queries for comparison in order to return a single dataset.

Using combined queries enables us to retrieve results from more than one query into a single table by comparing the rows of each query while a subquery compares a single object result.

Combined queries can use the following operators:

- **Union**: This will include the rows from both queries (this is also the default operator and is similar to the OR operator between query filters)
- **Intersection**: This includes the rows that are common to both queries (just like the AND operator between query filters)
- **Minus**: This includes the rows from the first query minus the rows from the second query

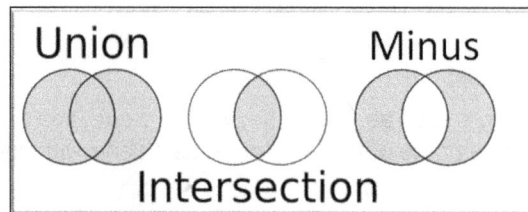

When building combined queries, the order, data type, and number of result objects has to be the same; however, there is no limitation to the number of query filters.

Getting ready

We are required to use the **Island Resorts Marketing** universe this time as our data provider to query customers who used hotel room service and restaurant services.

Since there is no method to perform such a query in a single step, we will create an intersection between two queries.

> Using **In list** in the product query filter will not return the required results as **In list** uses an OR operator between these list values.

How to do it...

We will create a query with one result object, **Customer**, and a query filter, **Service Equal to Hotel Room**. We will click on the **Add a combined query** button located on the top-left **Query Panel** toolbar, as shown in the following screenshot:

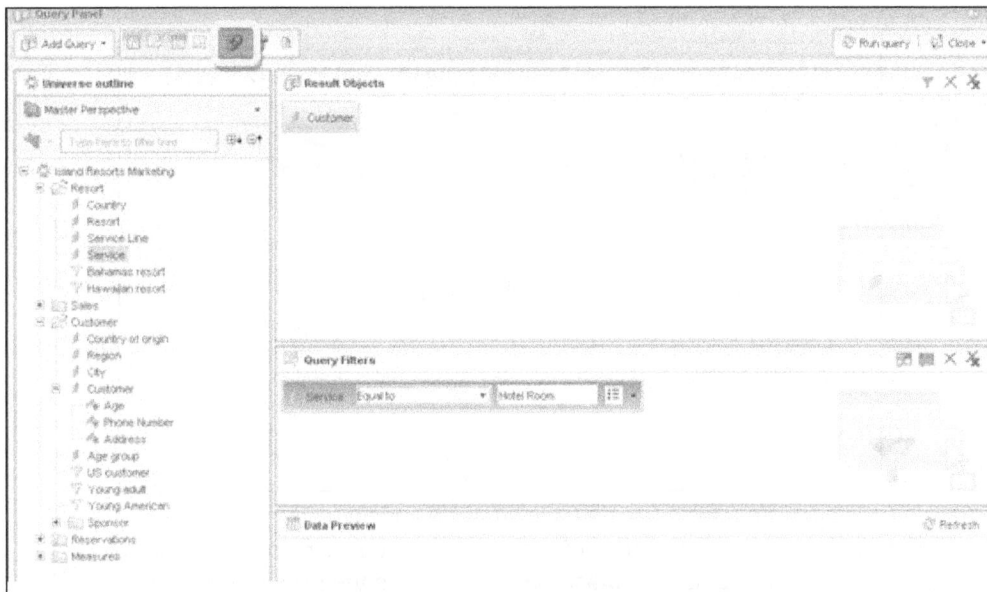

A second query will be created with the same result object. Note that switching between the queries is done by clicking on one of the gray bars on the bottom-left **Combined Query** panels, as shown in the following screenshot:

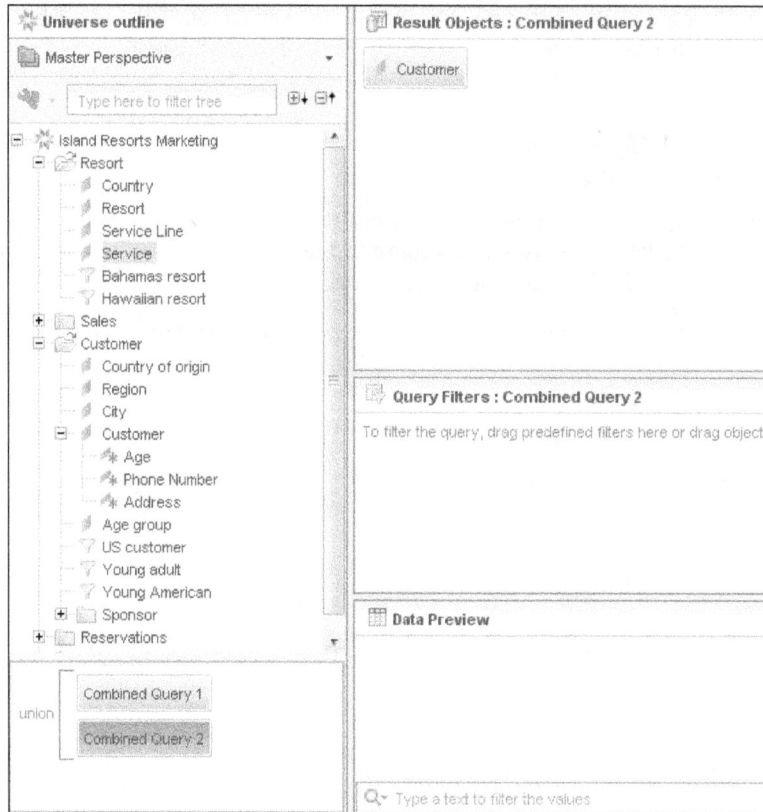

Furthermore, as explained earlier, the default combined query type created is **union**; by clicking on it, we will change it to **intersection**, as shown in the following screenshot:

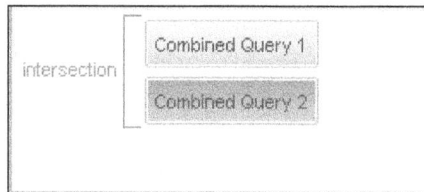

We will add another service query filter to the second query with the value **Restaurant**. We will click on the **Run query** button and get the following customer list:

Customer
Arai
Brendt
Kamata
McCarthy

Only customers who used the hotel room *and* the restaurant are in this list.

> When using intersection, all values of the rows returned by the objects have to be the same, including the measure objects. This means an intersection between queries can only compare the same values and can only retrieve distinct values.

Now, we want to edit the query so that it will return those customers who used the hotel room service but didn't use the restaurant service (a minus operation between the two queries). We will go back to **Query Panel** and click on the **minus** operator, as shown in the following screenshot:

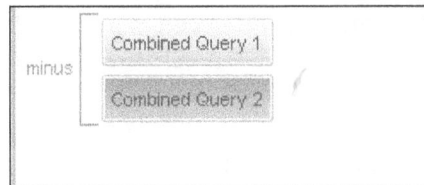

minus	Combined Query 1
	Combined Query 2

We will rerun the query and get the list of clients who didn't use a restaurant service but did use the hotel room service, as follows:

Customer
Diemers
Schiller

How it works...

Combined queries are the way to implement AND/OR/Minus relations between queries. A combined query compares the two queries result sets row by row and returns the relevant results depending on the type of operator between the queries.

Combined queries are great for answering business questions such as:

> ▶ Which customers bought a specific product but didn't buy another product (minus operation)?

> ▶ Which customers bought a specific product and bought another product as well (an intersection operation)? Since intersection can only compare queries with the same values another good example would be: which customers who ordered a product got it on the same day? (the order date and shipment date will be the same)?

> ▶ Which customers have a valid billing date or sale date (union operation)?

> Using union operation between queries is useful when we need to compare data between tables that aren't connected in the universe.

There's more...

You might wonder at some point how we can know for sure that the query worked as expected. We can be sure by creating another query that will fetch a specific customer service and checking the results against the original query.

See also

> ▶ For how to combine several queries at the report level, see *Chapter 8, Merging Data*

Adding another query

Building several queries in the **Query Panel** is a core functionality of Web Intelligence.

The ability to centralize several data aspects in the same report is considered in many ways the heart of reporting and analysis.

There are many scenarios where we would be required to build more than one query; the main reasons are presented as follows:

- The report needs to present different queries with different filters that can't be unified into one query (will create contradiction in the filters)

- There are also several contexts in the universe that require separation between the queries

> Contexts are structures that can be created in universes when a business question can be asked in several different contexts. For example, in the Motors universe, we can analyze the customer data in the sales context (who bought a car) and we can analyze the customer data in the rental context (which customer rented a car).
>
> Contexts are also created when there are data areas in the universe that are isolated from each other since they can't connect directly through the table structure for business and technical reasons; for example, we have a monthly sales table and a daily sales table that are not connected directly in the universe and can't be defined in the same query.

- The data required is originated in more than one universe

- The data required is originated in different data types and structures (a universe and an Excel sheet)

- The query is using data structures from universes that are not connected (lack of joins)

- We want to create another query for **quality assurance** (**QA**) purposes (usually a *lighter* query in terms of the number of filters)

Getting ready

We are required to add a second query; this query will fetch a different aspect of data from the same universe and analyze the sales per customer and his or her geographical additional data. The reason we are using two separate queries based on the same universe is because they have different granular levels of data as well as they are relating to two different data subjects based on different query filters.

How to do it...

We will add a new query by clicking on the **Add Query** button located on the top-left **Query Panel** toolbar. We will drag the **Category of Car**, **Maker**, and **Sales Revenue** objects, and a query condition sales revenue greater than 1 million, as shown in the following screenshot:

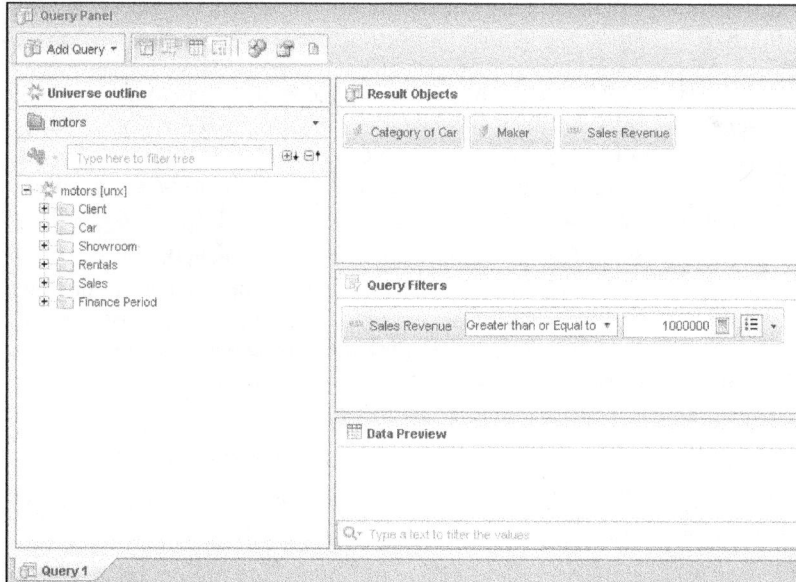

The **Universe** prompt screen will be launched. Just as we chose a universe in the first query, we will pick the **Motors** universe again, as shown:

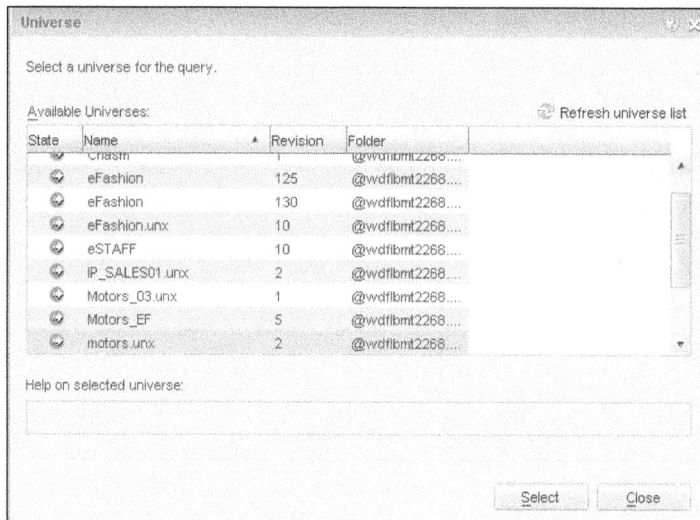

A second query tab will be created that will enable us to create the query. This query will deal with the customer data displaying the objects: **Client Name**, **Client Town**, **Client Country**, and **Sales Revenue**; and the query predefined filter **US Clients**, as shown in the following screenshot:

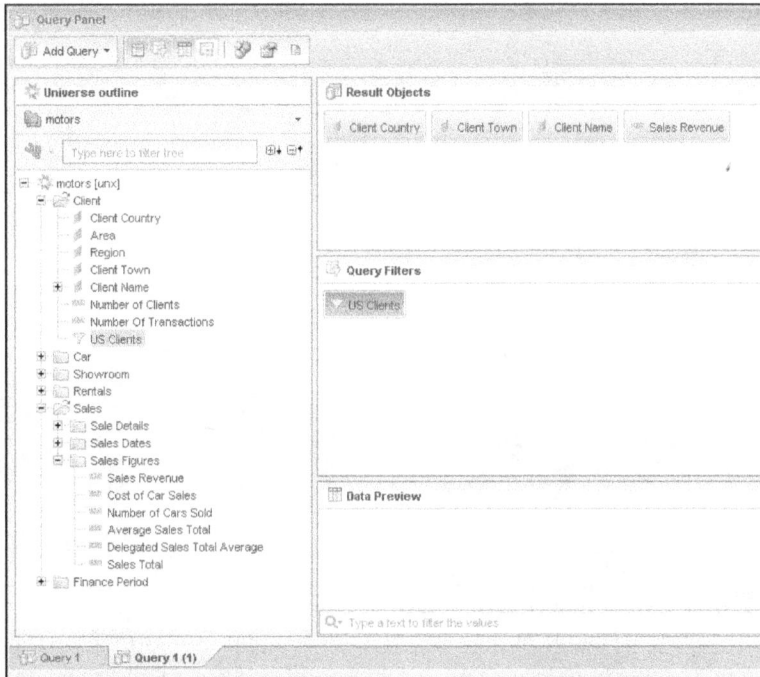

We will run the query. Before getting the results, an **Add Query** window will pop up, offering us three options. Have a look at the following screenshot:

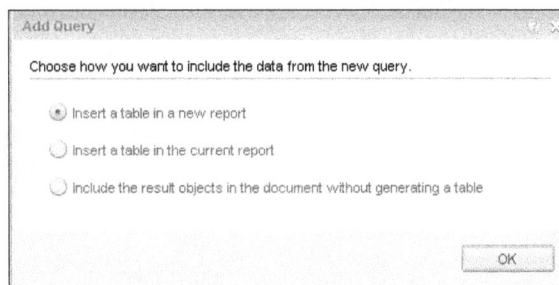

The three options are as follows:

▸ **Insert a table in a new report**: This will insert the new query data in a new report tab

▸ **Insert a table in the current report**: This will insert the new query data in the current report beside the existing query's result table

> ▶ **Include the result objects in the document without generating a table**: The returned objects and data will not be presented, but will be available for dragging-and-dropping later if the user needs to do so

We will pick the second option and get the second query result next to the first query table, as shown:

Category of Car	Maker	Sales Revenue
4X4	Leep	332,415
4X4	Scoobaru	188,512
COUPE	Austin Martini	891,819
COUPE	Fennari	670,876
COUPE	Forsche	233,298
COUPE	Lowtoos	475,940.5
COUPE	Rolls Choice	399,510
ESTATE	Valdo	527,940
OPEN TOP	Catorhammer	217,675
OPEN TOP	Fennari	1,640,192
OPEN TOP	Forsche	491,050
OPEN TOP	Lowtoos	222,304.5

Client Name	Client Town	Client Country	Sales Revenu
Abaunza, Howard	Chatham	United Kingdom	13,250
Answersen, Pamela	Malibu	USA	22,800
Barkley, John	London	United Kingdom	45,210
Barry, John	Dallas	USA	105,444
Benson, Jack	San Jose	USA	24,300
Blacksen, Karen	New York	USA	22,455
Bloomhead, Peter	Hollywood	USA	71,605
Blumenhein, Joe	Hollywood	USA	47,745
Bonnehammer, John	Hollywood	USA	155,005
Brent, Paul	Malibu	USA	315,964.5
Brown, Peter	Hollywood	USA	71,605
Carter, Sue	Boston	USA	39,995

How it works...

Creating another query is just as easy as creating the first one. Simply perform the same procedure one more time. After clicking on the **Add Query** button, we are walked through an already familiar universe screen to choose our next data provider.

Both of the reports are run and each query fetches its own dataset. As we have seen, the tables can be presented in the same report tab or in different report tabs.

When we are saving a Web Intelligence report, the query structure as well as the data in the presentation layer is saved.

There is no compulsion to combine the results of the different queries into one common table—it's all about the purpose of the report and the business user requirements. A business analyst might require a 360-degree report that displays a different aspect of the data in every tab of the report based on a different universe.

Note that when we refresh the report, we don't refresh the table and nor do we refresh the report tabs—it's the query that is being refreshed! As an outcome of the query refresh, all the visual components such as tables, charts, and cells are updated accordingly.

> You can refresh several queries with the same prompt as long as the text in all the prompts is the same and the objects which are used in the prompts share the same data type.

See also

> ▸ For information on how to combine several queries from different universes, see *Chapter 8, Merging Data*

Working with several queries

When working with several queries, it is recommended to work with conventions.

First of all, we would like to give a meaningful name to each query. This is important for several reasons, as follows:

- ▸ When the report consumes several queries, it is easier to know which query should be edited.
- ▸ Reports travel through time and users. They are changed over time and can lose track of their initial purpose. Working with conventions will keep the report as clear as possible.
- ▸ Theoretically, when running a report that is a combination of several queries, one or more queries can fail to retrieve results. By giving each query a name, it would be easier to identify which query is the problematic one. This is why it is recommended to not give generic names such as `query 1`, `query 2`, and so on.

How to do it...

We will be able to edit the query by right-clicking on the **Query** tab, as shown in the following screenshot:

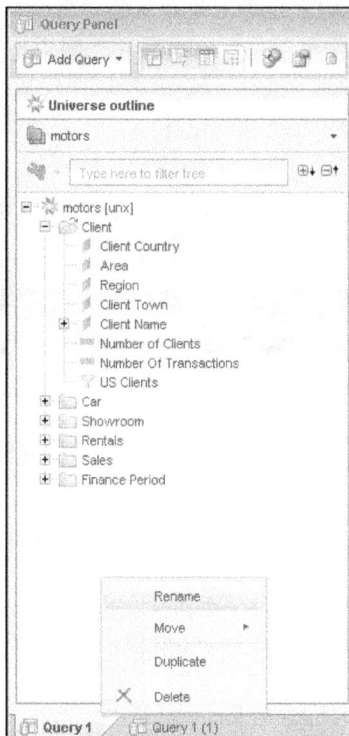

The **Rename** query pane will pop up and we will be able to give the query a meaningful name, as shown:

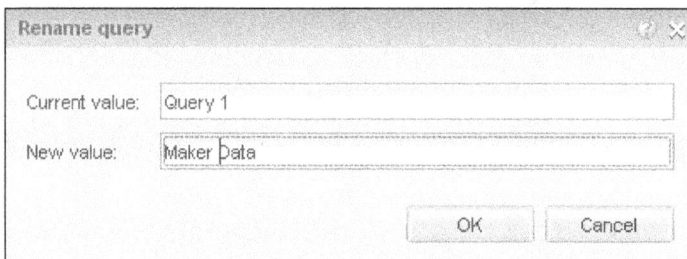

Now that both of the queries have a meaningful name, it will be much more organized and it will be easy to work with several queries.

There's more...

Besides renaming, there are several additional actions that can be performed as well:

- **Move**: The query can be moved left or right. When working with several queries, it can be useful to order them according to the data subjects.

- **Duplicate**: This option duplicates the query and is extremely helpful when we are building several queries that are similar to each other.

- **Delete**: When a query is no longer required, it can be deleted.

> Note that there is no undo option for this action or for the other actions in the **Query** panel.

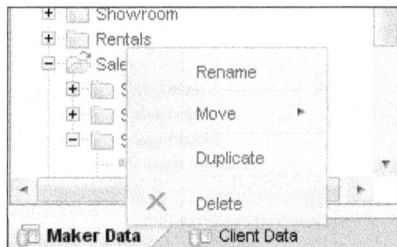

If we want to monitor all the query statistics, we should use the **Data** view in the report level. Here, we can see all the queries and their basic statistics such as duration, number of rows retrieved, and so on:

This panel is very important because it enables us to get all the query statistics in one place as well as manage them by right-clicking on one of the query names.

By double-clicking on the query name, we will switch to raw data display, which is similar to the preview pane in the **Query Panel**.

See also

- For more on how to manage each query property, refer to the next recipe, *Working with the query properties*

Working with the query properties

We can also manage query properties by navigating to the query options located on the **Query Panel**.

Getting ready

We want to edit the query properties as well as discover the available options.

How to do it...

In the main **Query Panel** toolbar, we will click on the query properties button located to the right of the combined query icon, as shown in the following screenshot:

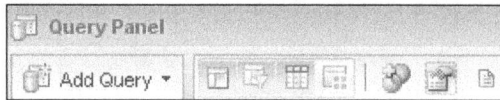

The **Query Properties** panel will appear, enabling us to change the query properties, as shown:

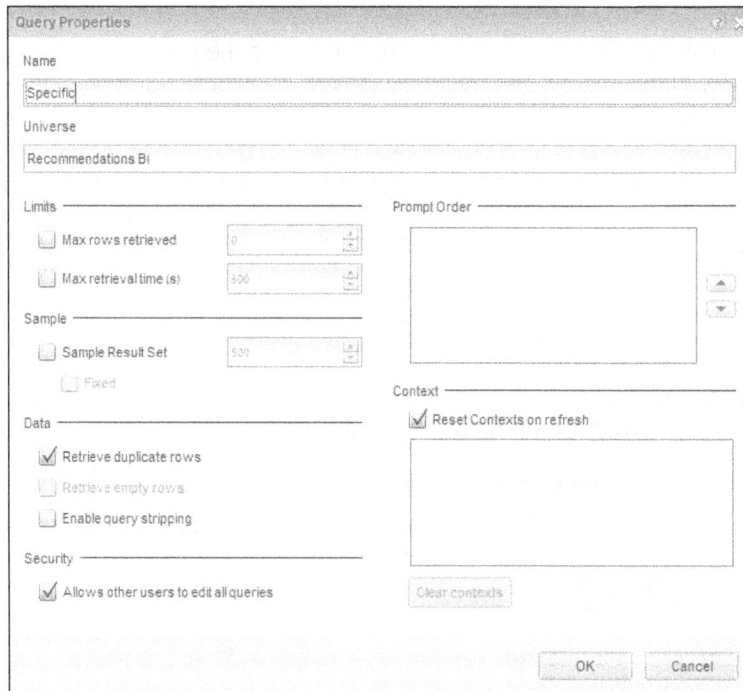

We can find the following options in this panel:

- **Name**: This is similar to the previous recipe's discussion.
- **Universe** This is the query source name.
- **Limits**: Using this, the number of rows in the query and the maximum retrieval time(s) can be limited; these limits can't exceed the universe definitions.

   This feature is mainly good for QA purposes and when we want to quickly apply formatting on a small amount of data while keeping the running time as short as possible. This option can't override the universe limitations or the database limitation, as it's not possible nor would it be logical to increase the number of return rows to 2 billion rows.

   Also note that query results can't be limited for real reporting as it will require the entire dataset to be fetched.

- **Sample**: This is a function that enables us to fetch fixed random results. As opposed to the **Limits** option that will always bring the same result, the **Sample** option will use random logic and fetch different rows each time (applied, of course, by the query result objects and filters).

   This feature is great for QA purposes and for supporting pilot requests from the business, such as sampling different client groups for the marketing department.

- **Retrieve duplicate rows**: When we are retrieving results, the same data can be repeated. This option eliminates duplicate values as it is checked by default. Unchecking this option will create a **Select Distinct** statement.

   Note that by default Web Intelligence doesn't present a duplicate row, which is the same row having the exact same values in all its columns.

   Usually, duplicated rows are eliminated when using measures that created aggregations as per the dimension values.

- **Retrieve empty rows**: This is an option that is relevant to OLAP data sources.
- **Allows other users to edit all queries**: This locks or enables the **Edit** icon in the report layer. By doing so, we prevent/allow other users to edit the query.
- **Query stripping**: This is a great option to improve the query performance. The **Query stripping** option indicates those objects that are included in the query but not used in the report. These objects should ideally be removed from the query.

> The **Query stripping** option is available for OLAP-based universes (UNX) and relational universes, including HANA from version 4.1.

- ▸ **Prompt Order**: Since prompts are arranged alphabetically by the prompt text, a custom prompt order can be defined to match the user preferences when the query is run.

- ▸ **Reset Contexts on refresh**: There are cases where the user is required to pick up a context before he or she runs the query, as shown in the following screenshot:

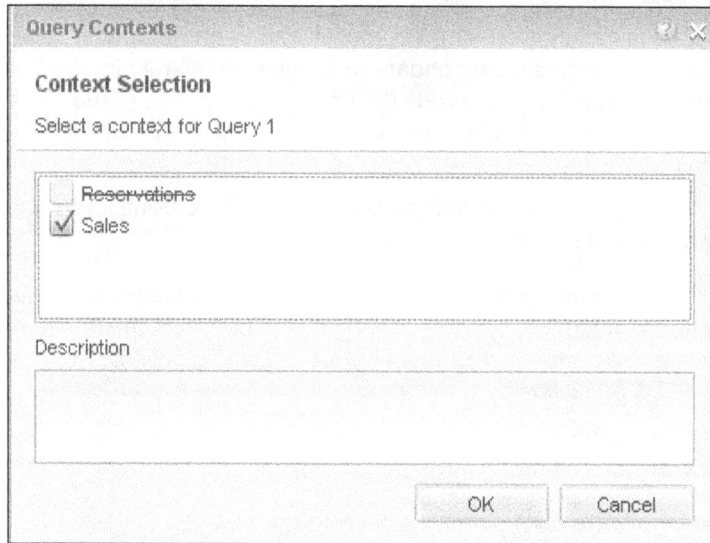

Unchecking this option will select the context that was chosen without prompting the **Context** screen anymore, as shown here:

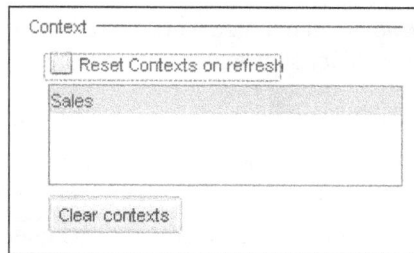

How it works...

As we have seen, the query properties are a set of options that the user can use to adjust the query for different purposes: better QA, prompt and context control, as well as performance improvements by using the **Query stripping** option.

See also

▶ For further information on how to quality-assure the results of a query, see
   Appendix, Applying Best Practices, QA, and Tips and Tricks to Our Reports

Using the data preview

The data preview is a useful option in the **Query Panel** when we want to get a preview of the
data; that is, see the raw data before it gets fetched and formatted in the table.

This option is great for getting a "sense" of the data, if the values we expect to be returned are
actually these.

This feature can also be useful when we want to make sure a specific value was returned
by the query but isn't shown in the report results for some reason, for example, a local
report filter.

Getting ready

We want to get the data preview before we run the report and get the results.

How to do it...

We will click on the **Refresh** option located to the upper-right corner of the
Data Preview window.

Now, we will be able to see that this pane is populated with the row data, as shown in the
following screenshot:

Data Preview						Result 1 ▼	🔄 Refresh
Country	Resort	Service Line	Service	Revenue	Number of g...		
France	French Riviera	Accommodat...	Bungalow	126240	140		
France	French Riviera	Accommodat...	Hotel Room	116790	106		
France	French Riviera	Accommodat...	Hotel Suite	320220	200		
France	French Riviera	Food & Drinks	Fast Food	28440			
France	French Riviera	Food & Drinks	Poolside Bar	46320			

🔍▾ Type a text to filter the values

How it works...

Data preview is another feature in the **Query Panel** that we can use to our benefit. Seeing
the row data before it's formatted, filtered, and so on in the report level can be very
informative in some cases when we want to get a better understanding of the data
regardless of its formatting.

There is more

The row data can also be previewed by using the **Data** option in the report level.

See also

▶   For more information on how to view the raw data, see *Chapter 3, Working Inside the Report*

Viewing the SQL

SQL stands for structured query language. It is code that is used for direct database querying when writing code using programming tools.

The universe outline generates SQL code as soon as objects are dragged-and-dropped into the **Result Objects** and **Query Filters** panes.

The user generates complex SQL code without understanding the nature of SQL.

As a best practice, the business user shouldn't access or deal with the SQL language, but on the other hand, it could be handy to get an idea of what's happening behind the scenes by viewing the SQL code. Of course, you need to be familiar with the SQL code and the table structure.

Viewing the SQL code is useful only for those users (Business Intelligence developers, advanced analysts, and the QA team) who are qualified to understand SQL code as well as have an understanding of the database structure.

We need a different type of join, that is, a special analytical or advanced SQL structure when we need to verify the origin tables of the objects, when we need to verify the validity of the SQL code, when we have SQL code and we want to debug it, and of course, the main reason—when we need to adjust and edit the SQL code since the universe structure doesn't support the SQL structure.

How to do it...

We will click on the **View Script** button located at the top of the **Query Panel** toolbar, as shown in the following screenshot:

The **Query Script viewer** window will be launched as shown here:

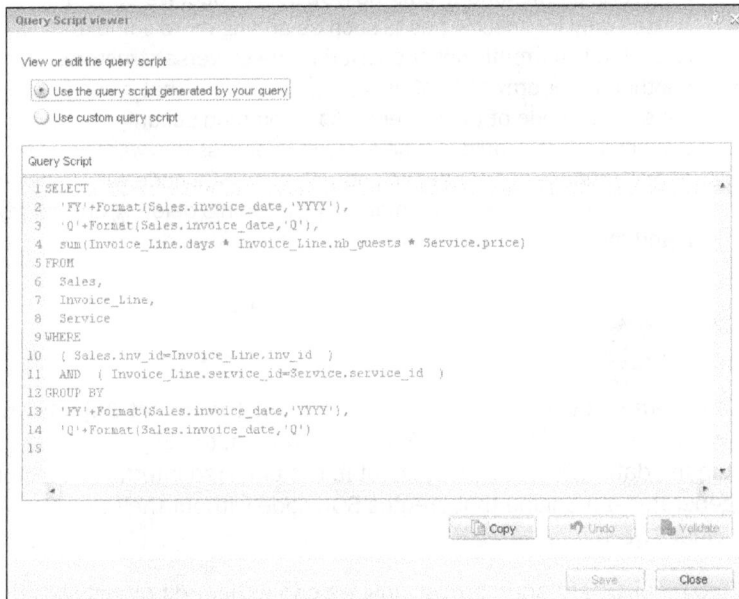

Switching to **Use custom query script** will enable us to copy and adjust the script if we need to use the SQL generated instead of writing it in one of the SQL programming tools, as shown in the following screenshot:

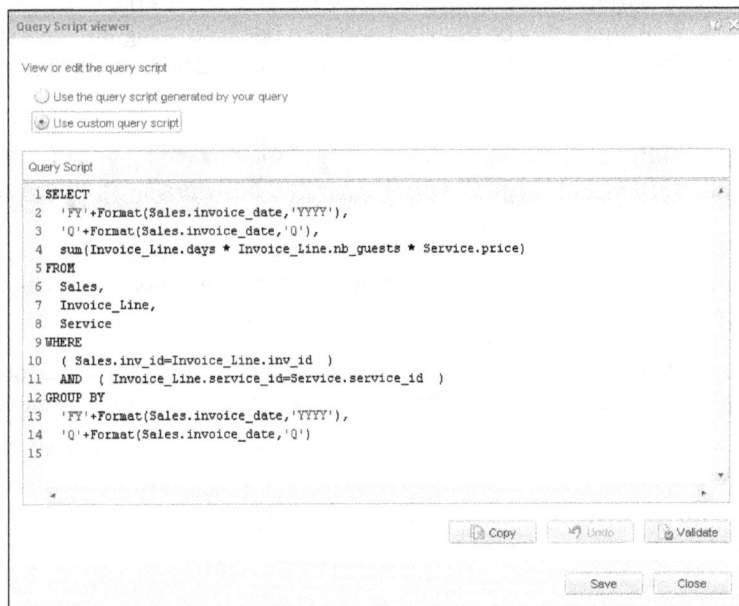

It's not recommended to edit the SQL query code. It's better if it is used only for specific needs such as adding more complex SQL code that is currently not supported in the universe structure. Another major drawback of using custom code is that it can overrun the security code of the universe. As a common security practice, business users should just be allowed to access this window with no permissions to change the code. Custom SQL code will be lost as soon as the query is edited manually by adding/deleting objects from it and the structure returns to the universe SQL code.

How it works...

The SQL code is generated by the objects the user drags to the **Result Objects** and **Query Filters** panes. When the user clicks on the **Run query** button, the SQL code is sent to the database to fetch the data. When we think about it, the universe interface is simply a drag-and-drop SQL generator—an engine that creates SQL code without the user knowing or understanding what SQL is.

Depending on the requirement and permissions, we can either edit or just view the existing code.

There's more...

In some of the projects that I have worked on, I was asked to enable business users to create free-hand reports. Well, that won't be required anymore because using free-hand SQL as a data provider is a planned feature that is supposed to be added to Web Intelligence by the end of 2014 (subject to changes).

Using other query results

Using other query results is an advanced method about how to restrict other queries based on other types of operands. This concept is similar to the subquery concept with some differences:

- The query doesn't generate SQL; rather, it uses the results returned by other query results (could be seen as a local function rather than a database function).

- Query results from other universes can be used (in a subquery, it is limited to the same universe).

- Other data providers such as Excel can be used too.

- The number of rows that the main query can process from the inner query is limited to 1,000 rows (the 1,000 value limit is a common limit for most of the databases; however, in some cases, it's possible to extend it to 3,000 or even 10,000 rows. It's advised to consult your database administrator or BI support team in case you require more than 1,000 values).

Getting ready

We are required to create a summarized query that will fetch the states with sales revenue greater than 7 million dollars.

Based on these query results, we would like to create a detailed query that will present the data for those states in the City level as well.

Note that this query can't be performed in one step because if we drag the State, City, and Sales Revenue objects, the query will be detailed in the City level when there is no city with more than 7 million dollars of sales revenue.

How to do it...

We will create the first aggregative query: sales revenue per state with sales revenue greater than 7 million, as shown in the following screenshot:

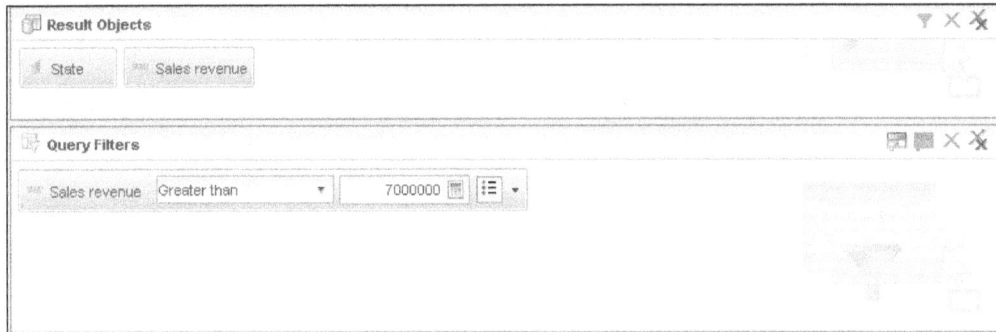

We will get the following results on running the query:

State	Sales revenue
California	$7,479,569
New York	$7,582,221
Texas	$10,117,664

Based on this list of states, we will create a second query that will extend this data and fetch the City level as well.

The second city will include the **City** dimension as well. In the query filter, we will use the **State** object. We will pick the **In list** operator since we are looking for more than one state, and in the operand we will pick the **Results from another query** option, as shown in the following screenshot:

In the next screen, we will choose the object from the query that we are required to compare via the **State** object, as shown here:

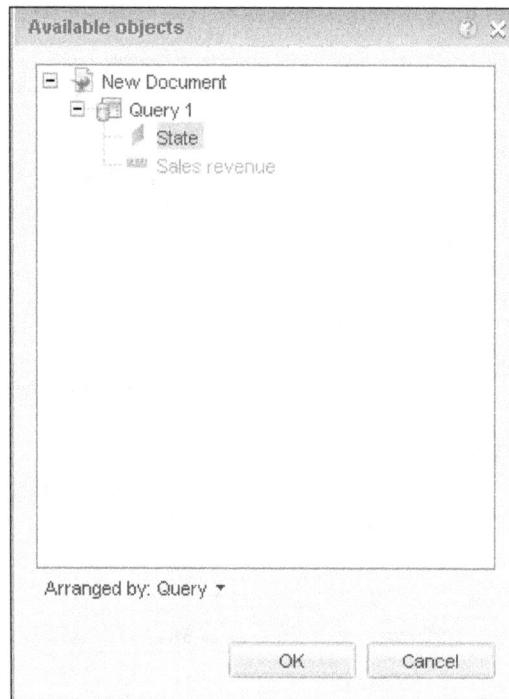

Picking the **State** object will finalize our filter:

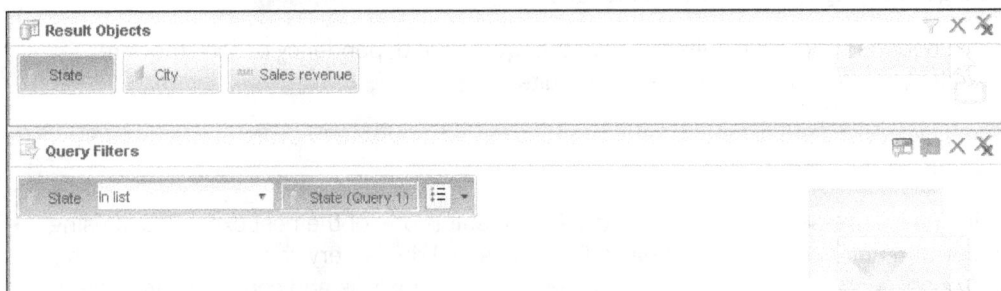

Result Objects		
State	City	Sales revenue

Query Filters		
State	In list ▼	State (Query 1) ≡ ▼

We will run the queries and get a city's detailed results based on our first query. Note that at the summarized level, we can see that the revenue is greater than 7 million although we fetched the **City** object as well, as shown in the following screenshot:

State	City	Sales revenue
California	Los Angeles	$4,220,929
	San Francisc	$3,258,641
California	**Sum:**	**$7,479,569**

State	City	Sales revenue
New York	New York	$7,582,221
New York	**Sum:**	**$7,582,221**

State	City	Sales revenue
Texas	Austin	$2,699,673
	Dallas	$1,970,034
	Houston	$5,447,957
Texas	**Sum:**	**$10,117,664**

How it works...

Using results from another query is similar to the subquery concept—using the first query for the benefit of the second.

The behind-the-scenes workflow can be thought of as the detailed query running on the `Sates with sales revenue greater than 7 million` table.

This means that the detailed query is using the aggregative query as its data source and not running directly against the entire database.

Both subqueries and the results from another query are dependency based—they are dependent on the inner query to return results.

There's more...

Basing your universe query upon an Excel file's result is one of the best examples of using results from another query. Creating an Excel personal data query can help us reduce the main query search criteria as well as enable advanced analysis and complementary data aspects that are sourced only in a personal data file. With this technique, we can base, for example, the query results only on the client IDs we are managing in our Excel file.

See also

> ▶ For more information on how to create a query based on an Excel file, see the *Merging data from different data sources* recipe in *Chapter 8, Merging Data*

Scope of analysis

Scope of analysis is a method to add objects that will not be displayed when the results are fetched, but will be used for additional analysis of more detailed levels of data.

This method is known as **drill**, and by using it, the user can define a data navigation path from high-level data to low-level data.

This has a dedicated panel in the **Query Panel** and can be activated by clicking on the **Scope of analysis** panel button.

Getting ready

We are required to activate the Scope of analysis panel as we want to explore its major options.

How to do it...

We will create a query that presents the **State**, **Year**, and **Sales Revenue** result objects.

By clicking on the **Scope of analysis** panel icon located to the left of the **Combined Query** icon, we will see the panel located at the bottom-right of the **Query Panel**, as shown in the following screenshot:

Note that the **Year** and **State** dimensions are appearing in the following panel:

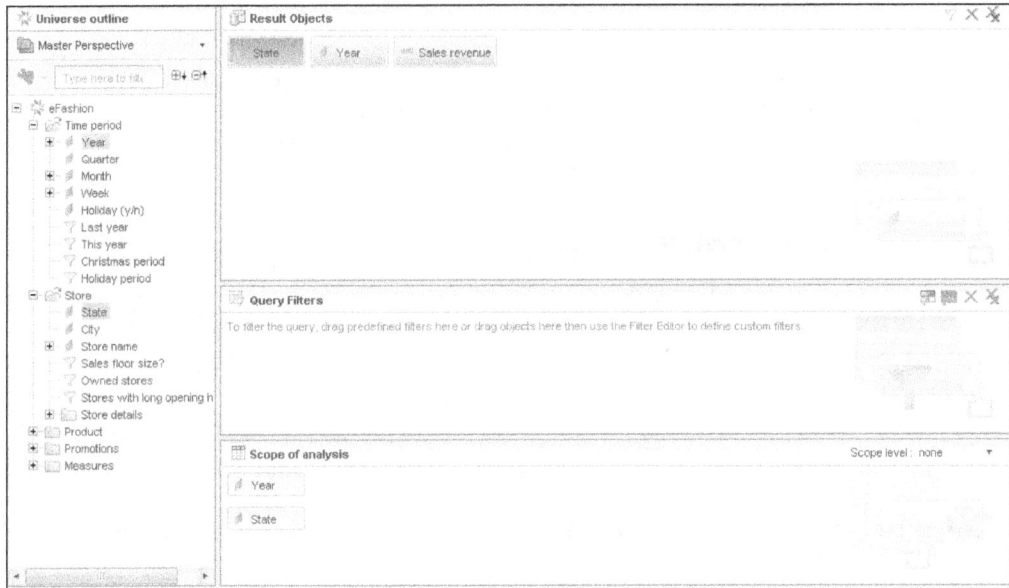

We can expand the scope of analysis objects by using a predefined or custom drill option, as shown in the following screenshot:

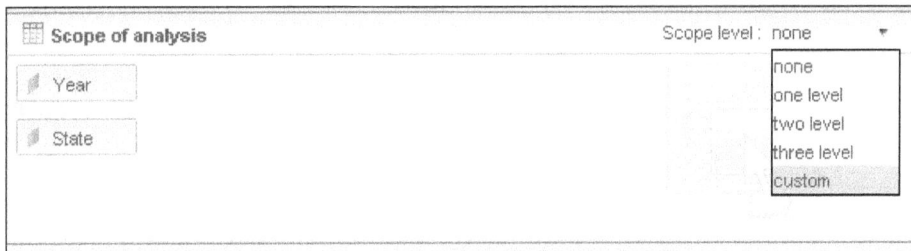

There are four main options in the dropdown of the **Scope of analysis** box:

- **one level**: This will fetch another object that is located one level below the chosen result object (**City** and **Quarter**)

- **two level**: This will fetch two more objects that are located up to two levels below the chosen result object (**City**, **Store name**, and **Quarter month**)

- **three level**: This will fetch three more objects that are located up to three levels below the chosen result object (**City**, **Store name**, **Quarter month**, and **Week**)

- **custom**: The user can add objects from any class in the universe outline, adjusting the scope to his or her specific requirements

> Note that scope of analysis is functional if there are hierarchies defined in the universe structure by the universe designer, as well as when there are cases where the dimension object doesn't have three more dimensions defined under it.

We will choose the **three level** option:

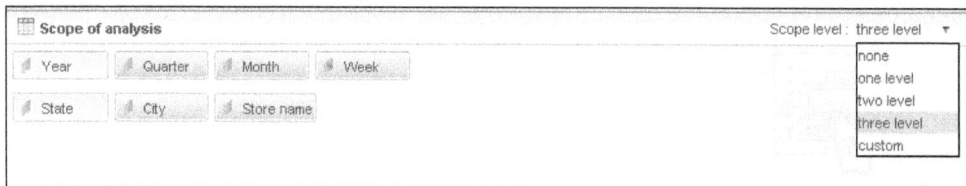

Scope of analysis				Scope level : three level ▼
Year	Quarter	Month	Week	none
				one level
State	City	Store name		two level
				three level
				custom

Note that the `store` class contains only two objects under the **State** object although we chose **three level**.

We will run the report and activate the **Drill** option. Note that the result object is the only one presented, but we can further analyze the data by zooming on a dimension object, as shown in the following screenshot:

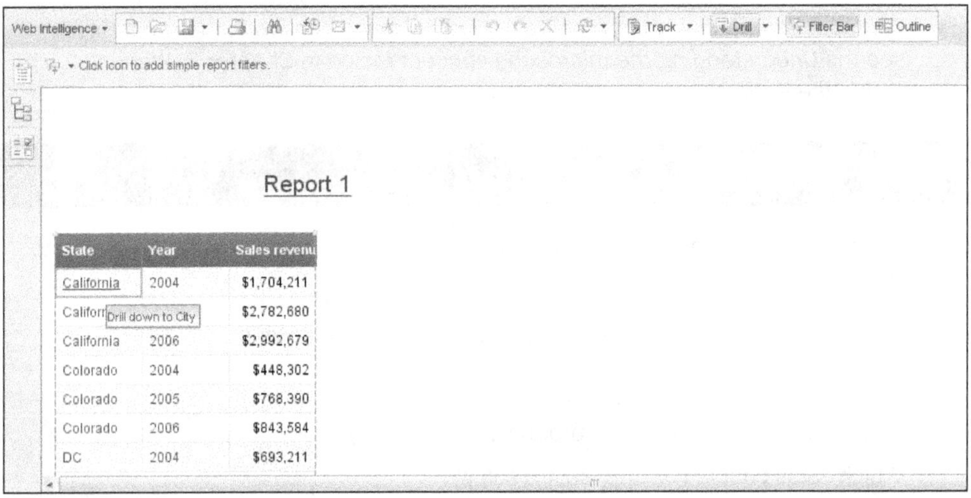

We will drill down to city-level data by choosing the **City** option, as shown here:

City	Year	Sales revenue
Los Angeles	2004	$982,637
Los Angeles	2005	$1,581,616
Los Angeles	2006	$1,656,676
San Francisc	2004	$721,574
San Francisc	2005	$1,201,064
San Francisc	2006	$1,336,003

How it works...

Scope of analysis enables us to define which objects will be used as drill objects.

By defining a specific level of scope or a custom one, we will be able to create an analysis patch that is drilling from high-level data to low-level data.

The objects that are placed in the **Scope of analysis** pane can only be of dimension type. Once the scope is set, these objects will be brought to the report as well, but will be stored locally in the report level, ready to be used for drilling.

See also

- For more information on how to work with the Drill option, see *Chapter 11, Using Drill*

- For more information on how objects are stored and behave in the report level, see the *Understanding the microcube concept* recipe in *Chapter 3, Working Inside the Report*

Using database ranking

Database ranking is an advanced query filter that can rank the query results according to a measure.

Ranking is good for classical business questions such as the following:

- Who are the top *n* customers by revenue?
- What are the top *n* most sold products?
- Which sales people had the least *n* sales?

Getting ready

We want to rank the top five best salespeople based on their sales revenue.

How to do it...

First, we will build our query by dragging-and-dropping the **Sales Person** and **Sales Revenue** objects. We will mark the **Sales Person** dimension objects and click on the **Add a database ranking** button located on the query filter's top right-hand side, as shown in the following screenshot:

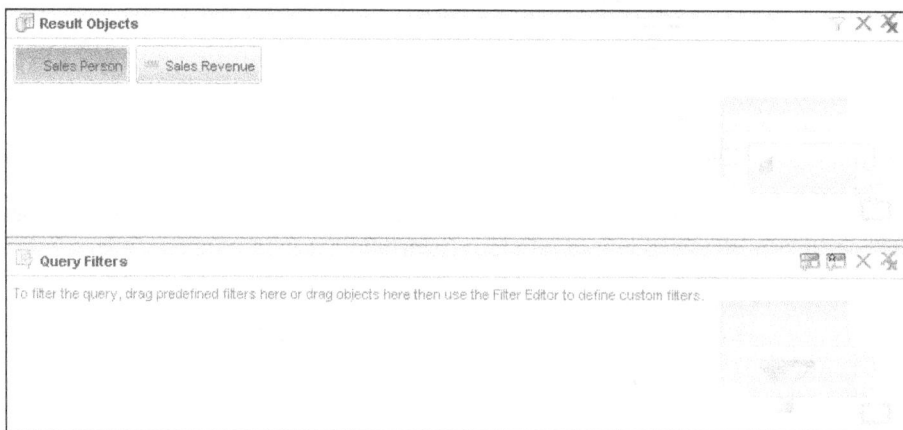

In the database ranking created filter, we will notice the following options:

▶ The ranking can be adjusted to **Top**, **Bottom**, **% Top**, **% Bottom** (that is, from the number of records):

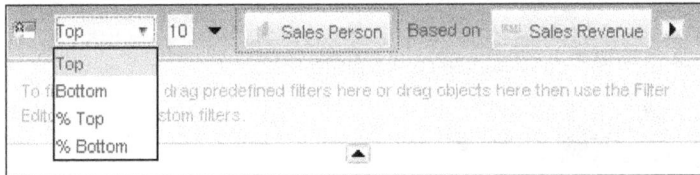

▶ The default ranking number is **10**, but it can be adjusted to any other number too as it can be changed into a **Prompt**, as shown:

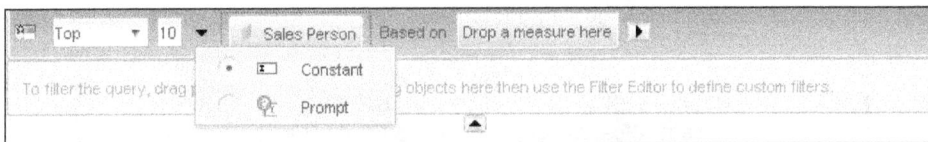

▶ The next parameter will be the measure we use to rank the **Sales Person** dimension according to the database ranking.

We will drag the measure object **Sales Revenue** to measure the area of the condition and adjust the top number to **5**, as shown in the following screenshot:

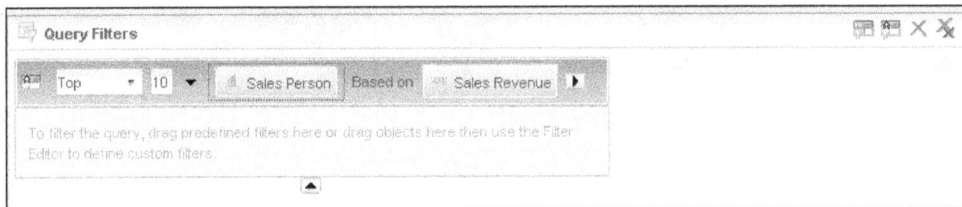

We will run the query and get the top five salespeople based on their sales revenue, as shown here:

Sales Person	Sales Revenue
Baker	441,594
Oneda	387,088
Larson	301,545
Makino	257,795
Weimar	222,910

How it works...

Database ranking is a function working at the database level, retrieving already ranked results to the report.

When adding such query filters, Web Intelligence modifies the SQL script and creates an analytical function that can process the ranking request.

There's more...

You can also add regular filters to the database ranking area and focus on a specific year's data.

You can also further extend the ranking option by using the optional **Ranked by** feature, which enables the additional dimension calculation context.

> Database ranking works only with databases that support the analytical ranking function, such as Oracle.

See also

▶ For more information on how to view rank data in the report level, see the *Ranking* recipe in *Chapter 6, Formatting Reports*

Using BEx queries

One of the new core capabilities of Web Intelligence is the integration with the SAP BW environment, which means that we can connect to BEx queries as well as to BW OLAP cubes.

Since this topic is worth an entire book by itself, I suggest that you should start with the following links in order to get some well-informed and detailed information regarding this subject: `http://scn.sap.com/community/bi-platform/businessobjects-bi-for-sap/blog/2013/06/09/sap-businessobjects-bi-4x-with-sap-bw-and-sap-bw-on-hana--latest-documents` and `http://scn.sap.com/docs/DOC-35444`.

Getting ready

We want to create a query based on one of our BEx queries in order to display the sales figures per division.

How to do it...

This time, when we select the data source, we will choose the **BEx** option. Right after that, we will need to choose the relevant BW connection for our query, as shown in the following screenshot:

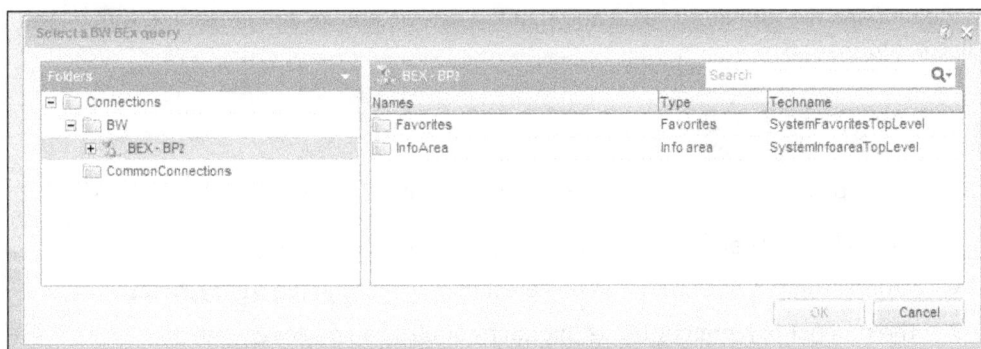

After choosing the connection, we will get a list of queries we can use. By clicking on the relevant BEx query, we will access its structure through the **Query Panel** in a way that is very similar to how we use the universe structure. The main difference is that the BEx query structure will be displayed in the report. Have a look at the following screenshot:

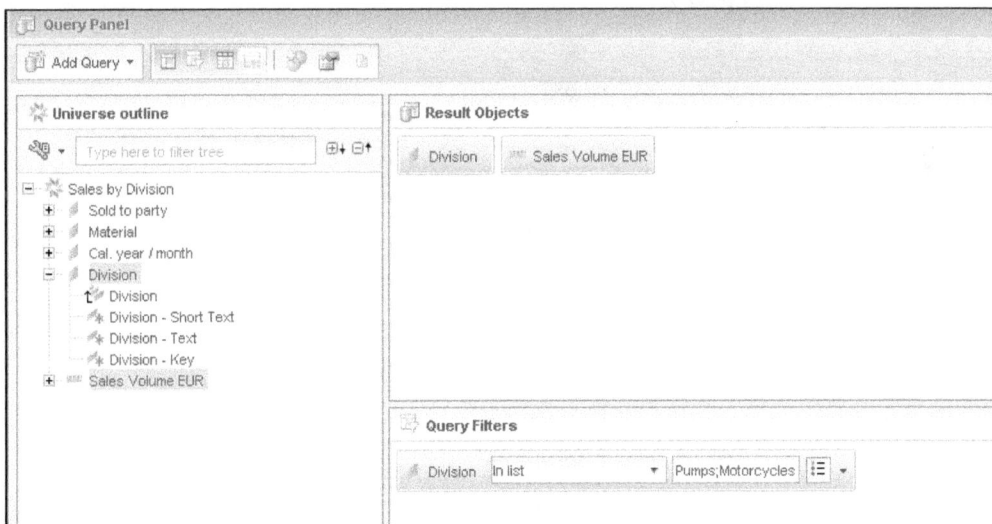

After dragging objects to the result and filter query panes, we can run the query and get the BEx query result in the report.

How it works...

The integration between SAP BusinessObjects and BW enables us to import all our BEx queries without the restriction of rebuilding them in Web Intelligence or creating a universe.

Once the BEx query is imported, we will be able to see that the key figures are presented with the unit and the formatted value and that the characteristics are presented with all the available information.

There's more...

What else is supported when using BEx as our data source? Have a look at the following:

> ▸ Hierarchy-level selection if we have variables in our BEx query
> ▸ Variables in the BEx query can be selected or ignored in the **Query Panel**
> ▸ The number of hierarchy levels (hierarchy depth) can be set as well

3
Working Inside the Report

In this chapter, we will cover the following recipes:

- ▶ Understanding the structure of the Report layer
- ▶ Understanding the concept of the microcube
- ▶ Working with the Left Pane panels
- ▶ Working with the report toolbars
- ▶ Navigating between the view modes
- ▶ The File and Properties tabs

Introduction

Building reports is what Web Intelligence is all about. While building a query lays out the data results into a table or a chart, there is another major phase involved in creating the report, and that is formatting and analyzing the results in the Report layer.

Data is formatted by interacting with several main toolbars and left-pane panel reports. The Report layer offers enhanced and rich capabilities such as filtering, sorting, calculating, creating alerts, ranking, and using different types of presentations such as tables, charts, and pivot tables, as well as implementing advanced capabilities such as creating complex variables and document linking and drilling.

Each report can be saved in the repository so that we can continue work on it, and when we save the report, it'll save the formatting as well, just as in any MS Office document. Reports are always combined from the query (/queries) or the data provider(s) and the table or charts that display and describe the data. When a Web Intelligence report is saved, both parts of the report, that is the query or data provider and the formatting applied, are saved.

In this chapter, we will cover the report toolbars; the different modes of the report; the main menus; and the panel structure, look, and feel.

Understanding the structure of the Report layer

After running a query, the data is presented in the Report layer. This main screen is structured from several main functional areas.

Getting ready

We want to get familiar with the report interface's main parts and elements in order to get a better understanding of how to work with a report.

How to do it...

We can interact with the Report layer using three different viewing modes: **Reading**, **Design**, and **Data**. These buttons are located in the toolbar at the top-right corner of the report.

The **Reading** mode is a view mode that enables minor functionalities, and it's fit for report readers who mainly refresh the report often as well as use simple filters to view the report results. The following screenshot shows the **Reading** mode:

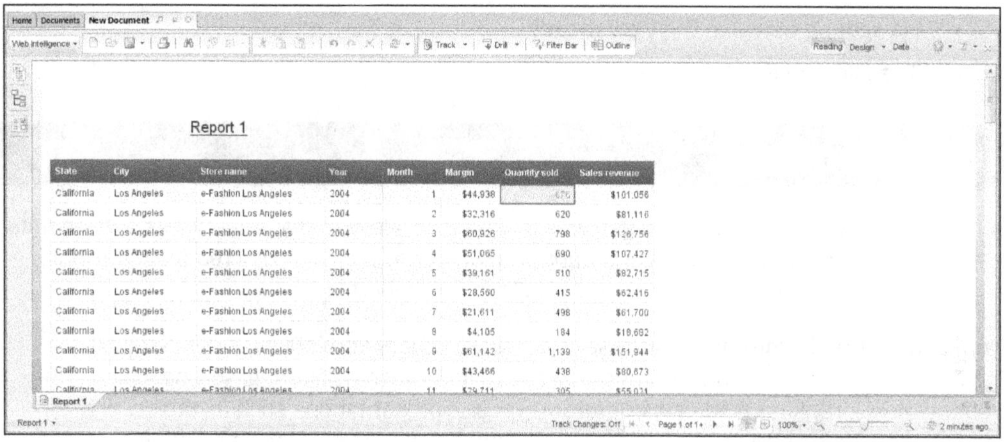

By switching to the **Design** mode, we get an enhanced and rich interface inclusive of all formatting capabilities. The following screenshot shows the report in the **Design** mode:

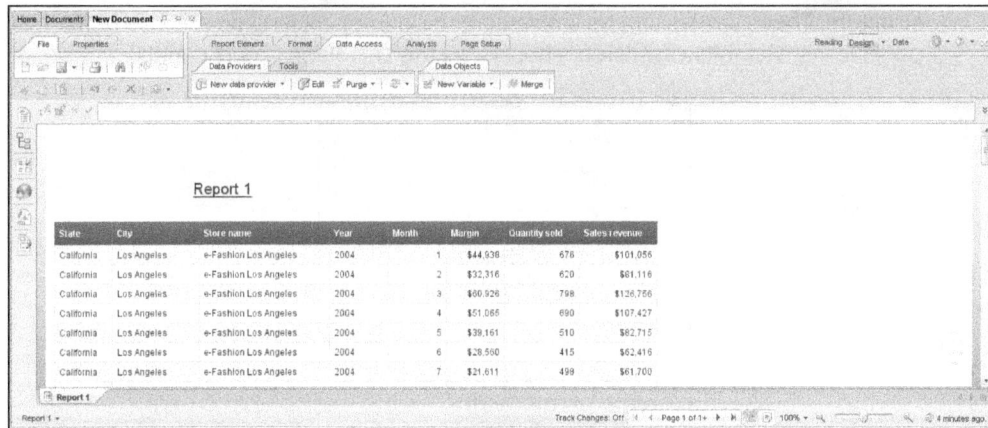

The Report layer is structured from the following main functional areas:

- ▶ **Main report toolbars**: These toolbars are located at the top-center portion of the window; these toolbars have a ribbon-style look and feel and are ordered by functional topics which are **Report Element**, **Format**, **Data Access**, **Analysis**, and **Page Setup**.

  Each main toolbar is structured from subtoolbars that enable further additional functionalities:

  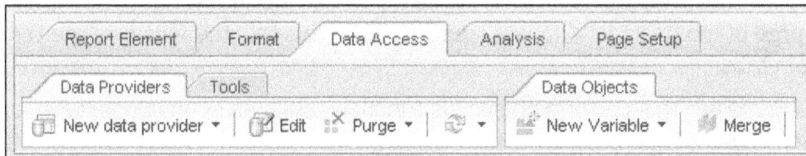

▶ **Left panes**: This includes six quick panels located to the left of the window that activate basic and important functionalities such as using available objects, using advanced filters (input controls) navigating in the report map, and the document structure. These panels can be activated or hidden by clicking on any one of the panel icons. The following screenshot shows the Left Pane report panels:

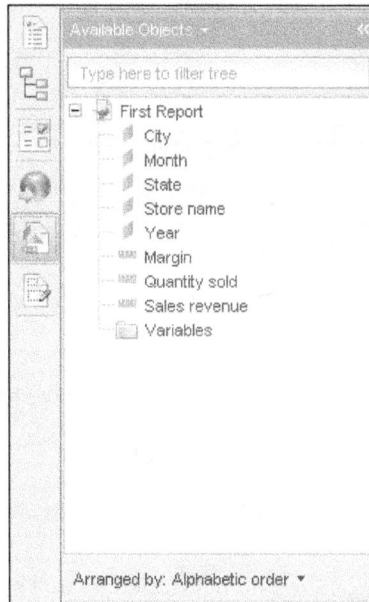

▶ **Report Tabs**: This tab is located at the top-left side of the window, and it is mainly in charge of the basic functionality report. Under this tab, the following are the two main tabs:

❑ **File**: This performs basic file functions such as open, close, save, undo, send, and others

❑ **Properties**: This adjusts the view options and the document properties

The following screenshot shows the **File** and **Properties** tabs:

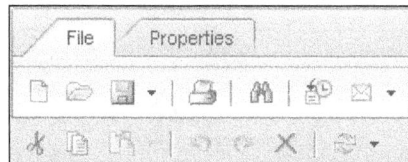

- ▸ **View mode buttons**: These buttons are located at the top-left panel and enable different view modes: **Reading**, **Design**, and **Data**. The buttons are shown in the following screenshot:

- ▸ **Status bar**: This is located at the bottom of the screen and enables navigation between the reports pages, quick view mode switch, refreshing the report, and zooming in of reports. The Status bar is shown in the following screenshot:

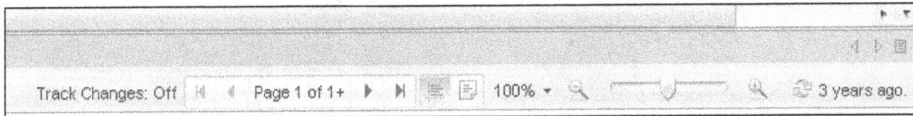

- ▸ **Main speed menu**: By right-clicking on the gray area located in any one of the bars, you will get a speed menu that enables quick access to the view modes and basic functions such as the **Filter Bar**.

How it works...

The Report layer is structured from several functional areas and enables us to address all types of tasks from its location, for example, whether formatting the report data, managing the file properties, or using the Left Pane panel to apply special functions to the report structure and data.

Understanding the concept of the microcube

Reporting and analysis are the main core functionalities of Web Intelligence. Web Intelligence report engine retrieves the data and stores it locally in a microcube report. The microcube can be described as a local structure of data, where every value of a dimension, attribute, or measure object can be sliced with any of the other object, or in more simple words, the user can display various types of aggregations and tables based on the data retrieved by the query. The following diagram is that of a microcube:

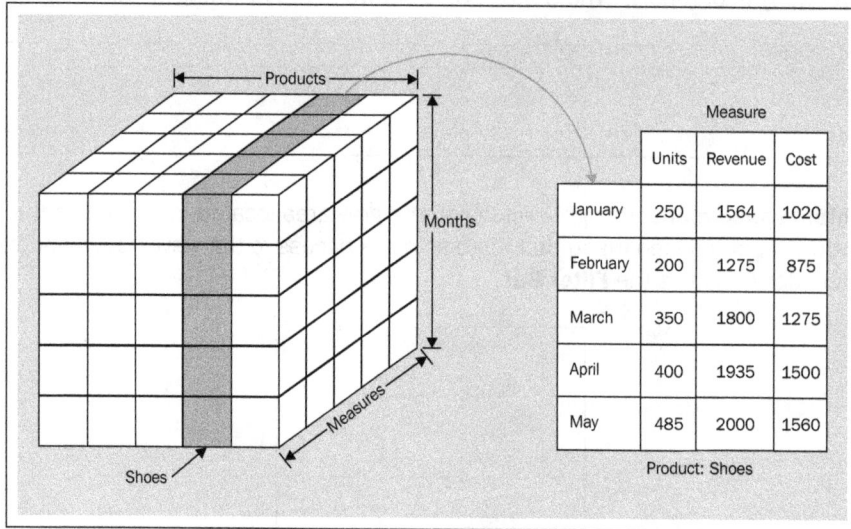

	Measure		
	Units	Revenue	Cost
January	250	1564	1020
February	200	1275	875
March	350	1800	1275
April	400	1935	1500
May	485	2000	1560

Product: Shoes

The data that was retrieved by the query is stored locally in the report and can be displayed by dragging-and-dropping the selected objects into the report. Retrieving data has nothing to do with displaying the data; a query can return huge volumes of data and many result objects, but none of them will be displayed. Usually, we will display the data in several tables or tabs, addressing different types of data levels.

So, why is this important to understand? It's because displaying data is a dynamic and flexible option where the user can choose what to display according to their requirements and not necessarily because of the query structure.

What is analysis?

Analysis can be defined in many ways and with many terms; however, in the context of Web Intelligence, it is creating different views from the same data. These views can either be detailed or summarized with all sublevels between them. We can distinguish between two general levels of data in terms of summarized or detailed.

By presenting data at a summarized level, we usually use few dimensions or attribute objects that are sliced with measure objects. By presenting detailed data, we can use more dimensions and attributes along with measure objects. The diagrammatic representation of the summarized and detailed levels of data is shown as follows:

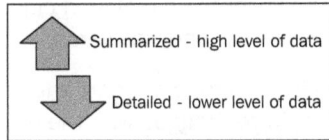

After the query's data is fetched, the data can be used in both levels, giving us the basic capabilities that will answer typical business questions such as the following:

▶ What is the sales revenue per year? (a summarized question)

▶ What is the sales revenue per customer and the invoice date? (a detailed question)

Getting ready

We will analyze the data from a different perspective, and create a summarized view of the data although the level of the query data is detailed.

How to do it...

1. From the Left Pane, we will choose **Available Objects** (the second option from the bottom).

2. We will mark the **Year** and **Sales revenue** objects by holding down the *Ctrl* key, and drag them to the report table area which is to the left of the detailed table that displays the sales revenue year wise. The resultant table is shown in the following screenshot:

3. Note that the sales revenue was automatically aggregated per the **Year** dimension and that although we can see many objects in the left-hand side pane, we are using just two of them for our new aggregative table.

How it works...

The Web Intelligence report engine can drop any type of presentation based on the data returned. As we have seen, although the granular level of data can be detailed, we can summarize it to high level views; the fewer the dimension objects used in the table, the more summarized the presentation will be, and vice versa.

When dragging-and-dropping certain objects, the report engine immediately projects the results as per the dimension(s) that were dragged with the measure, thus enabling the values of the measure objects to be presented in the relevant dimension object's level.

Dragging-and-dropping a summarized view can also be seen as creating subsets of the data from the original retrieved raw data. Our rule of thumb would be that the grand total of a revenue measure or net sales would be the same no matter what dimension or dimensions we will slice with it. The difference would be in the row level, where the measure is aggregated differently according to the dimension that was projected with it. This is why the nature of measures is dynamic and dependent on the dimension and attributes.

There's more...

When you are planning your report design, it's important to take into consideration the fact it can serve both the summarized and detailed purposes, even if the data is displayed in the same report tab or in separate report tabs. I have seen too many reports in my life that were created separately, or each table in them was based on a different query. The only reason for this is the lack of understanding of how the microcube works.

Also, it's advised to avoid common data-level mistakes, for example, don't use the customer ID dimension objects and then count them in the report only if you actually require to display the number of customers per product (if it's possible, use the aggregate measure **Number of Customers** in a universe).

See also

- ▸ *Working with the Left Pane panels* to understand how to work with the **Available Objects** panel in the Left Pane
- ▸ *Chapter 4, Working with Tables*, to understand how to insert tables in the report table area

Working with the Left Pane panels

The Left Pane panels are interactive panels that provide additional functionalities to the report and not just how to manipulate the data in it.

With the Left Pane report panels, the user can get important information regarding the report and query status, as we saw when we performed the drag-and-drop data tasks, and use advanced filters and navigate through the report structure.

Getting ready

We will explore the Left Pane panels' functionalities and options.

How to do it...

We will explore the Left Pane panels, starting from the top most one, as follows:

- **Document Summary**: This provides the report's metadata, which is categorized into several topics discussed as follows:

    - **General**: This includes **Type, Author, Creation date, Locale, Description, Keywords**

    - **Statistics**: This includes **Last Refresh Date, Last Modified, Last Modified By**, and **Duration of Previous Refresh**

    - **Document options**: This supplies information about the properties defined in the **Properties** report tab

    - **Data options**: This supplies information about the data options set in the report such as data tracking and merge dimension behavior

    - **Parameters**: In case the report uses a prompt, the values that were picked will be shown in this window.

    The preceding panels are shown in the following screenshot:

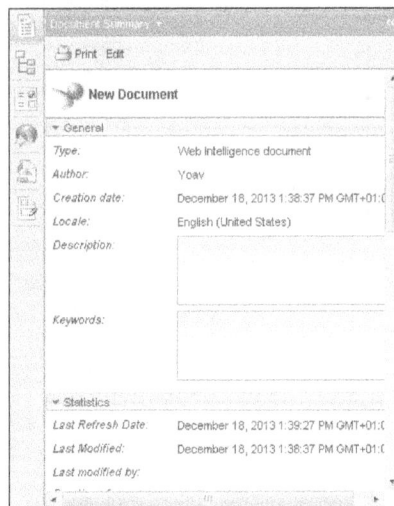

> You can edit the properties, keywords, and other file properties by clicking on the **Edit** button located to the right-hand side of the **Print** button under the **Document Summary** pane title.

▸ **Navigation Map**: This provides an easy Report tab navigation as well as section bookmark map. This is one of the most useful panes to obtain quick report navigation and provides a high-level view on the report structure. The **Navigation Map** panel is shown in the following screenshot:

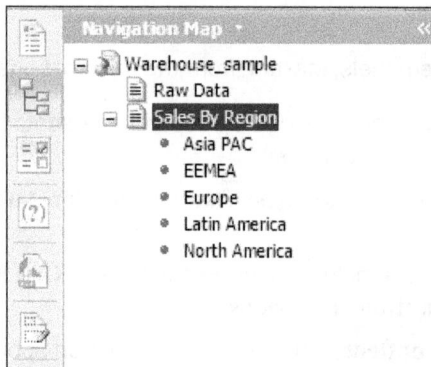

▸ **Input Controls**: This panel is used for creating custom filters by choosing a specific look-and-feel type filter from a list of components. The following screenshot shows the list box filter type which is a single value filter under **Input Controls**:

▶ **Web Services Publisher**: This enables us to turn tables in the report into web services that can be used in other BI tools of the SAP BI4 platform such as Dashboard Design and outside of the SAP BI platform.

▶ **Available objects**: This is one of the core functionalities that we have already discussed. It shows the result objects that were retrieved by queries, displays the variables created by the user, and enables to merge dimensions. This window is important because it enables us to create different views of the data as described in the former recipe. The objects in this panel can be sorted alphabetically or per query.

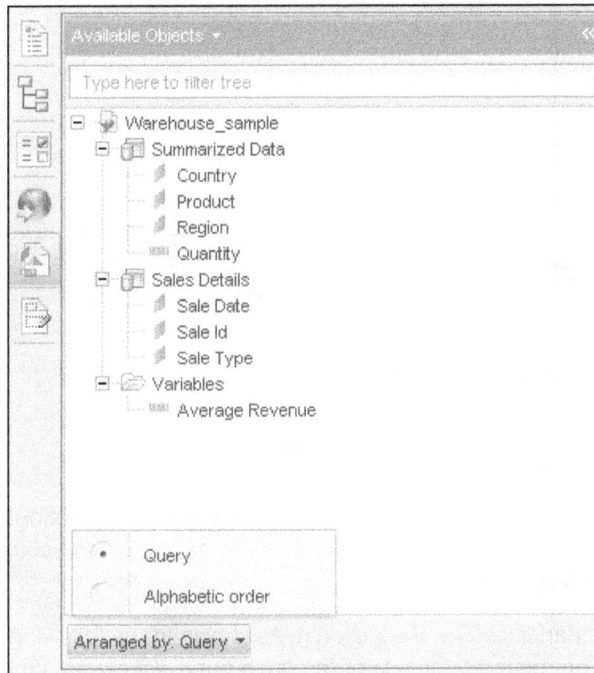

▶ **Document Structure and Filters**: This pane shows us the structure of all the tables and charts in all the report tabs, as well as indicating whether a single filter or multiple filters have been applied to the tables. Getting a preview of how each of the filters work is extremely useful when we are working with a report we didn't create and want to have a better understanding of its structure.

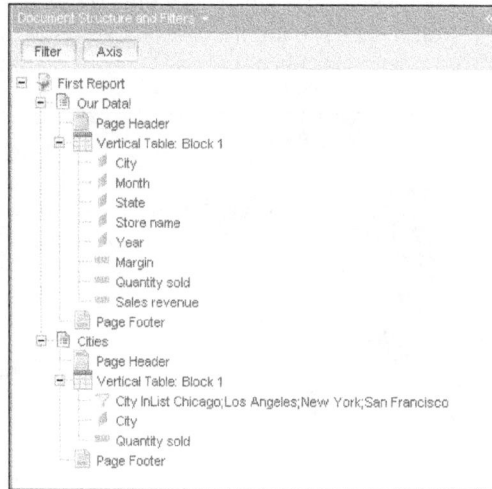

How it works...

As we have seen, the Left Pane report panels enhance the report functionalities by providing us additional information about the report as well as some basic and solid core functionalities such as the **Available Objects** pane.

We can activate each panel icon by clicking on it. As shown in the following screenshot, by clicking on the arrow on the top-right side of the open pane, we can minimize it:

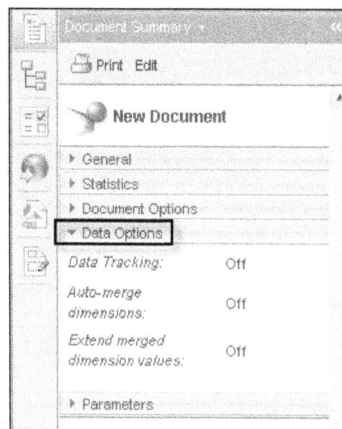

There's more...

While working with the view mode, we will get a thinner functionality fitted for the view mode. In this mode, we will have access only to these panels: **Document summary**, **Report map**, and **Input controls**.

See also

▶ For further reading on how to work with the input control, refer to the *Using input controls* recipe in *Chapter 7, Filtering the Report Data*

▶ *Chapter 4, Working with Tables,* for how to insert tables in the report table area

Working with the report toolbars

The main report interaction and functionality is conducted by using the report toolbars. These toolbars are used mainly to apply additional functionalities to the data in the report, format the report area, and perform advanced tasks of drill and data merging.

By using these toolbars, we can address various types of tasks ranging from a simple task such as formatting the table headers to advanced capabilities such as filtering, sorting, creating calculations, and editing the query. The toolbars are grouped according to the main functionality subjects and structured from the subtab areas. The toolbars are as follows:

▶ Report Element

▶ Format

▶ Data Access

▶ Analysis

▶ Page Setup

In this recipe, we will explain how to work with each of the toolbars and understand what type of task requires which type of toolbar.

Getting ready

We will focus on the working of the toolbars in the **Design** mode.

How to do it...

We will explore the report toolbars by getting to know them one by one as follows:

▶ **Report Element**: This toolbar is designed to insert different types of tables and charts as well as add other elements such as cell and sections into the report area. This toolbar is combined from four main tabs that are shown in the following screenshot:

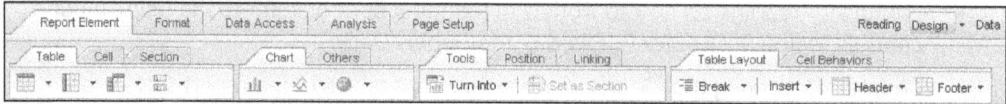

The first area is a combination of three subtabs and controls the different types of table presentations such as tables, charts, pivot, standalone cells, formula cells, sections, and breaks. Each one of them is discussed as follows:

❑ **Table**: The insertion of tables enables us to create different types of data presentations easily and quickly.

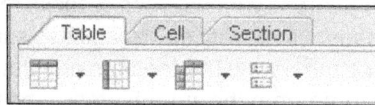

By clicking on an icon and dragging it to the report area, we will be able to create a new table.

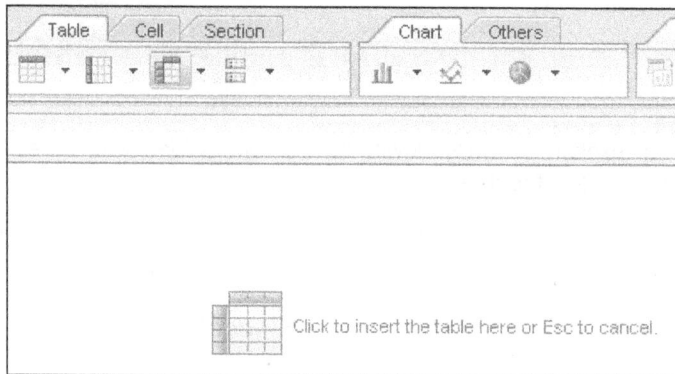

Click to insert the table here or Esc to cancel.

❑ **Cell**: This subtab enables us to insert predefined cells such as **Last Refresh Date**, **Prompt Summary**, and so on.

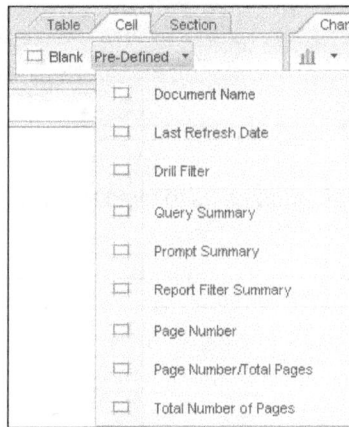

❑ **Section**: This subtab inserts sections that enable the grouping of data in a table or a chart.

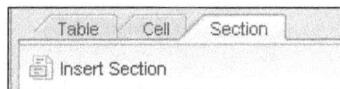

❑ **Chart**: This subtab enables the insertion of different visualization component such as lines, columns, and pie charts.

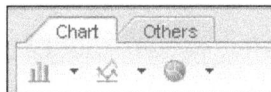

❑ **Others**: Apart from the basic chart types under the **Chart** subtab, this subtab contains additional chart types such as **Radar Chart**, **Tree Map**, **Tag Cloud**, and so on.

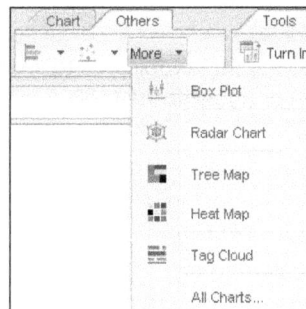

❑ **Tools**: This tab enables us to interact directly with an existing table in the report area and turn it into another type of presentation such as a pivot table or a chart, or turn a dimension or an attribute into a section.

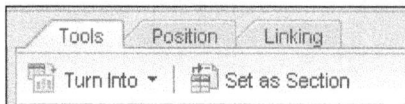

Tools	Position	Linking
🔲 Turn Into ▼		🔲 Set as Section

❑ **Position**: This tab enables us to align report elements such as cells, and position them properly.

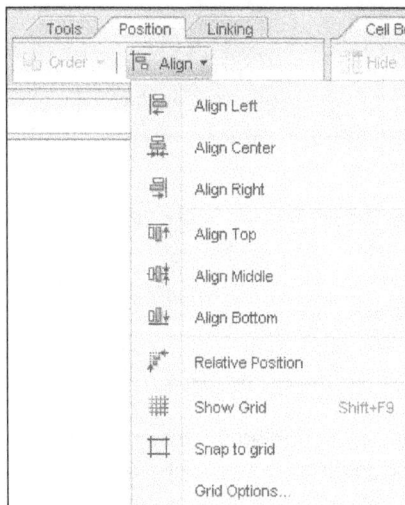

Tools	Position	Linking	Cell Be
Order ▼	Align ▼		Hide

🔳	Align Left
🔳	Align Center
🔳	Align Right
🔳	Align Top
🔳	Align Middle
🔳	Align Bottom
🔳	Relative Position
▦	Show Grid Shift+F9
🔲	Snap to grid
	Grid Options...

❑ **Linking**: This subtab helps us to create a link between components in the report (also, pass parameters between components) and a link between reports (also, pass parameters between different reports).

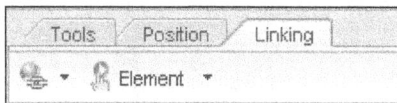

Tools	Position	Linking
🔲 ▼	🔳 Element ▼	

❑ **Table Layout**: This subtab enables us to set a break on a table column, to insert a column or a row to the table, and to show or hide the table header or footer.

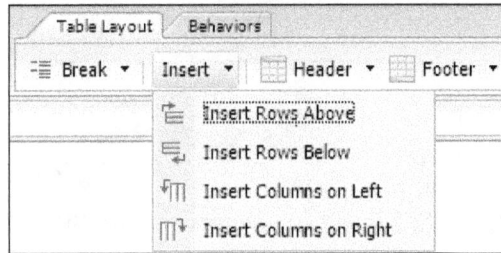

- **Behaviors**: This subtab can hide a dimension object column and set the table header and footer to repeat on every page.

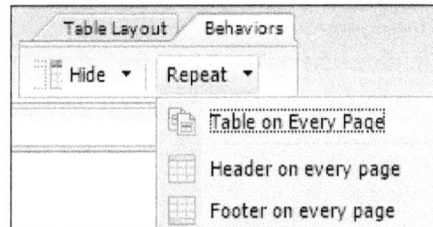

▶ **Format**: This toolbar helps us to format the text and numbers and their look and feel. It is very similar to MS Excel and MS Word formatting toolbars. This toolbar is a combination of four main tabs, as shown in the following screenshot:

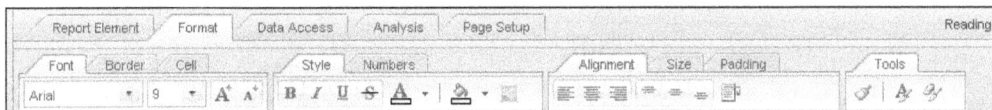

- **Font**, **Border**, and **Cell**: These subtabs help us to format the font, the border, and the cell.

  This is probably the most straightforward tab with some of its features being similar to MS office.

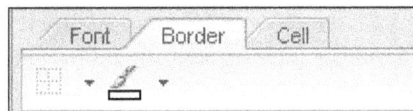

The following screenshot shows the **Cell** subtab:

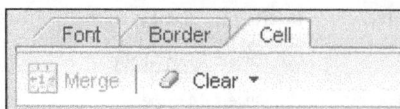

□ **Style**: This is the second subtab that controls the style formatting.

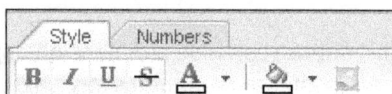

□ **Numbers**: This subtab is very handy when we are required to format a measure or a date object. The **Numbers** subtab is shown in the following screenshot:

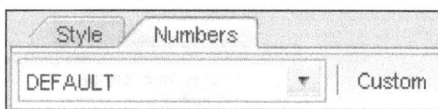

□ **Alignment**, **Size**, and **Padding**: These subtabs can format the text alignment, the size of the cell or column, as well as the padding of the text.

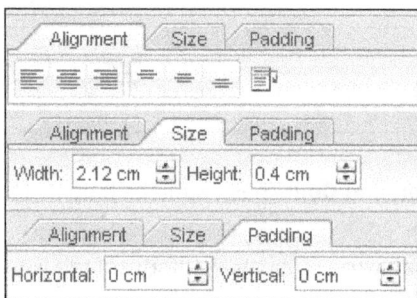

□ **Tools**: This subtab enables us to duplicate the formatting style, access the **Format Cells** window, and to clear the formatting of some text.

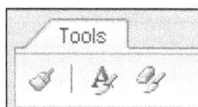

▶ **Data Access**: This is the most basic and important toolbar that can interact with a query. It enables us to edit, purge, and refresh the query, along with creating new variables and merging data between query dimensions. This toolbar is a combination of the two main tabs:

- **Data Providers**: This subtab enables us to create a new query, edit, purge, and refresh the query results.

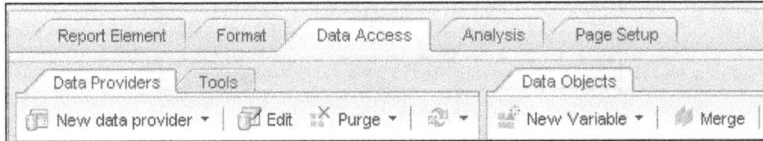

> Purging the query results is a very useful function as it enables us to save the report without the data. In cases where the data isn't relevant for the next refresh or the query returns large volumes of data, opening the report in a clean mode would be a better practice

- **Tools**: This subtab enables us to switch the query source universe and export the query results into CSV format.

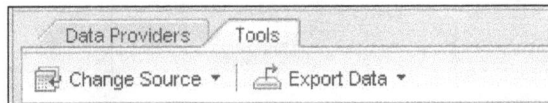

- **Data Objects**: This subtab enables us to create local variables in order to extend the report functionality and merge common dimensions between queries in order to unify several queries' data.

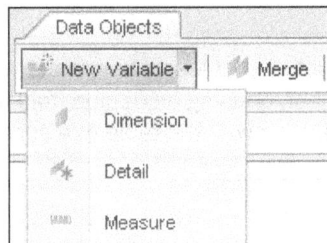

▶ **Analysis**: This toolbar enables us to perform the most common and important functionalities such as filtering, sorting, and creating calculations.

This toolbar is a combination of the following four main tabs:

❑ **Filters**: This subtab enables us to use different types of filters: a simple one, a top *n* filter, and custom filters such as input controls:

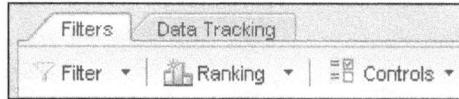

❑ **Data Tracking**: This subtab allows us to track data changes by comparing different query refresh results:

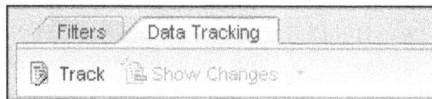

❑ **Display**: This subtab enables to use breaks and sorts, which are extremely useful when we are required to rearrange the data:

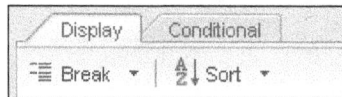

❑ **Conditional**: This subtab creates conditional formatting rules:

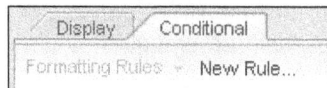

❑ **Interact**: This subtab enables us to interact with the data using Drill, an interactive filter bar, or using an outline (folding the data; a quick switch between a detailed view of the table to a sub total/total view):

- ❑ **Functions**: This subtab enables us to apply useful calculations such as **sum**, **count**, **min**, **max**, **average**, and **percentage**.

  These calculations can be mainly applied on measure objects and numeric data:

  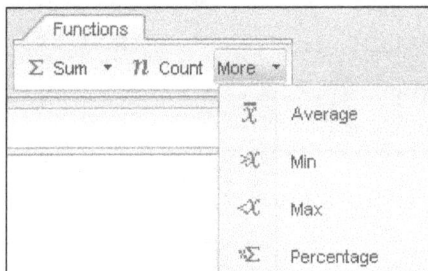

- ▶ **Page Setup**: This toolbar enables us to format the page layout, adjust the margins of the page, to define the page mode, and to manage the report tabs. This toolbar is a combination of three main tabs, as shown in the following screenshot:

  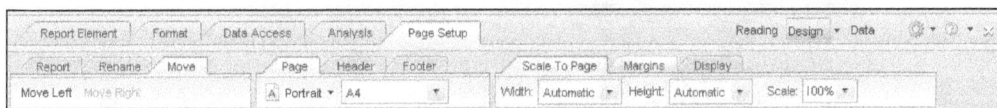

  - ❑ **Report**: This subtab enables us to manage reports with the options to create, duplicate, or delete reports:

    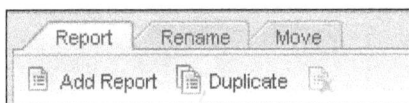

  - ❑ **Rename** and **Move**: These subtabs enable us to rename the report or change the report location:

    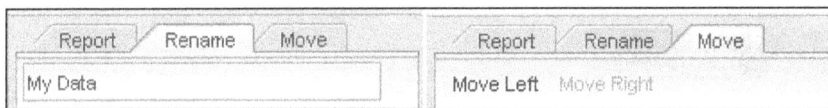

❑ **Page**, **Header**, and **Footer**: These subtabs enable us to choose the page type and adjust the header and footer margins:

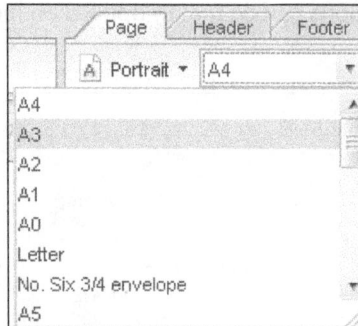

The following screenshot shows the **Header** and **Footer** subtabs:

❑ **Scale To Page**, **Margins**, and **Display**: These subtabs enable us to scale the page, set the page margins, and change the display mode of the report:

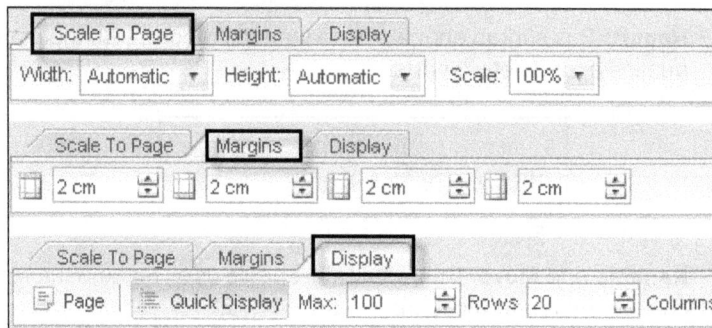

How it works...

The Reporting toolbars provide us with access to the entire report functionalities organized by different functionality subject areas, thus enabling the report developers with quick and easy access to every specific formatting task.

Working with the toolbars is the main method to apply formatting to the report as they hold the core functionalities of the report formatting capabilities.

Navigating between the view modes

There are three main view options in the Web Intelligence report interface. Each view mode is fitted for a different interacting type of the report and enables a different set of options.

How to do it...

Let's get familiar with the different view modes in the Web Intelligence report's main screen. On the top-right corner of the window, there are three buttons: **Reading**, **Design**, and **Data**. We will discuss each of the views as follows:

- **Reading**: This mode is fit for a lighter mode that can be refreshed. **Track**, **Drill**, **Filter Bar**, and **Outline** are its main options. This mode is more fit for a specific type of user: users who mainly refresh and view the report results. This is also the default view mode while accessing a report:

- **Design**: This mode, as we have already seen, gives access to a rich mode fit for report designers. When we switch to the **Design** mode, not only can we work with report toolbars and Left Pane panels, but we can also switch to the **Structure Only** mode.

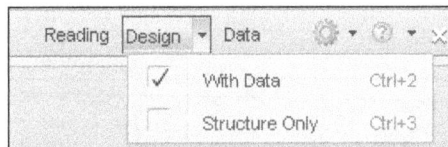

The **Structure Only** view can switch only to the structure of the report and not the data and the rest of the displayed components in the tables:

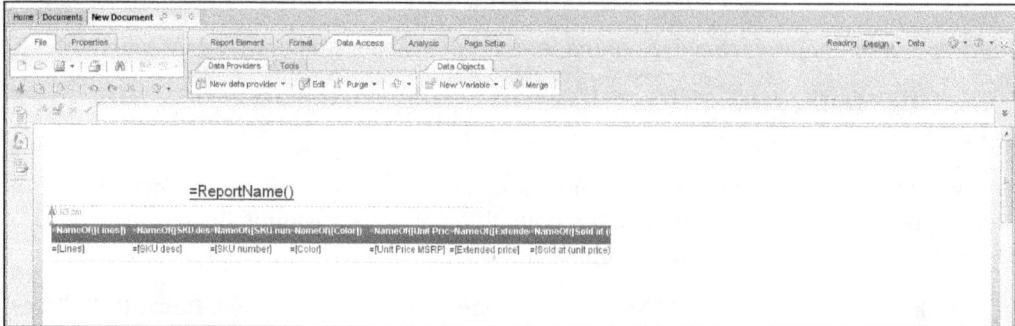

Working in the **Structure Only** mode is a better option when we require a better grip of the data structure, or validate that structure using a specific formula or a variable that is present in the table, or even locate hidden components in the report area.

> Working in the **Structure Only** mode is also useful when we want to apply formatting without checking its effect on the presented data and when the data can't be displayed for security reasons.

▶ **Data**: This mode shows us the basic information and statistics of a report, that is, the name of the query, the name of the data source, the refresh date, the query duration time, the status of the query, and the number of rows returned:

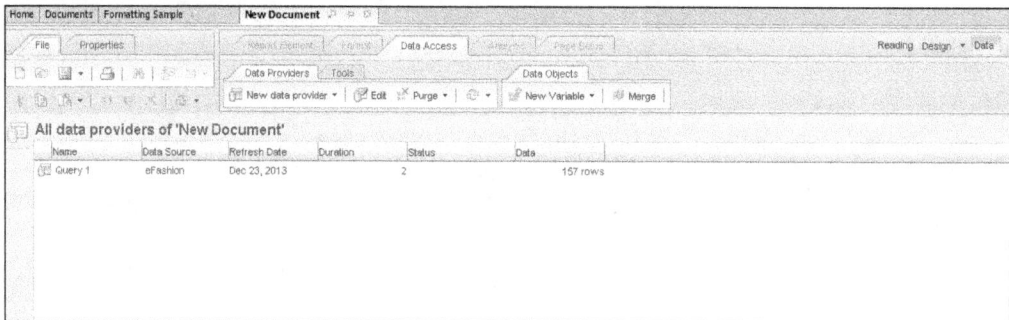

This view mode mainly enables us to validate whether the query has returned a specific number of results. Also, by double-clicking on the status row, we will be able to view the row data.

This option is extremely useful when we are required to validate whether a specific value was fetched by a query before it was formatted or filtered in the report area.

At the bottom of the **Data provider** screen, we can also activate a simple search engine that will help us to track any value more easily by pressing the *Ctrl* and *F* keys together.

How it works...

The view options simply enable us to address the right working and formatting mode as well as enable the relevant type of users to work with the right application mode.

The File and Properties tabs

In addition to the main formatting toolbars, the Left Pane panels and the speed menus, there are the **File** and **Properties** tabs.

These tabs are used for performing general tasks, such as saving, creating new reports, and adjusting the file properties on reports.

How to do it...

The first tab is the **File** tab, which enables several main functions, discussed as follows:

- ▶ **New**: This option helps in creating a new report
- ▶ **Open**: This option opens an existing report that was saved in the public or private folder
- ▶ **Save**: This option saves the report

- **Print**: This option enables us to print the report

- **Find**: This option searches for a specific value in the report

- **History**: This option shows the instance history in case the report was scheduled

- **Send**: This option enables the sharing of reports by sending it to another user, SAP BI user inbox e-mail, or an FTP server

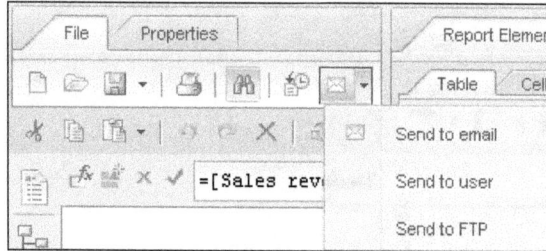

The **Properties** tab is a combination of the following three options:

- **View**: This option enables quick access to **Filter Bar**, **Outline**, **Formula Bar**, and show/hide the **Report Tabs** and the **Status Bar**

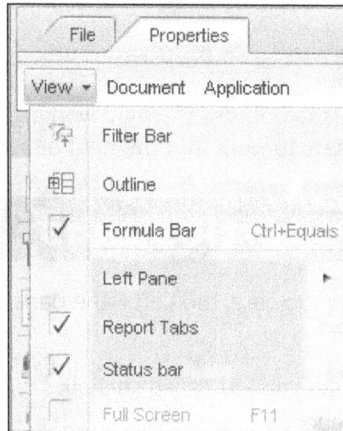

- **Document**: This option enables us to configure the properties of the report as well as add a description and keywords to the report.

  By clicking on the **Document** icon, a properties window will appear, which enables the following main options:

  - **Enhance viewing**: Using this option, the appearance of reports is optimized for onscreen viewing

- **Refresh on open**: When the document is opened it will immediately be refreshed and then run; this option is extremely useful when the report uses a prompt

- **Permanent regional formatting**: This option changes the regional settings of the report

- **Use query drill**: This option changes the drill behavior

- **Enable query stripping**: This option improves the query-running performance by sending only the objects that are actually used in the report tabs of the database

- **Hide warning icons in charts**: When charts have negative or inconsistent values, this option can be turned on or off

- **Auto-merge dimension**: This option automatically merges between the same dimension objects

- **Extend merged dimension values**: This option changes the merged dimension behavior into a "Full Outer Merge" behavior; similar to the desktop intelligence behavior, the merge behavior will be discussed in depth in *Chapter 8, Merging Data*

- **Merge prompts (BEx Variables)**: Based on the technical names of the BEx variables, prompts can be merged in case we have many of them

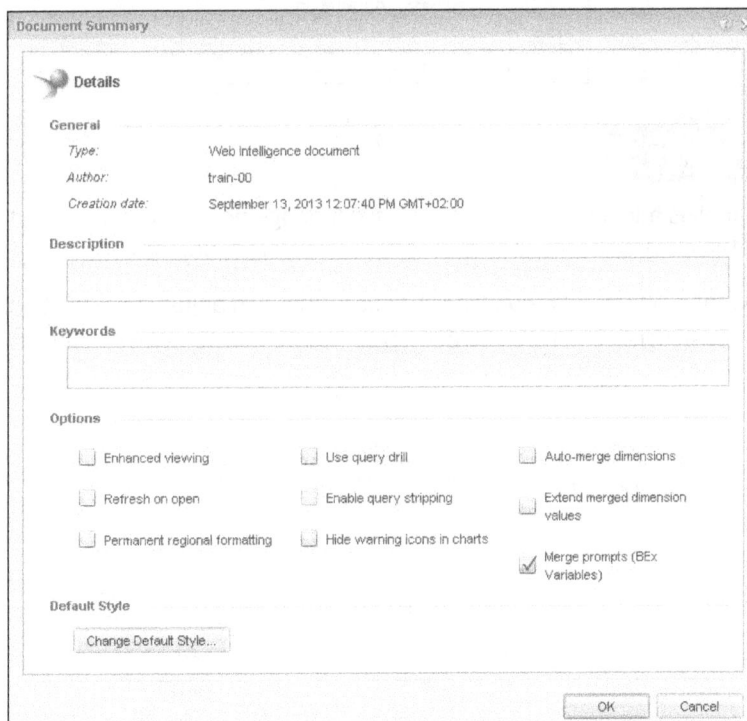

▸ **Application**: This option enables us to switch the **Measurement unit** to either **Inch** or **Centimeter**, and **Grid** to **Show grid** or **Snap to grid**

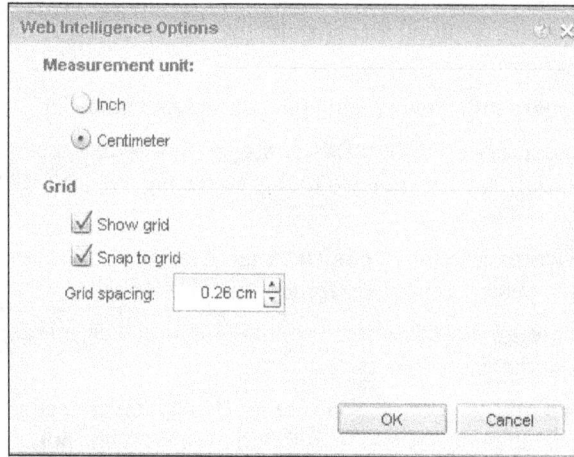

Below these subtabs, there is a simple taskbar that enables functions such as cut, copy, paste, undo, redo, and refresh.

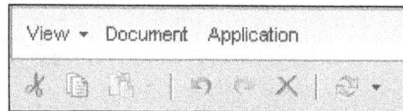

How it works...

The **File** tab supplies additional and necessary file management functionalities to the report by addressing the most basic tasks such as open, close, save, and new.

The **Properties** tab contains more advanced options that can adjust the report behavior in terms of viewing, merging, and refreshing the report.

4

Working with Tables

In this chapter, we will cover the following recipes:

- ▶ Getting to know the structure of tables
- ▶ Working with different table types
- ▶ Formatting tables
- ▶ Working with cross tables
- ▶ Hiding dimensions

Introduction

Data presentation is done mostly by using tables and charts.

Tables are the most basic structures that store the data in rows and columns.

Using tables is the most common way to organize and display the data that is retrieved by a query, either detailed or aggregative. In this chapter, we will learn how to work with the main table types: vertical, horizontal, cross table, and forms; learn which data type is best displayed by a specific table type; and how can you format the tables.

Getting to know the structure of tables

Although we have different types of tables, we can start from the basic and most common table type, which is the vertical table.

Getting ready

We want to get familiar with the basic vertical table structure and display some data in it.

How to do it...

As we have seen in *Chapter 2, Creating New Queries*, after the query retrieves the data, in most cases, the data will be displayed in a vertical table. Tables can also be created by dragging-and-dropping certain objects from the available objects pane or by using the report element toolbar.

By looking on at the table, we can distinguish between the following three main parts:

- The first row is the **table header** showing the column names and providing us the reference for which result object or a variable does the column stands for. The default color for the header is blue and it can of course be formatted.

- The second part is where is the data presented, which is the **table body**. This data area is combined from rows and columns. Each column represents a result object or a variable data, and a row presents a single common data of all the columns. This area is important because most of the common formatting actions are applied to it such as sorting and filtering.

- The third part is the **table footer**. This part will be presented if a calculation has been applied to one of the columns such as **Sum** or the option **Show Table Footer** has been applied, as shown in the following screenshot:

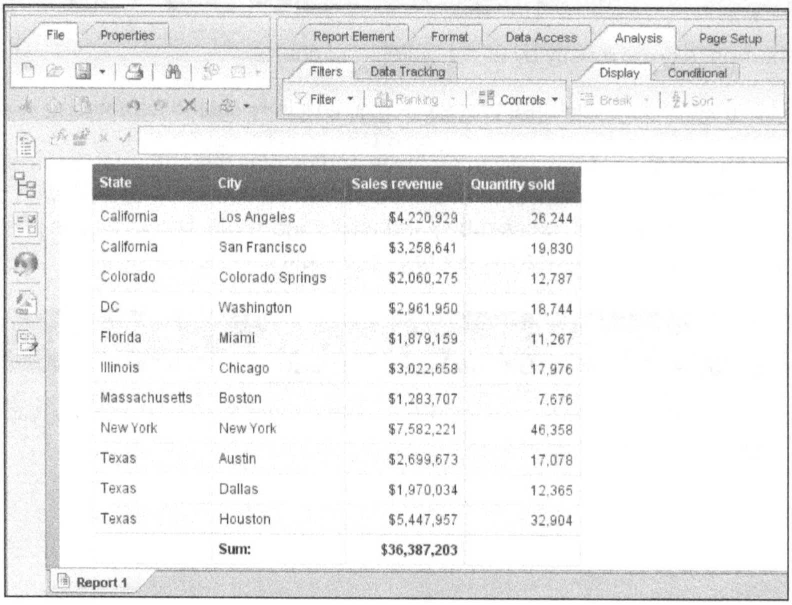

How it works...

The table is probably the most simple and basic structure that can be found in any data presentation environment. The table simply displays the data that was retrieved by the query. When we refresh the query, any table that is based on that query will display the updated data accordingly. It is important to understand that we refresh the data structure via the query and not the table.

There's more...

The table can be dragged-and-dropped into the report area, copied to another report tab, moved, or deleted. It's important to understand that in such cases the data will not be deleted but the graphical presentation of it—the table.

The order of columns in the table can be easily changed by marking a column. Then using drag-and-drop, we can either switch between columns or set them side by side. The different formatting results are caused by the location of the object we drag—when a rectangle appears inside the column, as shown in the following screenshot, we are dragging our object into it and then the column will be switched:

Fiscal Period	Year	Quarter
FY02	2002	Q1
	=[Quarter]	
FY02	2002	Q1
FY02	2002	Q1
FY02	2002	Q1

If we move our object to another column, then we can drag the object and locate it on the border between the columns until a small vertical rectangle appears, as shown in the following screenshot:

Fiscal Period	Year	Quarter
FY02	2002	Q1
FY02	2002=[Quarter]	Q1
FY02	2002	Q1

We can also easily move columns in the table by right-clicking on the table, choosing the **Assign Data** option, and then navigating to a panel that enables simple move options of the existing objects on the table, as shown in the following screenshot:

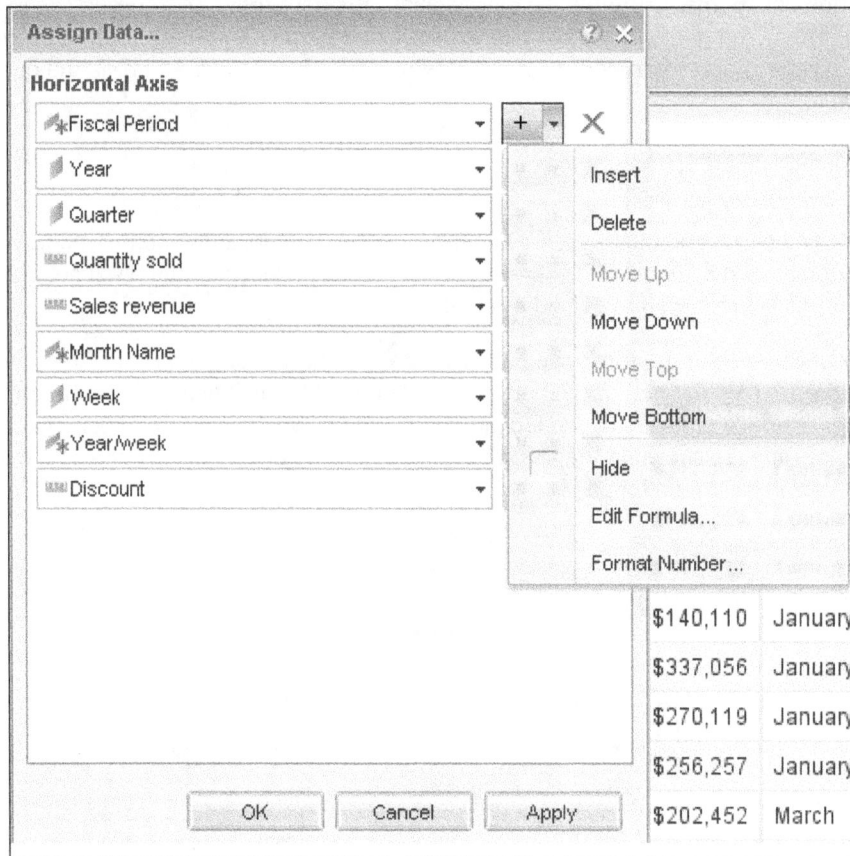

See also

▶ The remaining recipes in this chapter will explain the different manners in which vertical tables can be used

Working with different types of tables

There are four main types of tables. The most basic table type was already covered in the previous recipe, so we will deal with the remaining three types.

Getting ready

We want to learn how to use the different types of tables.

How to do it...

Perform the following steps to start using tables:

1. In order to insert a new table, we can use the **Report Element** toolbar, use the right-click button, and chose the **Insert** option from the menu.

2. Horizontal tables are structured in a way that the objects are located on top of each other; each row shows the object values and on the first left-hand side column, the object names are presented.

   This table is also knows as a **finance table** and it's more fitted for an aggregative type of data or *short* data as reading hundreds of values from left to right doesn't make sense. By using the **Report Element** toolbar, we can choose the horizontal table type, as shown in the following screenshot:

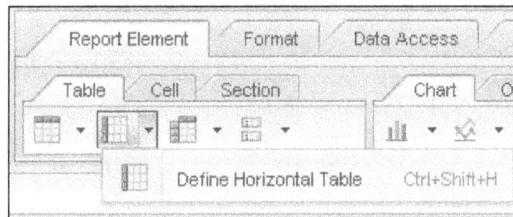

3. Then, drag the horizontal table into the report area in order to display an aggregative view of the data, as shown:

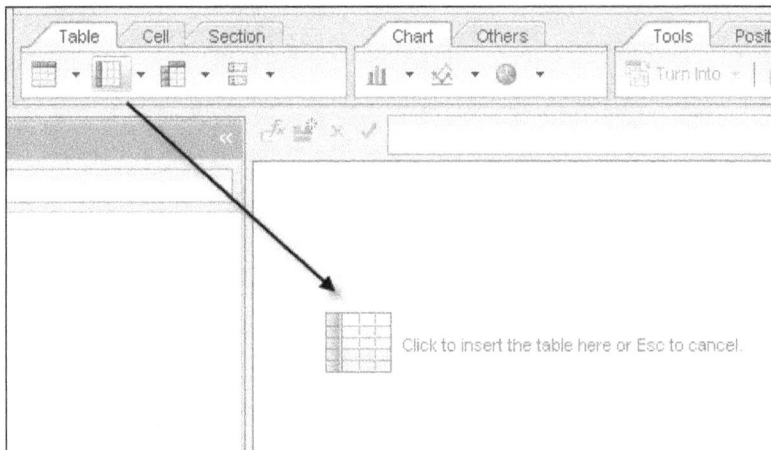

4. After inserting the table, the insert table screen will pop up and we will be able to choose the objects we want to present from the top right-hand side of the screen, as shown in the following screenshot:

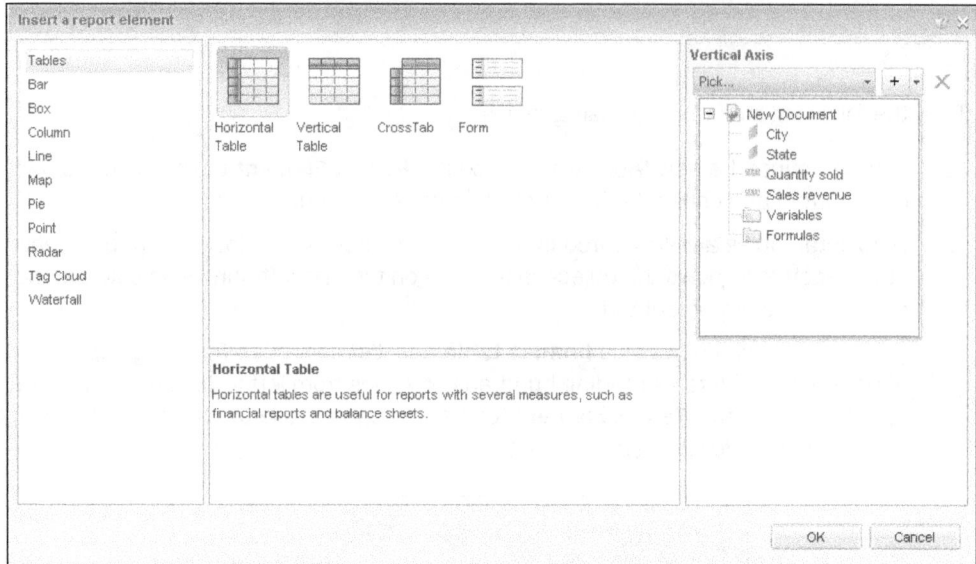

5. We will pick the **City**, **Quantity sold**, and the **Sales revenue** objects. Notice that by using the **+** sign, we will be able to expand our selection and add more objects to the Horizontal table, as shown:

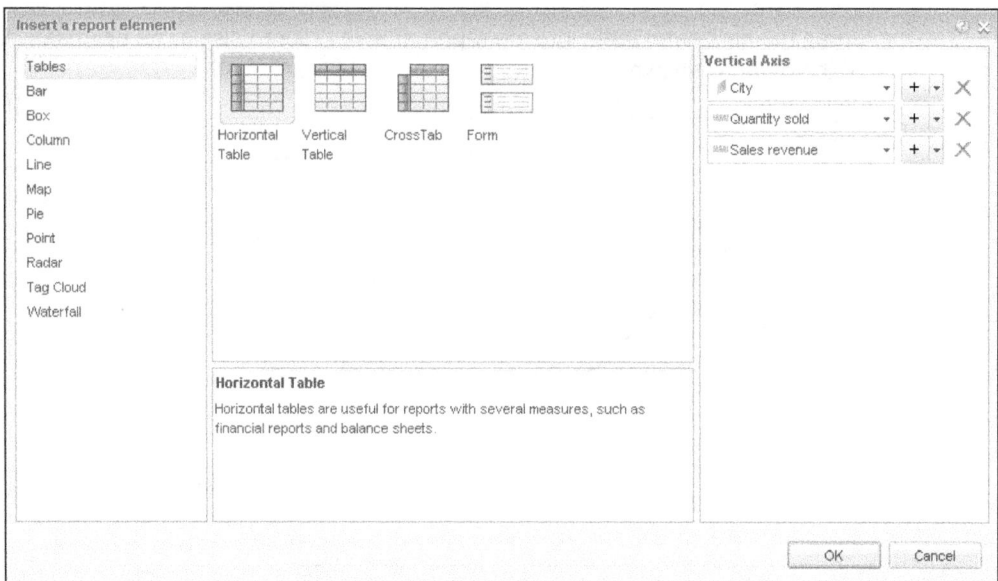

6. We will get a horizontal table such that all its result objects are displayed on top of each other, as shown:

City	Austin	Boston	Chicago	Colorado Springs	Dallas	Houston	Los Angeles	Miami	New York	San Francisco	Washington
Quantity sold	17,078	7,876	17,976	12,787	12,365	32,904	26,244	11,267	46,358	19,830	18,744
Sales revenue	$2,699,673	$1,283,707	$3,022,658	$2,060,275	$1,970,034	$5,447,957	$4,220,929	$1,879,159	$7,582,221	$3,258,641	$2,961,950

7. The next type of table is the crosstab table. The crosstab table is also known as a pivot table and a matrix table, and it is mainly used to display measure objects that are sliced by two or more dimensions or attribute objects. In a crosstab table, the column and the rows contain the dimension or attribute values, while the body of the table is storing the measure results.

8. In the following cross table, we can compare the sales figures by crossing the results between the **Year** and the **City** dimension objects, as shown in the following screenshot:

	2004	2005	2006
Austin	$561,123	$1,003,071	$1,135,479
Boston	$238,819	$157,719	$887,169
Chicago	$737,914	$1,150,659	$1,134,085
Colorado Springs	$448,302	$768,390	$843,584
Dallas	$427,245	$739,369	$803,421
Houston	$1,211,309	$1,990,449	$2,246,198
Los Angeles	$982,637	$1,581,616	$1,656,676
Miami	$405,985	$661,250	$811,924
New York	$1,667,696	$2,763,503	$3,151,022
San Francisco	$721,574	$1,201,064	$1,336,003
Washington	$693,211	$1,215,158	$1,053,581

9. The form type of table is good for data that is required to be detailed but grouped by a customer, invoice ID, or a product name. This table groups each set of unique rows into one section, as shown in the following screenshot:

Year	2004	
City	Austin	
Sales revenue		$561,123

Year	2004	
City	Boston	
Sales revenue		$238,819

Year	2004	
City	Chicago	
Sales revenue		$737,914

How it works...

By using the report toolbar or the speed menu, we can easily insert any type of table into the report area in order to present the different data types and support the different presentation requirements. Determining which table type is suited for which type of data can be answered by the following simple decision table:

#	Table type	Type Of Data
1	Horizontal table	Aggregative
2	Vertical table	Detailed and aggregative
3	Cross table	Aggregative
4	Form	Detailed and aggregative

See also

► Working with crosstab tables will be further discussed in the next recipe

Formatting tables

Tables can be formatted and adjusted according to the user requirements. Formatting the table not only enables to you change the look and feel of the table, but also enables you to control important table properties such as which type of rows will be displayed.

Getting ready

In order to format the table, we will use the right-click menu, as shown in the following screenshot. Notice that in order to get the proper menu, we are required to mark the table outline.

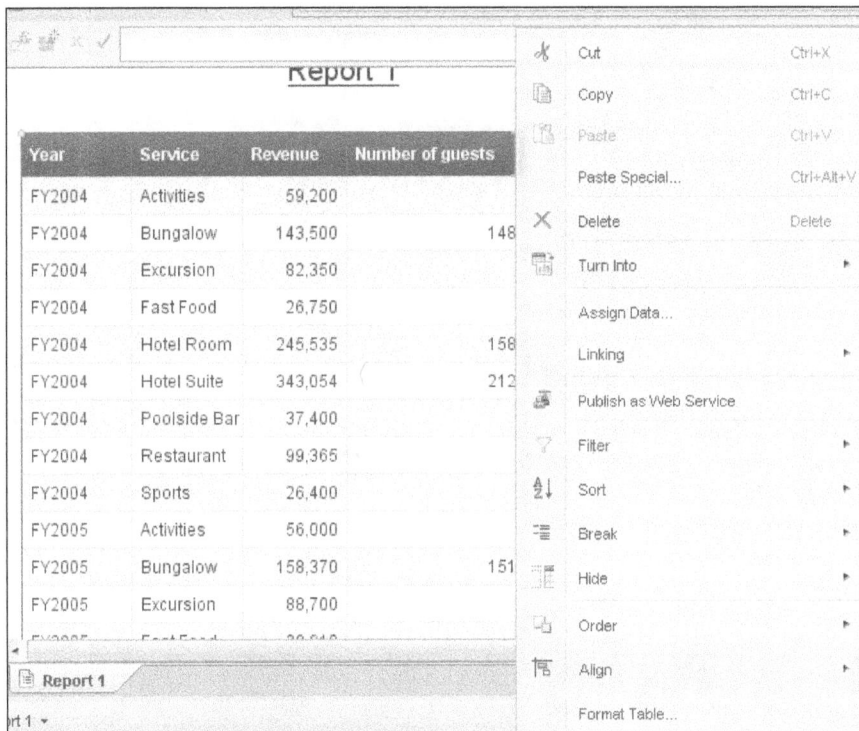

By choosing the last option in the speed menu, **Format Table**, we can access the formatting window that is structured from four main categories.

How to do it...

The tables can be formatted using the following four main categories:

- ▶ **General**: This category enables the control of the table row properties along with some other options, as shown in the following screenshot:

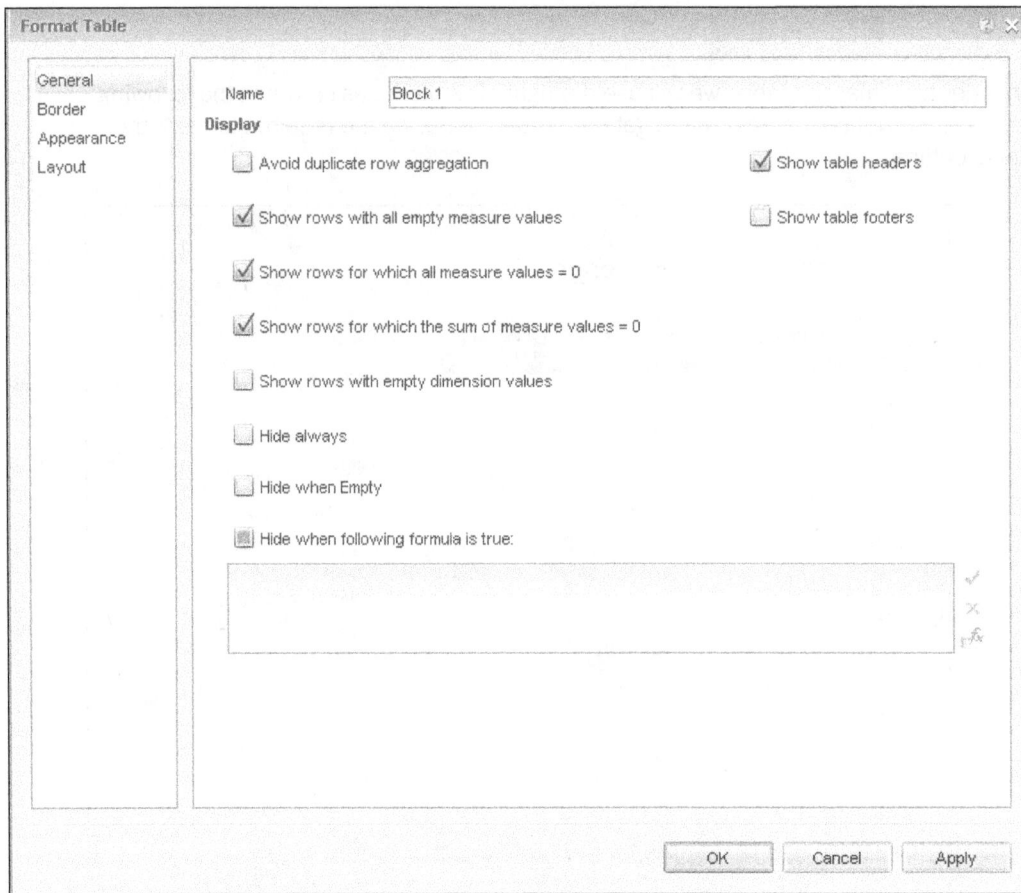

Format Table

General
Border
Appearance
Layout

Name   [Block 1]

Display

☐ Avoid duplicate row aggregation   ☑ Show table headers

☑ Show rows with all empty measure values   ☐ Show table footers

☑ Show rows for which all measure values = 0

☑ Show rows for which the sum of measure values = 0

☐ Show rows with empty dimension values

☐ Hide always

☐ Hide when Empty

☐ Hide when following formula is true:

    [   ] ✓ ✗ *fx*

OK   Cancel   Apply

Under the **General** category, there are options such as the following:

- ❑ **Name**: This option is used to name a table. It is helpful when we have several blocks in the **Report** tab and we want to distinguish between them better.

- ❑ **Display**: In this section, we can control the type of rows that can be displayed in the table.

- ❑ **Avoid duplicate row aggregation**: This is an important option; by default, Web Intelligence does not show a duplicate row. A duplicate row is a row that has the exact same values in all of its columns as shown in another row, usually when using a measure in the query values are grouped and duplication is eliminated. In dimensional-oriented reports, duplication can occur, since showing the same duplicate row will usually be meaningless. This option is unticked by default. In cases such as counting the whole rows, showing the whole duplicate rows can be meaningful.

- ❑ **Show rows with empty measure values**: In this case, we have a table with measure objects that include empty values as well the rows that will be hidden.

  For example, the following table contains a measure column with empty values:

Year	Service	Number of guests
FY2004	Activities	
FY2004	Bungalow	148
FY2004	Excursion	
FY2004	Fast Food	
FY2004	Hotel Room	158
FY2004	Hotel Suite	212
FY2004	Poolside Bar	
FY2004	Restaurant	
FY2004	Sports	
FY2005	Activities	
FY2005	Bungalow	151
FY2005	Excursion	
FY2005	Fast Food	

By unmarking this option, only rows with measure values will be shown:

Year	Service	Number of guests
FY2004	Bungalow	148
FY2004	Hotel Room	158
FY2004	Hotel Suite	212
FY2005	Bungalow	151
FY2005	Hotel Room	149
FY2005	Hotel Suite	225
FY2006	Bungalow	153
FY2006	Hotel Room	144
FY2006	Hotel Suite	211

- **Show rows for which all measure values = 0**: This is used to hide or show rows where all the values of the measure equals zero.

- **Show rows for which the sum of measure values = 0**: This is used to hide or show rows of a measure if all the values are zero.

- **Show rows with empty dimension values**: This is used to hide or show rows where the dimension value is empty.

- **Hide always**: This option hides the table.

- **Hide when Empty**: This hides the tables when there are no values returned by the query or as a result of filters.

- **Hide when following formula is true**: This enables you to hide the table if a specific formula is matched.

- **Show table headers**: This is used to show/hide the table headers.

- **Show table footer**: This is used show/hide the table footer.

> Notice that some of the hiding options of the measures will only take place if you have one presented measure in the table.

▶ **Border**: This category mainly controls the properties of the border lines of the table and includes properties such as style, thickness color, and the location of the border line. For example, by setting the style as plain, the thickness as medium, and applying it on the entire table outline, we will get the following result:

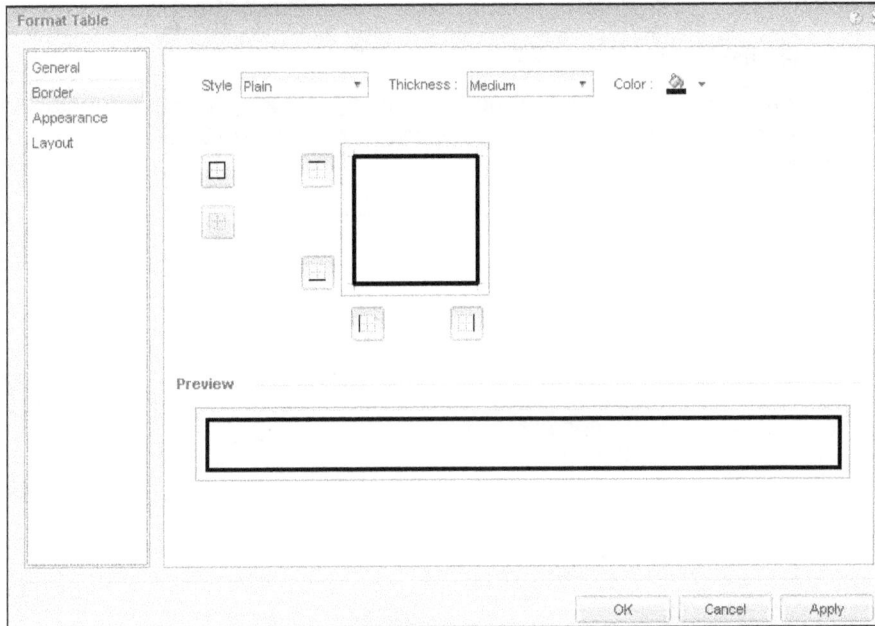

The result table will be similar to what is shown in the following screenshot:

Year	Service	Revenue	Number of gu
FY2004	Activities	59,200	
FY2004	Bungalow	143,500	148
FY2004	Excursion	82,350	
FY2004	Fast Food	26,750	
FY2004	Hotel Room	245,535	158
FY2004	Hotel Suite	343,054	212
FY2004	Poolside Bar	37,400	
FY2004	Restaurant	99,365	
FY2004	Sports	26,400	
FY2005	Activities	56,000	
FY2005	Bungalow	158,370	151
FY2005	Excursion	88,700	

[🔆 In order to apply border style to the columns, use the format cell option.]

▸ **Appearance**: This category is used to set the background of the table to a specific color, skin, or image. It enables us to control the spacing between the columns and to use alternate row shading.

For example, we will set the spacing and padding to **0.2 cm** in the horizontal and vertical properties along with a gray row color for the alternate row shading, as shown in the following screenshot:

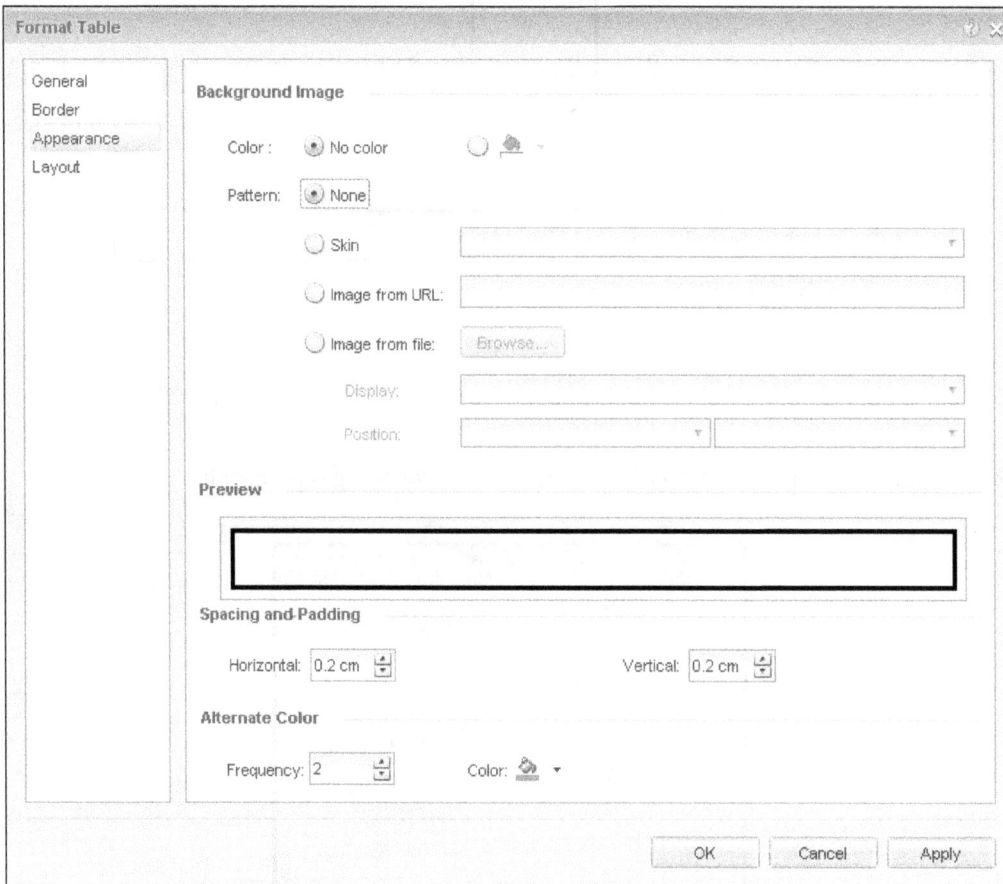

The result will be what is shown in the following screenshot:

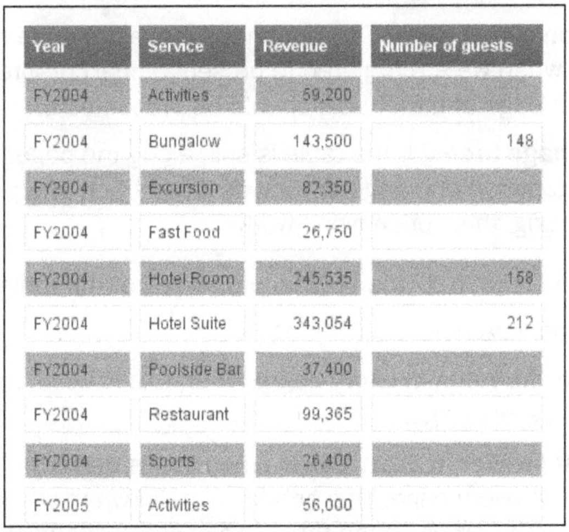

Year	Service	Revenue	Number of guests
FY2004	Activities	59,200	
FY2004	Bungalow	143,500	148
FY2004	Excursion	82,350	
FY2004	Fast Food	26,750	
FY2004	Hotel Room	245,535	158
FY2004	Hotel Suite	343,054	212
FY2004	Poolside Bar	37,400	
FY2004	Restaurant	99,365	
FY2004	Sports	26,400	
FY2005	Activities	56,000	

- **Layout**: This category defines the location of the table and the vertical and horizontal layout options of the table, as shown:

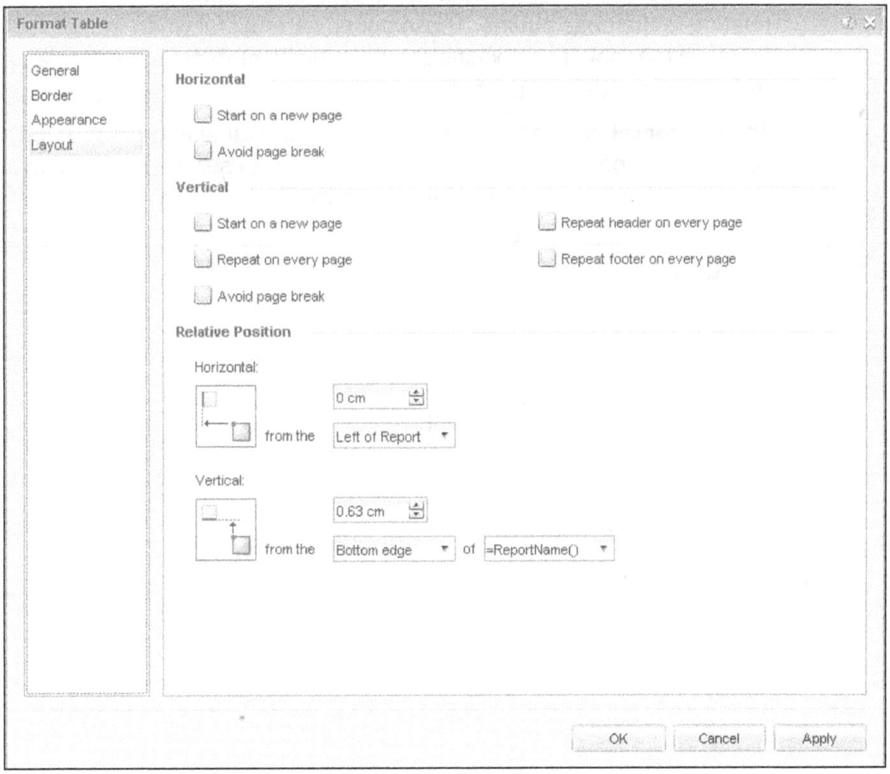

The **Horizontal** option controls the horizontal properties of the table. The options available under **Horizontal** are:

- **Start on a new page**: This option will move the table to the next page. It is useful when we are required to present a chart or a report explanation on the first page and the table should be presented on the next page.

- **Avoid page break**: If the table is split along the pages, then this option will fit the table on one page as long as it can fit on one page (if the table is two pages long, this option won't work).

The **Vertical** option controls the vertical properties of the table.

The additional options here are:

- **Repeat the table in every page**: When this is used, the table will repeat itself on every page.

- **Repeat header in every page**: When this is used, the table header will repeat on every page. This option is useful when we want to keep track of the column names as the table can continue along several pages.

- **Repeat footer in every page**: This option is useful when we are required to show the total sum on every page.

- **Relative position**: This enables us to position the table in a specific location relating to the page outline. These options are useful when we are required to locate the table in a specific position and want to maintain it as a part of the fixed formatting of the table appearance.

  The **Horizontal** position sets the position of the table to the left or to the right of the report. An additional option is used to set the table relative to the report, as shown in the following screenshot:

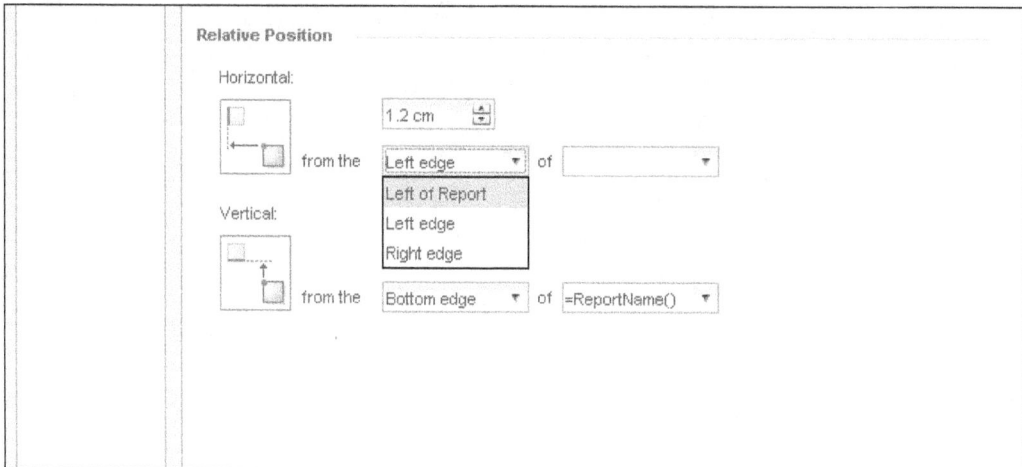

The **Vertical** position does the same to the vertical position. Both of these options are very useful when we have several tables in the report and we need to locate them in a relative position. So, when the upper table had "data growth", the extra rows won't cover the lower table but rather "push down" that table accordingly.

How it works...

The table format menu is a simple formatting window combined from several formatting categories; by using it, we are able to enhance the table's look and feel as well as control important viewing row behaviors.

Working with cross tables

Pivot tables are matrix tables aimed to slice a measure with two or more dimensions.

Pivot tables are great for presenting aggregative data, but provide additional value for the data analysis as they use the x and y axes. This enables us to cross the data and compare two dimensions or more.

Getting ready

In order to understand the pivot table capabilities, we will use a basic structure: two dimensions and one measure object.

How to do it...

In the following pivot table, we will be able to analyze data by the **Year** or **Quarter** dimension. In the pivot body table, the revenue measure is presented as follows:

	FY2004	FY2005	FY2006
Q1	256,860	275,030	258,726
Q2	272,490	282,886	266,441
Q3	288,993	291,050	304,654
Q4	245,211	258,274	285,909

X axis →

Y axis ↓

We can analyze each quarter row and view the increment/decrement in each year or analyze each year column and view the increment/decrement of the revenue along the quarter time progress.

Pivot tables are also great for showing what didn't happen. For example, let's analyze the following table:

City	Year	Revenue
Augsburg	FY2004	123,606
Augsburg	FY2005	145,300
Augsburg	FY2006	126,090
Berlin	FY2004	12,112
Berlin	FY2006	20,330
Chicago	FY2004	128,362
Chicago	FY2005	150,666
Chicago	FY2006	162,566
Cologne	FY2004	10,976
Dallas	FY2004	128,330
Dallas	FY2005	135,580
Dallas	FY2006	136,989
Dresden	FY2004	4,400

Note that there is no revenue for the city **Berlin** in the year **2005**.

We will transform this table into a pivot table by using the right-click menu: turn into crosstab and we will get the following result. Notice the "extra" year 2005 value showing us in which year Berlin didn't have any sales:

	FY2004	FY2005	FY2006
Augsburg	123,606	145,300	126,090
Berlin	12,112		20,330
Chicago	128,362	150,666	162,566
Cologne	10,976		
Dallas	128,330	135,580	136,989
Dresden	4,400		
Kobe	11,872		
Kyoto			16,720
Los Angeles	92,000	108,210	101,335
Magdeburg	67,850	78,330	76,730
Munich	129,658	127,584	131,282
New York City	8,420		
Osaka	4,700		
San Diego			18,715

So, from where did that null value come from?

This is simply a product of the pivot table that creates a cross between all the values of the *y* axis and all the values of the *x* axis, whether they have a match or not. In this manner, the pivot table creates a form of a Cartesian product, by showing us the "nonmatches" as well as the matches between the axes.

Note that the blank values were not fetched by the query, but are the products of the table structure.

> Since the null values are a product of the view mode of the table and not a real null value (like in a vertical table), they can't be filtered.

Another property of a pivot table is that since the rows and columns header show the dimension values, we could argue that it would be more useful to show the object names.

In order to do that, we will right-click on the pivot table and navigate to the **Format Table** window. In the **General** category, we will be able to see the **Show object name** option, as shown in the following screenshot:

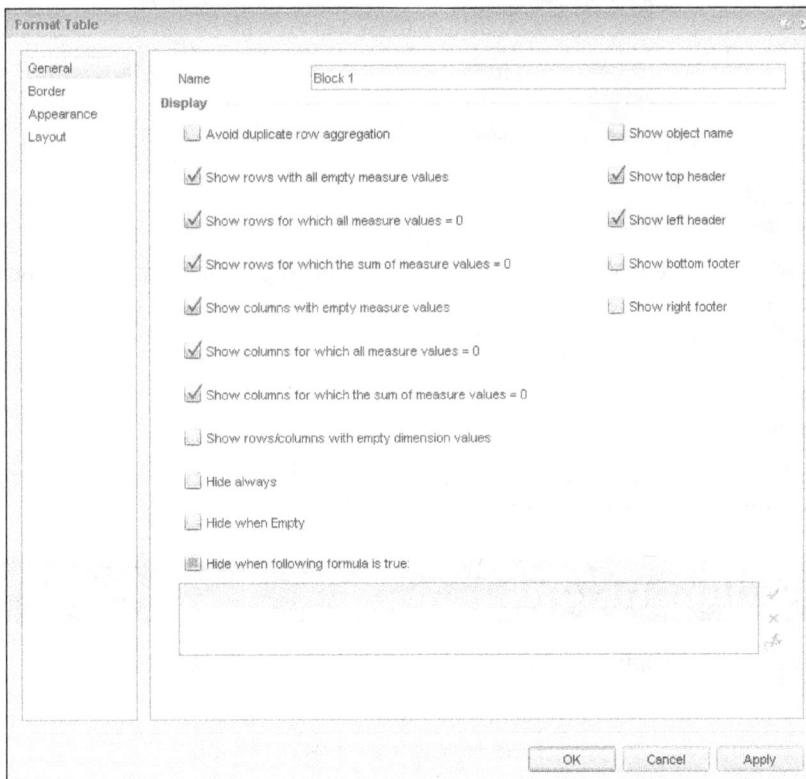

By ticking this option, the object name will appear in the cross table, as shown in the following screenshot:

[💡 It is better to use in the x axis a dimension with fewer values so that it can try to fit in a one-page view.]

Year	FY2004	FY2005	FY2006
City	Revenue	Revenue	Revenue
Augsburg	123,606	145,300	126,090
Berlin	12,112		20,330
Chicago	128,362	150,666	162,566
Cologne	10,976		
Dallas	128,330	135,580	136,989
Dresden	4,400		
Kobe	11,872		
Kyoto			16,720
Los Angeles	92,000	108,210	101,335
Magdeburg	67,850	78,330	76,730
Munich	129,658	127,584	131,282

How it works...

As we have seen, using a cross table is great for showing aggregative data as well as slicing it with two axes. This panoramic view can give us additional information that can't always be seen in a vertical or a horizontal table types.

See also

▶ For further information on how to use calculations in a cross table, refer to the *Calculations* recipe, in *Chapter 6, Formatting Reports*

Hiding dimensions

Hiding dimensions is an option that can be applied on dimension objects.

This option is useful when we don't want to show a specific object for viewing, for security reasons, or we don't want to change the aggregative level of the table.

Another reason could be that the dimension object is part of a complex calculation in the table and removing it may affect the formula result.

More reasons can be a dummy sort object (month number that we use to show the month names sorted chronologically) and a formula that returns 1/0 values that are used for a filter, but the values themselves don't hold a meaning.

Getting ready

We want to hide the **City** dimension object as well as understand what the difference is between deleting and hiding a dimension object.

How to do it...

We will right-click on the **City** object in the table and navigate to the **Hide** option, as shown in the following screenshot:

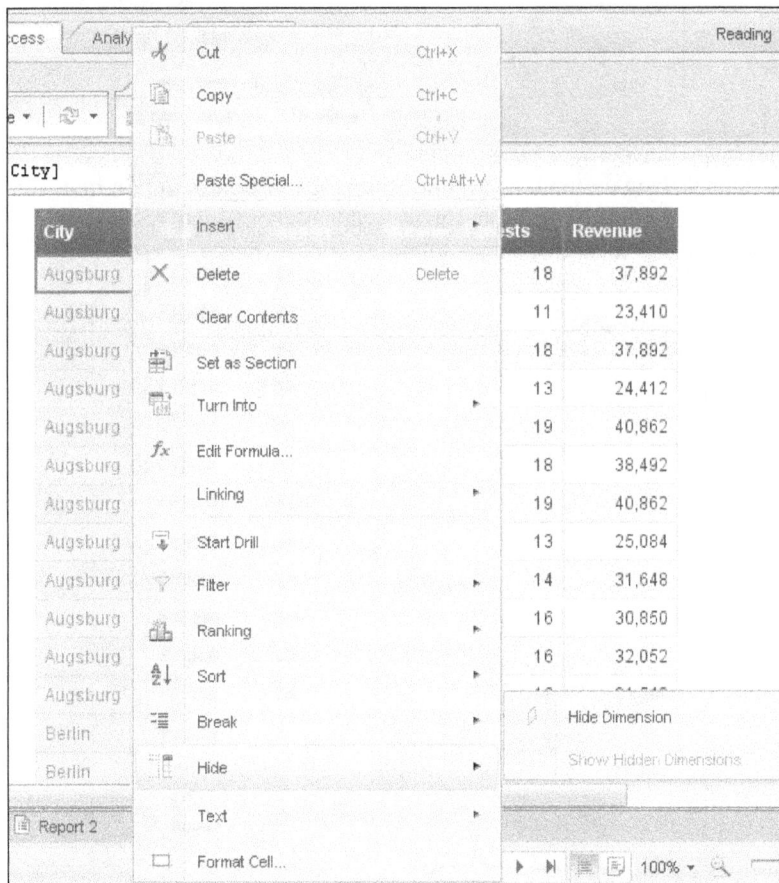

By choosing this option, the **City** column will be hidden:

Year	Quarter	Number of guests	Revenue
FY2004	Q1	18	37,892
FY2004	Q2	11	23,410
FY2004	Q3	18	37,892
FY2004	Q4	13	24,412
FY2005	Q1	19	40,862
FY2005	Q2	18	38,492
FY2005	Q3	19	40,862
FY2005	Q4	13	25,084
FY2006	Q1	14	31,648
FY2006	Q2	16	30,850
FY2006	Q3	16	32,052
FY2006	Q4	16	31,540
FY2004	Q2	6	12,112
FY2006	Q3		11,020

Notice that the aggregative level of the table hasn't changed, but if we delete the **City** dimension by right-clicking on the column and choosing the **Delete** option from the speed menu or drag-and-drop out the table into the available objects pane, the aggregative level of the table will be changed, as shown in the following screenshot:

Year	Quarter	Number of guests	Revenue
FY2004	Q1	127	256,860
FY2004	Q2	132	272,490
FY2004	Q3	134	288,993
FY2004	Q4	125	245,211
FY2005	Q1	132	275,030
FY2005	Q2	136	282,886
FY2005	Q3	132	291,050
FY2005	Q4	125	258,274
FY2006	Q1	122	258,726
FY2006	Q2	127	266,441
FY2006	Q3	130	304,654
FY2006	Q4	129	285,909

This is the whole difference between hiding and deleting/removing a dimension object from the table.

How it works...

Hiding dimension objects can be seen as painting the column in white; it's a formatting capability rather than a functional capability.

There's more...

In order to show the hidden objects, right-click on the table, choose the **Hide** dimension option, and then show hidden dimensions or navigate to the **Report Element** toolbar and choose the subtab **Cell Behaviors**.

5
Working with Charts

In this chapter, we will cover the following recipes:

- ▸ Working with the Line chart
- ▸ Working with different chart types
- ▸ Formatting charts

Introduction

Data can be displayed and analyzed through tables of different types, as we saw in the previous chapter.

When we are required to visualize data, charts are considered to be a very good solution as they enable us to explore business insights that a *flat* table isn't suited for.

While a table displays data in a basic, straightforward way, charts can *tell the story* of the data.

Charts enable us to visualize the data and create an analysis in a very clear way. For example, analyzing a sales trend with a time axis will be much clearer than using a table since a chart can graphically show the trend of the increase or decrease of sales over time.

Charts and visualization components are more suited to aggregative type of data because the graphical effect is lost in the volume of data when using detailed data.

Web Intelligence provides a set of various chart types that can be easily and quickly used to address different types of data visualization requirements.

In this chapter, we will demonstrate how to work with the core charts functionality and how to fit each chart to the type of data.

Working with the Line chart

There are many chart types we can use when we are creating Web Intelligence reports, but we would like to get a better understanding of which chart type we can use and when.

Getting ready

We will be analyzing the sales revenue by year in a graphical way that will display the sales trend.

How to do it...

We will first open the **Available Objects** panel on the left-hand side and perform the following steps:

1. From the **Available Objects** pane, we will drag-and-drop the **Sales revenue** and **Year** objects into the report area, as shown in the following screenshot:

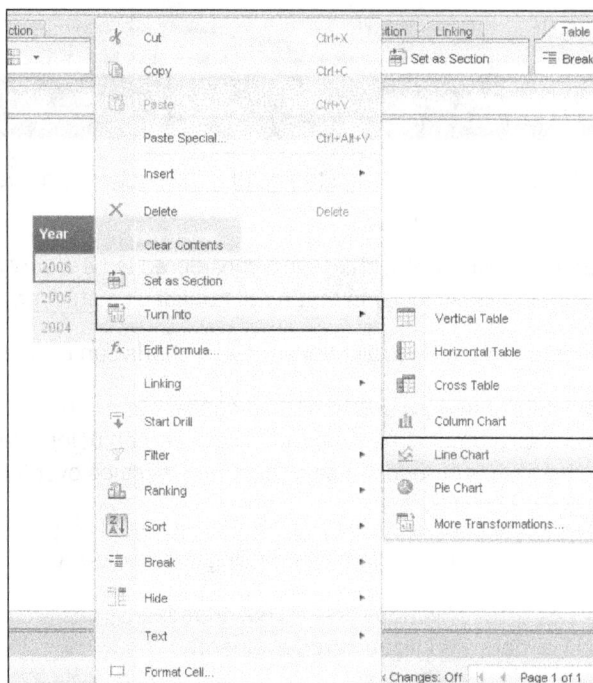

2. After the table is located in the report area, we will right-click on the table and navigate to **Turn Into | Line Chart** from the right-click menu.

3. We will get a line chart that will easily show us the sales revenue trend over the years, as shown in the following screenshot:

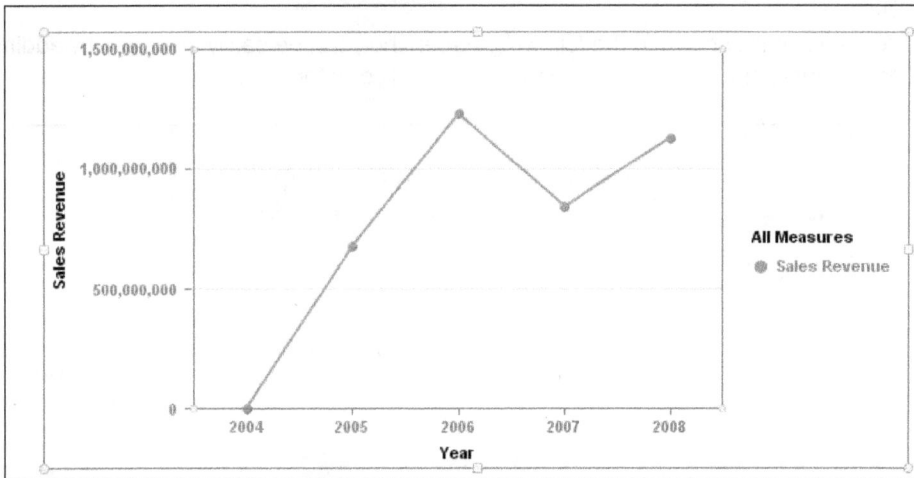

> You can display both charts and tables together by simply copying the table and turning the copy into a chart.
>
> When we create a chart, it's advised to add a description to it so that the data will be understood and in context. Adding a title to the chart is a simple practice that can be further improved by describing in which scale the numbers are displayed (millions and thousands).

4. Another way of creating a chart is to use the **Report Element** toolbar in the second tab, **Charts**.

5. The chart type can be changed by using the same option in the speed menu. By dragging the chart outline, it can be enlarged or minimized to suit the size requirements.

How it works...

Web Intelligence can translate an existing table to a chart. By dragging a table to the report area, you can transform it to any kind of chart type available in Web Intelligence.

There's more...

Charts are all about emphasizing and discovering the data trend, focusing on measure analysis and enabling us to compare several values.

The rule of thumb when using visualizations is that if the result of the chart isn't quickly realized by the user, or it fails to explain the *story* behind the data graphically, then we are probably using the wrong type of chart or the wrong type of data.

The current line chart, shown in the following screenshot, can be easily improved by adding a title, data values, and a better type of font, size, and color for the values:

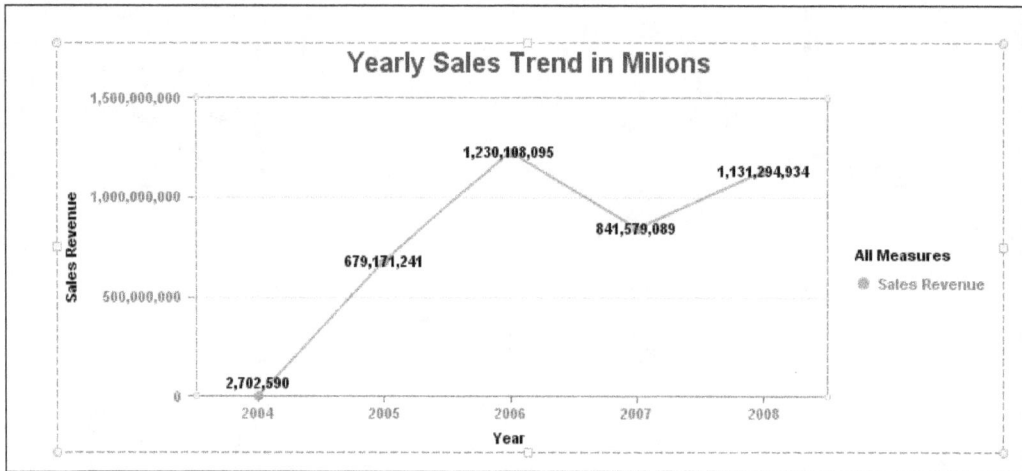

See also

▶ The next recipes will explain how to work with the different types of charts and how to format their results, including how to add a title and values to the chart

Working with different chart types

There are many types of charts suited for different kinds of data and analysis scenarios. This recipe will explore the various visualization types and explain which type of chart is best suited for the right task.

Web Intelligence provides 10 chart categories that can address different visualization requirements.

Getting ready

We want to explore the different chart types available and get a better understanding of what we can use.

How to do it...

By right-clicking on the existing line chart, we will choose the **More Transformations** option in order to get the entire chart types menu, as shown in the following screenshot:

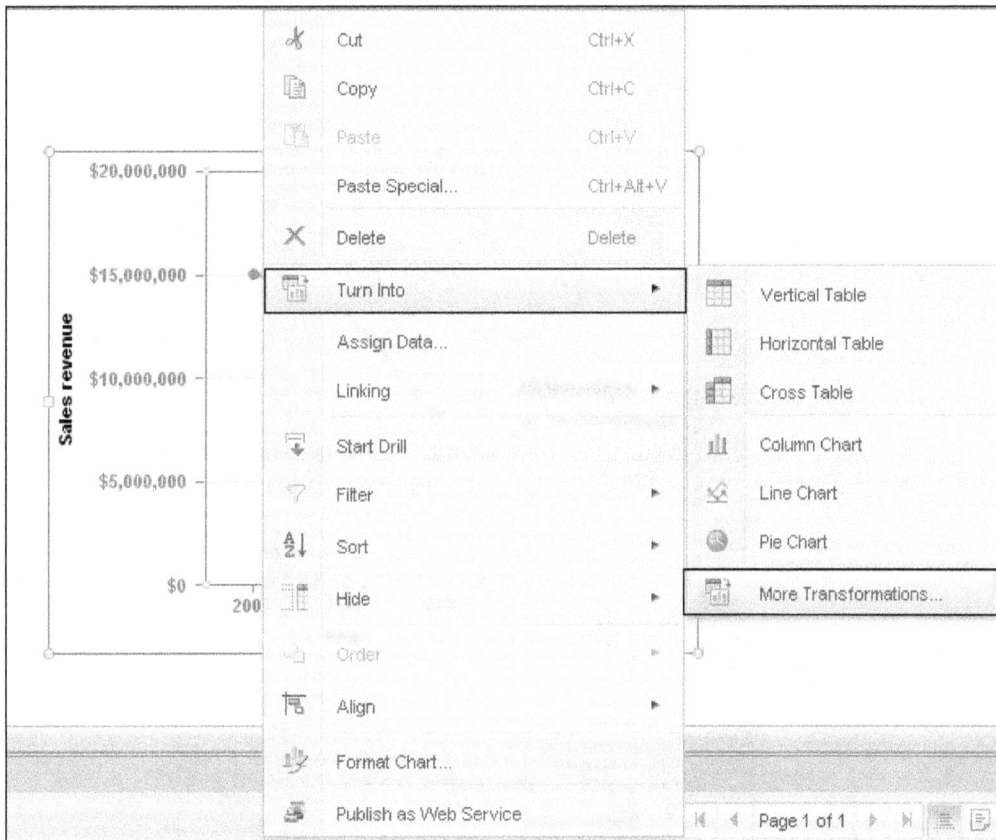

After choosing the preceding option, we will navigate to the chart and table type menu. By using this menu, we will be able to access each chart category located on the left-hand side of the screen as well as define which objects will be presented in the chart, as shown:

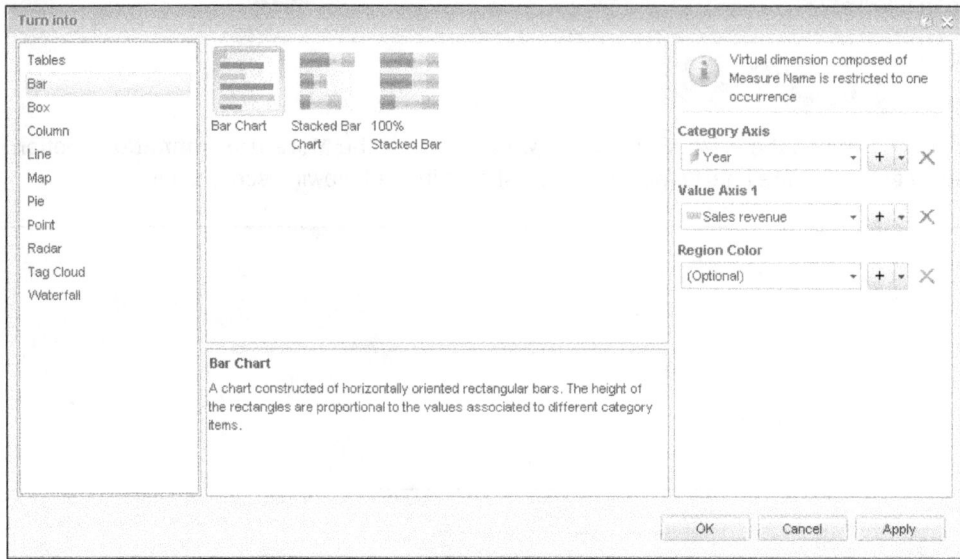

The preceding window offers the following chart types:

> ► **Bar Chart**: This chart is suited for data such as products or short time periods such as a year or quarters, as shown in the following screenshot:

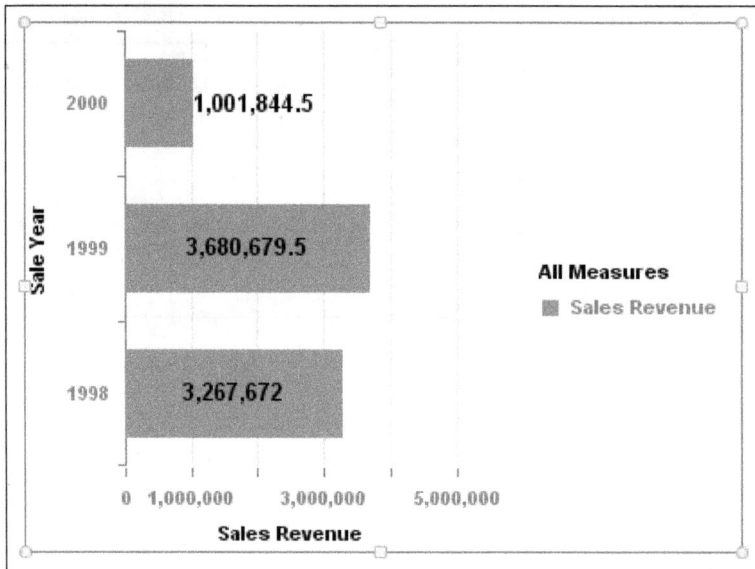

▶ **Box Plot Chart**: A box plot chart is a convenient way of graphically depicting groups of numerical data through their quartiles. Box plots may also have lines extending vertically from the boxes (whiskers), indicating variability outside the upper and lower quartiles, as shown in the following screenshot.

A box plot chart is made up of the following:

- Minimum
- Maximum
- First quartile
- Third quartile
- Median

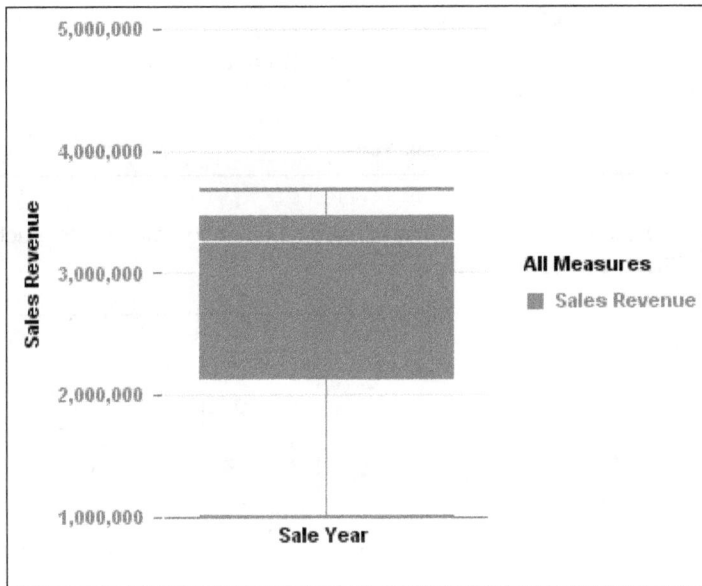

▶ **Column Chart**: This is perhaps the most common chart type, used for easily comparing sets of values over a period of time, as shown in the following screenshot:

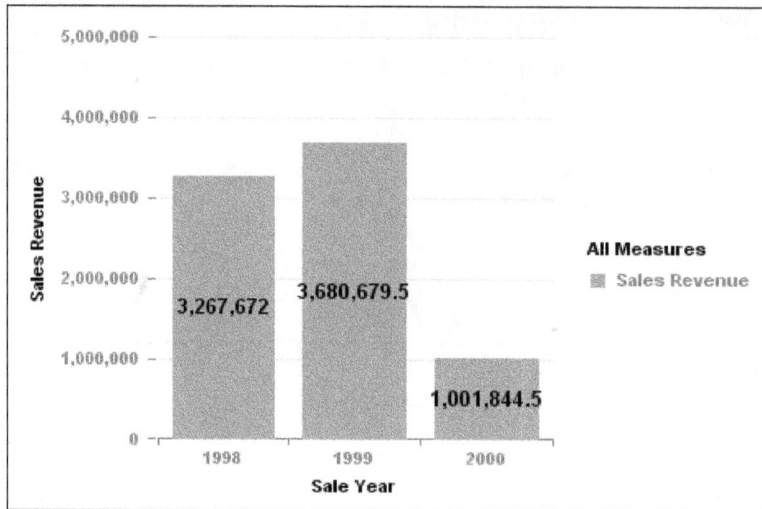

The **Column** category also contains various types of column charts, such as **Stacked Column Chart**, as shown:

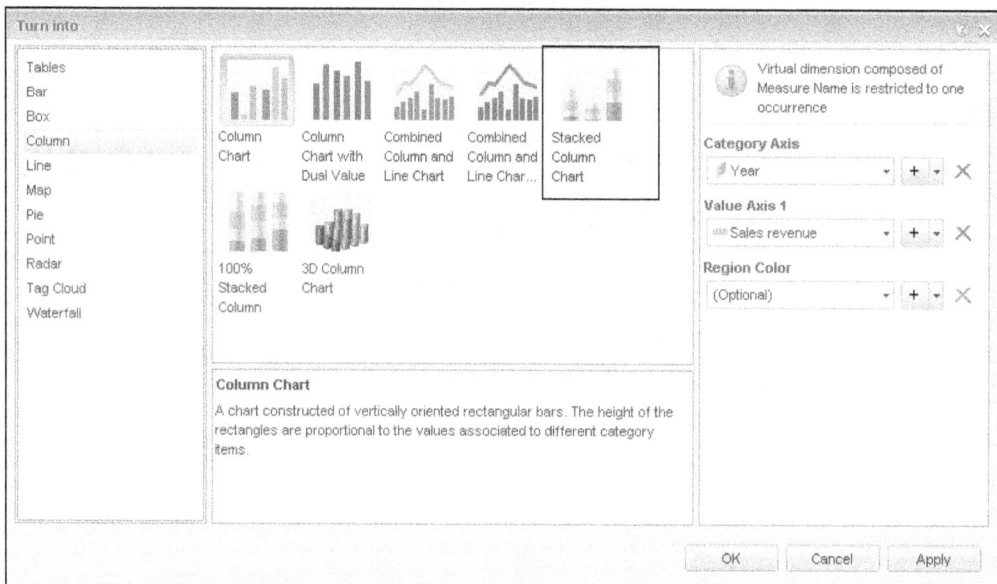

The **Stacked Column Chart** enables us to show different category values on top of each other. It also enables us to compare the totals.

In the following stacked chart, we have the quarters as the column values on top of each other, enabling us to compare each year's sales, as shown:

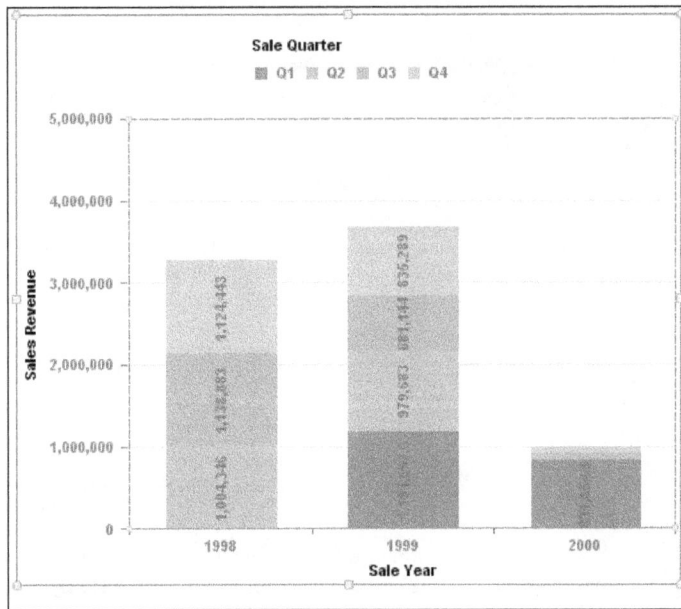

One of the most useful column chart types is **Combined Column and Line Chart**, as it enables us to compare and display several measures on the same *y* axis while applying a different chart type for each measure for a better and easier visual comparison. In this example, we chose **Combined Column and Line Chart**. Note that the data contains two measures, as shown in the following screenshot:

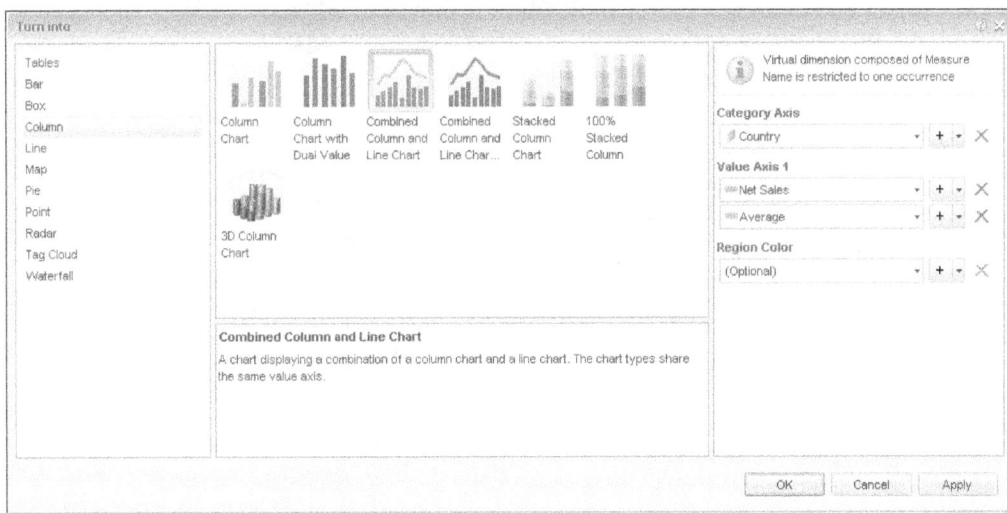

After applying this chart type, it will be easy to compare the net sales to the average net sales, an insight we can only get using this type of chart, as shown:

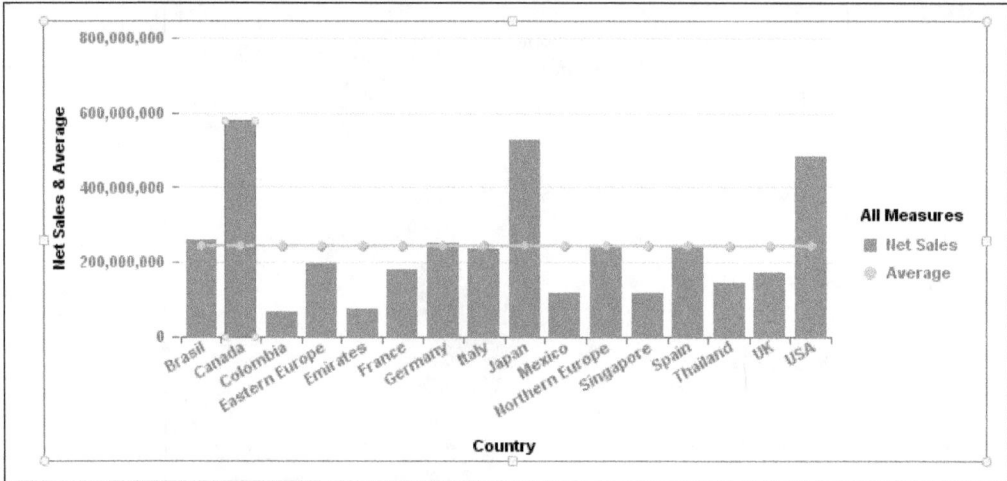

> When the data in the chart isn't chronological (country names, sales personnel), it's better to sort the data by the measure values.

The next sets of charts are as follows:

▸ **Line Chart**: This is very similar to a column or bar chart. A line chart is suited to visualize time trends data by using pick points connected by a line. We already used this type of chart in our first chart example.

▸ **Map Chart**: Tree and heat maps are charts that visualize data by dividing it into rectangles; the size of each rectangle represents the measure value of a dimension object. In this example, it is the year:

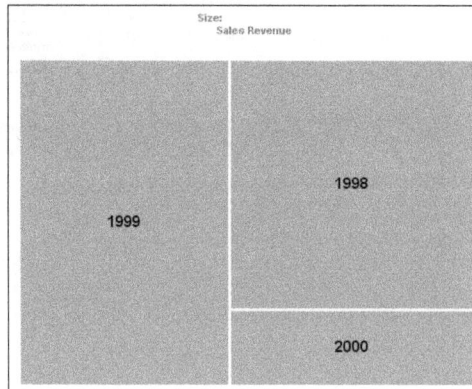

Heat maps work on a similar basis, but using red colors for the lower values and green colors for the top values.

The next sets of charts are as follows:

► **Pie Chart**: This is a sliced chart divided into several sectors. The pie chart represents the whole, each slice representing a part of the whole.

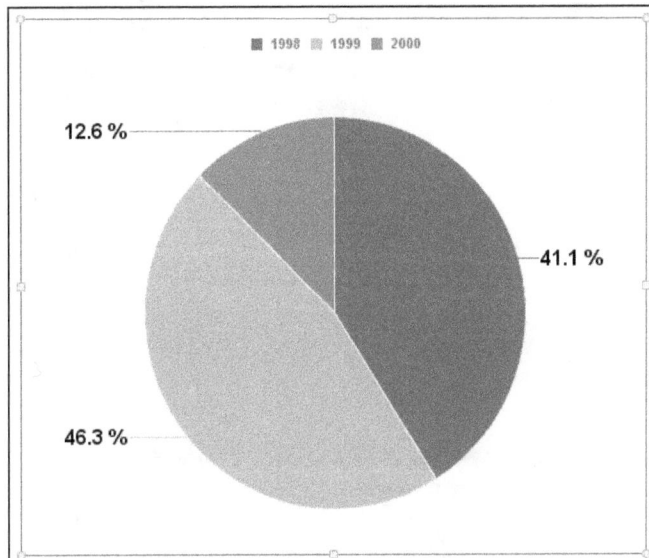

When working with pie charts, it's recommended to not display more than five or six values so that the visual effect is not lost. If you do have more than five to six values, then the rest of the values can be grouped into other single values. It's also better not to display a legend in a pie chart, but rather display the values with the labels in order to get the best display results.

▸ **Point Chart**: This category contains charts such as scatter, bubble, and polar charts. Bubble charts can analyze results using two measure axes and show the correlation between them; for example, analyzing market growth over time and the product price. Each bubble location will represent its place compared to these two variables. In the following bubble chart, we can analyze the quantity of products sold using another variable, **Discount**.

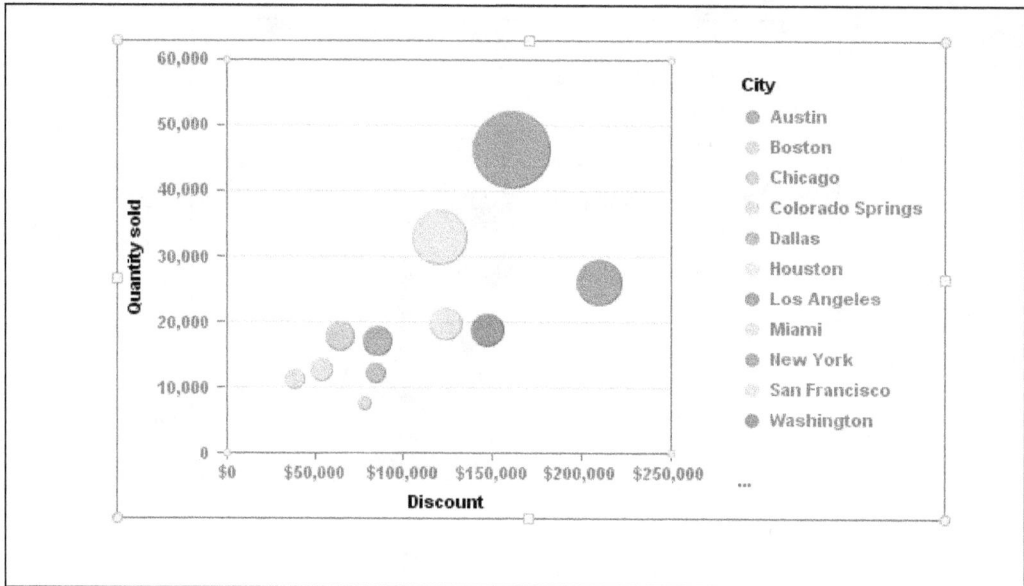

▸ **Radar Chart**: This chart is suited for scoring measurements and data that requires to be scaled with several variables/attributes. A radar chart can have several axes built to compare several scores. For example, in the following chart, we have three products that are measured by five different scoring criteria that are ranged between 1 and 5 (1 is the lowest and 5 is the highest score). By analyzing the scoring results, we can realize which product got a high or a low score compared to the other products. The following is a more panoramic analysis rather than a linear one:

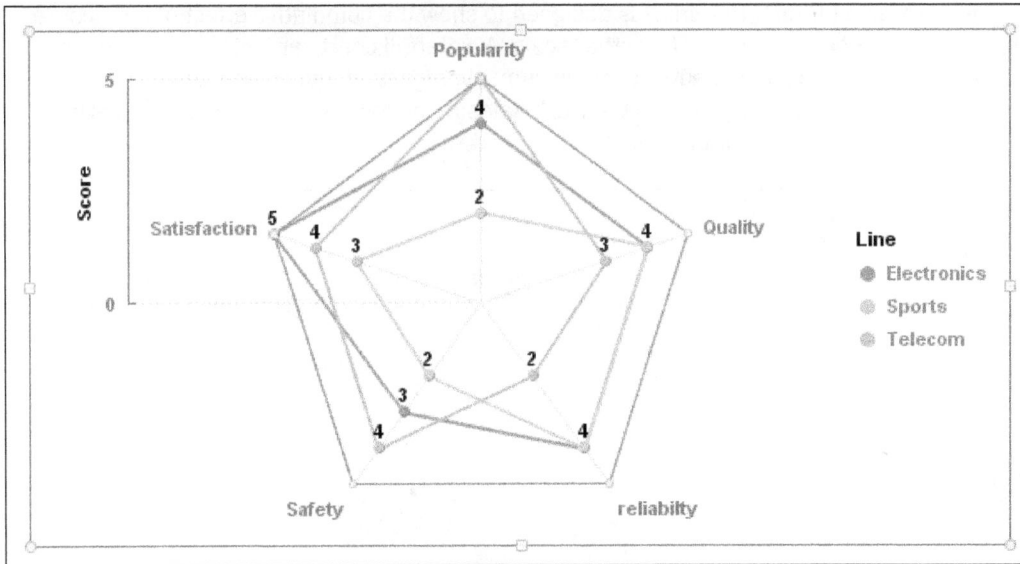

Multidimension charts such as radar and bubble charts are considered to be more complex and hard-to-read charts. Column and line charts are usually the most effective since they ease the use of chart types.

▶ **Tag Cloud**: This is one of the new visualization components we often see in websites, representing the results with words and the size of the word representing its ranking compared to the other values. In this example, we can see the results of sales per city. The tag cloud chart also enables us to use ranges to get a better analysis of the result, as shown:

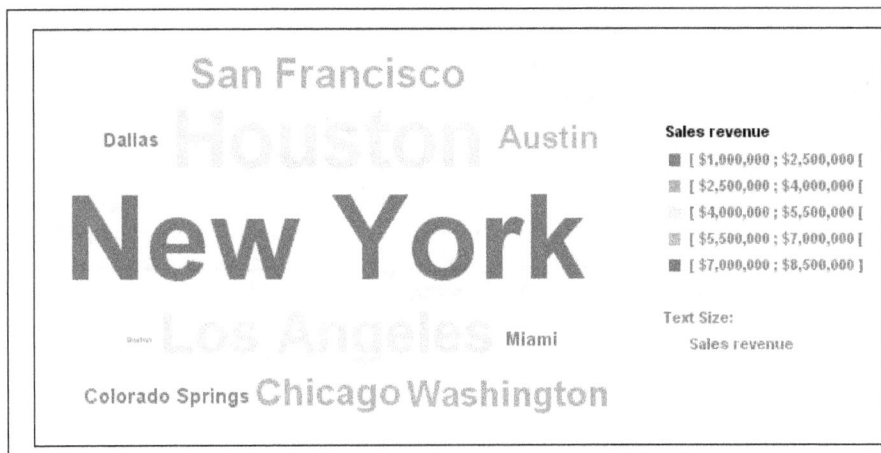

▸ **Waterfall Chart**: This chart is designed to show the cumulative effect of a measure over a period of time or any other scale. A waterfall chart can help us analyze the running totals of measures such as sum, average, and percentages. Notice that we are able to analyze each quarter's sales in the following chart, with the *y* axis representing the cumulative effect of the sales:

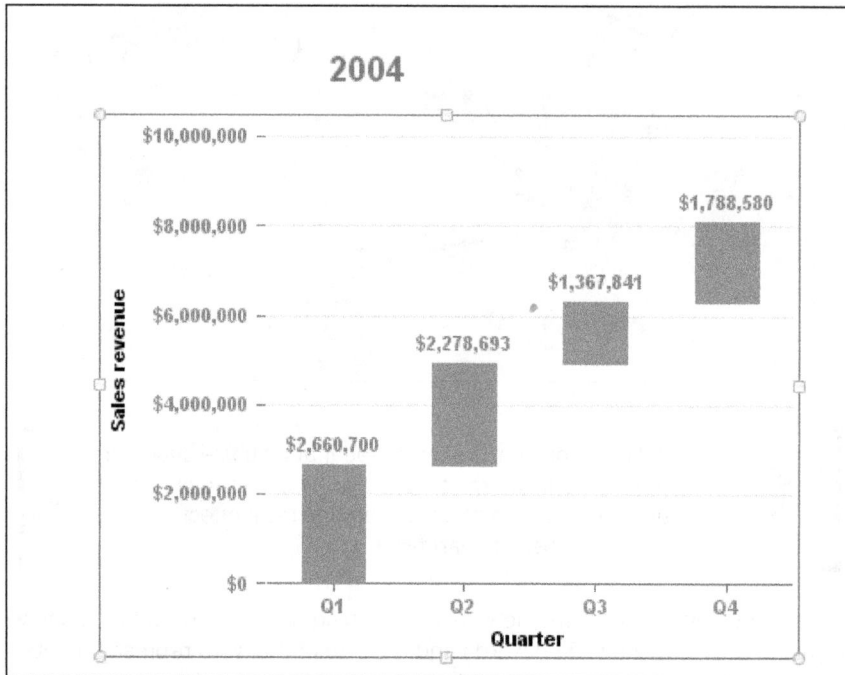

How it works...

By using the speed menu, we will be able to access various chart types that can deal with a different type of data and visualization requirement. Each chart can be applied to any kind of table or be displayed side by side with an existing table.

See also

▸ In order to create an interaction with the charts, such as using filters or passing a value from a table into a chart, see the *Using input controls* and *Using element links as filters* recipes in *Chapter 7, Filtering the Report Data*

Formatting charts

Charts can be edited and formatted using the **Format Chart** menu. Similar to the **Table Format** window, when we are required to format a chart, we will require more options enabling us to perform easy tasks such as formatting the font of the data values, editing the chart title, or using advanced features such as color value ranges.

Getting ready

By right-clicking on any chart type, we will navigate to the **Format Chart** menu:

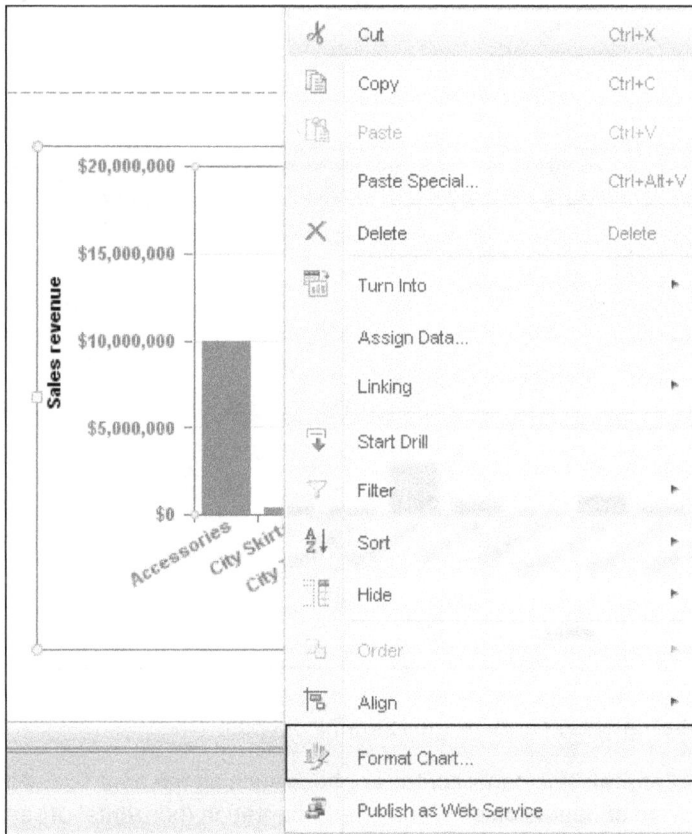

In the next window, we will be able to access the chart format properties.

How to do it...

The **Format Chart** window is organized into six main accordion-style categories:

▸ **Global**: This category contains the main chart-formatting options and is further organized into several formatting areas:

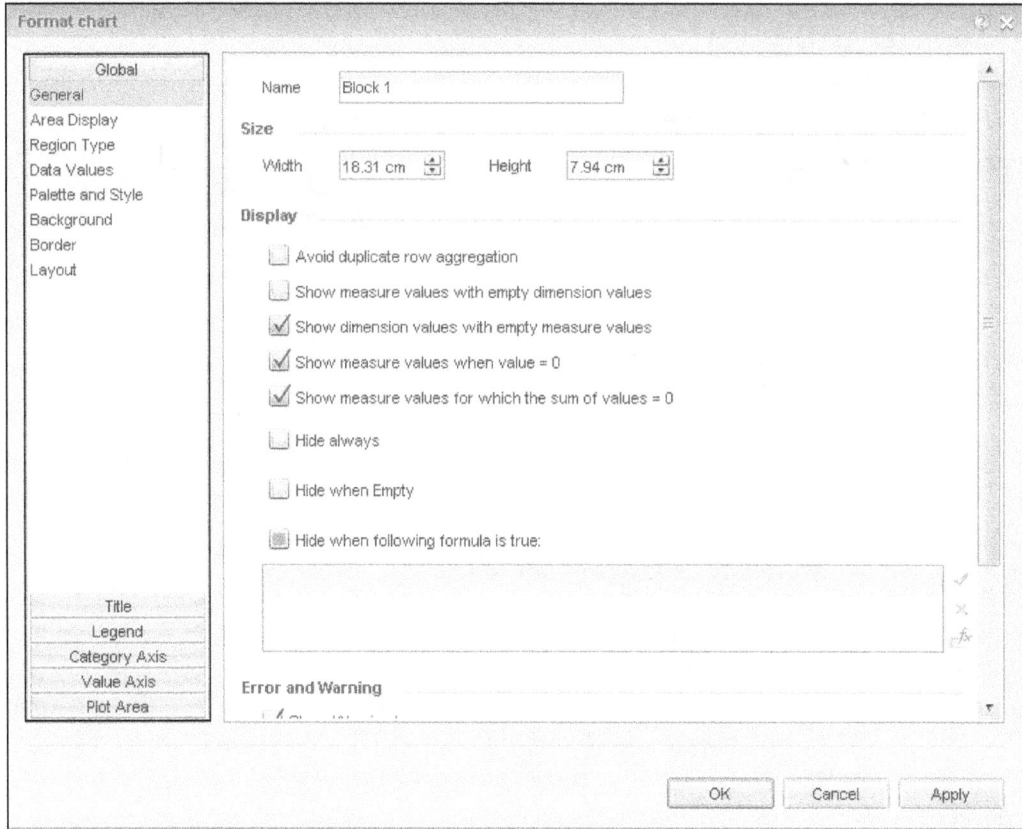

The **Global** category contains the following options:

❑ **General**: This panel controls options such as the area size of the chart, the type of data to display, and chart orientation (horizontal or vertical).

❑ **Area Display**: This panel mainly controls the visibility of the title, axes, values, and the legend. In this panel, the user can decide which part of the table they want to display, as shown:

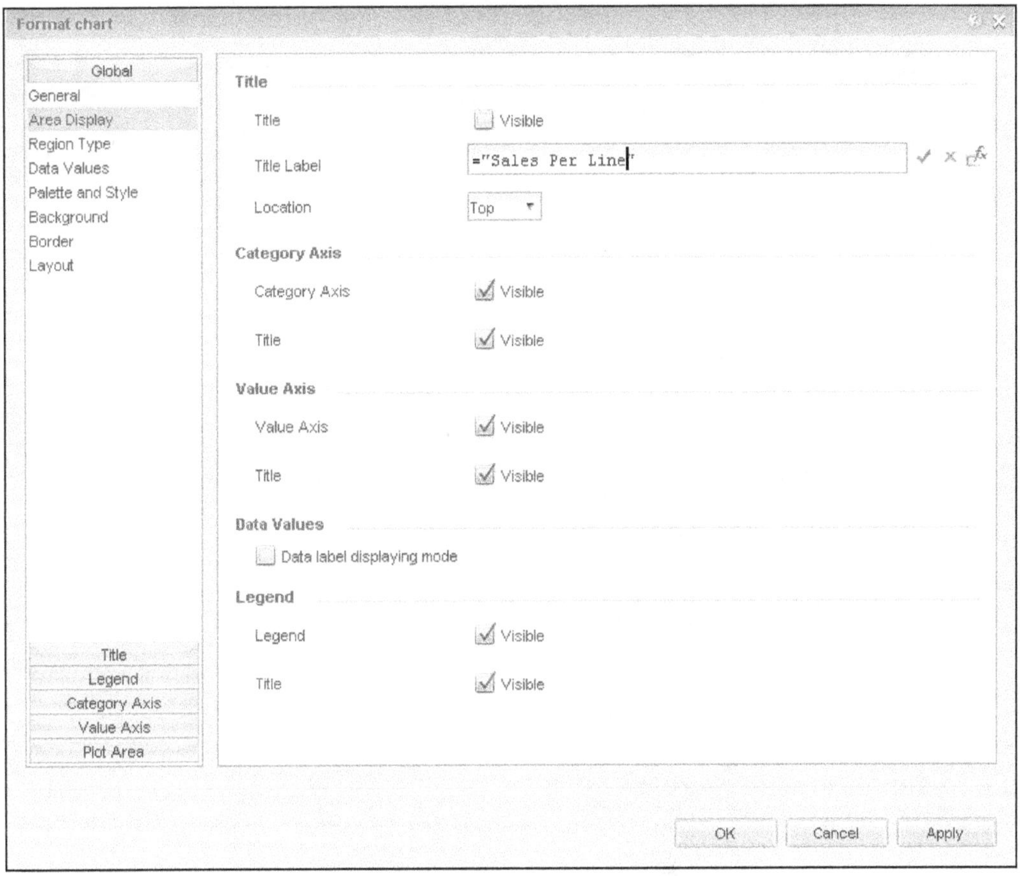

When displaying data values, it's not recommended to display long numbers in millions. For better display, it's recommended to divide the numbers by the relevant divider (for example, dividing the number 20 million by 1 million will give the number 20 rather than an eight-digit number).

□ **Region Type**: This enables us to quickly switch to other basic chart types such as bar, line, and surfaces. This option isn't available to all the chart types, as shown:

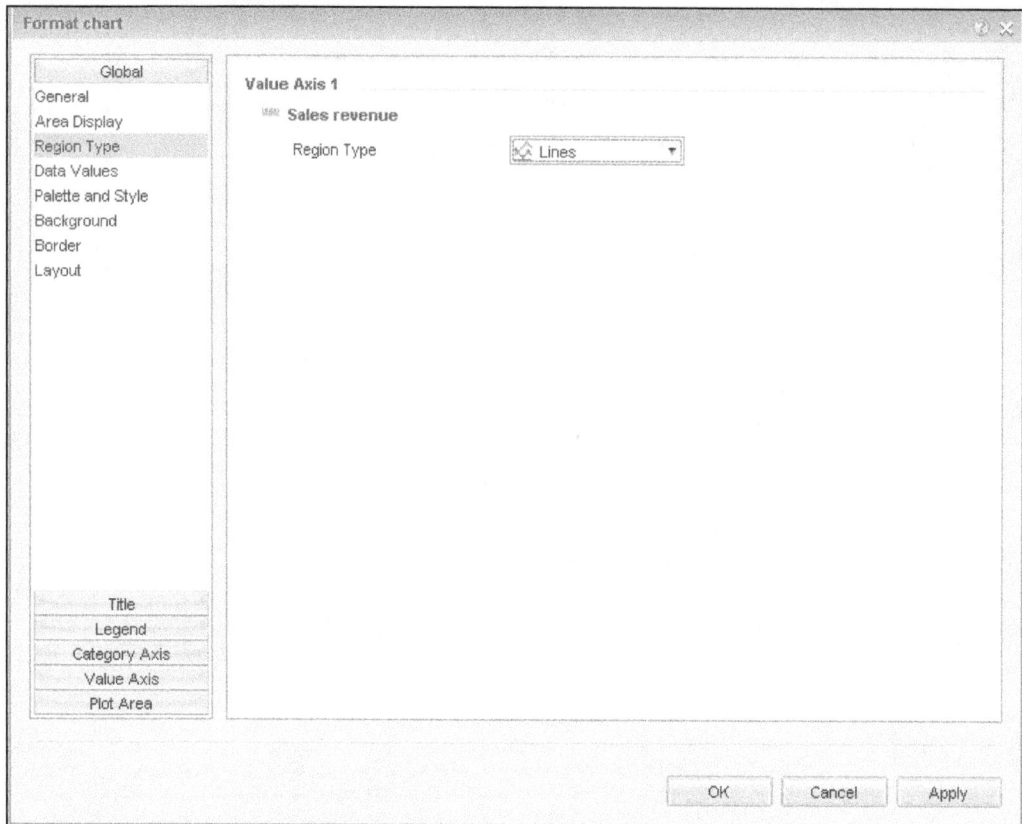

□ **Data Values**: This option enables us to format the values just as when using format cell and font options. In this tab, we can adjust the color, size, font type, orientation, and background of the values, as shown in the following screenshot:

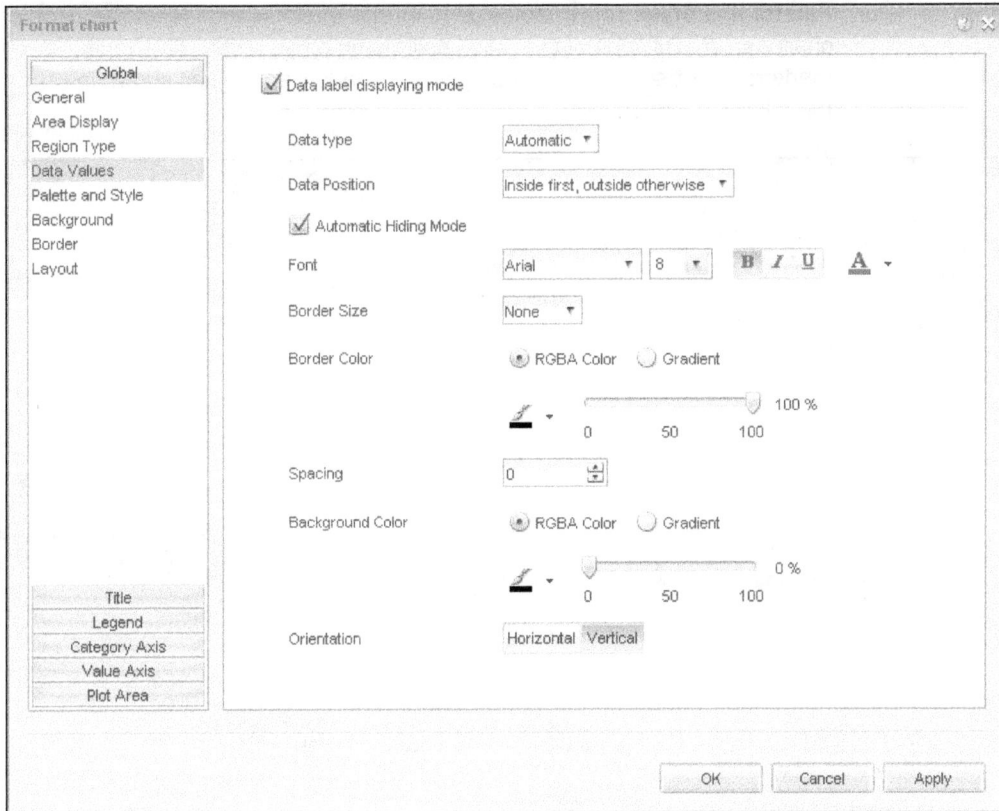

As a best practice, it is recommended to use a natural font color so that the values will be clear and easy to read. In the following chart, you can see that we are using black color values over a blue column chart, which makes the values very easy and clear to read:

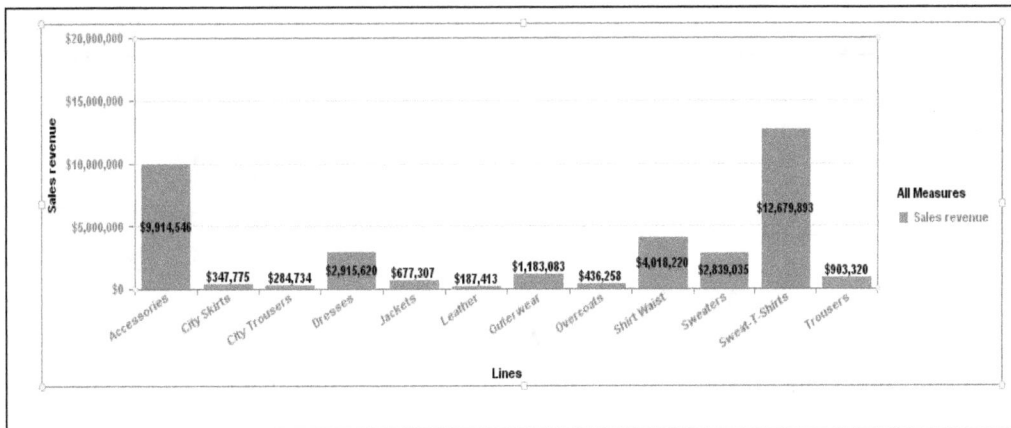

❑ **Palette and Style**: This enables us to format the look and feel of the chart's graphical capabilities, such as column color, width, 3D effects, markers, chart series style, and light and shadow effects, as shown in the following screenshot:

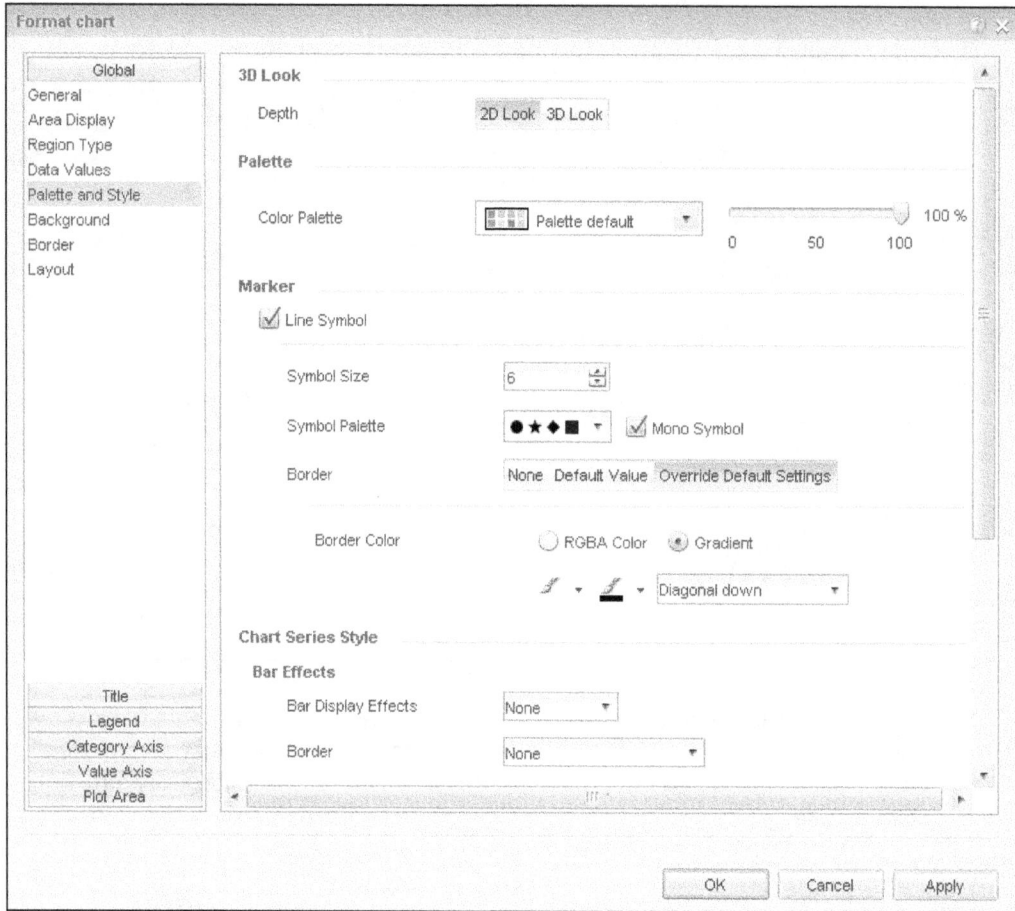

If we scroll a bit more, we will be able to see the rest of the window options:

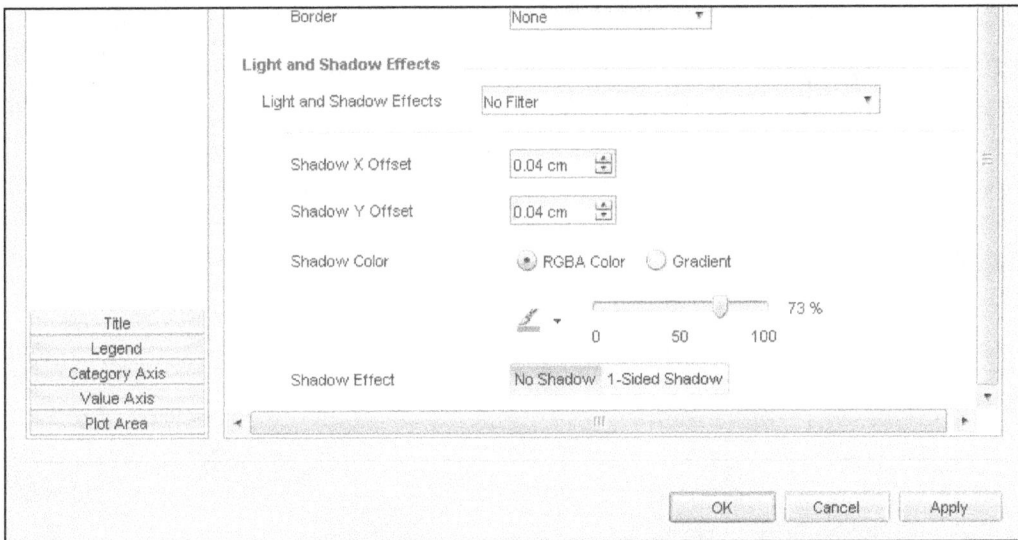

❑ **Background**: This enables us to format the chart background. Again, as with the color values, it is recommended to use natural colors and not strong live colors so that the chart keeps a clear, straightforward graphical approach, as shown in the following screenshot:

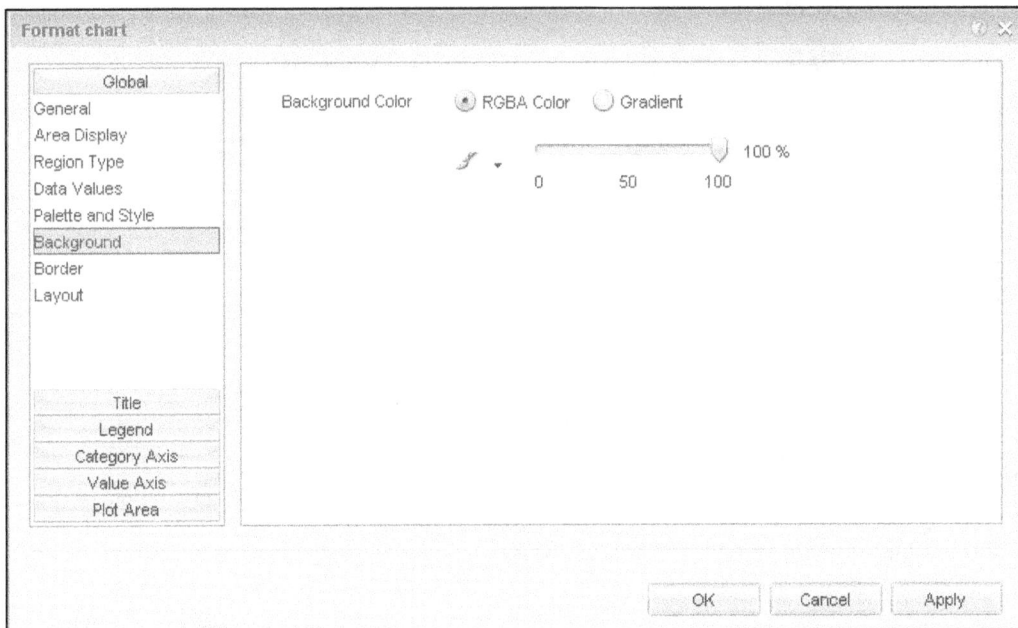

- ❑ **Border**: This outlines the chart area. This option is useful when we have several tables/charts in the same page and we want to create a better graphical isolation effect between the multiple elements, as shown:

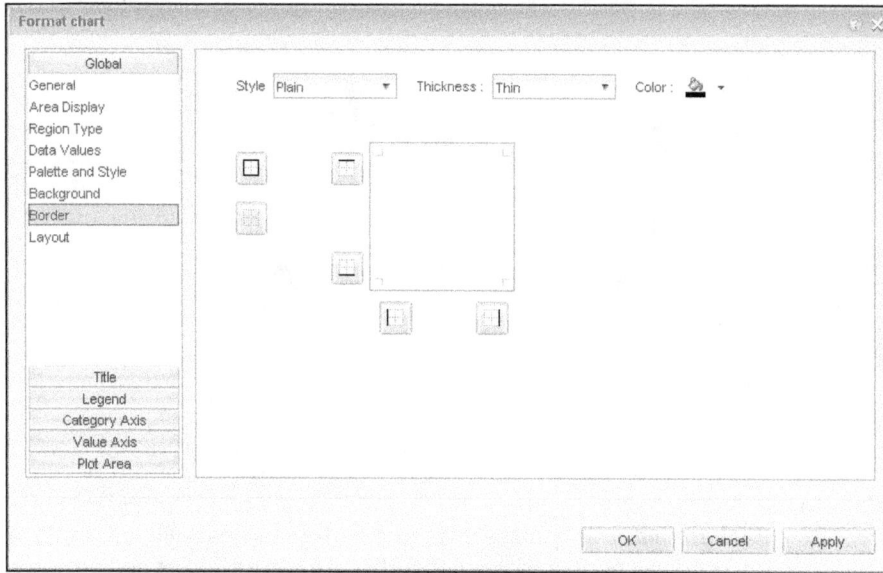

- ❑ **Layout**: This enables us to set the chart's horizontal, vertical, and relative positions, as shown:

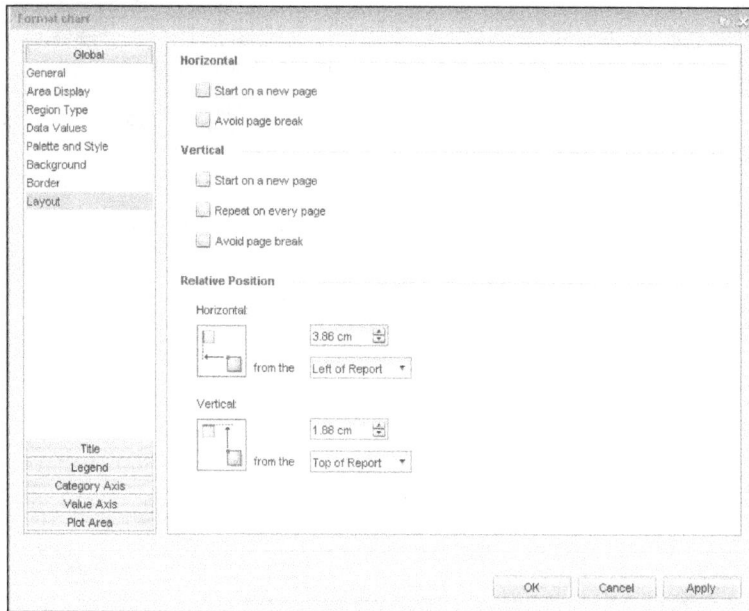

▶ **Title**: This category enables us to adjust title properties such as font size, text, borders, and background, as shown:

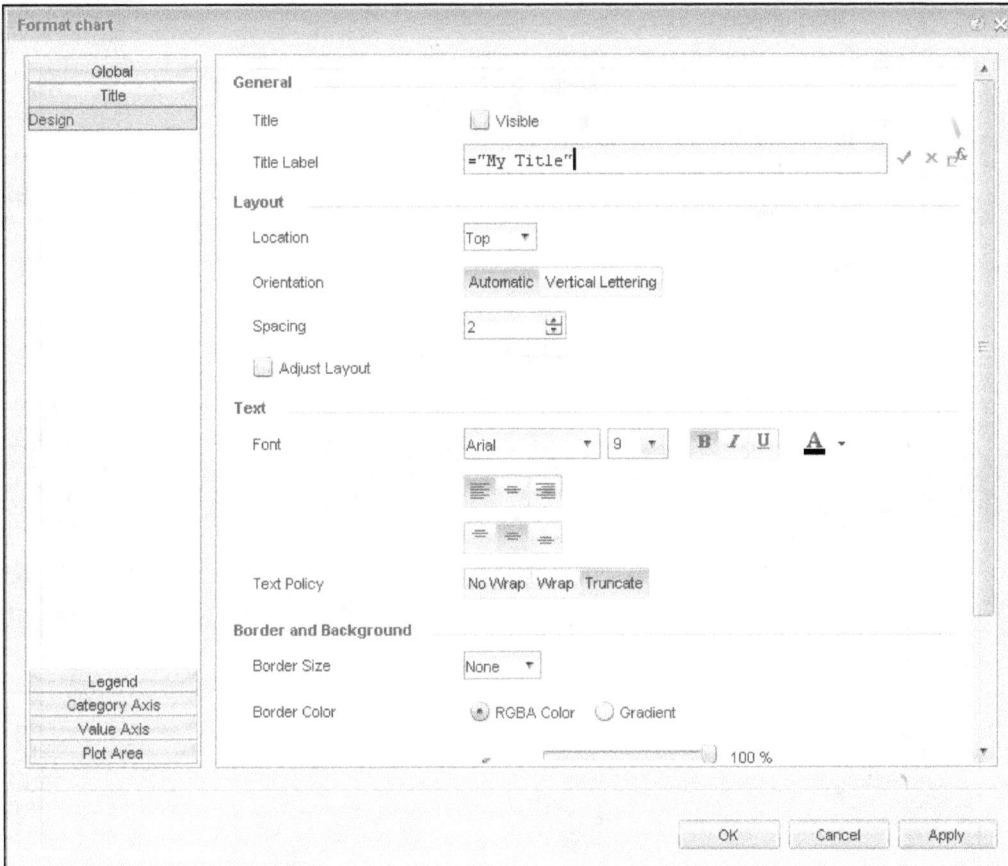

Format chart

Global	
Title	
Design	

General

Title   ☐ Visible

Title Label   `="My Title"|`   ✓ ✕

Layout

Location   Top ▼

Orientation   Automatic   Vertical Lettering

Spacing   2 ⬍

☐ Adjust Layout

Text

Font   Arial ▼   9 ▼   **B** *I* U   **A** ▾

Text Policy   No Wrap   Wrap   Truncate

Border and Background

Border Size   None ▼

Border Color   ● RGBA Color   ○ Gradient

100 %

Legend
Category Axis
Value Axis
Plot Area

OK   Cancel   Apply

▸ **Legend**: This category enables us to format the legend properties. The following are the options under **Legend**:

 ❑ **Design**: This formats legend properties such as layout, text, border, and background:

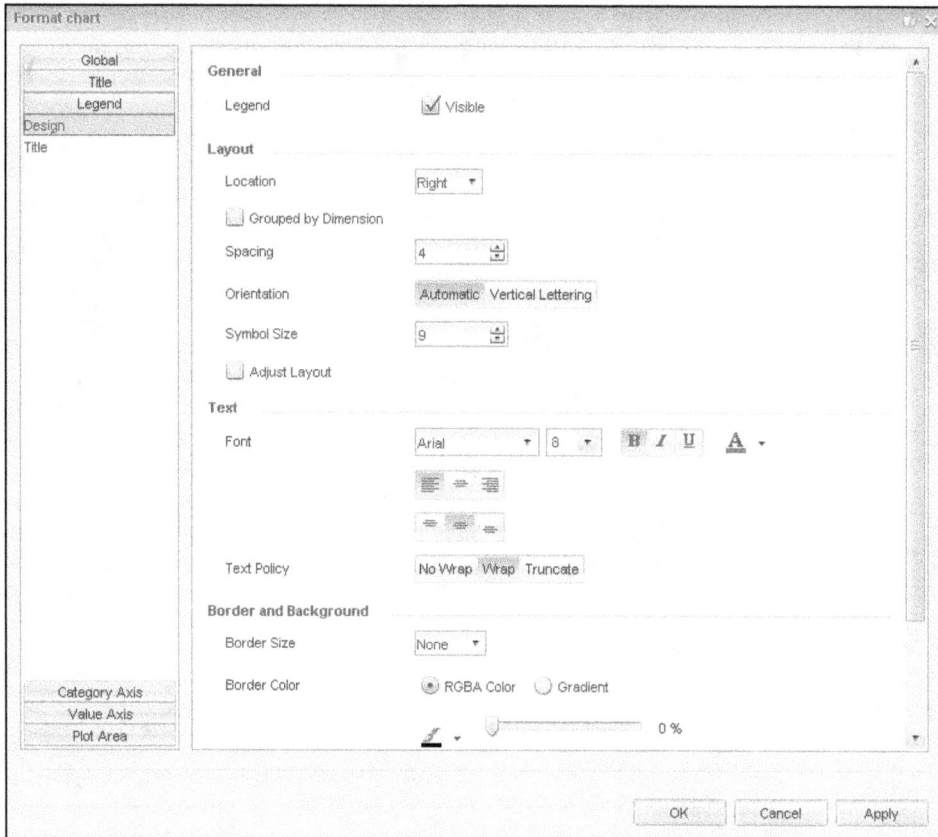

❏ **Title**: This enables us to format the title of the legend properties:

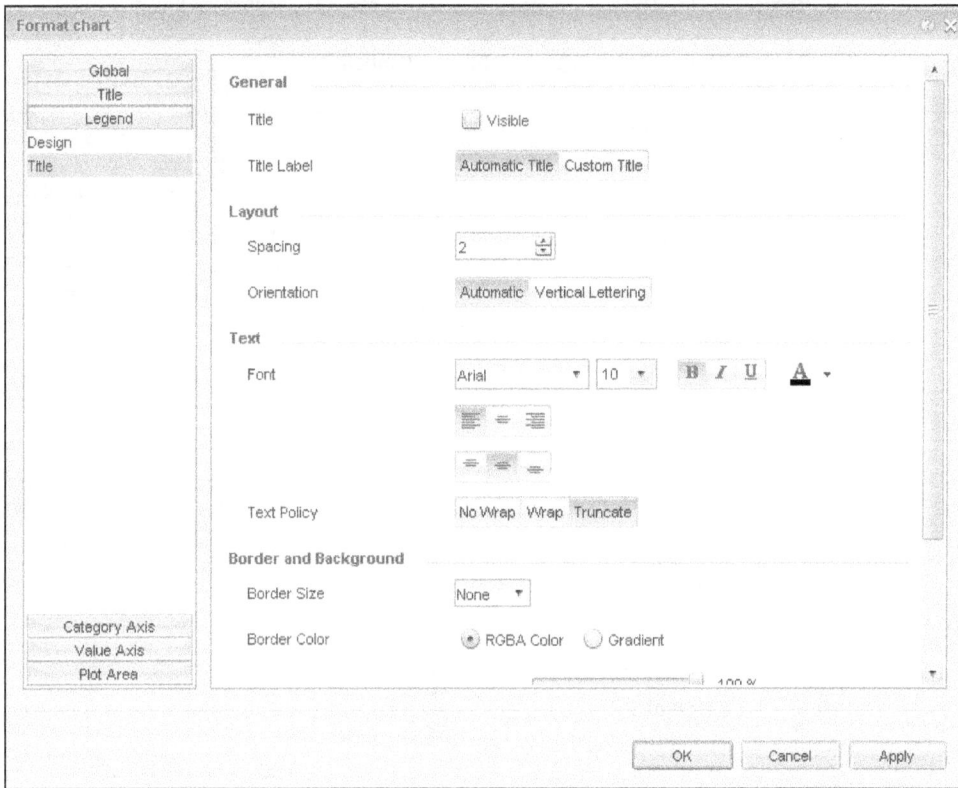

It is recommended to locate the legend to the right-hand side of the table. Use it when the chart has several measures and a legend is required to represent the different data colors, as shown:

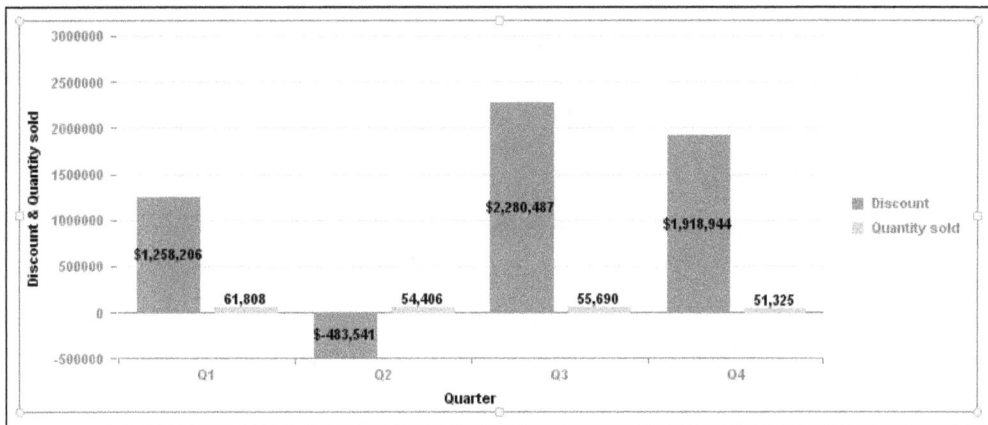

▶ **Category Axis**: This controls the *x* axis properties. It has the following options:

❑ **Design**: This enables us to hide/show the *x* axis category values, line, label, orientation, color, and text. In the layout area, you can also use the **Reverse order of the category axis** option, as shown:

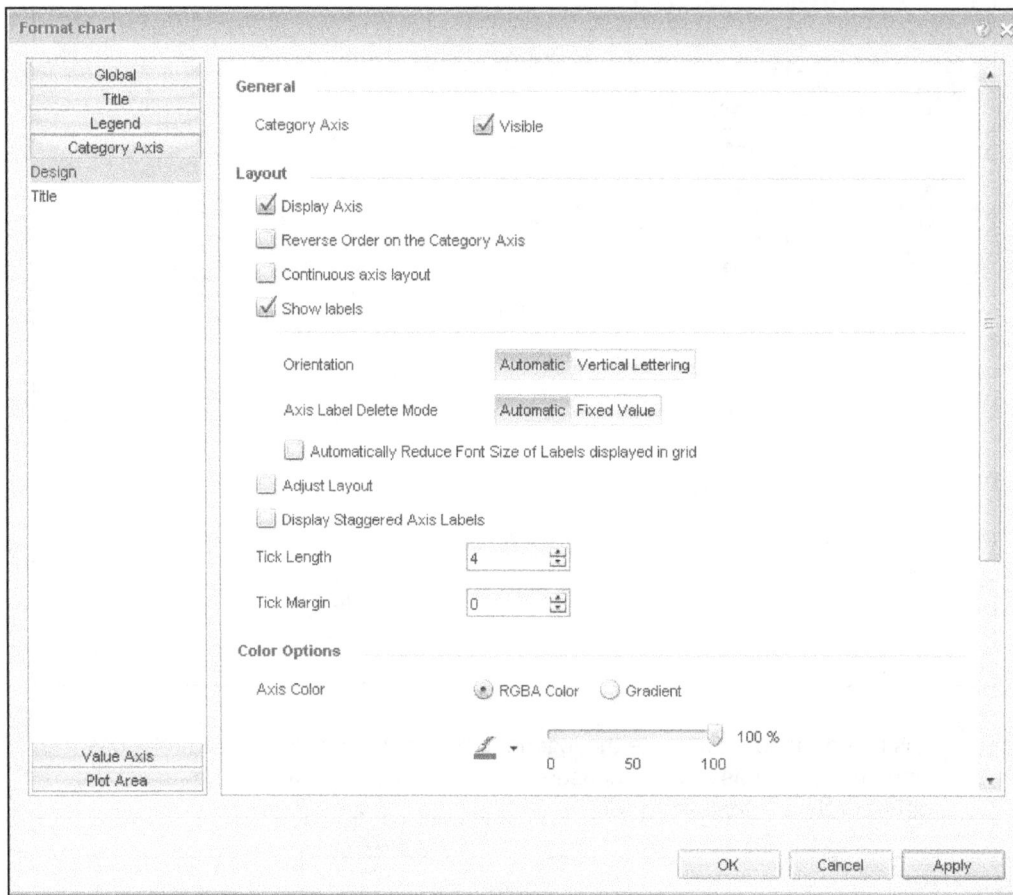

❑ **Title:** This enables us to control the *x* axis title properties such as title, text, layout, border, and background. The category values should be treated as any text should be—readable, clear, and without special formats, as shown:

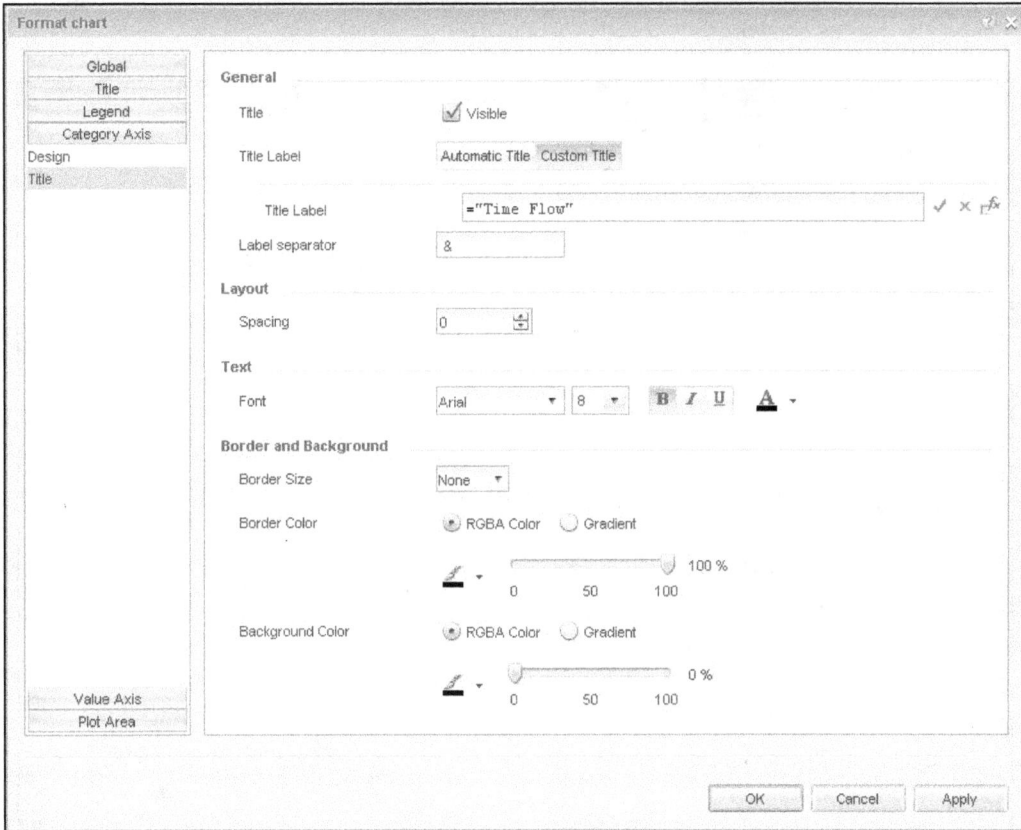

▸ **Value Axis**: This category enables us to format the *y* axis. It has the following options:

    ❑ **Design**: This is just like in the category values. This option enables us to choose chart behavior (stacked and unstacked), format the scale (linear and logarithmic), and choose layout, color options, text, and number formatting, as shown:

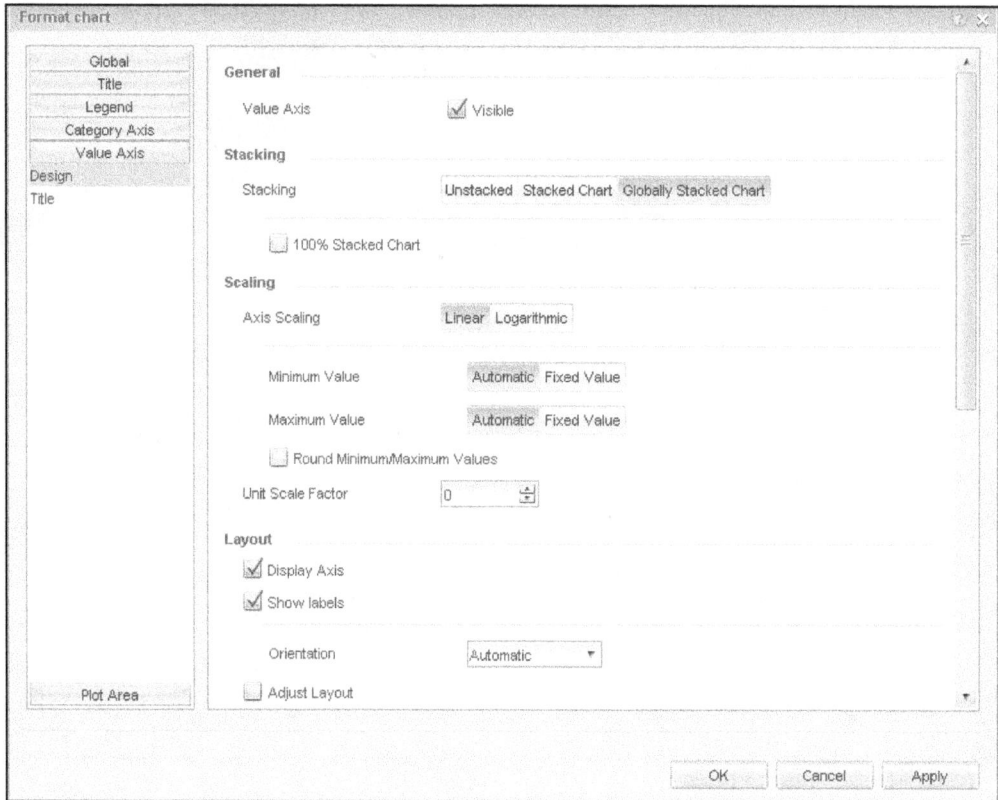

In the **Number** section, it's possible to apply the % sign to the values in case the scale is using percentages, as shown in the following screenshot:

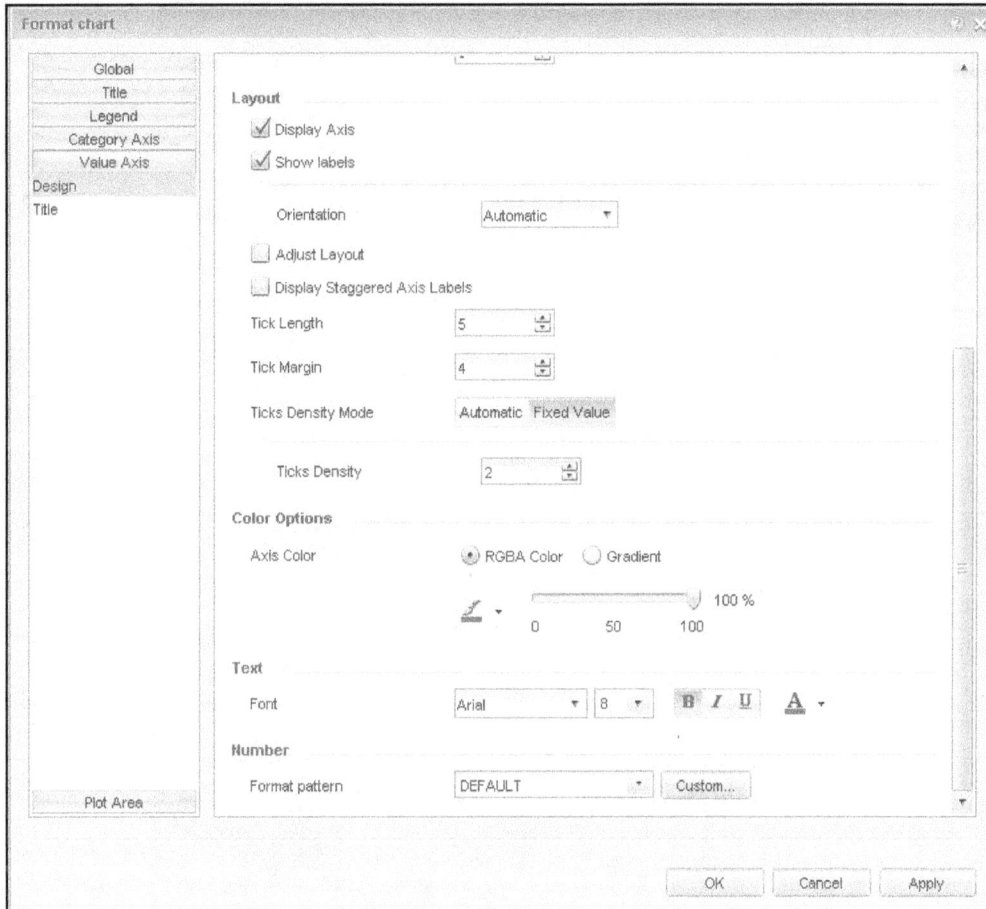

❑ **Title**: This option enables us to simply apply text formatting such as font size, layout, border, and background to the *y* axis title:

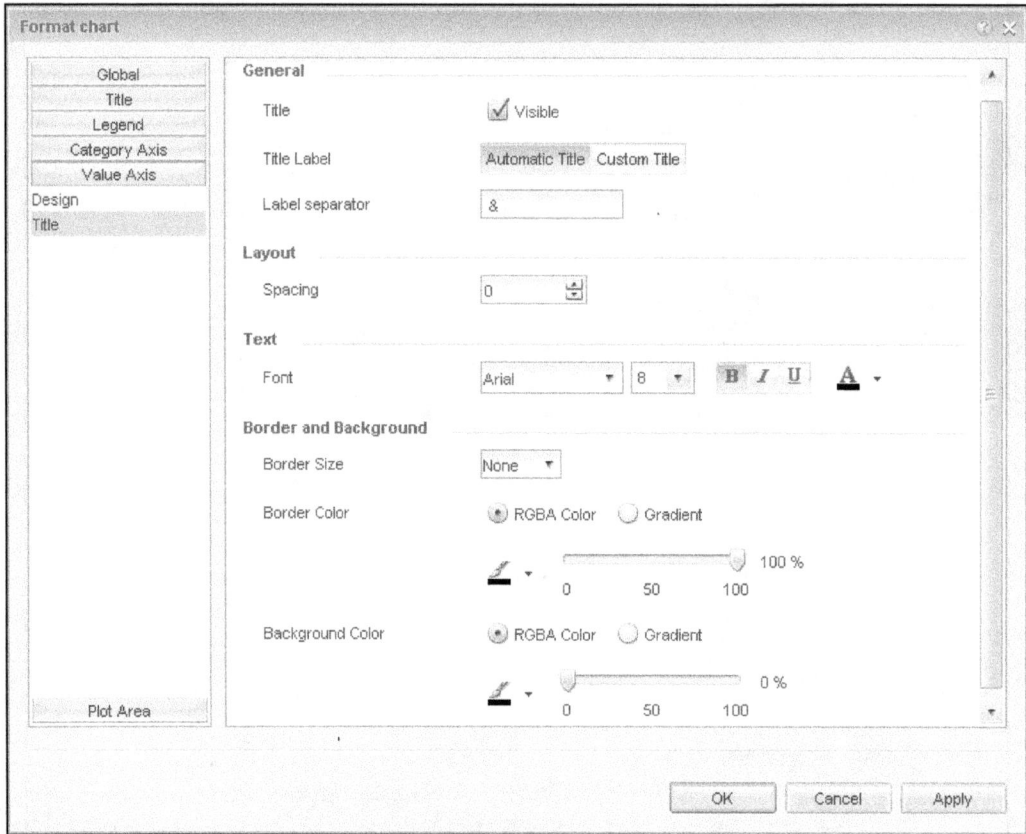

- **Plot Area**: This option enables us to format the plot area via the place where the chart is displayed:

  - **Design**: This option enables us to format the spacing between and within the chart bars. This option is useful when we are required to show several category values and we want to make them closer for better and easier comparison, as shown:

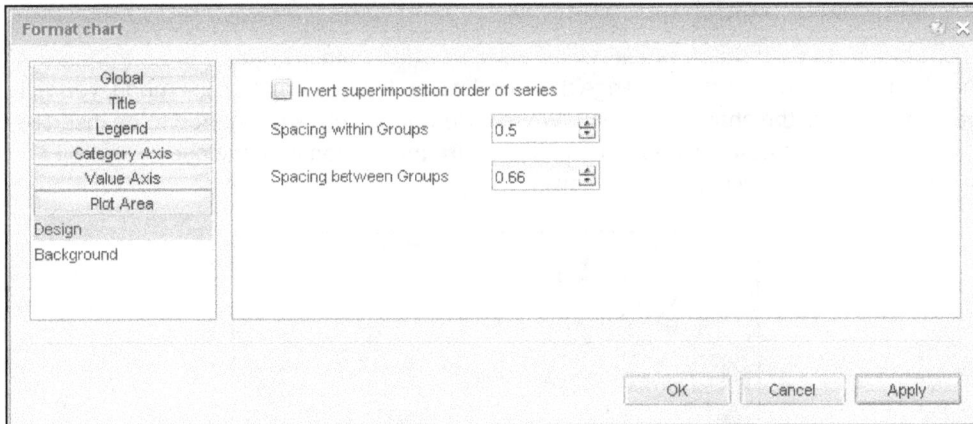

  - **Background**: This option enables you to format the *x* and *y* axes grid, the chart background color, and effect:

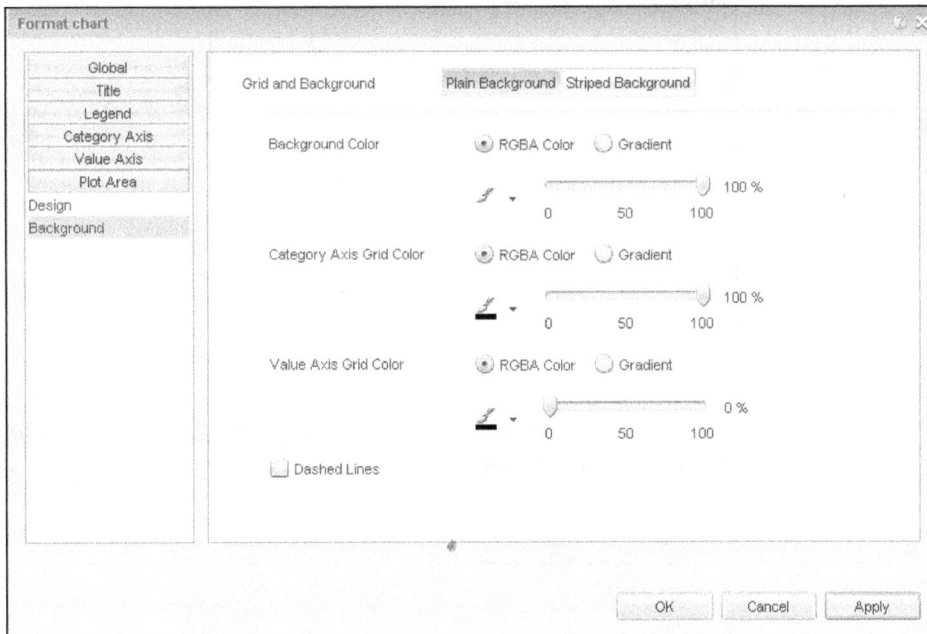

How it works...

As we can see, the **Format Chart** menu enables us to adjust the chart properties. By using a rich formatting menu that is structured from six formatting categories, we can easily access a specific formatting option and a specific formatting subject and activate a specific chart function.

There's more...

If the chart type requires you to change the **turn into** option in the right-click menu, you will have to navigate to the chart type menu. When different objects are required to be inserted into the chart, the **assign data** option under the **turn into** option in the speed menu will enable us to choose new objects, as shown:

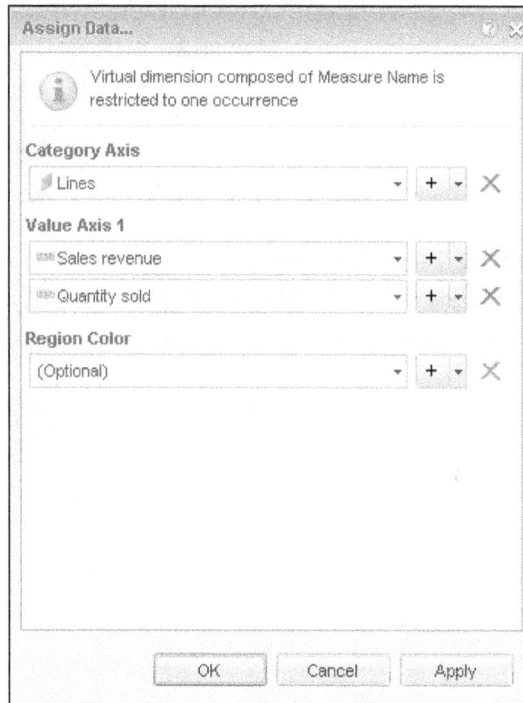

By using the **+** sign, we will be able to add new objects to the chart. By using the **X** sign, an object from the exiting chart can be unassigned.

6
Formatting Reports

In this chapter, we will cover the following recipes:

- ▸ Using sorts
- ▸ Using calculations
- ▸ Using sections and breaks
- ▸ Ranking
- ▸ Conditional rules
- ▸ Data tracking
- ▸ Outline and fold

Introduction

Traditionally, we can distinguish between two stages of work while interacting with the Web Intelligence reports:

- ▸ **Building the query**: This includes defining the query, dragging the result objects, and setting the query filters
- ▸ **Formatting the report**: After the data is retrieved by the query, we are no longer interacting with the database. We are formatting the results using the Web Intelligence toolbars, left-hand side panes, and the rest of the report functionality

Formatting report results is the main part of interacting with Web Intelligence reports.

The formatting layer holds many capabilities that enable the business user to perform basic tasks such as sorting, filtering, calculations, data aggregations, and more advanced tasks such as using complex formulas, performing drills, or even linking reports. Whatever we do in the report can't affect the query structure nor its performance.

There is no difference between performing a complex calculation to using a simple sort. Everything we do in the report is saved as long as we save the report and our formatting is saved as a part of the report.

The formatting layer is also very important because it enables us to complete the picture by extending the query results and adding calculations, with better presentation and *story telling* of the data.

For example, creating calculations or grouping the data in order to present the subtotals are actions that we can't always solve at the query level and require extra formatting.

In this chapter, we will provide the core formatting capabilities addressing the most common and useful actions to the report builders.

Using sorts

Sorts are one of the most useful features we can find in the Web Intelligence application.

Sorting provides a clear context to the data since it enables us to read the data in a much clearer way, especially when we are working with time or measure objects that require to be sorted chronologically or displayed starting from the top results.

With sorting, we can answer simple questions, such as who the top sales person was, or analyze our data starting from the most current one by the date or the year. We can also apply several sorts to our table or charts, which can be extra helpful.

Another basic requirement that we can apply by using sorting is to sort the data alphabetically from A-Z or Z-A.

Getting ready

We want to understand the sorting capabilities that we can apply to the data in our reports.

How to do it...

If we observe the data displayed in the table, as shown in the following screenshot, we notice that the data is already sorted:

Year	Quarter	Sales revenu
2004	Q1	$2,660,700
2004	Q2	$2,279,003
2004	Q3	$1,367,841
2004	Q4	$1,788,580
2005	Q1	$3,326,172
2005	Q2	$2,840,651
2005	Q3	$2,879,303
2005	Q4	$4,186,120
2006	Q1	$3,742,989
2006	Q2	$4,006,718
2006	Q3	$3,953,395
2006	Q4	$3,356,041

We can see that all the possible columns in the chart are sorted from A to Z: the **Year** and then the **Quarter** columns besides the **Sales revenue** column, which can't be sorted because the rest of the columns are already sorted.

The years are sorted from the first year to the last year, and the quarters are sorted as a secondary sort under the years.

This is the default sorting behavior that Web Intelligence applies to the data in tables in order to provide a basic, familiar display mode to the users.

In order to change this basic behavior of the sort to Z-A, we will mark the **Year** column in the table and navigate to the **Analysis** toolbar, and use the **Display** tab, which also controls the sorting options. Have a look at the following screenshot:

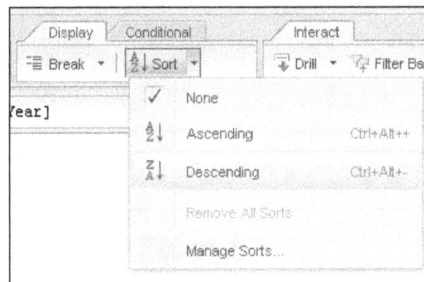

Display	Conditional		Interact	
Break ▾	Sort ▾		Drill ▾	Filter Bar

✓	None	
	Ascending	Ctrl+Alt++
	Descending	Ctrl+Alt+-
	Remove All Sorts	
	Manage Sorts...	

[ear]

The result of the sorting can be viewed in the following screenshot:

Year	Quarter	Sales revenue
2006	Q1	$3,742,989
2006	Q2	$4,006,718
2006	Q3	$3,953,395
2006	Q4	$3,356,041
2005	Q1	$3,326,172
2005	Q2	$2,840,651
2005	Q3	$2,879,303
2005	Q4	$4,186,120
2004	Q1	$2,660,700
2004	Q2	$2,279,003
2004	Q3	$1,367,841
2004	Q4	$1,788,580

Notice that the entire row as well as the table is sorted accordingly (unlike Excel where it's possible to sort a single column with no effect on the rest of the columns).

Now, we will add a secondary sort by marking the **Quarter** column and repeating the same steps we applied earlier. Have a look at the following screenshot:

Year	Quarter	Sales revenue
2006	Q4	$3,356,041
2006	Q3	$3,953,395
2006	Q2	$4,006,718
2006	Q1	$3,742,989
2005	Q4	$4,186,120
2005	Q3	$2,879,303
2005	Q2	$2,840,651
2005	Q1	$3,326,172
2004	Q4	$1,788,580
2004	Q3	$1,367,841
2004	Q2	$2,279,003
2004	Q1	$2,660,700

Notice that the second sort doesn't run over the first sort but is added to it.

In order to rearrange the sort direction, we can navigate to the **Manage Sorts** option. In the prompt window, we will be able to perform several sorting tasks:

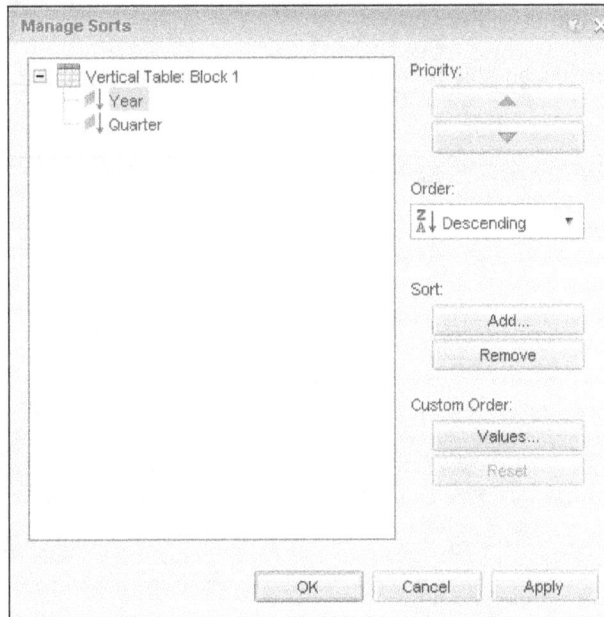

By using the **Priority** button in the top-right corner, we will be able to change the priority of the sort, that is, by double-clicking on the object or opening the order list, we will be able to change the sort direction.

If we are required to add another sort, then we can use the **Add** button. After clicking on this button, we will be able to choose additional objects to sort, as shown in the following screenshot:

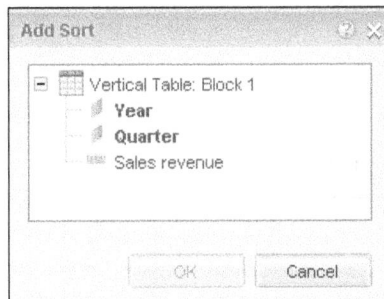

Notice that all the already sorted objects are marked in bold.

Another useful option is the **Custom Sort** option. This option is relevant when we want to sort the data according to our personal pick; for example, we would like to analyze the order of importance of specific customers first.

Another example could be a character type object that is required to be sorted chronologically, such as month name (January, February).

In the next window, we will be able to re-sort the object values according to our choice, as shown here:

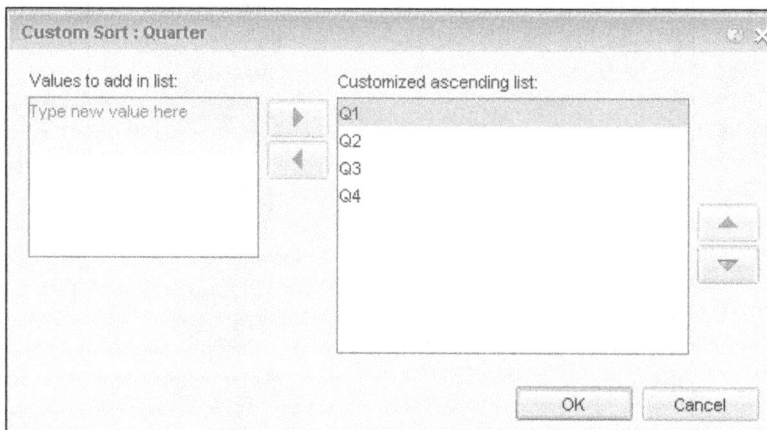

This option is more suited to a short list of values since sorting more than 30-40 values manually would be very difficult.

How it works...

The sort option changes the data direction and helps us to sort the data according to our choices. We can apply several sorts and manage them through the sort manager located under the **Analysis** tab.

There's more...

When we need to view which sorts have been applied to the table, we can click on one of the table columns and navigate to the sort options, which will be available as soon as we mark any one of the columns.

Using calculations

Using calculations is another useful feature that we can apply to the data.

Almost every report uses some kind of calculation: a total summation, a percentage, calculating the average sales across various products, or performing simple minimum or maximum functions—we can use it with measure, age, and date data.

Calculations are aimed to get the bottom line, that is, the understanding of how good or bad the results are, as they complete the picture of the data and a measurable analysis of the results provide the final insight.

How to do it...

We want to get familiar and use the calculations offered by the **Analysis** toolbar. By marking a measure column, the **Analysis** tab will become available, as shown in the following screenshot:

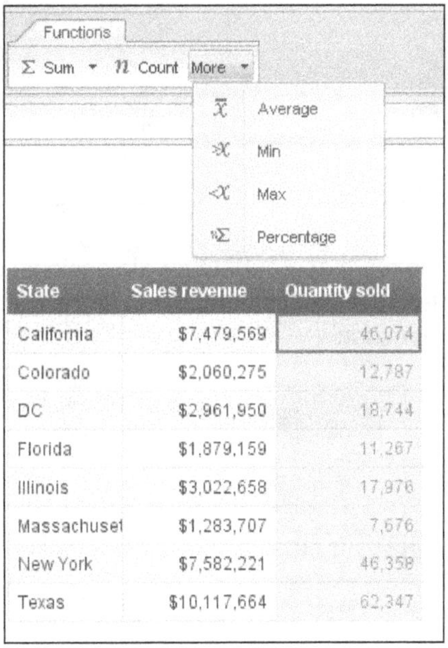

The following calculations can be performed on measure columns:

- ▸ **Sum**: This calculates the total values of a given measure.
- ▸ **Counts**: This counts the distinct values in a column. This calculation is extremely useful and can be used on dimension objects as well as for tasks that require counting the unique numbers of customers or orders.

- ▸ **Average**: This calculates the average value.

- ▸ **Min**: This calculates the minimum value.

- ▸ **Max**: This calculates the maximum value.

- ▸ **Percentage**: This calculates the percentage of each measure value in a separate column.

By clicking on the calculation in the preceding screenshot, footer rows will be added at the end of the marked measure along with the calculation name to the left-hand side of it, as shown in the following screenshot:

State	Sales revenue	Quantity sold	Percentage:
California	$7,479,569	46,074	20.64%
Colorado	$2,080,275	12,787	5.73%
DC	$2,961,950	18,744	8.40%
Florida	$1,879,159	11,267	5.05%
Illinois	$3,022,658	17,976	8.05%
Massachuset	$1,283,707	7,676	3.44%
New York	$7,582,221	46,358	20.77%
Texas	$10,117,664	62,347	27.93%
	Sum:	223,229	
	Average:	27,904	
	Min:	7,676	
	Max:	62,347	
	Percentage:		100.00%

Using the count function will be more appropriate for dimensional objects. In the following table, we will count the **Year** and **Quarter** columns and get the numbers **3** and **4** respectively, as shown in the following screenshot:

Year	Quarter	Sales revenu
2004	Q1	$2,660,700
2004	Q2	$2,278,693
2004	Q3	$1,367,841
2004	Q4	$1,788,580
2005	Q1	$3,326,172
2005	Q2	$2,840,651
2005	Q3	$2,879,303
2005	Q4	$4,186,120
2006	Q1	$3,742,989
2006	Q2	$4,006,718
2006	Q3	$3,953,395
2006	Q4	$3,356,041
3	4	

How it works...

By using the **Analysis** toolbar while marking a measure or dimension object, we can add a simple and quick calculation to our table.

There's more...

You can also use the right-click speed menu and navigate to **Insert | Calculations**.

In order to count the number of rows in the table regardless of which object is marked or whether its values are full or empty, you can use the `=count ([object]; all)` formula.

Using this formula will result in the same value no matter which column is marked, as the entire table has the same number of rows.

> The question as to which calculation is more suited, count or count all, depends on what we are trying to achieve. If we are trying to count the number of customers in a table, then we better use the count function and apply it on a unique object such as **Customer ID**. If we are trying to count how many appearances are in the table, then we better use the `count all` function.

See also

▶ For further information on how to create subtotals, please see the *Using sections and breaks* recipe. On how to create formulas and use them in the reports see *Chapter 9, Using Formulas and Variables*.

Using sections and breaks

Sections and breaks are two similar ways to group the data according to a specific dimension or an attribute object value.

Sections and breaks help us to create a better view of the data as well as apply logical grouping to it, for example, we can group the data in the report by the product type or the sales year. Last but not least, sections and breaks enable us to perform subtotals, which are a key calculation embedded in reporting and analysis.

Getting ready

We already have a table displaying the **Year**, **Quarter**, and **Sales revenue** data, and we want to apply a break on the **Year** dimension column in order to display the subtotals of each year.

How to do it...

In order to create a break, we can either use the **Analysis** toolbar and under it navigate to the **Display** tab, or simply right-click on the **Year** column in the table and use the **Break** option located in the speed menu, as shown in the following screenshot:

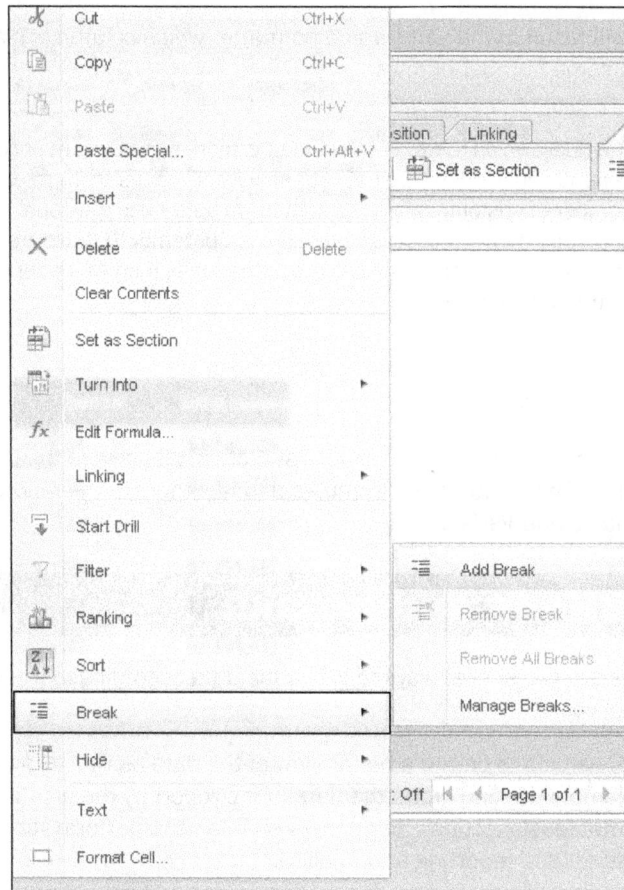

After we choose this option, the table will be separated according to the year values and will be displayed in a "subtable" structure, as shown in the following screenshot:

Year	Quarter	Sales revenue
2006	Q4	$3,356,041
	Q3	$3,953,395
	Q2	$4,006,718
	Q1	$3,742,989
2006		

Year	Quarter	Sales revenue
2005	Q4	$4,186,120
	Q3	$2,879,303
	Q2	$2,840,651
	Q1	$3,326,172
2005		

Year	Quarter	Sales revenue
2004	Q4	$1,788,580
	Q3	$1,367,841

Now, we have a totally different look and feel for the table. First, the values are grouped according to the **Year** column. Second, if we are required to create a subtotal, then we will be able to perform it.

Breaks can also be applied to more than one dimension or attribute object, and they enable us to display several hierarchy levels in a much easier and more convenient way.

> It isn't recommended that we perform more than 4-5 breaks, although technically there is no limitation, but the more the table is nested, the harder it will be to read.

Breaks can be managed by using the **Manage Breaks** option, as shown in the following screenshot:

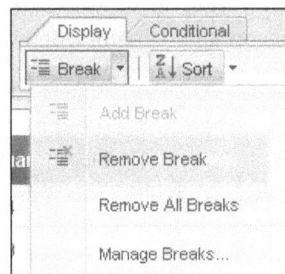

After navigating to the **Manage Breaks** window, we will have several break formatting options, as shown in the following screenshot:

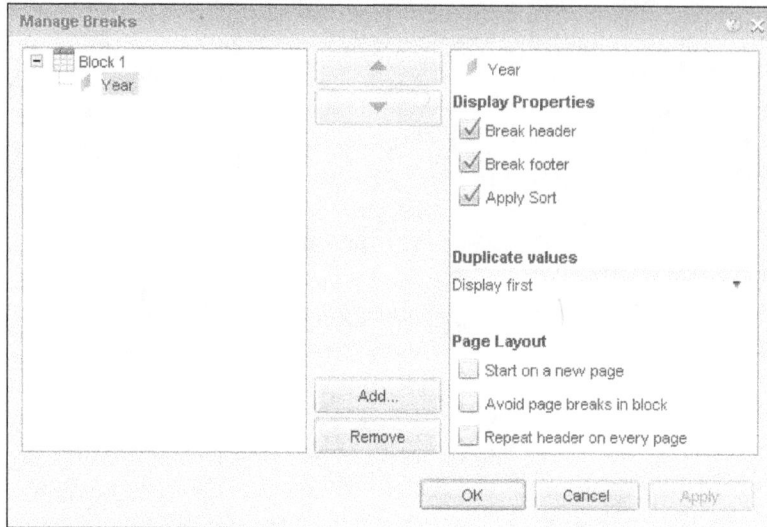

The following are the options:

- **Break header**: This removes or shows the break header
- **Break footer**: This removes or shows the break footer
- **Apply sort**: This enables sort on the break values
- **Duplicate values**: This drop-down list controls the behavior of the break values—we can display the break value in the first row, in all the rows, merge it, or repeat the value in every new page
- **Page layout**: This will start each break value in a separate page; this option is very useful when we are required to print in separate break value data and for better viewing options.
- **Avoid page breaks in block**: Each break block that can be viewed in one page will be avoided from being split across more than one page
- **Repeat header on every page**: This option will enable the break header to be repeated on every page; this option is useful when we want to keep track of the column names along with the continuous pages

Sections are another great way to implement table grouping according to a dimension or an attribute object value. In general, we can get the same effect of subtables as well as displaying the subtotals with breaks, but sections have several functionalities and look and feel differences.

We will right-click on the **Year** column and choose the **Set as Section** option, as shown in the following screenshot:

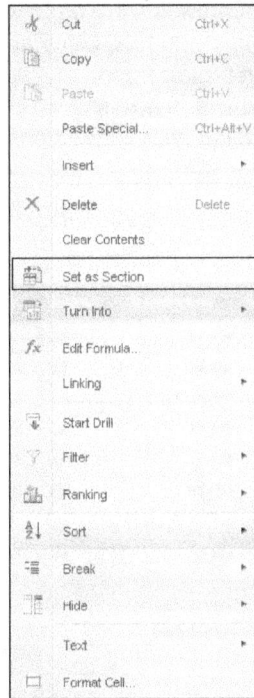

✂	Cut	Ctrl+X
▤	Copy	Ctrl+C
▥	Paste	Ctrl+V
	Paste Special...	Ctrl+Alt+V
	Insert	▸
✕	Delete	Delete
	Clear Contents	
▦	Set as Section	
▦	Turn Into	▸
fx	Edit Formula...	
	Linking	▸
▽	Start Drill	
▽	Filter	▸
▥	Ranking	▸
▤↓	Sort	▸
▤	Break	▸
▤	Hide	▸
	Text	▸
▢	Format Cell...	

The following result will be a sectioned report where each value of the **Year** column will appear as a master cell above each table:

2004

Quarter	Quantity sold	Sales revenue
Q1	18,136	$2,660,700
Q2	14,408	$2,278,693
Q3	10,203	$1,367,841
Q4	10,331	$1,788,580

2005

Quarter	Quantity sold	Sales revenue
Q1	21,135	$3,326,172
Q2	17,152	$2,840,651
Q3	19,224	$2,879,303
Q4	22,344	$4,186,120

The look and feel as well as functionality provided by sections are different as the section cell isn't a column that is displayed as part of the table.

When using a section, the hierarchical view is more intuitive and clear, and we get to save some room if we have a table with many columns. Other advantages that the section holds is that if we are required to group non-table components such as charts, then sections will be the appropriate solution. One more point—when using the left-hand side panel, we can navigate to the **Report Map** pane and get a bookmark view of the sections, as shown in the next screenshot.

This option is extremely useful when we have several levels of sections, for example, year and quarter, then, in these cases, it will be very easy to navigate to a specific value. Have a look at the following table:

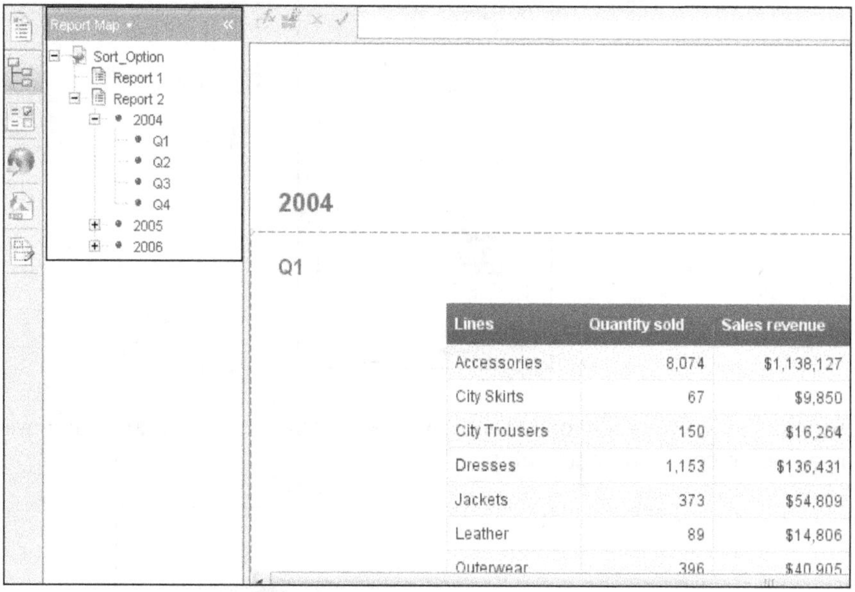

In order to delete the section, we can right-click on the section cell, and then the **Delete cell only** and **Delete section and cell** options will be available. In order to format a section, we can right-click on the section area and navigate to the **Format Section** option, as shown in the following screenshot:

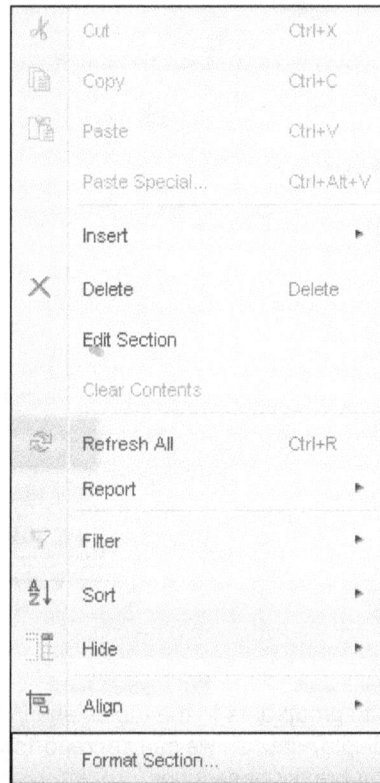

✂	Cut	Ctrl+X
	Copy	Ctrl+C
	Paste	Ctrl+V
	Paste Special...	Ctrl+Alt+V
	Insert	▶
✕	Delete	Delete
	Edit Section	
	Clear Contents	
⟳	Refresh All	Ctrl+R
	Report	▶
▽	Filter	▶
ᴬ↓	Sort	▶
	Hide	▶
	Align	▶
	Format Section...	

In the **Formatting Section** window, we can use the following options:

- **General**: This is used to adjust the section cell size, bookmark a section, and hide the section when a condition is met (empty section cell or empty block)
- **Appearance**: This section is used to adjust the cell color, color pattern, and skin
- **Layout**: Similar to a break, we can adjust the section layout along the pages using options such as **Start on a new page**, **Repeat on every page**, and **Avoid page break**

The **General** option is displayed in the following screenshot:

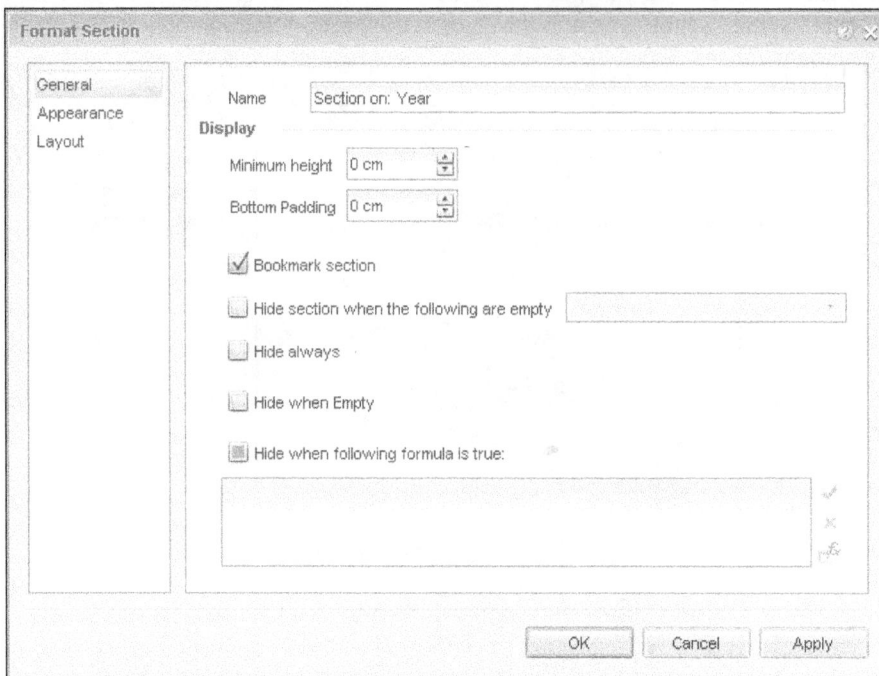

How it works...

Breaks and sections enable us to group data in the tables and in the charts. This is the most common and useful option to display data as we can get reports with many rows that can be spread over several pages, using breaks or sections.

After enabling a break or a section, every calculation that we perform will be calculated in the section/break area for each of the section/break blocks.

There's more...

Measures can't be turned into sections or breaks as they are always grouped according to the dimensional data presented in the table.

Another major difference between breaks and sections is that breaks can display the subtotal as well as the grand total; with sections, we can only calculate the subtotals.

Ranking

Ranking is a top/bottom filter that enables displaying of the top or bottom *n* best results of a dimension object based on a measure.

One of the most basic questions that a business user can ask is "who are the top 10 customers based on their amount of purchases this year?"

How to do it...

We have a table displaying the **Line** and the **Sales revenue** data in which we require to rank only the top five best lines.

The rank icon is located under the **Analysis** toolbar, in the **Filters** subtab, and can also be accessed by right-clicking on the table and navigating to **Ranking | Add ranking**.

The following **Ranking** window will appear:

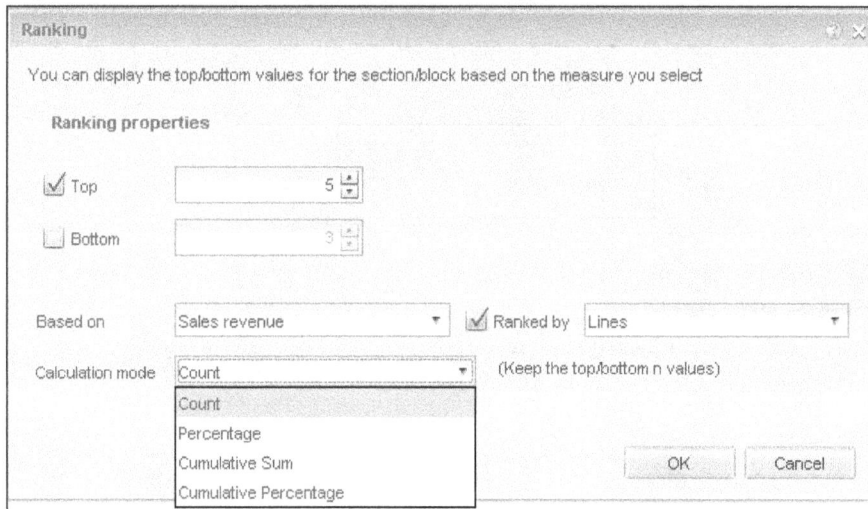

The **Ranking** window offers the following options:

- ▶ **Top**: Here, we can adjust the number of top values we require to filter; the default value is three and can be adjusted by using the arrow signs. If there are two values returning the same result, both of them will be presented and counted as the same rank.

- ▶ **Bottom**: This does the same as the **Top** option but for the bottom values.

- ▸ **Based on**: Here, we can choose the measure from a drop-down list that the rank will be based on. Measures that don't appear in the table but were returned by the query can also be used here.

- ▸ **Calculation mode**: Here, we can choose the type of calculation: **Count**, which is the most common and practical one, **Percentage** of the total values, **Cumulative Sum**, and **Cumulative Percentage**.

- ▸ **Ranked by**: In this drop-down list, we will choose the dimension object that the ranking will take into account.

We will choose the top five, based on the sales revenue measure and ranked by the lines. The result will be that only the top five lines will be filtered and presented, as shown in the following screenshot:

Lines	Sales revenue
Sweat-T-Shirts	$12,679,893
Accessories	$9,914,546
Shirt Waist	$4,018,220
Dresses	$2,915,620
Sweaters	$2,839,035
Sum:	**$32,367,313**

How it works...

Ranking behaves as an advanced filter, enabling us to filter the top or the bottom rows of a specific dimension according to a measure object.

There's more...

When using ranking, the dimension values are also sorted according to the measure values; this action overrides any existing sorts that already exist in the table.

Only one of ranking can be applied to a table. If we need to perform several rankings, then we can turn the objects into a section, and then we can rank by the section and by another object in the table. Another way is to concatenate several objects into a variable in the report and rank by this new variable.

See also

▸ For further information on how to use other types of filters see *Chapter 7, Filtering the Report Data*

▸ For further information on how to create variables see the *Using variables* recipe in *Chapter 9, Using Formulas and Variables*

Conditional rules

There are cases when we are required to focus on specific types of data or values that appear only in some of the rows that were retrieved with the entire dataset.

A sales business user will want to focus on the rows where the sales decreased more than 15 percent, and a business user working in a bank will want to focus on the loans that were greater than 100,000 dollars.

In order to perform this kind of analysis, we will use conditional rules that will enable us to highlight the result or any set of rows that holds a particular significance for our analysis through the report's data and visually emphasize it.

Getting ready

We want to highlight all the rows in the table whose product quantity is greater than 50; this will result in marking those rows only and help us to focus on more relevant results while analyzing the data.

How to do it...

We will navigate to the **Analysis** toolbar and under it to the **Conditional** tab, as shown in the following screenshot:

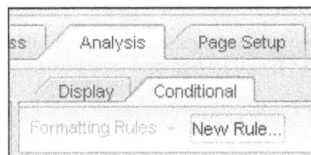

By clicking on the **New Rule** option, we will switch to the **Formatting Rule Editor**. Here, we can use the following options:

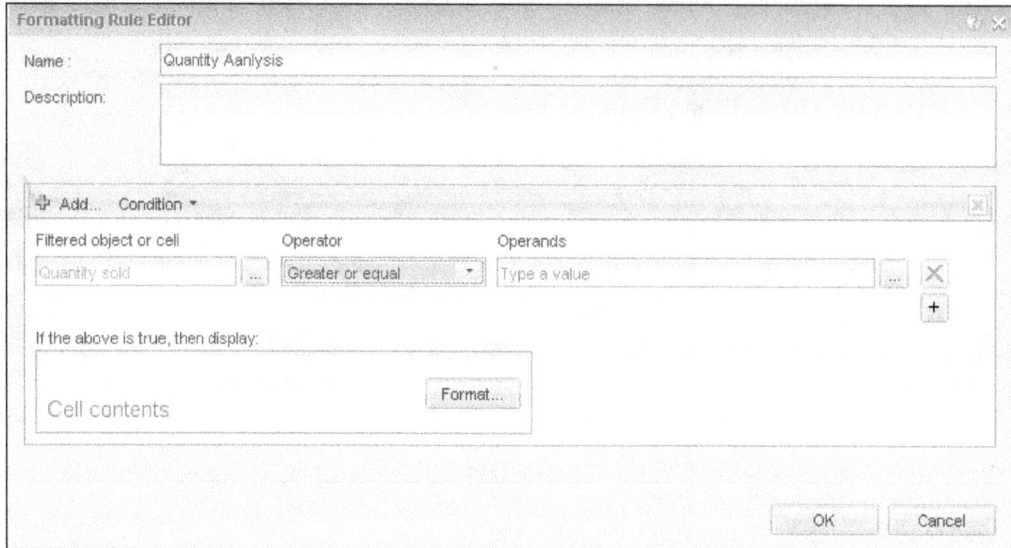

▸ **Name**: Using this, we can name the alerter. This option is useful if we want to make our report more clear, and if we have several alerts, naming them will make it easier to know which alerter we should edit.

▸ **Description**: We can add an account (A/C) description to the alert.

▸ **Add**: This will add another alert rule that will result in an OR relation with the other alert rules.

▸ **Condition**: Here, we have two options that enable us to create a condition rule using the rule editor, which is the first option, or by creating a formula, as shown in the following screenshot. The formula editor is useful when we are required to create a rule based on a custom formula and not on an existing object or calculation.

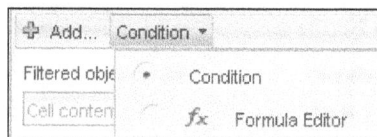

- ▶ **Operator**: This is similar to the query filter. We can also use operators such as equal to, between, and others in our conditional rule.

- ▶ **Operands**: We can either type a value or choose an object from the existing report objects, so we can even compare two objects. By clicking on the three-dots sign, the list of available objects to compare will pop up, as shown in the following screenshot:

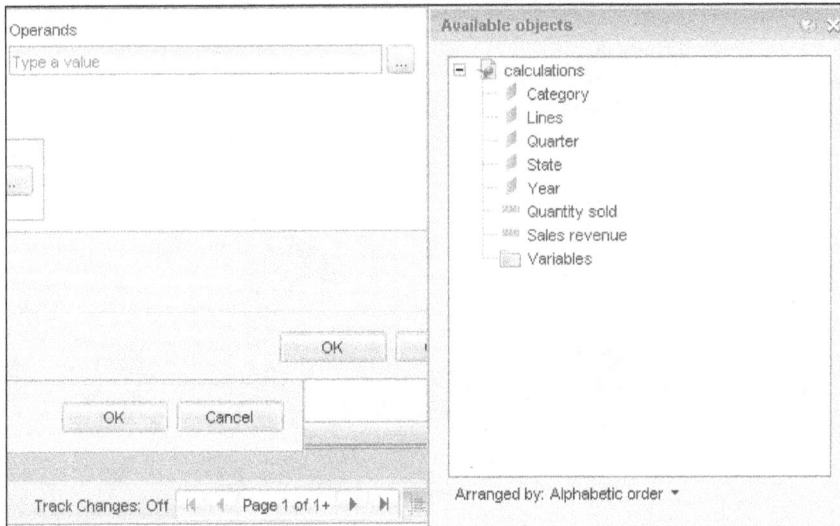

- ▶ **Display area**: Under the rule editor, we can get a preview of the highlighted result and use the format cell editor to format the results.

We will pick the **Quantity sold** object and the greater than or equal to operator, and type 50 in the constant area. Using the format button, we will be able to navigate to the **Text** category in the format window and adjust the font size and color to our requirement, as shown in the following screenshot:

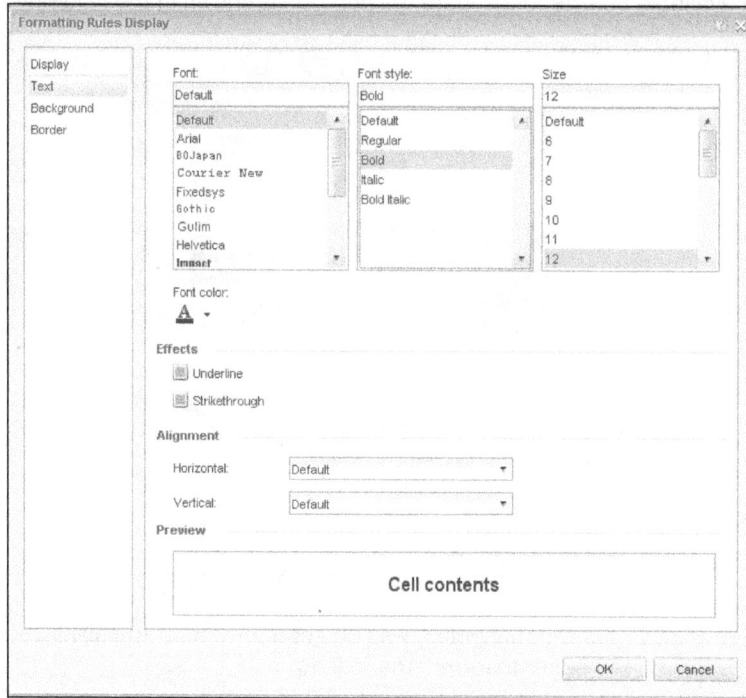

The finalized condition will look like the following screenshot:

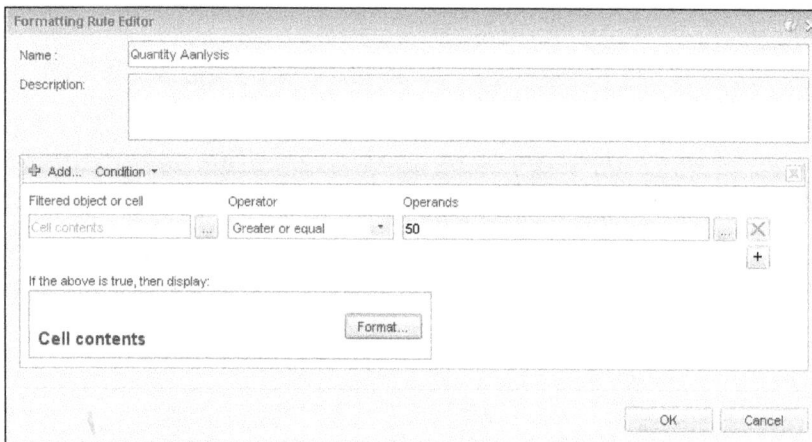

And the quantity values will appear accordingly, as shown in the following screenshot:

Year	Quarter	State	Category	Sales revenue	Quantity sold
2004	Q1	California	2 Pocket shirts	$13,906	72
2004	Q1	California	Belts,bags,wallets	$31,385	232
2004	Q1	California	Bermudas	$1,085	10
2004	Q1	California	Boatwear	$8,278	55
2004	Q1	California	Cardigan	$21,029	122
2004	Q1	California	Casual dresses	$1,646	14
2004	Q1	California	Day wear	$2,866	21
2004	Q1	California	Dry wear	$2,259	15
2004	Q1	California	Evening wear	$18,229	148
2004	Q1	California	Fancy fabric	$3,650	25
2004	Q1	California	Full length	$2,634	15
2004	Q1	California	Hair accessories	$5,615	32

Editing the formatting rule is done by navigating to the **Manage Rules** option located on the left-hand side of the conditional tab.

How it works...

Conditional formatting uses a type of IF logic: if a certain condition is met, then instead of 1/0 result or a text returned, the result can be simply formatted according to what we adjust in the **Format** window.

There's more...

In order to apply the formatting rule on other columns, we can mark the column and choose the alerter name from the conditional tab, and it will be applied accordingly, as shown in the following screenshot:

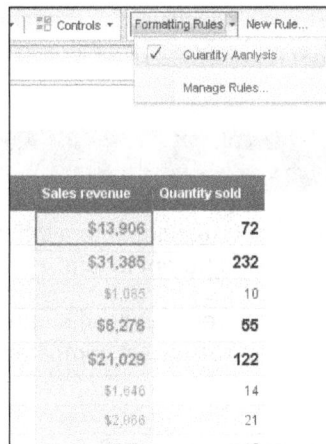

Sales revenue	Quantity sold
$13,906	72
$31,385	232
$1,085	10
$8,278	55
$21,029	122
$1,646	14
$2,866	21

If we add another condition using the **+** sign located on the right-hand side, the AND operator will be the operator created between the rules. If we are required to set an OR relation between the conditions, we will use the **Add** option located in the top-left corner, as shown in the following screenshot:

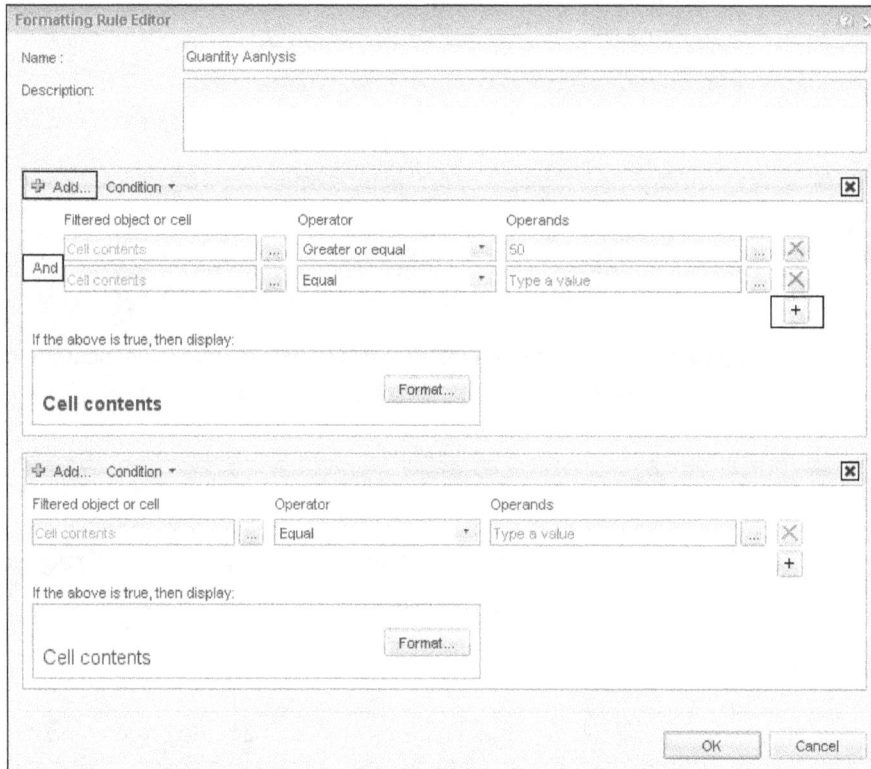

> You can create up to six conditions in the same formatting rule; if you require more, simply create another separate formatting rule.

Data tracking

Data tracking follows the theme of formatting rules with a difference, that is, its formatting results are determined by comparing two different results.

Data tracking is used to compare two different result sets returned by the query; a basic comparing scenario would be the current results set compared to the previous results set.

With data tracking, we can analyze changes over time and are able to track increments and decrements of changes along measures and dimension values.

A classical business question can be delivered by a weekly sales report checking whether there was a decrease or an increase in the current week's sales compared to the previous week.

Getting ready

We want to compare the sales results growth and number of cars sold from last year to the current year by analyzing the measures per car maker and quarter.

How to do it...

After getting last year's data, we will first adjust the data tracking options so that we can easily analyze the current year results.

By navigating to the **Analysis** toolbar and then to the **Data Tracking** tab, we will be able to adjust the data tracking options, as shown in the following screenshot:

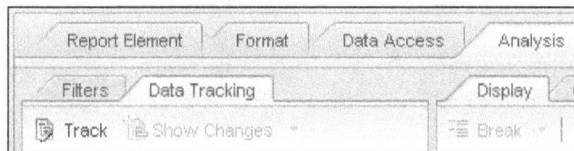

Upon clicking on the **Track** button, the **Data Tracking** window will pop up.

This window is combined from two main tabs:

  ▶ **Data**: Here, we can define the context of the track. The default behavior is set to off, but we can adjust it to be compared with the last data refresh, which will probably provide a more common scenario. The other option is to compare with data from a specific date, which can be a useful option if we require the comparison to work against a fixed date.

▶ We can also make adjustments as to which reports the data tracking will be applied. After doing so, you can also use the **Refresh data now** option, as shown in the following screenshot:

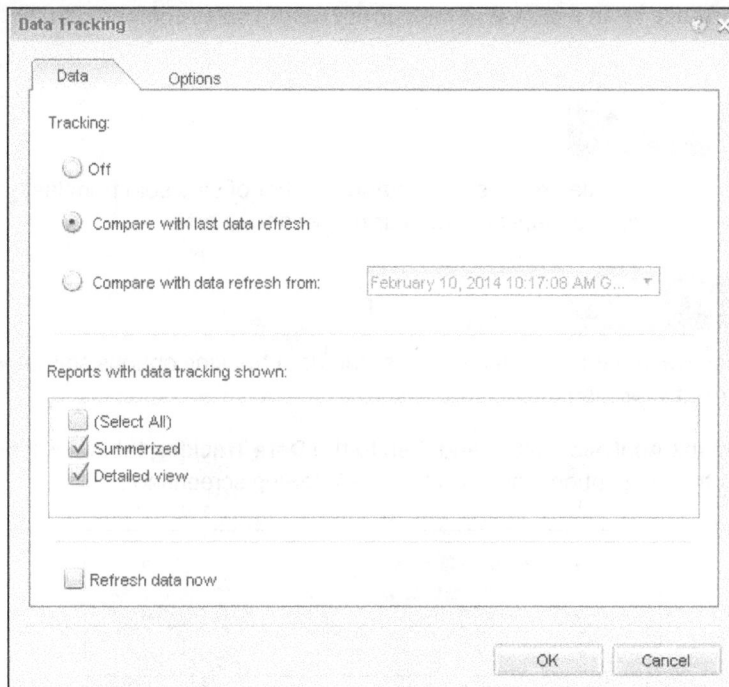

▶ The second tab is the color legend options that will enable you to define and adjust the decrement/increment of result colors as well as the increase/decrease of units.

This tab defines the behavior format of each object type: dimensions, detail objects, and measures.

▶ **Dimensions**: This includes insertion of new values and deletion of existing values.

▶ **Details**: The changes in general in detail objects can be adjusted here

▶ **Measures**: Here is the real deal; we can adjust the format of the increased and the decreased values. Traditionally, in data formatting, red stands for bad results or a result that requires to be monitored, while green usually stands for a good result, as shown in the following screenshot:

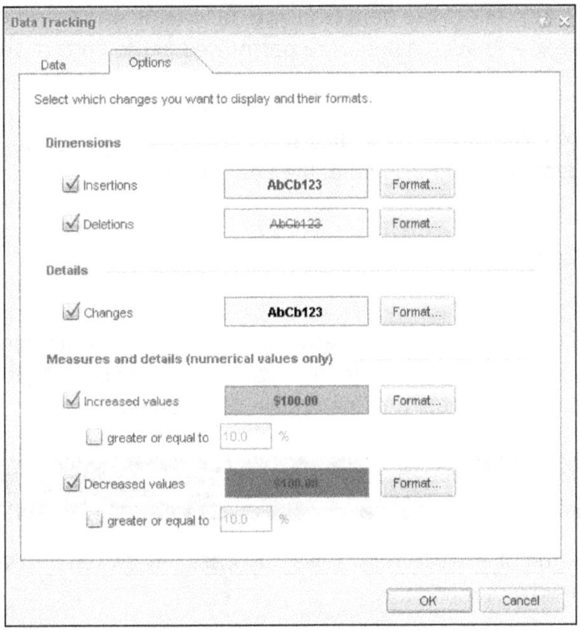

In this scenario, we will keep up with the already default format setting as we serve our analysis and choose the option **Compare with last data refresh**.

We will now run the report on the current year data and get the track highlighted. Have a look at the following screenshot:

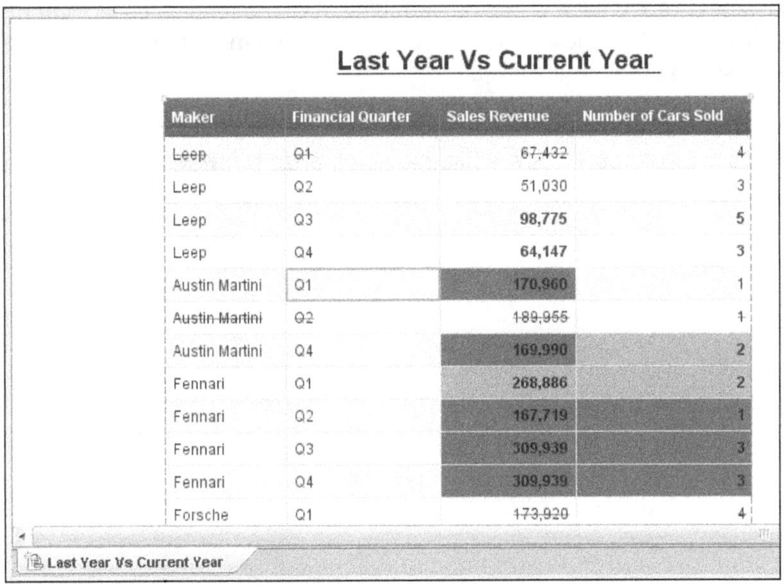

As we can see, the results reflect the data tracking definitions and some values such as the second row are deletions—no such sales were performed in the current year.

> You can also edit the data tracking by accessing it through the status toolbar located at the bottom-center part of the screen.

How it works...

The data tracking option compares two different query refresh results, formats the results, and helps us to get a better analysis of the increase and decrease ranges while using the color legend to immediately identify the changes in the results.

Outline and fold

When we use a sectioned or a break report, we can basically switch between the detailed views to the summarized footer level.

There are reports that require a specific interaction such as starting with a summarized view and viewing the detailed level when the business user needs to, depending on the summarized results.

The outline is a quick, simple switch between a summarized and a detailed view in the same table.

A classical business report case would be switching from the total sales of a car maker to the detailed invoice and date level, focusing on each sales amount, helping the sales team analyze their results at the invoice level.

Another reason why we would use the outline is because detailed reports can take time to scroll in order to get to a specific row, while the summarized view will show us the high-level outcomes directly.

Getting ready

After running a detailed report that presents the sales per maker, invoice ID, and sales date, we will add a break on the maker column and a sum calculation to view the sales subtotals, as shown in the following screenshot:

Maker	Sale Invoice ID Number	Sale Date	Sales Revenue
Austin Martini	1001	1/10/04	170,959.5
	1014	3/18/05	84,995
	1019	6/15/03	189,955
	1067	4/10/04	170,959.5
	1080	2/18/05	84,995
	1085	9/15/03	189,955
Austin Martini		**Sum:**	**891,819**
Maker	Sale Invoice ID Number	Sale Date	Sales Revenue
Catorhammer	1132	4/21/03	17,505
	1141	12/14/03	23,995
	1142	1/9/04	23,995
	1143	2/10/04	11,925
	1147	6/12/04	22,995

How to do it...

Through the **Analysis** toolbar, under the **Interact** tab, click on the **Outline** button, as shown in the following screenshot:

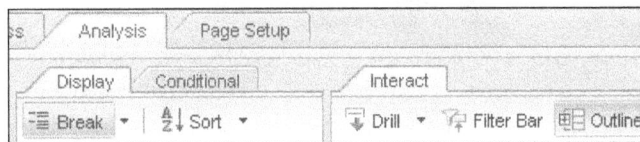

We will be able to fold or unfold the exiting table, as shown in the following screenshot:

Maker	Sale Invoice I	Sale Date	Sales Revenue
Austin Martini	1001	1/10/04	170,959.5
	1014	3/18/05	84,995
	1019	6/15/03	189,955
	1067	4/10/04	170,959.5
	1080	2/18/05	84,995
	1085	9/15/03	189,955
Austin Martini	**Sum:**		**891,819**
Maker	Sale Invoice I	Sale Date	Sales Revenue
Catorhammer	1132	4/21/03	17,505

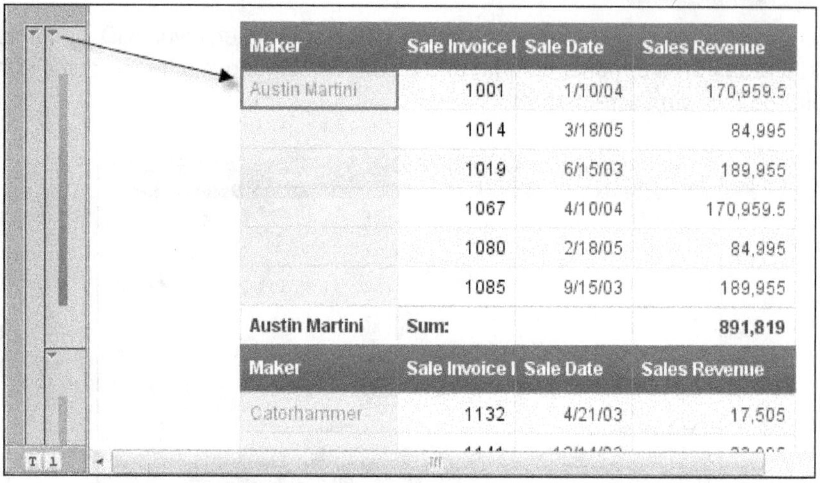

The folding area on the left-hand side of the table will enable us to fold a specific break area, and to focus on the subtotal, we can fold all the breaks, or show just the total of the sales revenue.

Upon clicking on the left-hand side inner arrow, we will be able to fold the specific break on the right-hand side of it, as shown in the following screenshot:

Maker	Sale Invoice I	Sale Date	Sales Revenue
Austin Martini	**Sum:**		**891,819**
Maker	Sale Invoice I	Sale Date	Sales Revenue
Catorhammer	1132	4/21/03	17,505
	1141	12/14/03	23,995

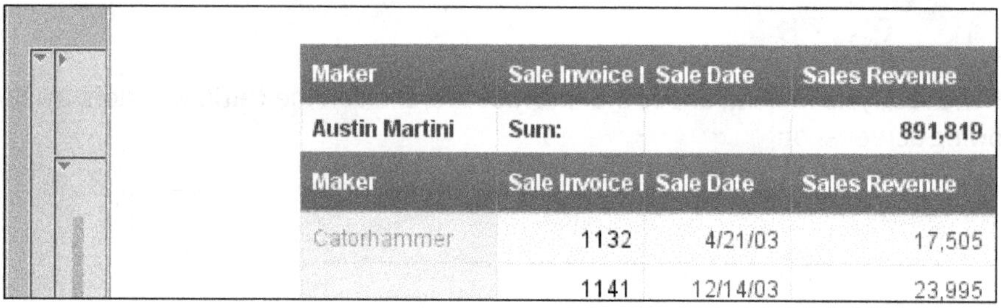

Clicking on the **1** button located in the bottom-left corner will result in folding all the breaks and show only the subtotal:

Maker	Sale Invoice I	Sale Date	Sales Revenue
Austin Martini	Sum:		891,819
Maker	Sale Invoice I	Sale Date	Sales Revenue
Catorhammer	Sum:		217,675
Maker	Sale Invoice I	Sale Date	Sales Revenue
Fennari	Sum:		2,311,068
Maker	Sale Invoice I	Sale Date	Sales Revenue
Forsche	Sum:		724,348
Maker	Sale Invoice I	Sale Date	Sales Revenue
Jaggular	Sum:		768,634

By clicking on the **T** button located at the left-hand side of the **1** button, we switch to the total sum view of the table:

Total Revenue :	7,950,196

The more nested break levels we have, the more buttons we will get accordingly.

By clicking on the arrows at the left-hand side of each break, we will be able to return to the detailed view of a specific break value or to the entire table by clicking on the **1** button again.

> Using the outline can also be managed in the reading mode window.

How it works...

The outline enables us to switch between the data levels of the table, summarized or detailed, by working with the left-hand side outline folding options.

Working with the fold buttons instead of working with the available objects and switching each time to a different table view, the outline enables us to create a more *live* interaction with the report data.

See also

▸ For further information about how to switch between data levels in the report, see *Chapter 11, Using Drill*

7
Filtering the Report Data

In this chapter, we will cover the following recipes:

- ▶ Applying a simple filter
- ▶ Working with the filter bar
- ▶ Using input controls
- ▶ Working with an element link

Introduction

Filtering data can be done in several ways. As we saw in *Chapter 2, Creating New Queries*, we can filter the results at the query level when there is a requirement to use a mandatory filter or set of filters that will fetch only specific types of rows that will correspond to the business question; otherwise, the report won't be accurate or useful.

The other level of filtering is performed at the report level. This level of filtering interacts with the data that was retrieved by the user and enables us to eliminate irrelevant rows.

The main question that arises when using a report-level filter is why shouldn't we implement filters in the query level?

Well, the answer has various reasons, which are as follows:

- ▶ We need to compare and analyze just a part of the entire data that the query retrieved (for example, filtering the first quarter's data out of the current year's entire dataset)
- ▶ We need to view the data separately, for example, each tab can be filtered by a different value (for example, each report tab can display a different region's data)

- We need to filter measure objects that are different from the aggregative level of the query; for example, we have retrieved a well-detailed query displaying sales of various products at the customer level, but we also need to display only the products that had income of more than one million dollars in another report tab

- The business user requires interactive functionality from the filter: a drop-down box, a checklist, a spinner, or a slider—capabilities that can't be performed by a query filter

- We need to perform additional calculations on a variable in the report and apply a filter to it

In this chapter, we will explore the different types of filters that can be applied in reports: simple ones, interactive ones, and filters that can combine interactivity and a custom look and feel adjusted by the business user.

Applying a simple filter

The first type of filter is a basic one that enables us to implement quick and simple filter logic, which is similar to the way we build it on the query panel.

Getting ready

We have created a query that retrieves a dataset displaying the **Net Sales** by **Product**, **Line**, and **Year**. Using a simple filter, we would like to filter only the year **2008** records as well as the **Sports Line**.

How to do it...

Perform the following steps to apply a simple filter:

1. We will navigate to the **Analysis** toolbar, and in the **Filters** tab, click on the **Filter** icon and choose **Add Filter**, as shown in the following screenshot:

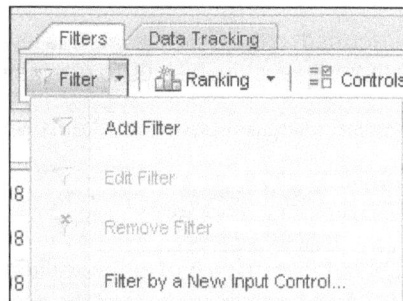

2. In the **Report Filter** window, as shown in the following screenshot, we will be able to add filters, edit them, and apply them on a specific table or on the entire report tab:

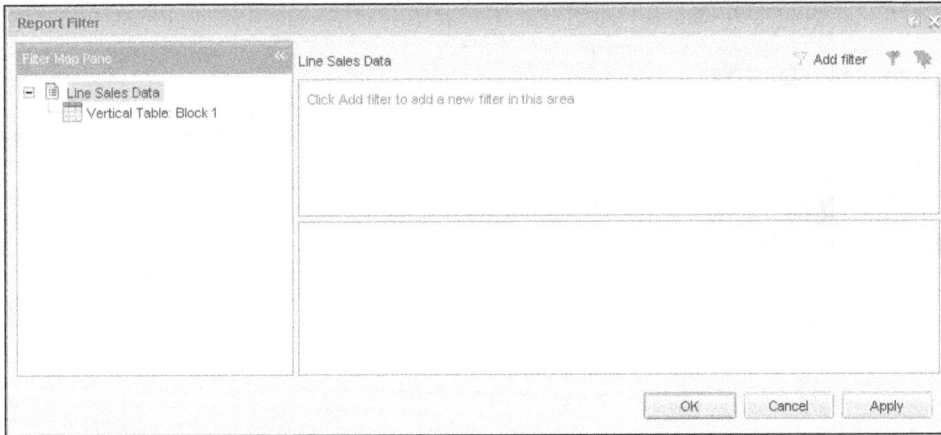

3. By clicking on the **Add filter** icon located in the top-left corner, we will be able to add a condition. Clicking on this button will open the list of existing objects in the report; by choosing the **Year** object, we will add our first filter, as shown in the following screenshot:

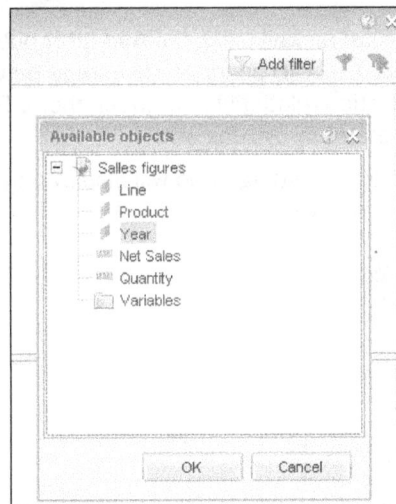

4. After we choose the **Year** object, a filter condition structure will appear in the top-right corner of the window, enabling us to pick an operator and a value similar to the way we establish query filters, as shown in the following screenshot:

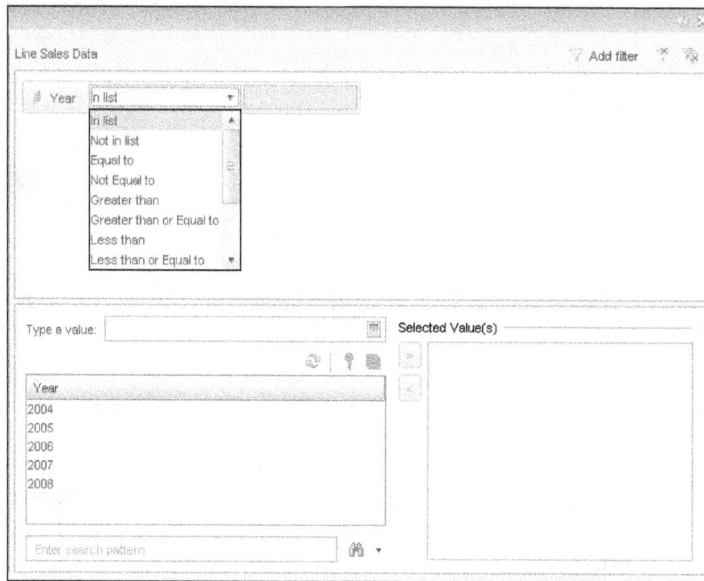

5. We will add a second filter as well using the **Add filter** button and adding the **Line** object to the filter area. The AND operator will appear between the two filters, establishing an intersection relationship between them. This operator can be easily changed to the OR operator by clicking on it.

6. The table will be affected accordingly and will display only the year 2008 and the **Sports Line** records, as shown:

Year	Line	Product	Net Sales	Quantity
2,008	Sports	Berta Golf Clubs	23,291,520	28,617
2,008	Sports	Clone Golf Clubs	10,155,950	24,787
2,008	Sports	Crochet Cycling Gloves	45,479	3,699
2,008	Sports	Descent Competition Bicycle	79,163,960	48,506
2,008	Sports	Golf Balls	1,389,644	85,252
2,008	Sports	No Name Skis	17,936,215	42,490
2,008	Sports	Pumpit Tennis Shoes	2,837,486	34,704
2,008	Sports	Rappel Mountain Bicycle	16,059,155	40,856
2,008	Sports	Romeo Hybrid Bicycle	29,994,744	45,934
2,008	Sports	Ski Boots	8,776,012	51,948
2,008	Sports	Ski Mask	515,866	40,615
2,008	Sports	Slamit Tennis Racket	5,994,890	36,664
2,008	Sports	SuperBounce Tennis Balls	352,772	43,155
2,008	Sports	Tees	607,065	98,868
2,008	Sports	Triump Pro Cycling Helmet	3,432,080	100,152
2,008	Sports	Tushuss Skis	24,825,135	41,948

7. In order to edit the filter, we can either access it through the **Analysis** toolbar or mark one of the filtered columns, enabling us to get an easier edit using the toolbar or the right-click menu, as shown in the following screenshot:

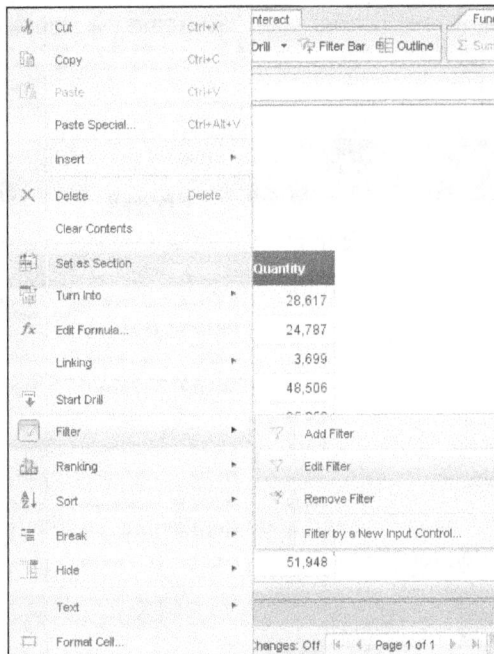

How it works...

The report filter simply corresponds to the values defined in the filtered set of conditions that are established by simple and easy use of the filter panel. The filters can be applied on any type of data display, table, or chart.

Like the query filters, the report filters use the logic of the operators AND/OR as well and can be used by clicking on the operator name.

> In order to view the filters that have been applied to the report tabs and tables, you can navigate to the document structure and filter's left-hand side panel and click on the **Filter** button.

There's more...

Filters can be applied on a specific table in the report or on the entire report.

In order to switch between these options, when you create the filter, you need to mark the report area. To create a report-level filter or a specific column in a table, you need to filter a specific table in the report tab.

Working with the filter bar

Another great functionality that filters can provide us is interaction with the report data.

There are cases when we are required to perform quick filtering as well as switch dynamically between values as we need to analyze different filtered datasets.

Working with the filter bar can address these requirements simply and easily.

Getting ready

We want to perform a quick dynamic filtering on our existing table by adding the **Country** dimension object to the filter bar.

How to do it....

Perform the following steps:

1. By navigating to the **Analysis** toolbar and then to the **Interact** tab, we will click on the **Filter Bar** icon:

   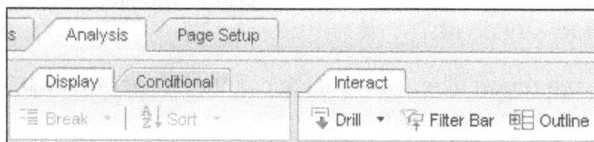

2. By doing so, a gray filter pane area will appear under the formula bar with a guiding message saying **Drop objects here to add report filters**, as shown in the following screenshot:

   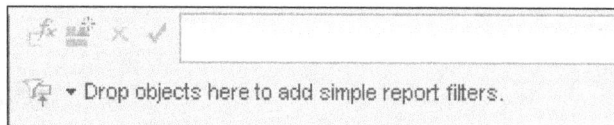

3. In order to create a new filter, we can either drag an object directly to the filter pane area from the **Available Objects** pane or use the quick add icon located in the filter bar on the left-hand side of the message.

4. In our scenario, we will use the **Available Objects** pane and drag the Country dimension object directly to the filter bar:

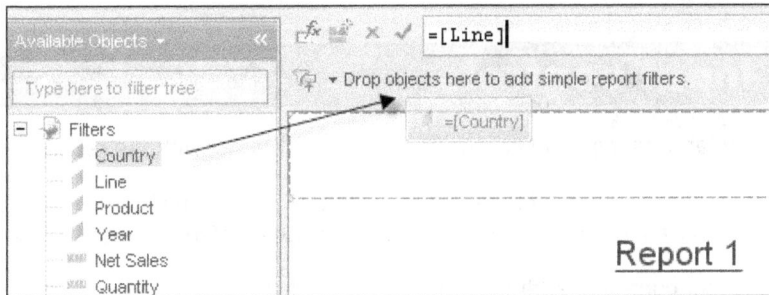

5. By adding the **Country** object to the filter bar, a quick drop-down list filter will be created, enabling us to filter the table data by choosing any country value:

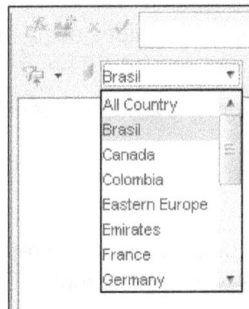

6. This filter will enable us to quickly create filtered sets of data using the drop-down list as well as using an interactive component that doesn't have to be in the table.

How it works...

The filter bar is an interactive component that enables us to create as many dynamic filters as we need and to locate them in a single filtering area for easy control of the data, and they aren't even required to appear in the table itself.

> The filter bar is restricted to filter only single values; in order to filter several values, we will need to either use a different type of filter, such as input control, or create a grouped values logic.

There's more...

When we drop several dimension objects onto the filter pane, they will be displayed accordingly; however, a cascading effect of filters (picking a specific country in the first filter and in the second filter seeing only that country) will be supported only if hierarchies have been defined in the universe.

Using input controls

Input controls are another type of filter that enable us to interact with the report data.

An input control performs as an interactive left-hand side panel, which can be created in various types that have a different look and feel as well as a different functionality.

We can use an input control to address the following tasks:

- Applying a different look and feel to the filter—making filters more intuitive and easy to operate (using radio buttons, comboboxes, and other filter types)
- Applying multiple values
- Applying dynamic filters to measure values using input control components, such as spinners and sliders
- Enabling a default value option and a custom list of values

Getting ready

In this example, we will filter several components in the report area, a chart and a table, using the **Region** dimension object. We will be using the multiple value option to enhance the filter functionality.

First, we will navigate to the input control panel located in the left-hand side area as the third option from the top and click on the **New** option.

How to do it...

Perform the following steps:

1. We will choose the object that we need to filter with the table and the chart, as shown in the following screenshot:

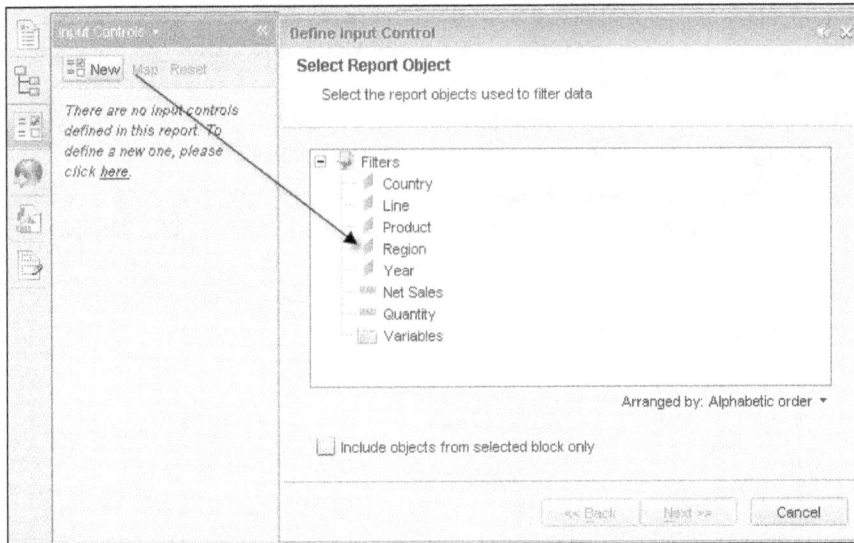

2. After choosing the **Region** object, we will move on to the **Define Input Control** window.

3. As mentioned earlier, input controls enable multiple-value functionality, and in the **Choose Control Type** window, we will choose the **Check boxes** input control type, as shown in the following screenshot:

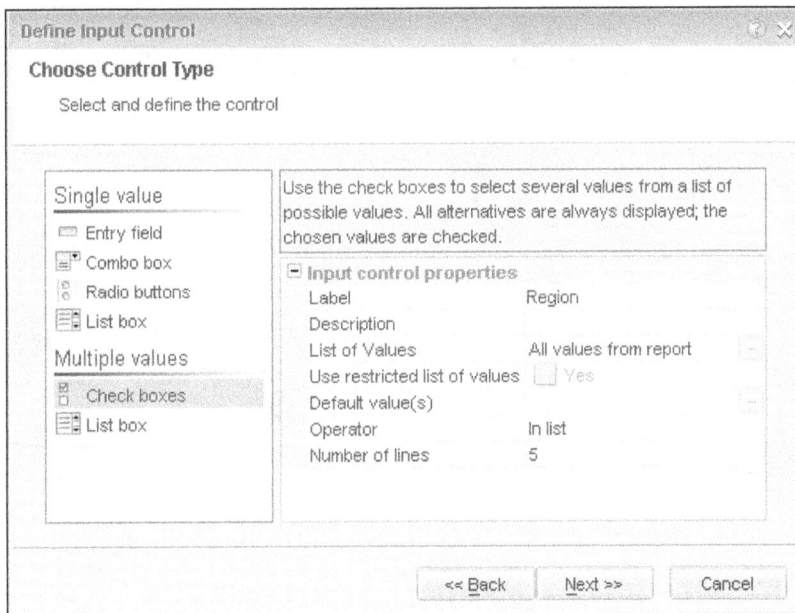

4. In the input control properties located at the right-hand side, we can also add a description to the input control, set a default value, and customize the list of values if we need specific values.

5. After choosing the **Check boxes** component, we will advance to the next window, choosing the data element we want to apply the control on.

6. We will tick both of the components, the chart and the table, in order to affect all the data components using a single control, as shown in the following screenshot:

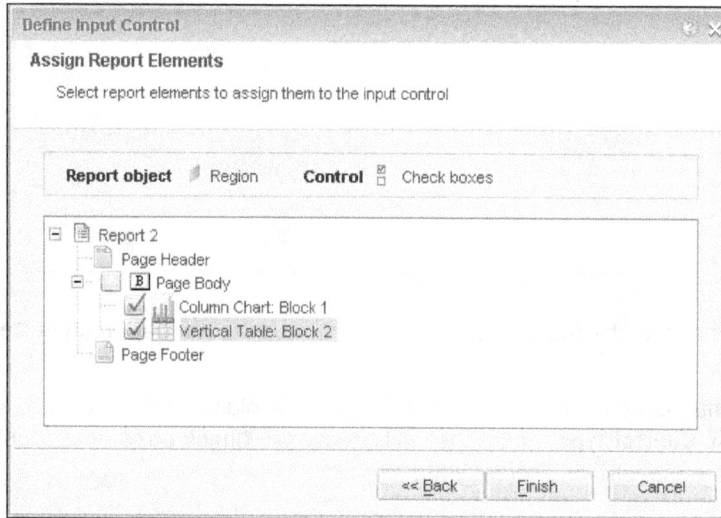

7. By clicking on the **Finish** button, the input control will appear at the left-hand side:

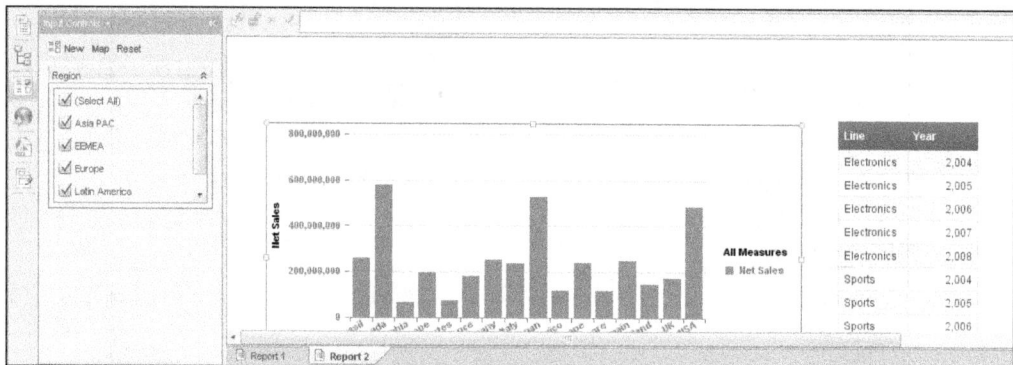

8. We can easily change the selected values to all values (**Select All**), one, or several values, filtering both of the tables as shown:

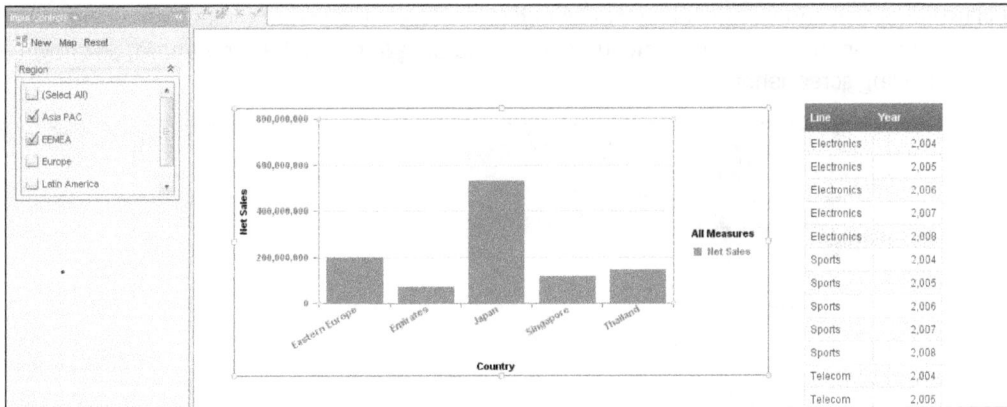

How it works...

As we have seen, input controls act as special interactive filters that can be used by picking one of them from the input control templates, that is, the type that is the most suitable to filter the data in the report. Our main consideration when choosing an input control is to determine the type of list we need to pick: single or multiple.

The second consideration should be the interactive functionality that we need from such a control: a simple value pick or perhaps an arithmetic operator, such as a greater or less than operator, which can be applied to a measure object.

There's more...

An input control can also be created using the **Analysis** toolbar and the **Filter** tab.

In order to edit the existing input control, we can access the mini toolbar above the input control. Here, we will be able to edit the control, show its dependencies (the elements that are affected by it), or delete it, as shown in the following screenshot:

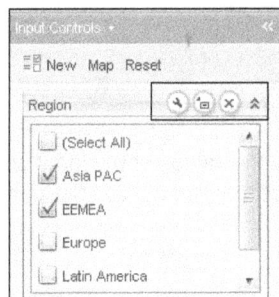

We can also display a single informative cell describing which table and report a filter has been applied on.

This useful option can be applied by navigating to the **Report Element** toolbar, choosing Report Filter Summary from the **Cell** subtoolbar, and dragging it to the report area, as shown in the following screenshot:

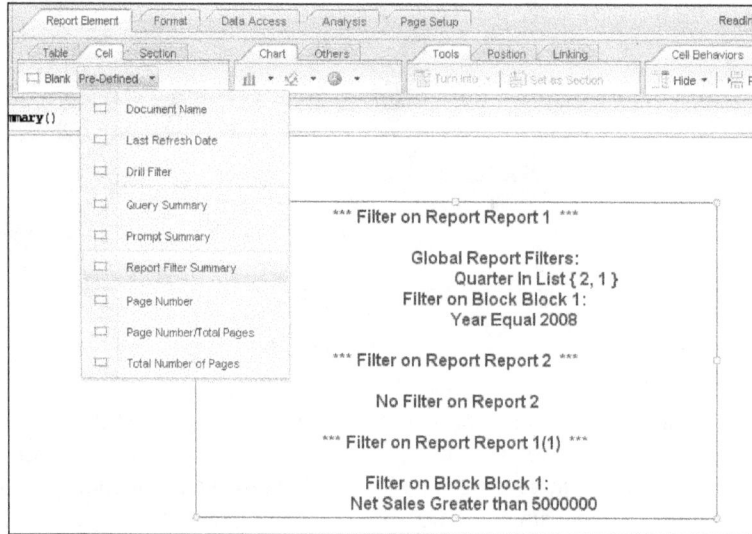

By clicking on the **Map** button, we will switch to a graphical tree view of the input control, showing the values that were picked in the filter as well as its dependencies:

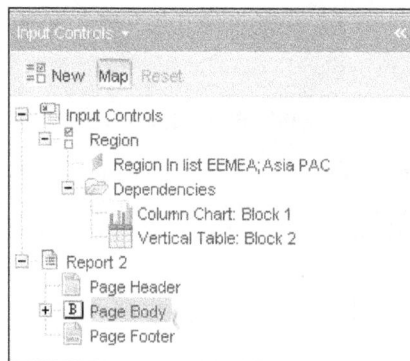

If you need to display the values of the input control in the report area, simply drag the object that you used in the control to the report area, turn it into a horizontal table, and then edit the dependencies of the control so that it will be applied on the new table as well.

Working with an element link

An element link is a feature designed to pass a value from an existing table or a chart to another data component in the report area.

Element links transform the values in a table or a chart into dynamic values that can filter other data elements.

The main difference between element links and other types of filtering is that when using an element link, we are actually using and working within a table, keeping its structure and passing a parameter from it to another structure.

This feature can be great to work with when we are using a detailed table and want to use its values to filter another chart that will visualize the summarized data and vice versa.

How to do it...

Perform the following steps:

1. We will pass the **Country** value from the detailed table to the line quantity sales pie chart, enabling the business user to filter the pie dynamically while working with the detailed table.

2. By clicking on the **Country** column, we will navigate in the speed menu to **Linking | Add Element Link**, as shown in the following screenshot:

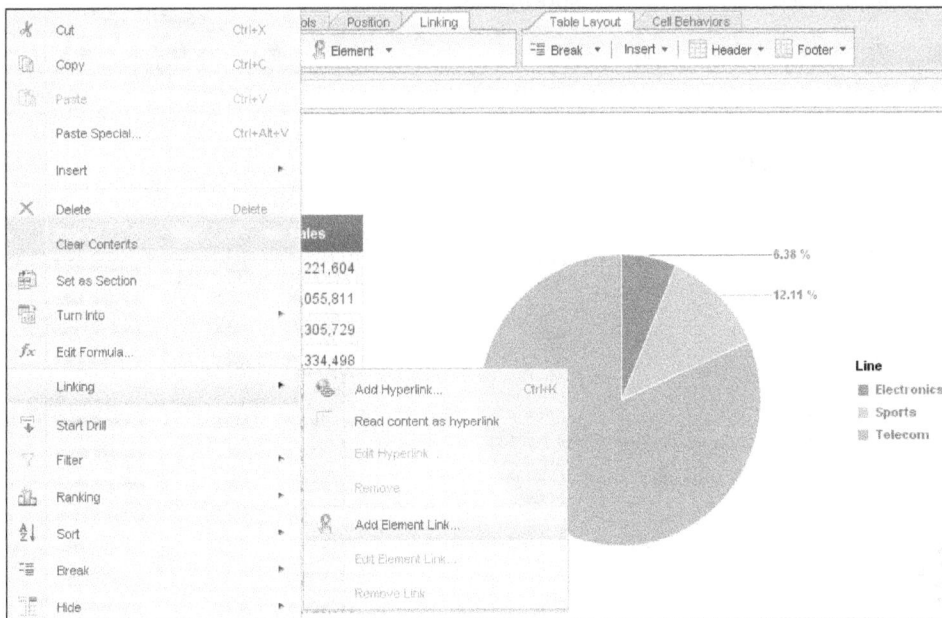

3. In the next window, we will choose the passing method and decide whether to pass the entire row values or a **Single object** value. In our example, we will use the **Single object** option, as shown in the following screenshot:

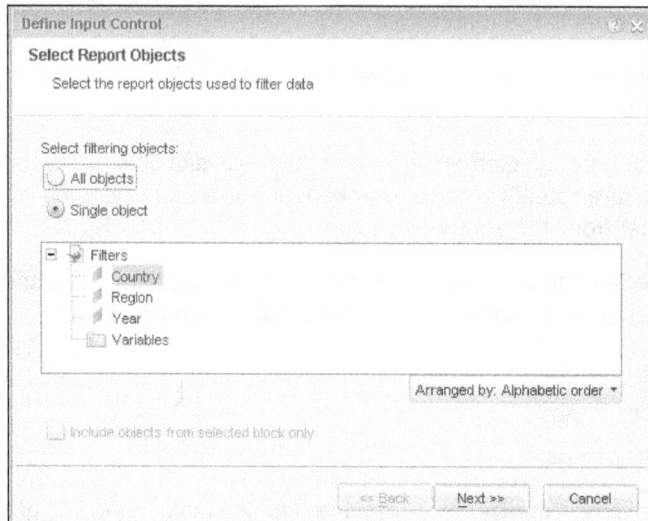

4. In the next screen, we will be able to add a description of our choice to the element link.

5. And finally, we will define the dependencies via the report elements that we want to pass the country value to, as shown in the following screenshot:

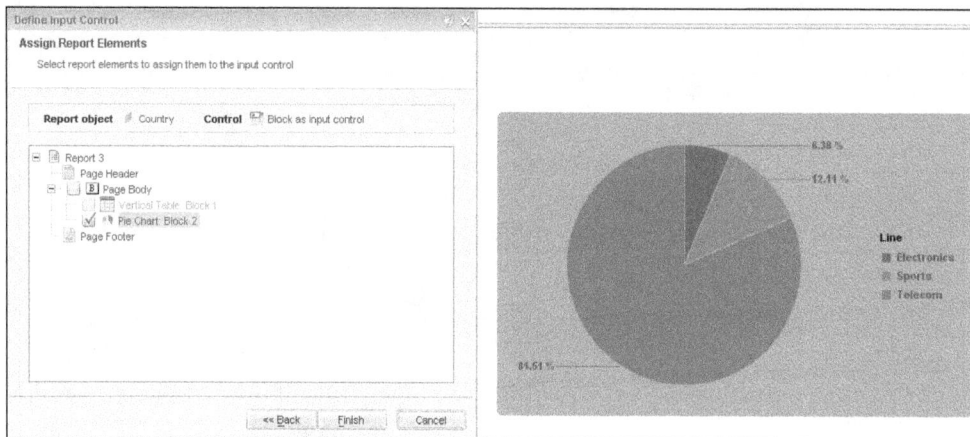

6. By clicking on the **Finish** button, we will switch to the report view, and by marking the **Country** column or any other column, we will be able to pass the **Country** value to the pie chart, as shown in the following screenshot:

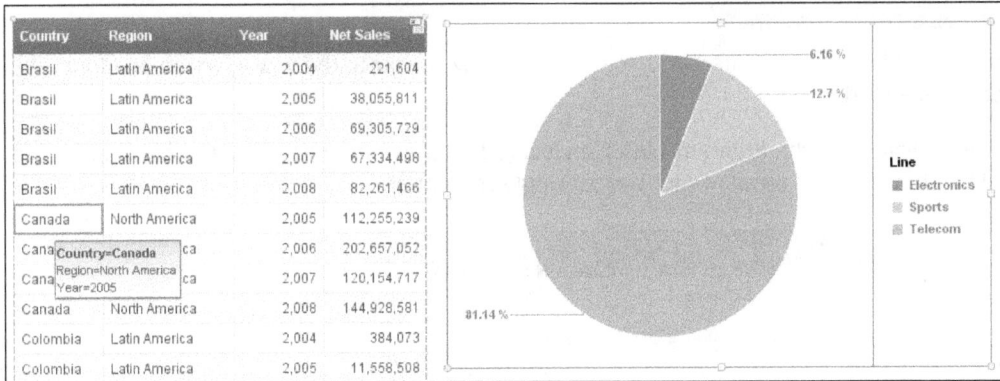

Country	Region	Year	Net Sales
Brasil	Latin America	2,004	221,604
Brasil	Latin America	2,005	38,055,811
Brasil	Latin America	2,006	69,305,729
Brasil	Latin America	2,007	67,334,498
Brasil	Latin America	2,008	82,261,466
Canada	North America	2,005	112,255,239
Cana	Country=Canada ca	2,006	202,657,052
Cana	Region=North America ca Year=2005	2,007	120,154,717
Canada	North America	2,008	144,928,581
Colombia	Latin America	2,004	384,073
Colombia	Latin America	2,005	11,558,508

Pie chart labels: 6.16 %, 12.7 %, 81.14 %

Line
- Electronics
- Sports
- Telecom

7. By clicking on a different **Country** value, such as **Colombia**, we will be able to pass it to the pie and filter the results accordingly:

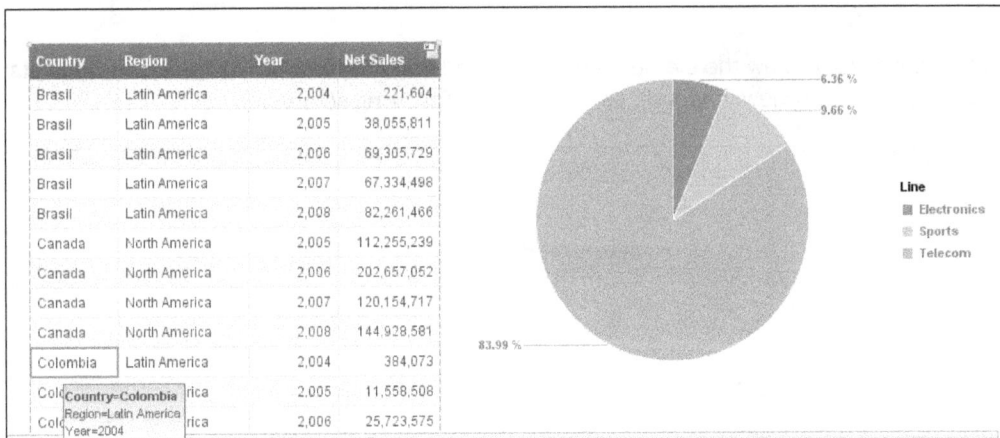

Country	Region	Year	Net Sales
Brasil	Latin America	2,004	221,604
Brasil	Latin America	2,005	38,055,811
Brasil	Latin America	2,006	69,305,729
Brasil	Latin America	2,007	67,334,498
Brasil	Latin America	2,008	82,261,466
Canada	North America	2,005	112,255,239
Canada	North America	2,006	202,657,052
Canada	North America	2,007	120,154,717
Canada	North America	2,008	144,928,581
Colombia	Latin America	2,004	384,073
Col	Country=Colombia rica	2,005	11,558,508
Col	Region=Latin America rica Year=2004	2,006	25,723,575

Pie chart labels: 6.36 %, 9.66 %, 83.99 %

Line
- Electronics
- Sports
- Telecom

8. Notice that the pie chart results have changed and that the country value is marked in bold inside the tooltip box, showing the column that was actually used to pass the value.

How it works...

The element link simply links the tables and other data components. It is actually a type of input control designed to work directly from a table rather than a filter component panel or a bar.

By clicking on any country value, we simply pass it to the dependency component that uses the value as an input in order to present the relevant data.

There's more...

An element link can be edited and adjusted in a way similar to the way in which an input control is edited.

By right-clicking on the **Element Link** icon located on the header of the rightmost column, we will be able to edit it, as shown in the following screenshot:

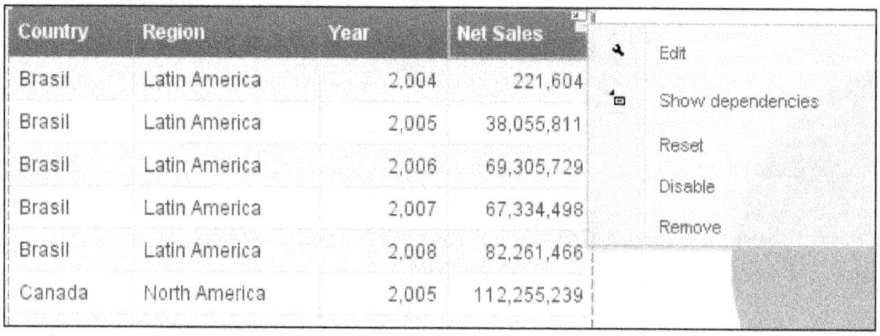

Country
Region
Year
Net Sales
Brasil Latin America 2,004 221,604
Brasil Latin America 2,005 38,055,811
Brasil Latin America 2,006 69,305,729
Brasil Latin America 2,007 67,334,498
Brasil Latin America 2,008 82,261,466
Canada North America 2,005 112,255,239
Edit
Show dependencies
Reset
Disable
Remove

Another good way to view the element link status and edit it is to switch to the **Input Controls** panel where you can view it as well, as shown in the following screenshot:

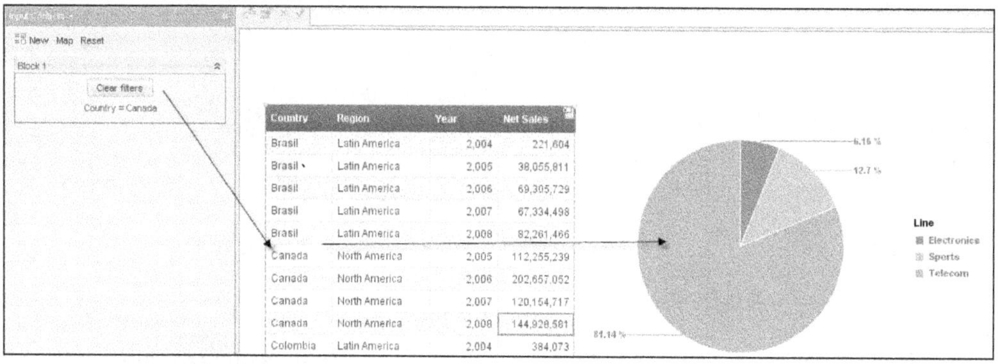

New Map Reset
Block 1
Clear filters
Country = Canada
Country
Region
Year
Net Sales
Line
Electronics
Sports
Telecom

8
Merging Data

In this chapter, we will cover the following recipes:

- ▸ Merging data from several queries
- ▸ Understanding the merge logic
- ▸ Merging data from different universes
- ▸ Merging data from different data sources
- ▸ Filtering matched values
- ▸ Troubleshooting aggregation problems
- ▸ Extending the data synchronization

Introduction

One of the key and core functionalities in Web Intelligence is the ability to create several queries in the same report and then merge their data into one common table, crosstab, or chart.

The requirement to view different aspects of the data as well as compare different datasets enables us to analyze the data in a completely new way compared to analyzing different data levels of granularity and aggregation.

Merging data is used to address and solve many common and generic data challenges, such as:

- ▸ Creating several queries that involve different sets of conditions that can't be met in the same query (for example, comparing different time frames).

- Comparing and combining datasets that originated in different universes. For example, let's say we would like to analyze the sales data of our customers based on the **Sales** universe as well as their billing data based on the **Billing** universe. By performing such cross-universe reports, we will be able to analyze the billing and sales data in a single row.

- Connecting to external data sources, such as Excel and text files that originated in a filesystem or a file created locally by an analyst. For example, let's say we would like to retrieve customer retention data and compare it to our expected goals kept and maintained in an Excel file.

- Creating a merge between queries with *full outer join* logic that can't be performed through the universe structure or is performance cost expansive.

- Working with multiple datasets and queries originating from different sources in a single place (for example, universe and Excel files).

In order to merge two or more data providers, we are required to use at least one common dimension object in order to connect the data providers.

The common dimension must have the same data type (number, date, and character) and the same format, but doesn't need to have the same name (for example, Customer ID in one query and Customer Number in another).

In general, it would be advised to merge all the common dimensions, but there are some cases in which we are required to merge only certain common dimension objects.

Merging data from several queries

In this recipe, we will learn and explain in depth how to merge data as well as about the dimension merging capabilities and behavior. Creating several queries from the same universe can help us resolve many data issues that can't be answered by using a single query:

- If the queries contain contradicting sets of conditions that require separation.

- Different time frames.

- Requirement to perform the union of two sets of data without the limitations of combined queries.

- Using different granularity data that can't be combined in a single query (monthly aggregative data and daily data).

- Using the *outer join* logic—depending on the database, the data warehouse design, and the universe structure, for some business questions, we require to display *unmatches* between certain data values. A good example for this kind of business question would be, "In which months were certain products not sold?".

Getting ready

We require to compare the current year's quantity sold data to the holiday period's quantity sold in the current year.

Since we are comparing two different time periods, we will create two separate queries that will correspond to each time frame and bring them to the report.

The goal of this comparison is to get the ratio between the holiday period's quantity sold per line to the current year's quantity sold.

How to do it...

Perform the following steps:

1. We will create two queries the same way we learned in the *Adding another query* recipe in *Chapter 2, Creating New Queries*.

2. The second query, **Holiday period**, will be very similar to the first one—only the holiday period will be added there additionally, as shown in the following screenshot:

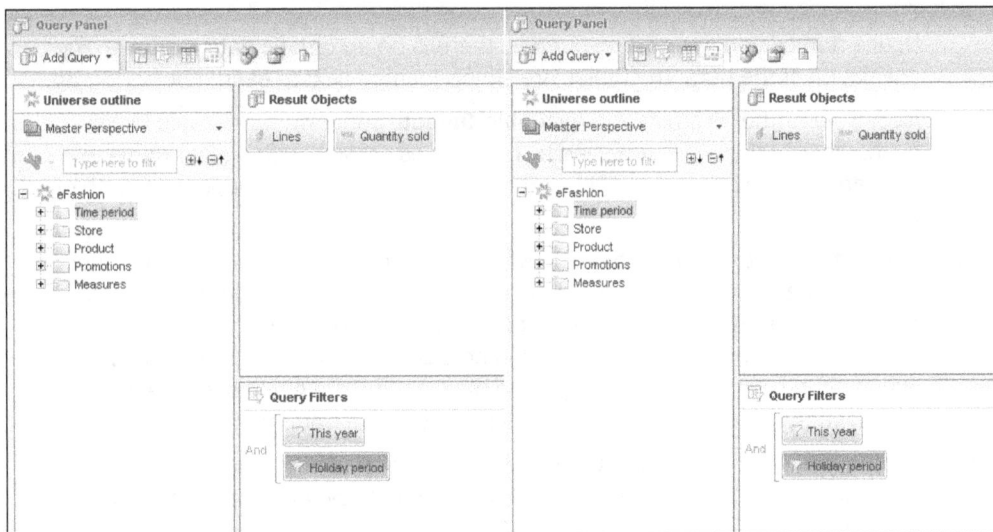

3. Adding another query isn't a complex process. It's simply performing the same procedure another time. We can just click on the first query tab, duplicate it, and edit the copied query. This feature can of course save query building time, but it is fitted to situations when we have a very similar query structure.

4. After running both of the queries, we will get the following two tables in our report:

Available Objects ▾		=[Current Year].[Lines]	
Type here to filter tree			

Report 2

Lines	Quantity sold	Lines	Quantity sold
Accessories	12,572	Accessories	2,465
City Skirts	1,171	City Skirts	173
City Trousers	511	City Trousers	26
Dresses	9,477	Dresses	1,642
Jackets	1,871	Jackets	207
Leather	230	Outerwear	46
Outerwear	259	Overcoats	2
Overcoats	505	Shirt Waist	1,421
Shirt Waist	9,223	Sweaters	2,204
Sweaters	11,221	Sweat-T-Shirts	7,933
Sweat-T-Shirts	41,780	Trousers	310
Trousers	1,476		

5. Notice that by bringing several queries, there is no automatic data merge or any unification of the data; the tables are simply located next to each other.

6. Also, if we further examine the **Available Objects** pane, we will be able to view all the objects that were retrieved by the queries as well as the query name in the parentheses appearing right next to the object name that appears in both of the queries.

7. We will be able to easily distinguish which object originated in a particular query by the query name, which is also one of the reasons why it is important to give the query a proper name. The query name will appear only beside common object names. Distinguishing between the queries can be easily done not just by the query names wrapping the common objects, but also by switching the **Available Objects** pane to the **Arranged by query** option, which is located at the bottom of the pane.

8. Another thing we can notice is that the queries fetched different datasets. In our example, we can see that in the right-hand side holiday table data, **Leather** doesn't appear.

9. Since this product line didn't have any sales during that time period, by navigating to the **Available Objects** pane, we will mark both of the common dimension objects by holding the control key down.

10. By right-clicking on the objects, the **Merge** option will appear, as shown in the following screenshot:

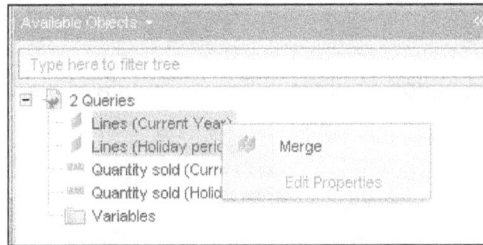

11. Upon clicking on the **Merge** option, both of the line dimensions will be grouped under a third main object. This new main object will enable us to merge the two tables.

12. We will drag the new **Lines** object into a new report, and both of the measure objects as well. Thus, we will get a single table displaying the merged data, as shown in the following screenshot:

Lines	Quantity sold	Quantity sold
Accessories	12,572	2,465
City Skirts	1,171	173
City Trousers	511	26
Dresses	9,477	1,642
Jackets	1,871	207
Leather	230	
Outerwear	259	46
Overcoats	505	2
Shirt Waist	9,223	1,421
Sweaters	11,221	2,204
Sweat-T-Shirt	41,780	7,933
Trousers	1,476	310
Sum:	**90,296**	**16,429**

The result is a single table displaying the entire datasets with no duplications. Notice that in the row displaying the **Leather** line data there is an empty value at the second **Quantity sold** column, which is the quantity data from the **Holiday period** query. This null value is a product of matching the queries. Data merge simply searches for this value in both of the queries by returning null for an unmatched value.

We can now view, analyze, and apply functions to one single table. When the report is refreshed, both of the queries will be sent to the database. The queries will retrieve the results and the new single table will correspond to the data changes like any other table or data element would. As you can see in the preceding screenshot, it's a bit confusing if the column name doesn't hold a distinct value, therefore in such cases it's recommended to name the column header in such a way that the business user will be able to distinguish between the two similar column names.

How it works...

The **Merge** option uses a common object to connect the data of the queries or any other legitimate data source.

The merge behaves as a union operator between the datasets, and as we have seen, doesn't display duplicate values.

Since the merge creates a common object that displays all the values, there is no need to drag both of the common dimension objects as well.

In the case there is no match between one or more values of one of the datasets with the other one (as in the case of the **Leather** product row), the cell will be displayed as empty.

The type of the merge operator can be changed and adjusted to the business user-specific requirements in order to filter and match only specific dataset rows.

> Merging data doesn't work as a simple join between tables; it is recommended that we merge all the common objects in order to obtain the best results.

There's more...

The data merge option enables us to mash different data sources into one table regardless of their origin. By doing so, we allow the user to view, analyze, and work on their data in one centralized report.

Let's examine another example that will demonstrate how to check in which regions there weren't any sales.

We will create two queries: the first will show the sales revenue per region, and the second one will fetch the region list.

We will get the following result tables:

Region	Sales Revenue		Region
East Coast	874,843		East
England	1,194,450		East Coast
Northern States	866,239		England
South States	1,091,335		North
West	99,051		Northern Ireland
West Coast	3,824,278		Northern States
			Scotland
			South
			South States
			Wales
			West
			West Coast

We can see that the right-hand side table displays a larger region list as this list isn't restricted to regions that have sales revenue.

We will use the merge technique this time from the main **Data Access** toolbar, as shown in the following screenshot:

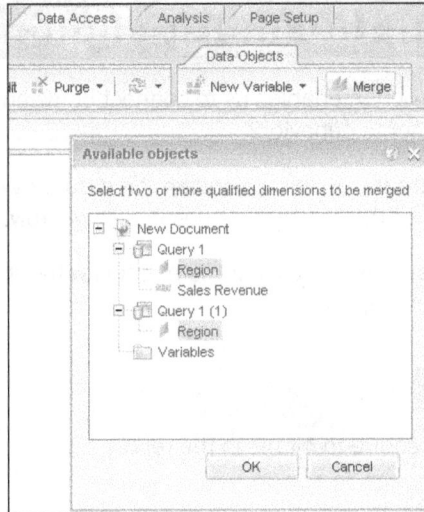

We will drag the **Region** common dimension and the **Sales Revenue** object into the report area and get the merge result of the two datasets, as shown in the following screenshot:

Region	Sales Revenue
East	
East Coast	874,843
England	1,194,450
North	
Northern Ireland	
Northern States	866,239
Scotland	
South	
South States	1,091,335
Wales	
West	99,051
West Coast	3,824,278

As we have seen earlier, the null or empty cells in the **Sales Revenue** column represent rows uncommon to both of the queries.

See also

▸ To further understand how the **Merge** option can be adjusted, follow the *Understanding the merge logic* recipe

Understanding the merge logic

As we have seen, the **Merge** option enables us to connect between several datasets, but what are the rules applied to the merge behavior?

The **Merge** option basically creates a union between the data providers. As we have seen, the effect is a full union that shows the common values in a single row.

Let's reverse the procedure and examine what the effect is without a merge and what other type of merge operators we can apply.

Getting ready

We have two tables that we require to merge in the report.

How to do it...

Let's have a look first at both of the tables' data.

We have a table with unique and common values, and both already have a global sum in each tables' footer.

Let's drag an unmerged dimension this time and see what the effect is.

We will drag the **City** dimension object twice, once from each query, and the results will be the following:

We can see there are two missing aspects:

- The measure values are not aggregated at the row level but are displaying the total result in each row
- We can't see the entire merge of both of the city dimension values

This result, of course, isn't correct, but we can now realize clearly what the results are when there is no merge between the data providers.

After establishing the merge between the two datasets, we will get the union results, as shown in the following screenshot, similar to what we saw in the previous recipe with a minor difference that in this result set both of the queries don't match each other completely; therefore we are getting empty values for both of the measures:

City	Revenue	Sales revenue
Augsburg	394,996	
Austin		2,699,673.2
Berlin	32,442	
Boston		1,283,706.6
Chicago	441,594	3,022,658.4
Cologne	10,976	
Colorado Spr		2,060,275.2
Dallas	400,899	1,970,034.2
Dresden	4,400	
Houston		5,447,956.9
Kobe	11,872	
Kyoto	16,720	
Los Angeles	301,545	4,220,928.8

Besides the union operator, we can use a left or right union operator. This kind of merge means that we are taking only one dataset (one of the tables) and finding their matched and unmatched values from the second dataset.

In the following example, from each query, the common dimension was dragged along with a measure from the same query and another measure from the second query, as shown in the following screenshot:

City	Quantity sold	Revenue
Augsburg		394,996
Berlin		32,442
Chicago	17,976	441,594
Cologne		10,976
Dallas	12,365	400,899
Dresden		4,400
Kobe		11,872
Kyoto		16,720
Los Angeles	26,244	301,545
Magdeburg		222,910
Munich		388,524
New York City		8,420
Osaka		4,700
San Diego		18,715
San Francisco	19,830	4,380
Tokyo		652,919
Washington D.C.		10,704
Yokohama		359,808

As you can see, only values from the first query are displayed along with their corresponding matching and unmatching values.

If we take the common **City** dimension from the second query, we will get the same effect, as shown in the following screenshot:

`=[Query 2].[City]`

City	Quantity sold	Revenue
Austin	17,078	
Boston	7,676	
Chicago	17,976	441,594
Colorado Spr	12,787	
Dallas	12,365	400,899
Houston	32,904	
Los Angeles	26,244	301,545
Miami	11,267	
New York	46,358	
San Francisc	19,830	4,380
Washington	18,744	

As we can see again, dragging a specific common dimension object creates a sort of right or left outer join logic.

How it works...

The merge uses a common dimension object to connect and synchronize the data from the datasets; without it, there is no row-to-row measure synchronization.

By choosing one of the common dimension objects (the specific dimension objects can be described as *sons* while the common main object can be described as *father*), we can establish the relevant synchronization between the datasets, and, as described earlier, it is recommended that we merge all the common dimensions to get the best results.

There's more...

Another operator that can be established between the datasets is the one that will display only the matched values from both of the queries (an intersection operator).

This means that only if the city values appear in both of the queries should they be displayed.

This operator is achieved using filter logic, which will be described in the *Filtering matched values* recipe.

Merging data from different universes

Merging data from different universes is done in the same way that we build several queries from the same universe.

The differences are minor, as follows:

▶ The name of the common object can be different (customer ID and customer number)

▶ We will be using the **Add Query** option rather than the duplicate query

How to do it...

We wish to retrieve data from the Sales universe and the Customer Data universe.

From the Customer Data universe, we will choose the **Year**, **Quarter**, and the **Number of Customers** objects using the **Add Query** button located at the top-right corner of the **Query Panel**. We will add another query from the Sales universe, and we will retrieve the **Year**, **Quarter**, and the **Sales revenue** objects, as shown in the following screenshot:

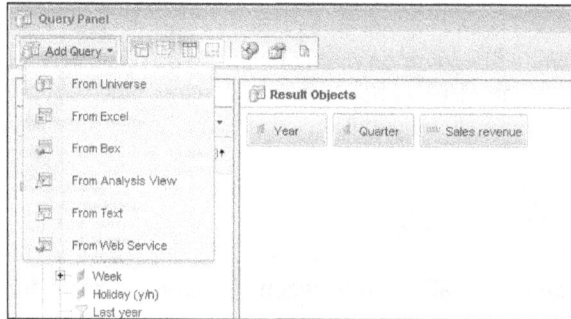

After running the queries, we will get the following two tables:

Year	Quarter	Number of Customers	Year	Quarter	Sales revenue
2004	Q1	127	2004	Q1	$2,660,700
2004	Q2	132	2004	Q2	$2,279,003
2004	Q3	134	2004	Q3	$1,367,841
2004	Q4	125	2004	Q4	$1,788,580
2005	Q1	132	2005	Q1	$3,326,172
2005	Q2	136	2005	Q2	$2,840,651
2005	Q3	132	2005	Q3	$2,879,303
2005	Q4	125	2005	Q4	$4,186,120
2006	Q1	122	2006	Q1	$3,742,989
2006	Q2	127	2006	Q2	$4,006,718
2006	Q3	130	2006	Q3	$3,953,395
2006	Q4	129	2006	Q4	$3,356,041

We will merge the **Year** common dimension and drag the common dimension object, along with the two measures, to a new report tab, as shown in the following screenshot:

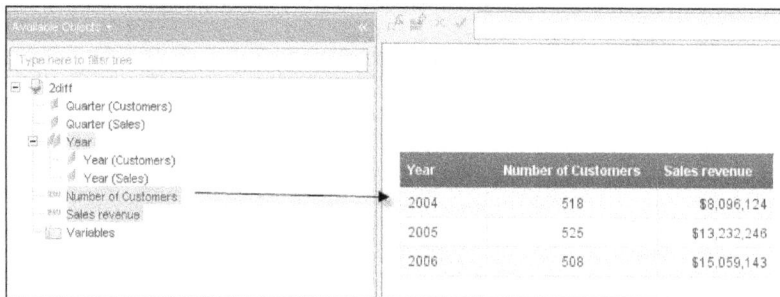

Year	Number of Customers	Sales revenue
2004	518	$8,096,124
2005	525	$13,232,246
2006	508	$15,059,143

We will also add the **Quarter** dimension to the existing table and get the following results. Notice that the **Sales revenue** values are repeating themselves for each quarter value.

Year	Quarter	Number of Customers	Sales revenue
2004	Q1	127	$8,096,124
2004	Q2	132	$8,096,124
2004	Q3	134	$8,096,124
2004	Q4	125	$8,096,124
2005	Q1	132	$13,232,246
2005	Q2	136	$13,232,246
2005	Q3	132	$13,232,246
2005	Q4	125	$13,232,246
2006	Q1	122	$15,059,143
2006	Q2	127	$15,059,143
2006	Q3	130	$15,059,143

This is because the datasets are merged at the **Year** level and not at the **Quarter** level.

Since the most detailed level of each query is aggregated in the **Year** and **Quarter** dimension objects, we are seeing unsynchronized measure values.

Since we took the **Quarter** dimension object from the **Customers** query, the **Number of Customers** measure is displayed correctly, but the **Sales revenue** coming from the second query is not displayed correctly since we are missing another merge dimension object.

We will merge the **Quarter** dimension as well; drag the common object to the table and the **Sales revenue** values will be synchronized at the **Quarter** level as well, as shown in the following screenshot:

Year	Quarter	Number of Customers	Sales revenue
2004	Q1	127	$2,660,700
2004	Q2	132	$2,279,003
2004	Q3	134	$1,367,841
2004	Q4	125	$1,788,580
2005	Q1	132	$3,326,172
2005	Q2	136	$2,840,651
2005	Q3	132	$2,879,303
2005	Q4	125	$4,186,120
2006	Q1	122	$3,742,989
2006	Q2	127	$4,006,718
2006	Q3	130	$3,953,395
2006	Q4	129	$3,356,041

How it works...

We have already seen how the merge logic works in the previous recipe. Another major part of the merge behavior is merging all the common dimension objects as they perform as levels of data synchronization. Merging the **Year** dimension enabled us to merge the data at the yearly level, adding the quarter to the merge enabled us to go another level down to a more detailed level of data; this is exactly what merging a certain dimension is.

There's more...

When merging datasets, it is best to use a *strong* common dimension. What is a strong merge dimension? It is a dimension at the most detailed level of the query. Therefore, it can "climb up" when we are synchronizing higher levels of data as well as match the data at its most detailed level.

Merging data from different data sources

Another common and useful scenario is merging data from different sources.

Besides the universe structure and BEx queries, we can find the Excel and text file data sources almost in every information environment.

Using Excel files comes with the job as it is one of the most common and useful data sources for business users' working environments.

Using Excel as the data source in Web Intelligence reports enables the business user to centralize different data sources with their different look and feel in the same table as well as enjoy the preferable drag-and-drop capabilities of Web Intelligence.

The data stored in the Excel files could originate from a filesystem, a daily automatic output, an ERP or a CRM system, or a local file of one of the business users.

Using the merge logic, we will be able to create one table out of several different data sources.

Getting ready

We will use an Excel file containing the estimated quantity sold per line of products. The data coming from this file will help the business user to compare the real quantity sold figures based on the eFashion universe compared to their local file.

How to do it...

First, we will build the universe query retrieving the **Lines** and **Quantity sold** objects.

Using the **Data Access** toolbar, we will navigate to the **New data provider** option and click on the **From Excel** option, as shown in the following screenshot:

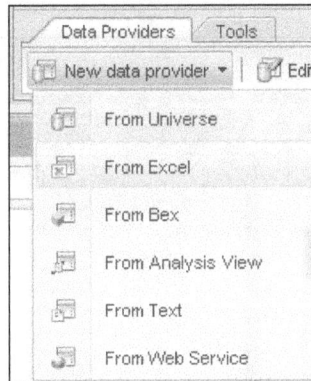

In the **Select a data source** window that will appear, we will navigate to the Excel file in the location it is saved, as shown in the following screenshot:

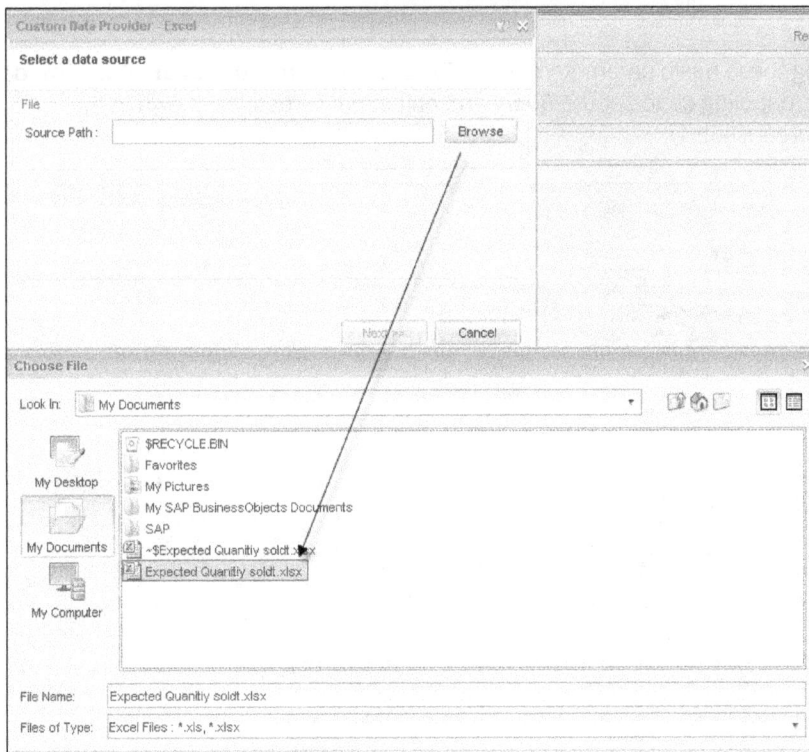

After choosing the Excel file, we will move to the parameters window. Here, we can see the file location, define data areas in the Excel file that we want to retrieve, or define the first row as column name, as shown in the following screenshot:

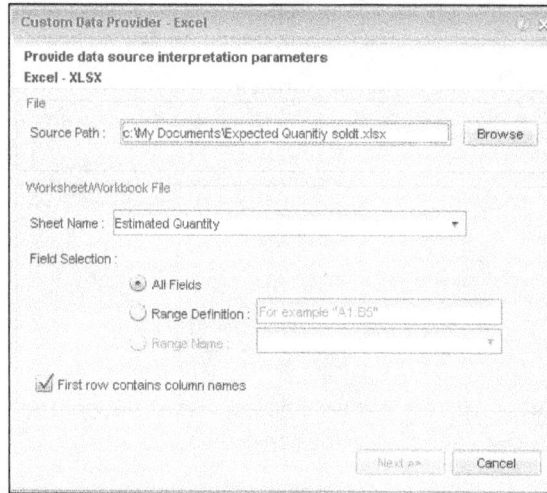

After setting these basic parameters of the Excel data source, the **Query Panel** window will appear, enabling us to set the query and object properties, as shown in the following screenshot:

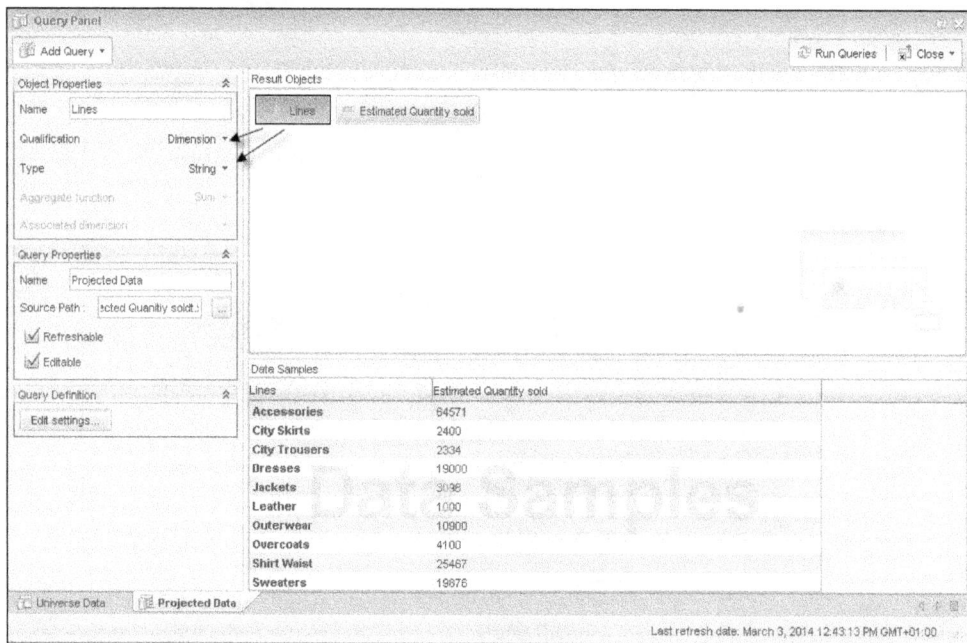

In this query panel, we can:

- ▸ Set the object qualification (dimension, attribute, and measure)
- ▸ Define the query name
- ▸ Remap the file location
- ▸ Set the edit/refresh option on the query

We will run the query, get the corresponding data in our report, and then use the **Merge** option and drag the common line dimension objects along with the two measures, as shown in the following screenshot:

Lines	Estimated Quantity sold	Quantity sold
Accessories	64,571	64,541
City Skirts	2,400	1,895
City Trousers	2,334	1,777
Dresses	19,000	20,257
Jackets	3,098	4,009
Leather	1,000	1,063
Outerwear	10,900	9,421
Overcoats	4,100	2,113
Shirt Waist	25,467	22,597
Sweaters	19,876	18,312
Sweat-T-Shirt	70,900	71,639
Trousers	6,230	5,605

Now, we can turn this table into a chart and get a better visual comparison between the two measures, as shown in the following screenshot:

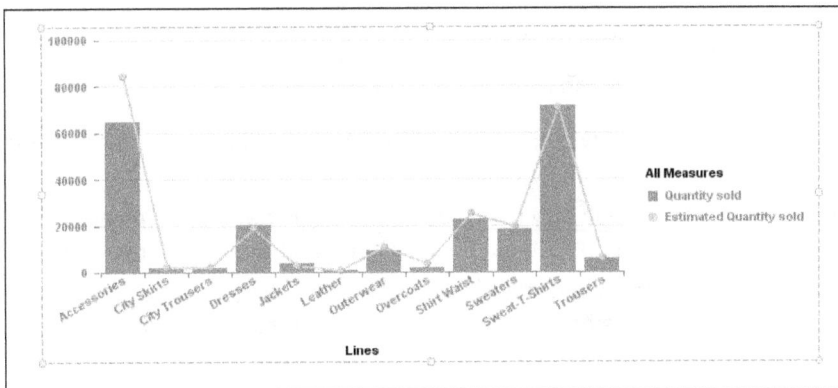

> [💡 If any changes are made in the Excel file, then they will reflect in the report data just as any other data source.]

How it works...

Web Intelligence enables us to connect to external files such as Excel files and import their data.

The spreadsheet can be seen as a local database where the data is stored, and as long as we are retrieving flat data from the file or mapping specific ranges of data in the Excel file, we are good to go.

By retrieving the Excel data, we are making the data analysis process simpler as we don't require two different applications to work on the same slice of data.

> [💡 Excel files can also be imported to our data warehouse and transformed into universe tables.]

There's more...

Excel files can also be used in a query condition. See the *Using other query results* recipe in *Chapter 2, Creating New Queries*.

In this method, we can use the Excel file result as the basis for the universe query list of values just as a subquery.

Filtering matched values

Another relation between datasets would be to filter only the matched values.

The main operators available when merging the datasets are:

- ▸ **Union**: This unifies the two datasets whether or not they have common values; this operator is similar to a full outer join.
- ▸ **Right union**: This unifies only the values that exist in dataset A with all the common and uncommon values of dataset B. This operator is similar to a right outer join.
- ▸ **Left union**: This unifies only the values that exists in dataset B with all the common and uncommon values of dataset A. This operator is similar to a left outer join.

These operators are good for these scenarios, but if we need to find only the common values of the datasets, we will need to use some filter logic.

Getting ready

We will use an already merged set of data originating from two different universes—Customer and Sales data—merging the **City** dimension with the **Number of Customers** and **Sales Revenue** measures.

How to do it...

If we look closely at the data displayed, we will reach the understanding that a common value for both of the datasets is any city value that contains values for both of its measure columns, as shown in the following screenshot. Any other state when only one of the measures has a value will stand for an uncommon value to both of the datasets.

City	Number of Customers	Quantity sold
Augsburg	191	
Austin		17,078
Berlin	6	
Boston		7,676
Chicago	241	17,976
Cologne	4	
Colorado Spr		12,787
Dallas	158	12,365
Dresden	4	
Houston		32,904
Kobe	6	
Los Angeles	163	26,244
Magdeburg	133	

In order to filter only the common values, we will be using simple filter logic that will state that if both of the measures are not empty (not null), then those corresponding rows will be displayed.

How to use filters was described in depth in *Chapter 7, Filtering the Report Data*. Here, we will be using a simple filter that will state that the **Number of Customers** and **Sales Revenue** measures are not null:

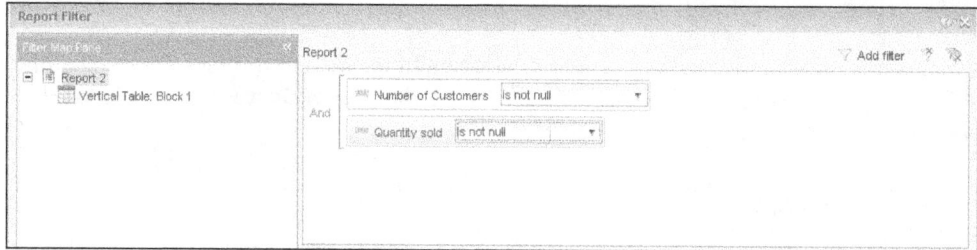

The result of these filter conditions will be the following screenshot, in which only common rows are displayed:

City	Number of Customers	Quantity sold
Chicago	241	17,976
Dallas	158	12,365
Los Angeles	163	26,244
San Francisco	6	19,830

How it works...

By applying very simple filter logic that looks for values in both of the measure objects, we are capable of filtering in only common values.

Once this logic is applied to the table, it will remain so and be updated according to the data changes.

> In order to filter only the uncommon values, we only need to adjust the filter operator to the null operator.

Troubleshooting aggregation problems

As we saw in this chapter, we can merge several datasets (data providers) in the same report into one table.

As long as we have the same common dimensions or we are able to merge data relying on the same number of common dimension objects, the results in the table will be projected correctly.

However, we might face some trouble when we try to merge data from datasets that don't have the same common dimensions.

This case can be very common as we will find ourselves many times building queries that don't match each other in all the aspects and objects.

Different queries can have a different granularity level or a different detail level. We can't expect a highly summarized query returning sales figures at the product level to be merged properly with a detailed query displaying data at the customer, invoice data, and product level.

Getting ready

Let's have a look at the following scenario.

We will be using two queries based on the Motors universe; the first query will fetch the **Number of Clients** per **Client Country** and **Area**, and the second query will retrieve the **Number of Cars Sold** per **Area**, as shown in the following screenshot:

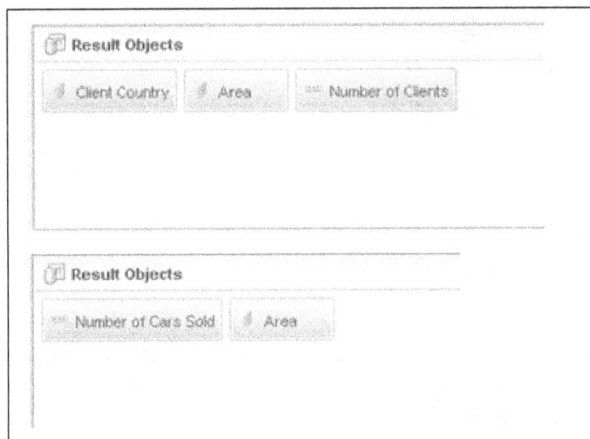

How to do it...

Perform the following steps:

1. We will merge the **Area** common dimension object and create a single table based on the two datasets:

Client Country	Area	Number of Cars Sold	Number of Clients
France	Paris		10
United Kingdom	Bedfordshire	3	2
United Kingdom	Berkshire	22	24
United Kingdom	Buckinghamshire	4	4
United Kingdom	Hertfordshire	2	2
United Kingdom	Kent	1	2
USA	CA	68	56
USA	IL	6	12
USA	MA	4	10
USA	MI	7	8
USA	NY	9	12
USA	TX	15	22
	Sum:	141	164

2. So far, so good. Now we will drag out the **Area** dimension and we are left only with the **Client Country** dimension. As soon as we do that, the measures will roll up to the **Country** level, and the results will be as shown in the following screenshot:

Client Country	Number of Cars Sold	Number of Clients
France	141	10
United Kingdom	141	34
USA	141	120
	141	164

3. Notice that the **Number of Cars Sold** measure isn't projected correctly as the queries are merged at the **Country** level. The **Number of Clients** is okay since it's based on the **Client Country** query.

4. In order to fix this problem, we will use the `forcemerge` function. This function enables *rolling up* the problematic measure using the missing dimensions affecting the measure results.

5. Using the formula bar, the **Number Of Cars Sold** column will be marked and wrapped with the =forcemerge ([Number Of Cars Sold]) syntax, as shown in the following screenshot:

Client Country	Number of Cars Sold	Number of Clients
France	141	10
United Kingdom	141	34
USA	141	120
	141	164

6. The result of the function will be adjusting the measure results to the **Client Country** level and displaying it correctly, as shown in the following screenshot:

Client Country	Number of Cars Sold	Number of Clients
France		10
United Kingdom	32	34
USA	109	120
	141	164

How it works...

The forcemerge function can deal with situations where we have hierarchical data that can be summed up as long as we have merged the lower-level dimension object.

The nature of the measure objects is to roll up or down along with the dimensions displayed with them. This function simply extends the context of the calculation by taking all the data from the unmatched query and enabling the problematic measure to roll up.

The forcemerge function can help us to roll up the measure values but not to roll them down as it uses a higher level of hierarchy (in this case, the **Client Country** contains the **Area** values so that the measures can roll up).

The reason why the forcemerge function worked for us is because the queries were merged at the **Area** level. In our first query, we also fetched the **Country** dimension so that each **Area** value was capable of being summed up through the **Country** dimension associated with it.

There's more...

Cases can be more problematic, and the `forcemerge` function will not deal well with non-unique values.

To get the best results, it is recommended that we use unique values and avoid null dimension values at the merge level as it may cause issues when using the `forcemerge` function.

Extending the data synchronization

As we saw in the previous recipe, queries can be unequal in terms of numbers of common dimensions.

As an axiom, we can claim that the more uncommon dimension objects we have, the more complex it is to display the common data.

In such cases, we will require additional functionality in order to display the common data.

In general, when we have more than one uncommon dimension object, we get a notification while trying to drag it into the table that is incompatible.

Let's have a look at such a case and learn how to resolve it.

Getting ready

We will create two queries based on the Data Warehouse universe: a **Sales Revenue** per **Client Name** and **Client Country** query, and another query that will fetch the **Client Name** and the **Sale Date**, as shown in the following screenshot:

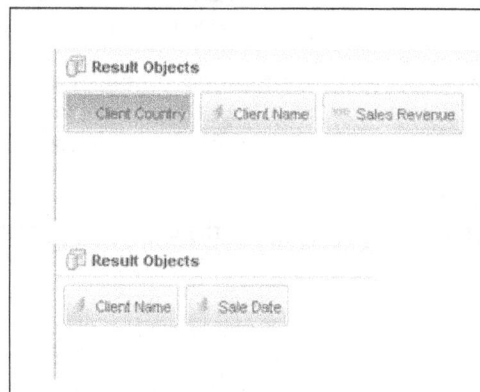

How to do it...

Perform the following steps:

1. We will merge the **Client Name** dimension object and drag it along with the client country name.

2. When we try to add the **Sale Date** as well, we will get the notification **Cannot drop here – the object is incompatible**, as shown in the following screenshot:

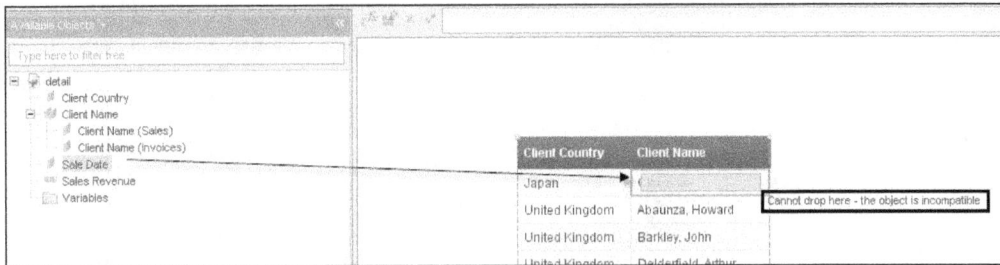

3. This is because we have more than one uncommon dimension (**Country** and **Sale Date**).

4. Our solution to this kind of problem will be to create a local variable in the report based on the **Sale Date** dimension object—only that we will create it as an attribute object associated with its merge dimension object.

5. First, we will create the new variable using the **Create Variable** button located on the formula bar toolbar. Upon clicking on this button, the **Create Variable** dialog box will appear.

6. Here, we will create a new object based on the **Sale Date** object. We will name the new object Q2.Sales Date and set its qualification to an attribute type of object, as shown in the following screenshot:

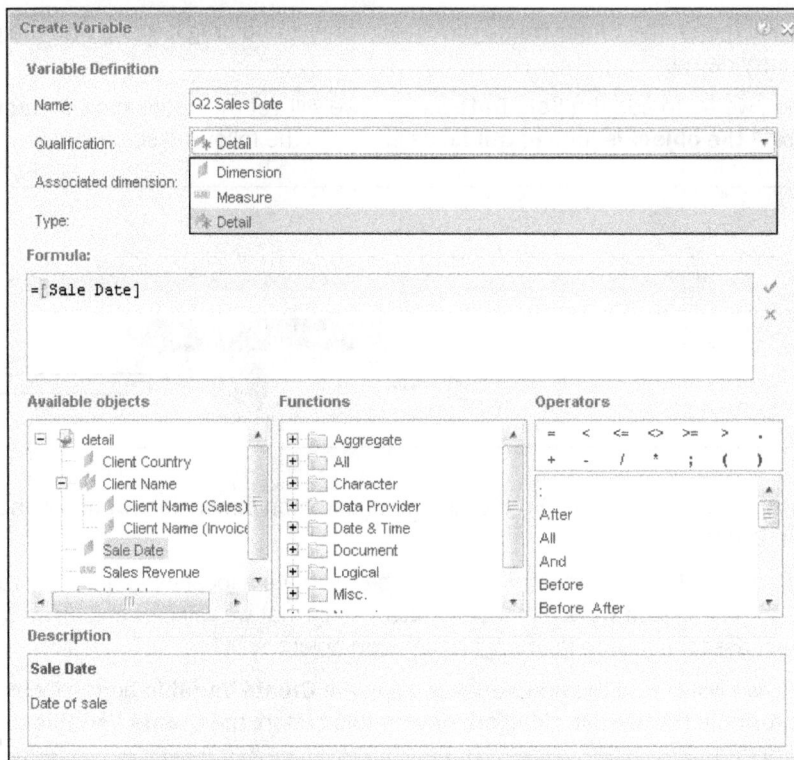

7. In order to make the new object compatible with the rest of the data, we will associate it with the **Client Name** object based on the same query and the basis for the merge with the second query data, as shown in the following screenshot:

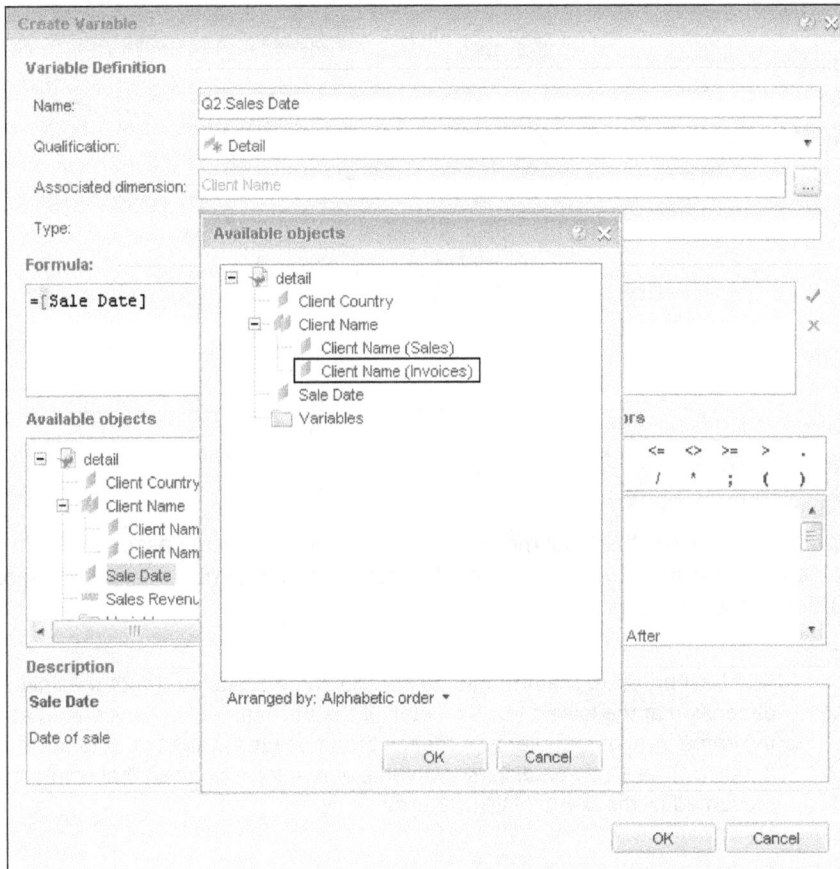

8. A new object will appear in the **Available Objects** pane under the **Variables** folder.

We will now be able to drag this object and add it to our table, as shown in the following screenshot:

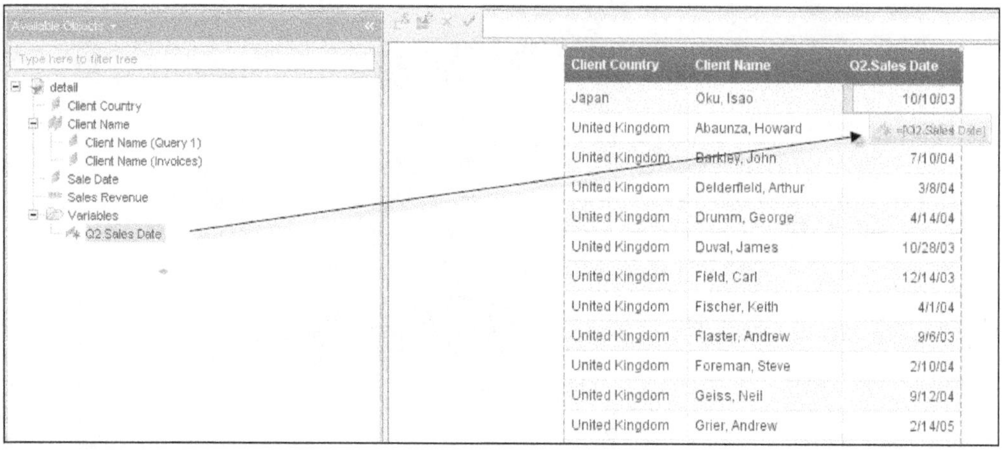

How it works...

The object we created uses the local merge dimension object by being associated with it. We were able to extend its connectivity using the method that makes the uncommon object available through the common object.

> As a best practice, the attribute object should be associated with the linked dimension at the lowest level of detail. If the attribute object isn't stated at the same level of granularity, it means that it doesn't make the data more detailed. There may be display problems of *many-to-one* rows that would be presented by the #MULTIVALUE error.

See also

▶ To read further on how to use variables and formulas, see *Chapter 9, Using Formulas and Variables*

9
Using Formulas and Variables

In this chapter, we will cover the following recipes:

- ▶ Using formulas
- ▶ Working with variables
- ▶ Using aggregate functions
- ▶ Using character functions
- ▶ Using data provider functions
- ▶ Using date and time functions
- ▶ Using document functions
- ▶ Using logical functions
- ▶ Using misc functions
- ▶ Using numeric functions
- ▶ Using extended syntax

Introduction

Using formulas and functions in a report helps us extend the report functionality and address simple and complex report requirements.

While a query is based on a universe, a BEx query, or a datafile, it's still restricted to the data source structure. Formulas and functions enable us to add calculations and perform additional analysis as well as address data issues that the database may not support or that are too "report specific".

Another good reason why functions and formulas are important is that they can result in better performance as they are performed only on the report's data, which always holds a smaller dataset rather than query-retrieved data from much larger structures.

The business user can have various types of functionality requirements, from creating a simple, aggregative function that will calculate a rolling 12-month average to more complex functions that calculate the time difference between two dates in hours and seconds.

Web Intelligence contains function libraries that can be applied to the main data aspects: aggregative functions, time functions, numeric functions, character functions, and many more.

Functions can also be used to perform if and then logic and create variables that can be used globally in the report.

In this chapter, we will learn how to create formulas, use functions, create variables in various ways, and understand how to reuse them in our reports while implementing best practices.

Using formulas

Formulas can be used whenever we need to add an additional calculation to the data or use an in-built function from the function libraries.

Let's take a look at how we can create different types of formulas, which will serve different purposes in our reports.

Getting ready

Our report data contains the **Number of Customers** and **Number of Orders** measures and the **Country** and **Region** dimensions; we want to add an average calculation that will display the average number of orders.

We first add a column to the right-hand side of the **Number of Orders** column using the right-click menu and by navigating to the **Insert** option and then choosing **Insert column on right**, as shown in the following screenshot:

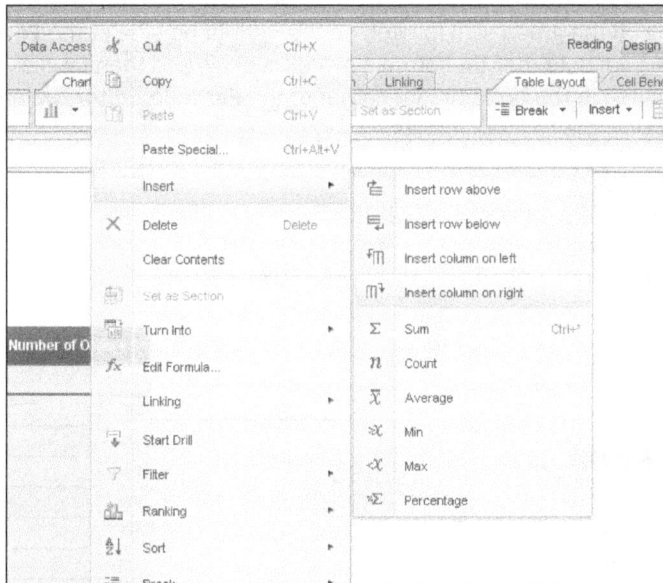

After adding the new empty column, we mark it and click on the **Formula Editor** button located on the top left of the formula bar.

How to do it...

Perform the following steps:

1. By clicking on the **Formula Editor** button, we switch to the **Formula Editor** window where we will write the formula.

2. The formula editor window is made up of four main parts:

   - **The top center part**: We write the formula here
   - **The left-hand side**: This consists of the list of available objects that can be used in the formula
   - **The middle part**: This consists of the function library grouped by subject areas
   - **The right-hand side**: This lists the operators that can be used in the formulas

3. We create a simple average formula by dividing the number of customers with the number of orders.

4. In order to write the formula, we will simply double-click on the objects located in the objects list and use the divide sign located on the **Operators** bar. The formula will look like `=[ Number of Orders]/[ Number of Customers]`, as shown in the following screenshot.

5. By clicking on the green sign located on the right-hand side of the **Formula Editor** window, we validate that the formula syntax is okay, and then by clicking on the **OK** button located in the bottom-right corner of the **Formula Editor**, we are able to switch back and view the formula results:

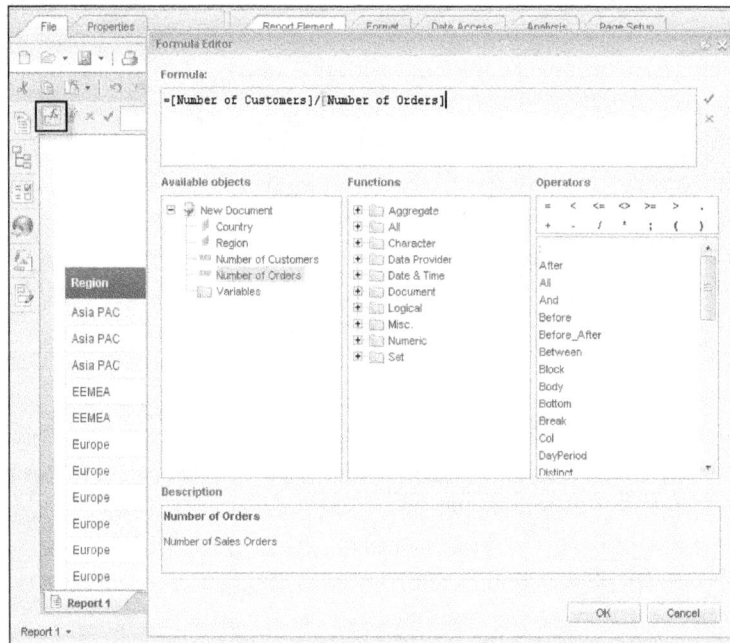

6. We are now able to analyze the average orders per region and country and apply other report functions on this calculation, such as the sorting function, as shown in the following screenshot:

Country	Region	Number of Customers	Number of Orders		Quantity
Brasil	Latin America	8	629	78.63	1,523,448
Canada	North America	12	713	59.42	3,519,001
Colombia	Latin America	4	203	50.75	401,100
Eastern Euro	EEMEA	8	483	60.38	1,196,729
Emirates	EEMEA	4	196	49	443,101
France	Europe	8	511	63.88	1,122,674
Germany	Europe	8	603	75.38	1,466,726

7. Let's have a look at another formula that uses an in-built function. We navigate to the **Misc** functions library and choose the `LineNumber()` function. This function will enable us to add the row number to the table, as shown in the following screenshot:

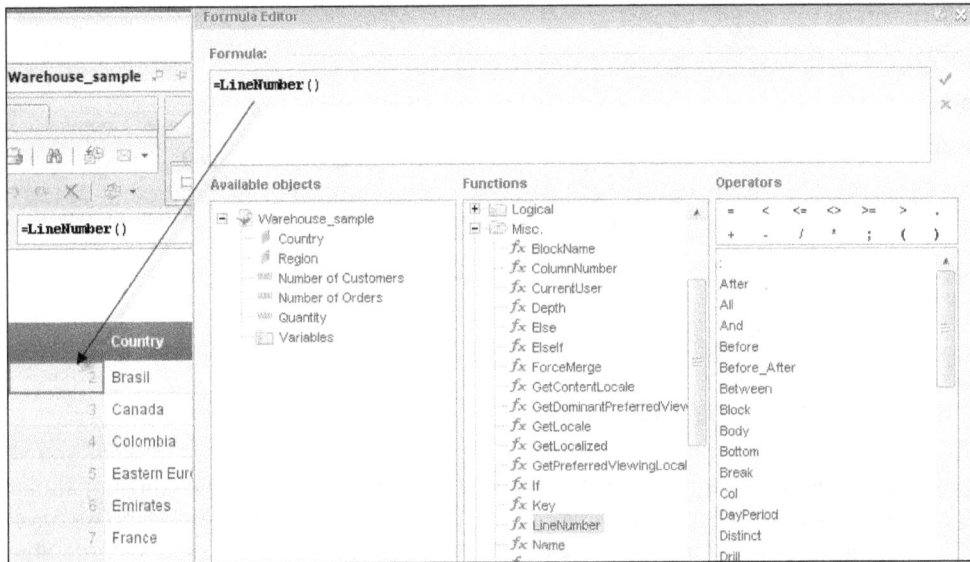

8. This formula doesn't require any further syntax; by simply clicking on it, we are able to add it to the **Formula** area.

> Note that the line number values start at 2 because the column header is counted as well; in order to adjust the formula so it will start at 1, you can apply the `=LineNumber() -1` syntax.

How it works...

The formula calculates a measure result, returns a value according to its use and type, or creates a better format for an existing object.

Business users can navigate to the **Formula Editor** and create a new "homemade" calculation or enhance the data by adding a build on functions.

See also

▶ For a detailed explanation of the various types of in-built functions, see the next nine recipes

Working with variables

A variable is simply a formula turned into a local object that can be viewed and used from the **Available objects** pane and treated just as any other object that exists in the report and was retrieved by the query.

Another way to define a variable is that it is a formula that has a name.

During creation, a formula inserts its result into a specific and usually a single column; to build a variable is just like saying that we have created a global formula in the report that can easily be used in every report tab, table, and chart.

There are several advantages to creating a variable compared to a formula:

▶ We can reuse a variable easily without needing to copy and paste or recreate the formula

▶ Variables can be used in filters, ranking, and conditional formatting, while formulas can't

▶ When creating a variable, we can give it a business term rather than dealing with a long and sometimes complex syntax; this option is even more useful when we have a complex calculation that is combined from several parts, and it would be preferable to create the variable from several subvariables

▶ Variables can be accessed from a common folder in the **Available objects** pane, which provides a centralized, easy way to manage and maintain them

Getting ready

We want to turn our formula of the average number of orders into a variable and then use it in a new aggregative table that we will create.

How to do it...

Perform the following steps:

1. We mark the column that displays the formula values and click on the **Create variable** button located on the left-hand side of the **Formula** bar:

	Country	Region	Number of Customers	Number of Orders		Quantity
2	Brasil	Latin America	8	629	78.63	1,523,448
3	Canada	North America	12	713	59.42	3,519,001

=[Number of Orders]/[Number of Customers]

2. After we click on the **Create variable** button, the **Variable Editor** window pops up. In this window, we name the formula `Average Number of Orders`, then set its **Qualification** field to **Measure** as it divides two measure objects, and finally, click on the **OK** button:

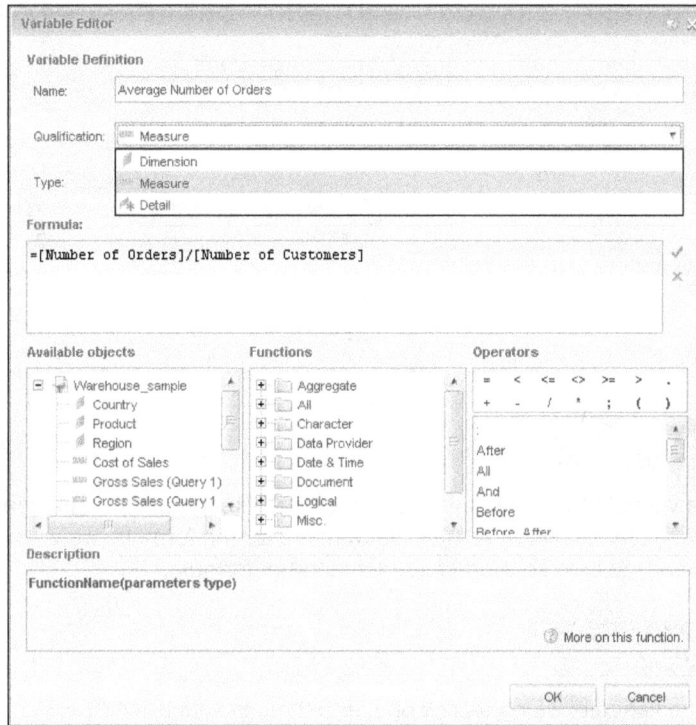

3. The result is a local object that we will be able to identify and use in the **Available Objects** pane, and it will also appear in the column we just marked:

4. Now, in order to reuse this object, we simply drag it and use it in any way we want. We already learned how to interact with the objects that exist in the report, so if we wish to display the average per country, we simply drag both the required objects and the average is projected at the **Country** level:

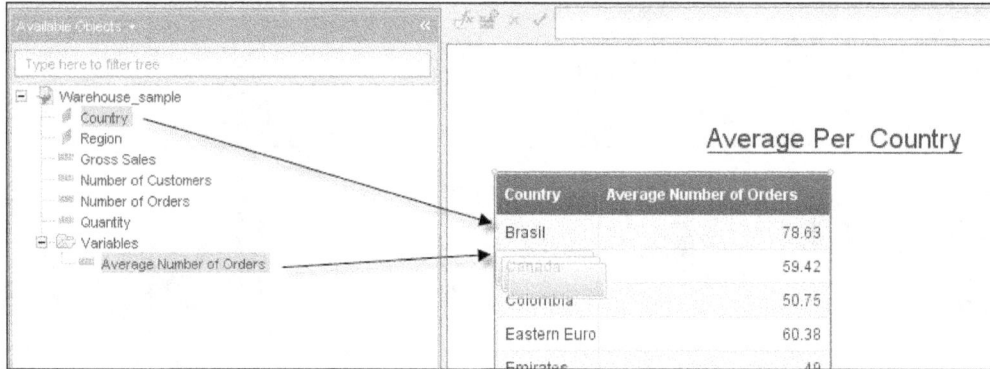

How it works...

The creation of a variable turns the formula into a local object that can immediately be used in the report table and tabs. Once we have set a name for the formula, we will find it under the variables folder ready to be displayed or used in another formula.

There's more...

In order to edit the variable, we right-click on it and then choose the **Edit** option as shown in the following screenshot:

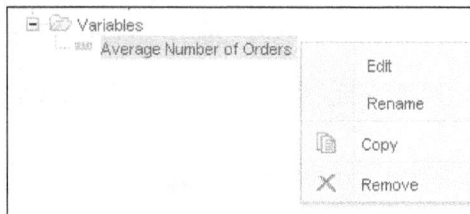

Another important note is that in order to create a new variable, we are not restricted to first creating the formula in a column and then defining it as a variable.

We may as well access the **Create Variable** option located in the **Data Objects** tab in the **Data Access** toolbar, create the variable, and then use it in the report according to our requirement, as shown in the following screenshot:

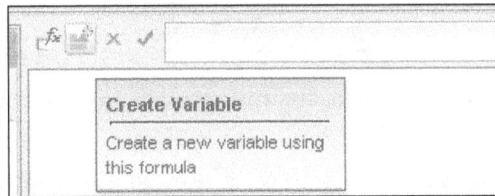

Using aggregate functions

Aggregate functions are used whenever we want to perform calculations on measure objects. This isn't always the case as we can also perform a count calculation on a dimension or an attribute object.

We distinguish between two main uses of aggregative functions as follows:

▶ A summarized aggregative function returns the result in the footer or in a single cell, such as **Sum** or a **Max** calculation

▶ A row-level calculation shows the aggregative result, such as the percentage

The main aggregative functions are as follows:

▶ **Sum**

▶ **Average**

▶ **Min/Max**

▶ **Percentage**

▶ **Count**

How to do it...

The count function counts each unique value once, so if we have 10K rows that contain only seven different values, the result of count will be 7.

If we need to count the number of rows in a table, regardless of whether a value exists in a specific row or not, we use the count all syntax.

As we know, every formula starts with the equals to sign, so we basically use the count syntax and add the all option to it so it will look like =count([Object];all).

This will result in us having to count all the rows in the table.

So basically, the `count` function is more suited to count the number of clients, while `count all` is more suited to count the number of purchases (assuming we are counting all the purchase dates or any other object that is not unique).

Another useful function is `RunningSum`. This function belongs to the accumulative functions family, such as `runningcount, average, product`, and others.

This formula is great when we want to display the accumulative effect of a measure, such as the gross sales for one quarter of the year.

The formula syntax will look like `=RunningSum ([Gross Sales])`.

Also, the results are that for each continuing quarter, we will see the accumulative results of the current and previous quarters, as shown in the following screenshot:

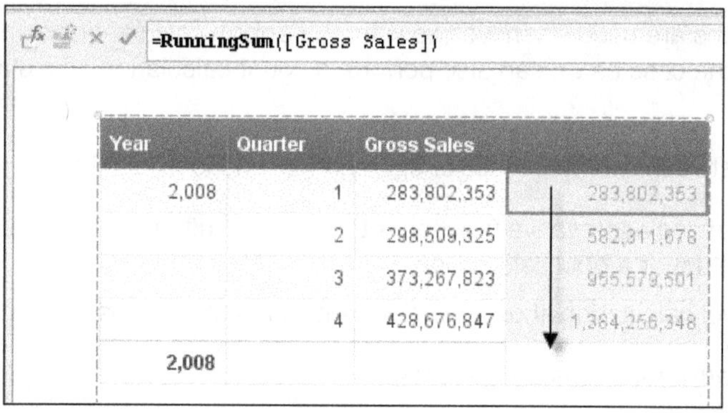

Year	Quarter	Gross Sales	
2,008	1	283,802,353	283,802,353
	2	298,509,325	582,311,678
	3	373,267,823	955,579,501
	4	428,676,847	1,384,256,348
2,008			

`=RunningSum([Gross Sales])`

How it works...

The aggregative functions are used to calculate all types of figures. Using the aggregative function folder, we can apply various and common calculations to the displayed data.

See also

▸ While the main aggregative functions have been described in the recipe, there are, of course, others. For further reading and examples on how to use aggregative functions, refer to the *Using extended syntax* recipe

Using character functions

Character functions can be applied mainly on character objects (non-numeric or date objects), but they can also be used to convert a date or numeric object into a string (character type) object.

Character functions are mainly used to manipulate string objects.

For example, we might want to combine two string objects into one, such as a customer's first and last name, return just part of the string, and so on.

The main character functions are as follows:

- ▶ `Left`: This returns the leftmost character in a string
- ▶ `Right`: This returns the rightmost character
- ▶ `Concatenation`: This combines two character strings
- ▶ `Match`: This searches for a specific character or a combination of characters inside a string
- ▶ `Replace`: This replaces a character or set of characters inside a string

How to do it...

Perform the following steps:

1. We create a couple of useful formulas on a simple customer query list based on the **Data warehouse** universe.
2. The first one creates an index from the customer name; by doing so, we turn the formula into a variable and even use it as a section for better and easier data grouping.
3. We use the `Substr` function; this function gets a part of the string using three parameters: the string, starting point, and how many characters from that point should be displayed.
4. In this example, we create an index from the customer name by returning the first value.

5. The formula syntax will be `=substr([Customer];1;1)`, and the result will be as shown in the following screenshot:

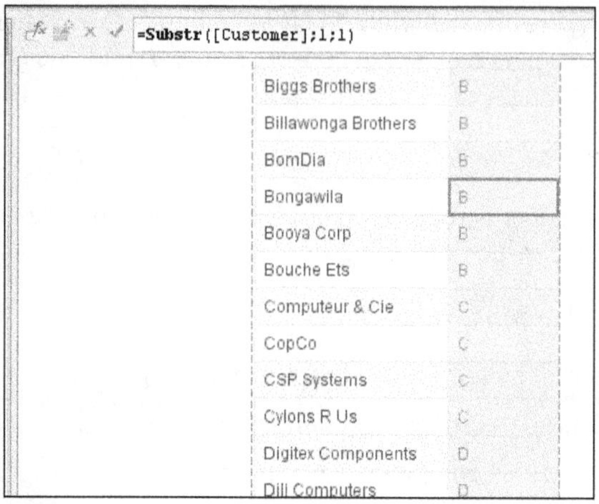

6. Note that the formula uses the number `1` as the starting point, and in the next argument, it uses `1` again as how many characters from that point to display.

7. Another function that we can use is to convert a date into a string in order to combine it with text, such as `Sales Date`. The reason we are using the date in a string is because we can't combine different data types unless we convert one of them to match the other one.

8. Our formula will look like `="Sales Date"+" - " +FormatDate([Date];"MM/dd/yyyy")`. Note that we are using the + sign in order to combine the text and space between the two sides of the formula.

The results will look like the following:

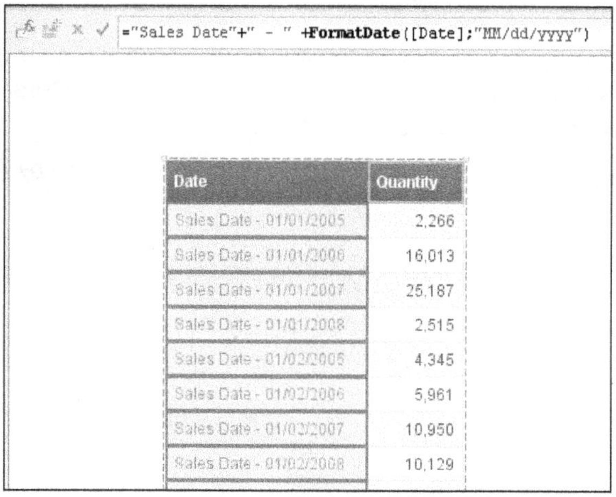

9. The first part of the formula is simple text that is bound in double quotes and combined with the conversion formula using the + sign.

10. The `Formatdate` function gets the **Date** object as the main parameter and the format of the converted date as the second parameter.

> Converting dates into a string in tables isn't recommended as we will lose the sorting capabilities, and in the case we need to calculate new time portions, it is more suitable to use the time conversions in standing free cells.
>
> We can also use the `Concatenation` formula in order to combine the two text objects, for example, `= Concatenation ([First Name];[Last Name)].`

How it works...

As we saw earlier, the character functions can be applied to string objects and can assist us whenever we need data manipulation or data type conversion.

The more complicated the string object is (a remark field, unstructured text, or uncommon formats of dates, strings, and numbers), the more we will require text manipulation.

Using data provider functions

Data provider functions provide us with data that relates to the query, such as the universe name, number of rows retrieved, data provider type, and more.

Data provider functions aren't useful in the report tables or charts as part of the data displayed but rather as **metadata** that relates the report frame and its context.

The main data provider functions are as follows:

- `LastExecutionDate`: This provides the last refresh date of the report (this action is recorded when the document is saved; otherwise, it keeps the last refreshed time of a saved version of the report)

- `NumberOfRows`: This is a function that returns the number of rows returned by a query

- `UniverseName`: This function returns the universe name that the query is based on

- `UserResponse`: This function is one of the most common and useful functions, and it returns the values picked in a prompt.

- `DataProviderType`: This determines whether the data provider is based on universal or personal data

How to do it...

We create the following functions:

► A single cell formula that displays the number of rows returned by the query, the formula will get the square brackets for any of the retrieved objects of the query as a parameter = `NumberOfRows([Country])`

The result will look like the following screenshot:

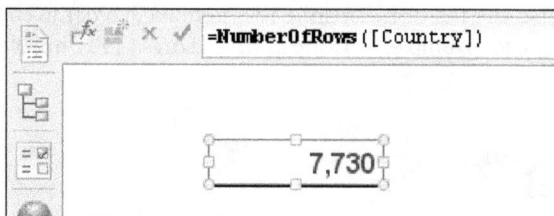

► Another good function is `UniverseName`; it uses any object returned by the = `UniverseName ([Region])` query.

The result will look like the following screenshot:

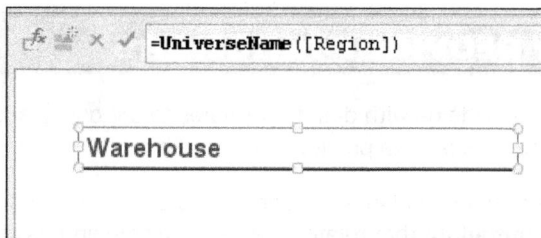

How it works...

The data provider functions help us get better information about our data, query, and its origin. This set of functions simply makes the report more oriented, clear for the business user, and updated.

Using date and time functions

Date and time functions are the most important functions as the main data context of analysis is time.

Date and time functions can convert dates into time portions, calculate time differences between dates, and be the basis for advanced time filtering, such as current week, last month, and other time portions.

The main date and time functions are as follows:

- ▶ `CurrentDate`: This returns the current data value; it is great for calculating time differences.

- ▶ `Daysbetween`: This calculates the number of days between two dates (the order date and arrival date).

- ▶ `Todate`: This converts a string object into a date type object. This option is great for when we have string objects that we need to sort chronologically or use in other date calculations.

- ▶ `Relativedate`: This function is very useful for when we are required to add or subtract days from a date; for example, we might be required to check which free offers that were issued to the customers have exceeded their 30-day validity.

- ▶ `Year`, `Quarter`, `Month`, `Week`, and `dayname`: These are used to create a specific time portion from a date object.

How to do it...

Let's examine the several date and time functions.

Let's check how many days are between the order date and the delivery date; this calculation will help us better analyze our efficiency and measure orders that have exceeded X number of days.

The formula gets two parameters: the start date and the end date.

We create the `=DaysBetween([Order Date];[Delivery Date])` formula in a new column.

The result will look as follows:

Order Id	Order Date	Required Date	Delivery Date	Days Gap
1,536	9/22/05	10/5/05	12/15/05	84
255	2/14/05	2/27/05	3/31/05	45
5,725	10/15/07	10/28/07	10/31/07	16
5,523	8/29/07	9/11/07	9/11/07	13
254	2/16/05	3/1/05	2/28/05	12

In the **Days Gap** column, we are able to see the number of days that have passed between the start and end dates.

Note that the **Days Gap** object doesn't calculate weekends or holidays, which can be considered nonworking days.

In order to subtract the number of weekends, we create a formula that will calculate the number of weekends in the period between these dates:

```
=Truncate((DayNumberOfWeek([Order Date])+[Days Gap]) /7 ;0
```

This formula converts the order date to the day number in the week and then adds to it the number of days passed between the order date and delivery date; so for example, if Sunday is the first day of the week, it will be 1 + the number of days passed.

We divide the result by 7, which is the number of days present in a week.

Then, if we multiply the result by 2, which is the number of days in a weekend, (as known so far...), we will get the number of nonworking days.

The formula will look like = (Truncate((DayNumberOfWeek([Order Date])+[Days Gap]) /7 ;0))*2.

The result will look as follows:

```
fx ✕ ✓  =[Days Gap]-(Truncate((DayNumberOfWeek([Order Date])+[Days Gap]) /7 ;0))*2
```

Report 5

Order Id	Order Date	Required Date	Delivery Date	Days Gap		Number of Days passed without weekends
1,536	9/22/05	10/5/05	12/15/05	84	24	60
255	2/14/05	2/27/05	3/31/05	45	12	33
5,725	10/15/07	10/28/07	10/31/07	16	4	12
5,523	8/29/07	9/11/07	9/11/07	13	4	9

Calculating the nonworking days can be crucial as fees and customer compensation can be determined by this calculation.

Another useful function that can help us transform this detailed table into a summarized one is converting the order date into a year format so that we can analyze the number of orders in a yearly view.

The formula for this function is =Year([Order Date]).

The result will look as follows:

How it works...

The date functions can convert dates into different time portions; basically, we can construct all the common time portions from a single date. As we saw earlier, we can also perform time calculations that will result in a difference of days.

The time calculations can also be very helpful when we need to calculate the seniority or time difference in minutes.

Using document functions

Document functions provide us with useful information regarding the report (and not with the query as in the data provider functions).

If we need to display who created the report, when the report was created, what the query structure is, or the report tabs that we have filters on, then document functions are the right function category to use.

Just as we saw in the data provider functions, we won't apply the document functions to the report data, but rather display it or use it for informative tasks, which will make our report friendlier and easy to understand.

The main document functions are as follows:

- ▶ `DocumentAuthor`: This provides the name of the report creator
- ▶ `DocumentCreationDate`: This provides the date when the report was created
- ▶ `DocumentName`: This provides the name of the document
- ▶ `QuerySummary`: This returns the query structure (results objects and conditions) and query statistics
- ▶ `DocumentPartiallyRefreshed`: This states whether the report returned partial results; this function corresponds to a report that exceeded the universal parameter limits of time and number of rows that can be fetched or a report that was partially refreshed by the user

> Some of the document functions such as the report author and creation date can also be accessed through the **Document Summary** panel under the **General** section.

How to do it...

Perform the following steps:

1. We create several document functions; the first function is the `PromptSummary` function that will enable us to display the values that were filled in the query prompts in a single cell.

2. The formula syntax is the function name (`=PromptSummary`).

   The result will be displayed in a cell, as follows:

   ```
   *** Query Name:Query 1 ***

   Enter values for Country: USA; Canada; UK; Spain; Brasil
   Enter values for Year: 2,007; 2,008; 2,009; 2,010; 2,011
   ```

   In the cell, we can see the prompt answer in each separate row about which values were picked by the business user.

> The prompt function displays the values that were picked in the prompt but not the ones that were actually retrieved by the query.

3. Another very useful formula is `ReportFilterSummary`. This function displays the entire report filter status in a single cell, which means that we are able to identify the report tab and table or any other component that a filter has been applied on.

4. This option is very useful since the report can be changed over and over during its "life cycle" and move through different users and changes. Having the entire filter data displayed can be very helpful to understand the report data.

5. The formula syntax will be = `ReportFilterSummary`. The result will look as follows:

```
*** Filter on Report Time Slice analysis ***

        Filter on Block Block 1:
            Year In List { 2007 }

*** Filter on Report Variables ***

No Filter on Variables

*** Filter on Report Time calculations ***

Filter on Block Block 1:
    Days Gap Is Not Null

*** Filter on Report Report 6 ***

No Filter on Report 6
```

6. The cell can be displayed in the report as an informative cell above the table or better suited in a separate report tab as it's information regarding the report and not the report's data.

How it works...

The document functions can return the report metadata and add relevancy and important information regarding the query, report state, and basic data such as report name to the report.

The functions can be used as a cell, report title, and function in a report selection criteria and an explanation tab.

There's more...

Some of the document functions can be accessed through the **Report Element** toolbar and inserted directly as single cells in the **Report** area, as shown in the following screenshot:

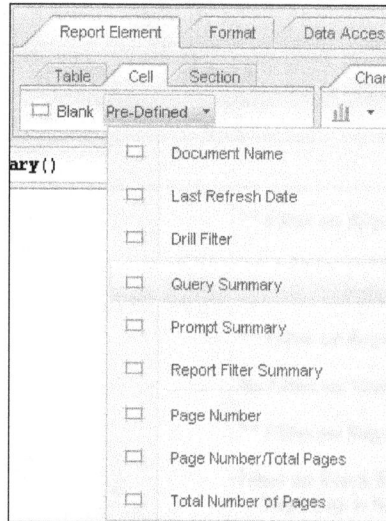

Using logical functions

Logical functions return a true or false answer that can be used in IF statements.

Logical functions return Boolean values such as 1/0, which is equal to true/false.

These functions are usually used to return a value that will be used inside a variable for filtering purposes or as indicators that we can use for sorting or display purposes.

For example, we can check whether the sales net gross measure contains a value or not and create a filter according to the result that the function will return.

The main logical functions are as follows:

- ▸ IsDate: This returns a Boolean value if the value is a date
- ▸ IsNumber: This returns a Boolean value if the value is a number
- ▸ Isnull: This returns a Boolean value if the value is null (this function works with all types of data: numeric, string, and date)
- ▸ IsString: This returns a Boolean value if the value is a string

How to do it...

Perform the following steps:

1. We have a table with two measures, but don't have a value in each row. We want to identify these rows that contain a value in each measure object column.

2. We use the formula =IsNumber([Future guests])And IsNumber([Number of guests]).

   Note that we used the AND operator since we need to validate the two measure objects.

3. The result, after we have added a sort to the formula column, will look as follows:

Service	Number of guests	Future guests	
Bungalow	452	12	1
Hotel Room	451	43	1
Activities		5	0
Excursion		3	0
Fast Food		2	0
Hotel Suite	648		0
Poolside Bar		1	0
Restaurant		28	0
Sports		8	0

4. The formula can be transformed into a variable that we can later use to filter the table according to the 1/0 values.

5. We might as well create a sum calculation on the new formula column and get how many rows had values in both of the measure objects.

How it works...

The logical functions create indicators that can be used to filter and flag specific rows. These functions are sort of simplified "if and then" logic as they require minimum syntax.

Using misc functions

Misc functions are a group of functions that can be applied for various tasks.

The most common function in this category is the `IF` logical operator, which we will demonstrate in this recipe, and there are other functions that can provide us additional and useful information about the report, such as report name and number of pages.

Some other functions we already discussed and demonstrated are `LineNumber` in the *Using formulas* recipe of this chapter and the `forcemerge` function in *Chapter 8, Merging Data*.

The main misc functions are as follows:

- ▶ `IfThenElse`: This is an operator we can use to create a Boolean statement
- ▶ `Forcemerge`: This adds the missing dimensions into the calculation context when we are synchronizing data providers
- ▶ `LineNumber`: This returns the number of the row in a table
- ▶ `Nameof`: This provides the name of the objects, usually displayed in the column header
- ▶ `NoFilter`: This ignores the filter applied to a table and displays the calculated value without the filter applied to it
- ▶ `NumberOfPages`: This returns the number of pages in the report
- ▶ `Previous`: This displays the previous value; it is useful when we need to calculate the increase or decrease percentages

How to do it...

Perform the following steps:

1. We create a formula that will help us analyze the day gap in our order date table using an `IF` statement.

2. Our formula will check which rows the day gap exceeded 20 days delay, and if so, it will return the text message **Above 20 days**. If the result was equal or less than 20 days, then the formula will return **Ok**.

3. Our formula syntax will be =`If([Days Gap]>20;"Above 20 Days";"Ok")`.

4. In a simple if and then statement, we don't need to use the "then, else" syntax, but rather, we use the simple "then" syntax of the semi period.

   The result in the report will appear as follows:

5. If we require a nested `IF` statement, for example, if we need to create ranges of 1-5 days, 6-10 days, and so on, we use the following syntax:

```
=If [Days Gap] Between (0;5) Then "0-5"
ElseIf
[Days Gap] Between (1;6) Then "1-6"
ElseIf
[Days Gap] Between (1;6) Then "7-20"
Else "More than 20 days "
```

6. Another great formula is the `Previous` function; this formula is used to return the previous value, which is the basis for calculating the increase or decrease of a measure over time.

7. In the following example, we calculate the increase/decease of **Gross Sales**.

The formula syntax will be `=[Gross Sales]/Previous([Gross Sales]) -1`.

The result will be the following:

8. The formula's first part is the current quarter's gross sales divided by the previous value.

    We subtract 1 from the formula because the first row has no previous value, and if we don't subtract, then the second row will be calculated as an increase compared to a null row.

> The first row's **-100%** value can be eliminated using if and then logic, such as `=If [Year]=Previous([Year]) Then [Gross Sales]/ Previous([Gross Sales]) -1`.

9. Another calculation issue that the misc functions can solve for us is that when we have a filter applied on a table that contains percentage calculations, the percentages will be affected from the filters.

10. In order to display the values, while keeping their initial state, we wrap the `NoFilter` function around the percentage calculation.

11. For example, we have a table that displays the **Quantity** per **Country**; we need to filter the country, but present the percentages of the quantity regardless of the filtering.

    The formula syntax will be `=NoFilter(Percentage([Quantity]))`.

12. In the following table, we can see the difference between the filtered measure columns and the measures that have been applied the `NoFilter` function:

`=NoFilter(Percentage([Quantity]))`

Filtered countries :Brasil;Canada;Spain

Country	Quantity	Filterd	With Nofilter Function
Brasil	849,855	25.51%	16.08%
Canada	1,620,934	48.66%	30.66%
Spain	860,113	25.82%	16.27%
	Percentage:	100.00%	

How it works...

The misc functions provide us with additional calculation capabilities; more information about the report; and advanced functions, such as `forcemerge`.

Using these functions requires a bit more technical skill, but as we saw in this recipe and in other chapters, these functions can come in handy in solving complex report issues.

Using numeric functions

Numeric functions can be used to perform mathematical calculations and common calculations such as rounding and ranking.

The main numeric functions are as follows:

- `Abs`: This returns the absolute value of the number (this is useful if we have negative values that we need to display as positive)
- `Ceil`: This rounds up a number
- `Floor`: This rounds down a number
- `Mod`: This returns the remainder from a division calculation
- `Round`: This rounds a number according to the level of rounding
- `Tonumber`: This converts a string into a number
- `Truncate`: This truncates a number according to the number of digits we require to truncate
- `Rank`: This ranks a measure by dimension

How to do it...

Perform the following steps:

1. We create a rank function that will display each year's ranking based on the **Net Sales** measure.

   The rank formula will use two parameters: the measure that we require to rank and the dimension that we want to base our ranking on.

   The formula syntax is `=Rank([Gross Sales];[Year])`.

   The table will be displayed as follows:

	=**Rank**([Gross Sales];[Year])	

Year	Net Sales	
2004	749,192	5
2005	291,246,429	4
2006	542,545,103	1
2007	388,671,205	3
2008	514,937,891	2

2. Now, we may also add a sort by the formula column and present the results in a more convenient way.

3. The rank function can also be fitted to cases when we require ranking that will state the higher the result is the lower the ranking would be.

4. This scenario is good for cases such as errors, rejections, malfunctions, and other measures where the higher they are, the negative effect on the business is higher as well.

5. We can adjust any rank formula by adding the top/bottom operator.

6. In this example, we have the **Customer** and **Number of Calls** options, where the more phone calls the customer has the lower the ranking should be as it reflects an unefficient customer care: =rank([Number Of Calls];[Customer];Bottom).

7. The bottom operator can be found in the operator list in the **Formula** window.

How it works...

The numeric functions provide various mathematical calculations that can be applied mostly on measure objects and numeric type objects. Although this category has a wide number of functions, practically, we will use just a few of them, as mentioned earlier in the main functions area, depending on the type of data and user requirements, of course.

Using extended syntax

Besides the regular calculations that we can apply and display in tables, we can use a different kind of calculation that uses contexts to perform the calculation.

The calculation engine of Web Intelligence treats measures in two main ways:

▶ It projects the measure value in the row level. This is what we will normally do with the measures in the report, drag them with dimensions and get their results per the dimension/s values (dynamic aggregative qualification)

▶ It creates a calculation that will display the total, average, min, or max in the table footer as a single cell (a "fixed" aggregative qualification)

Another way to use measures would be to change their context for the following reasons:

▶ We need to display a measure, the level of calculation of which is different from the data level that is displayed

▶ We need to filter the table according to the subtotals (not a simple row filter)

▶ We need to "fix" a value in order to compare it with the rest of the values, such as average, in order to check which value is greater, less than, or equal to it

There are other purposes as we focus on the common uses of the extended syntax.

How to do it...

Perform the following steps:

1. We need to compare the **Net Sales** column to the average **Net Sales** result in order to analyze the years in which the net sales were above or below the average.

2. We use the extended syntax by adding the **IN** operator to the output context. The formula syntax will be =Average([Net Sales]) In Report.

3. Since every aggregative function is displayed at the row level by default, taking into consideration all the dimensions that are displayed in the table, the IN report additional syntax will calculate the average at the report level, which is the same as saying calculate the average in the entire table level. In the following result table, note the difference between using the extended syntax to just using an aggregative function:

Year	Net Sales	Without Extended syntax	Extended syntax
2004	749,192	749,192	347,629,964
2005	291,246,429	291,246,429	347,629,964
2006	542,545,103	542,545,103	347,629,964
2007	388,671,205	388,671,205	347,629,964
2008	514,937,891	514,937,891	347,629,964
Average:	347,629,964		

4. If we need to explain what the difference between the extended syntax is to regular syntax in a nutshell, then it is a fixed value versus a dynamic value.

5. Now, we will be able to perform the comparison between net sales and average sales.

6. The additional syntax that we added to the formula was added in the output context. This is the context that defines where the aggregative function will be calculated (report, block, body, or section).

7. We use the output context when the level of data in the table is more detailed for the measure that we want to calculate.

> We use the output context when the level of data in the table is more detailed for the measure we want to calculate, or to say it in a more simple way, we use the output context when we want to exclude objects from the calculation result although they appear in the table.

8. We explore another example; this time, we come across a table that displays the region and quantity. We need to calculate the minimum quantity per region according to the country values.

9. We create two tables; the left one is the more detailed one that displays the **Region**, **Country**, and **Quantity**. On the left-hand side, we display a more aggregative table that displays the quantity per region.

10. We use the left-hand table for QA purposes so we can make sure we are calculating the minimum quantity per region correctly. Refer to the following screenshot:

Region	Country	Quantity
Asia PAC	Japan	3,024,789
	Singapore	689,907
	Thailand	850,857
Asia PAC	**Min:**	**689,907**

Region	Quantity
Asia PAC	4,565,553
EEMEA	1,639,830
Europe	7,983,897
Latin America	2,635,786
North America	6,291,753

Region	Country	Quantity
EEMEA	Eastern Europe	1,196,729
	Emirates	443,101
EEMEA	**Min:**	**443,101**

11. We formulate the following calculation that will enable us to display the minimum quantity per country based on the country level as well (=Min([Quantity] In ([Region];[Country]))).

This part of the formula is the input context; the input context determines which objects will affect the calculation.

The formula takes in its context the dimensions that are needed to affect the minimum calculation. We are simply saying to calculate the minimum quantity for the region and country level of aggregation.

> We use the input context when the level of data in the table is more aggregative for the measure we want to calculate, or to say it in an even more simple way, we use the input context when we want to include objects in the calculation although they aren't displayed in the table.

12. In the new, calculated column, we are able to see that the results are correct by comparing them to the detailed table on the left-hand side, as shown in the following screenshot:

Region	Country	Quantity
Asia PAC	Japan	3,024,789
	Singapore	689,907
	Thailand	850,857
Asia PAC	**Min:**	**689,907**

Region	Quantity	
Asia PAC	4,565,553	689,907
EEMEA	1,639,830	443,101
Europe	7,983,897	1,008,078
Latin America	2,635,786	401,100
North America	6,291,753	2,772,752

Region	Country	Quantity
EEMEA	Eastern Europe	1,196,729
	Emirates	443,101
EEMEA	**Min:**	**443,101**

Note that this time, we used a different syntax, adding the additional dimension objects that the minimum was calculated by into the same bracket.

How it works...

The extended syntax can enable us to change the default aggregation behavior and address two main issues:

▶ A detailed aggregative result being displayed although the table data level is more aggregative

▶ An aggregative result being displayed although the table data level is more detailed

There's more...

Another last useful operator is the **Where** operator, which can be found in the list of operators in the **Formula Editor**. This operator is used mostly to restrict a measure result in case a specific dimension or attribute value is matched.

This operator is limited to one value restricting the measure, but on the other hand, we don't need to display the dimension or attribute object in the table.

For example, we have a country per number of customers table which we require to calculate in the table footer how many customers were there in the year 2008.

The syntax is quite simple; first, we place the measure in the formula, and right after it, we place the `Where` operator that will condition the year with the 2008 value (`=Number Of Customers Where ([Year=2008])`).

The result will appear at the table footer as shown in the following screenshot:

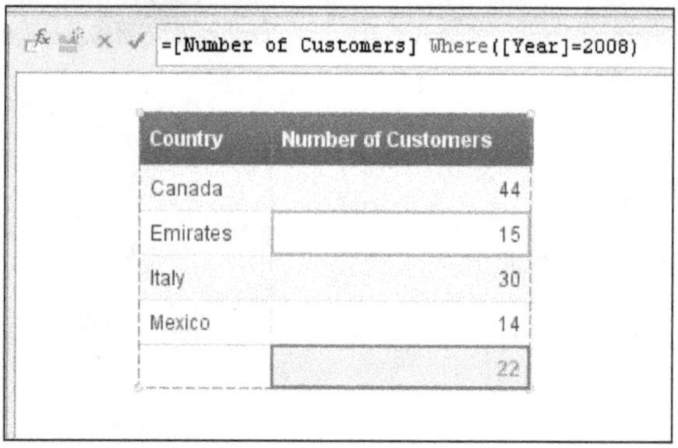

Notice that although the **Year** object isn't part of the table, it is used as a condition restricting the measure results and that is the main reason why to use a `Where` operator. Usually, the dimension or attribute we are using in the `Where` operator won't appear in the table.

10
Using Hyperlinks

This chapter contains the following recipes:

- ▶ Connecting reports
- ▶ Passing parameters between reports
- ▶ Linking to a web page
- ▶ Creating and editing hyperlinks manually

Introduction

The hyperlink is a feature that enables us to connect between reports or to create links to external sources, such as websites or even CRM and ERP web applications.

The main usability of hyperlinks is connecting between reports.

Connecting between reports has several advantages:

- ▶ We can navigate between reports that have different granularity levels (summarized and detail).
- ▶ We can navigate between reports based on different universes.
- ▶ We can pass specific values from the master report to the *drilled* report, so we can analyze a wider range of data just when we require.
- ▶ We can reuse existing reports in the repository and connect to them from our reports.
- ▶ We can create reports that will use conditional formatting and highlight, for example, specific products whose sales are below the target and use the hyperlink in order to further investigate why those products had low volume of sales. For example, we can switch to a detailed report that will display when and by whom the products were bought and explore the differences in the detailed level of data.

- ▶ We can create a URL link that the user can use in order to directly access a specific report in the repository without the need to navigate to a specific folder.

- ▶ Hyperlinks can be placed in an external portal or simply used from the user favorites in his or her web browser.

- ▶ The reports can also be integrated this way in **SAP Enterprise Portal**.

Hyperlinks can also be used to connect to the following SAP BI applications:

- ▶ Crystal Reports

- ▶ Interactive Analysis documents

- ▶ Advanced Analysis workspaces

- ▶ BI launch pad workspaces

- ▶ Dashboard Design objects

In this chapter, we will discuss how to implement hyperlinks while using best practices.

Connecting reports

We can create links between reports by using the **Add Document Link** feature.

A hyperlink is basically a URL that can pass a value or values between reports or simply build a connection between them as any other link would do.

This option is also known as **OpenDocument**, which also allows us to connect between SAP BusinessObjects BI applications or to program the link.

Before we start, the **Add Document Link** option is available only when the view mode is set to web panel mode by changing the preferences of Web Intelligence and must be set prior to it.

Getting ready

We need to create a hyperlink from our master report to another report.

Our master report is build on the **eFashion** demo universe that contains sales and quantity figures of various products. In our current table, we are displaying the **Year**, **Month**, **Sales Revenue** and **Quantity Sold** objects.

We will create the link in the report title, above the displayed data, so we can use it as a "trigger button" to switch to another report.

How to do it...

Perform the following steps:

1. We will create a simple cell by using the **Report Element** toolbar and choose **Cell** from the **Blank** cell option subtab, as shown in the following screenshot, and type `Click here in for switching to the visualization report`:

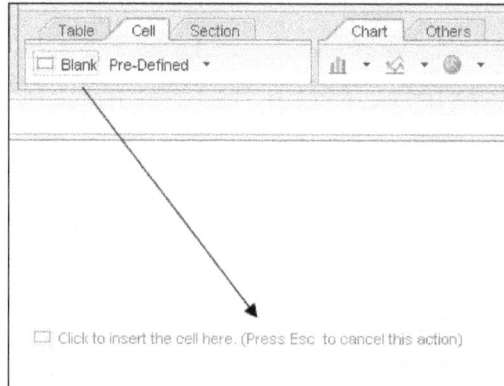

2. Now, we will right-click on the text cell, choose the **Linking** option from the speed menu, and then select **Add Document Link**:

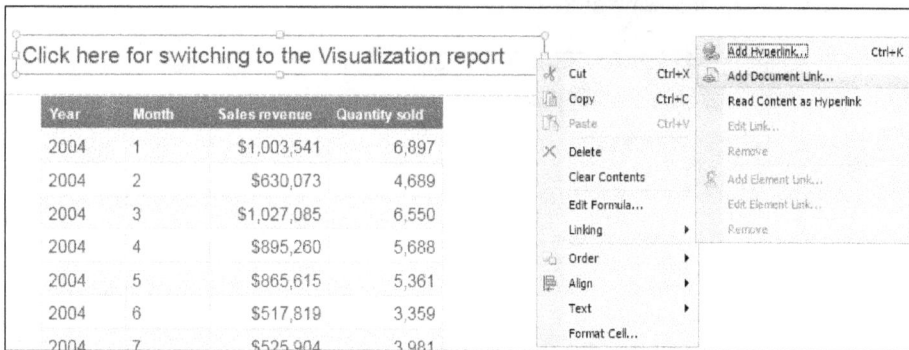

3. After choosing this option, the **Create Hyperlink** window will appear. By using the **Browse** button we will navigate to the folder in which the report is located and choose the report, as shown in the following screenshot:

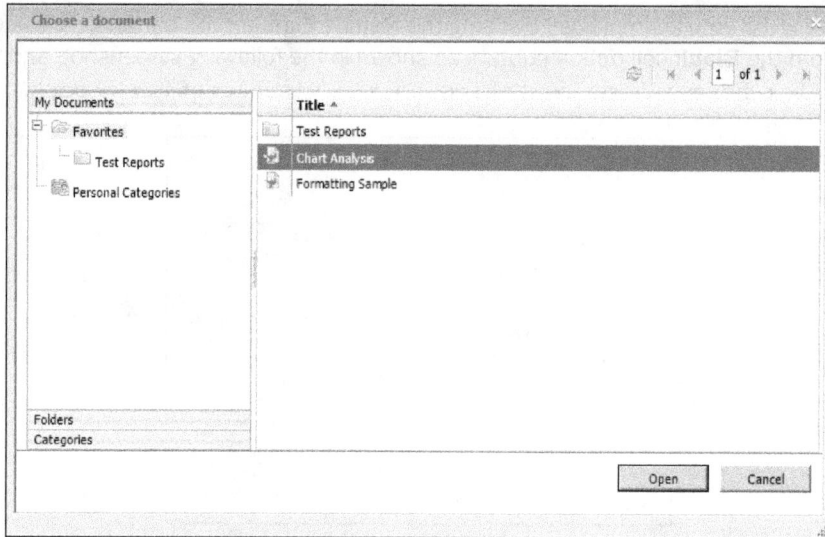

4. We will click on the **Open** button and switch to the **Link to document** properties window. In this window, we will be able to define and set the hyperlink definitions, as shown in the following screenshot:

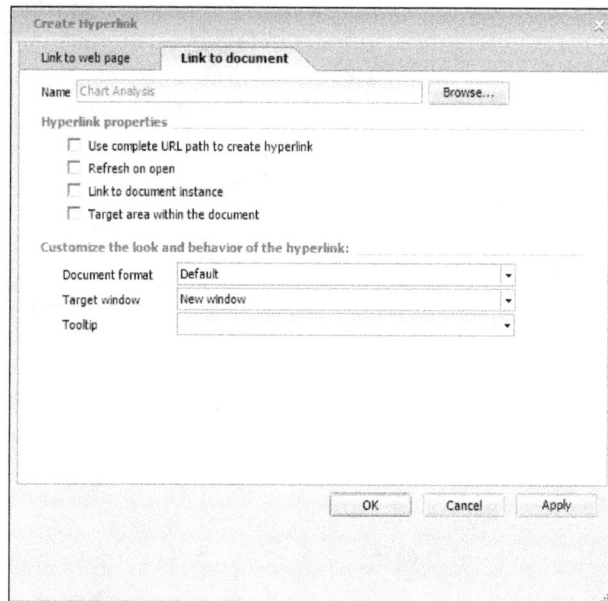

5. After clicking on **OK** the title cell will turn into a hyperlink, and by clicking on it, we will be able to open the **Chart Analysis** report. Notice that in the formula bar, we can see the URL code created although the title cell displays text, as shown in the following screenshot:

6. Now, by clicking on the title link cell, our report will be open in another web browser tab (this option can be adjusted in the **Create Hyperlink** editor):

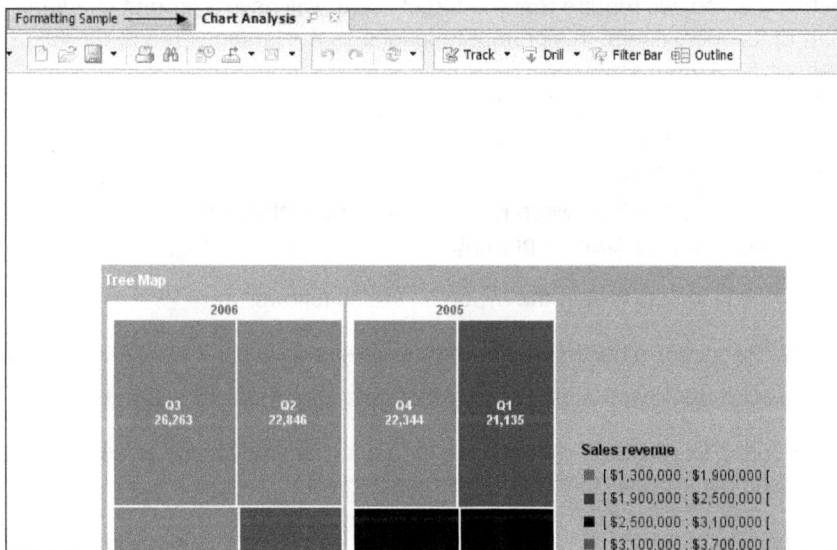

How it works...

The **Document Link** feature is a URL code generator that can access the report in its repository location and can turn a simple cell or a value in a column into a URL link that can connect reports or to the other SAP BI applications hosted in SAP BI4.

By using a parameter manger (the created hyperlink) we can set our destination, its way of opening, and the type of format we need it to open in.

See also

▸ In order to learn which parameters and options are available in the **Create Hyperlink** window, refer to the *Passing parameters between reports* recipe

Passing parameters between reports

The hyperlink's core functionality and main use is to pass parameters between reports as we have already seen in the previous recipe. This capability allows us to pass a specific value to another report no matter whether the reports are based on the same universe or not (as long as we have common objects, we can connect them directly).

In order to pass parameters, we need to know the following two prerequirements:

▸ We require a common value that the **master report** can pass to the **target report**, which is the same as in merged data providers. The value needs to be in the same type (for example, numeric to numeric object)

▸ In this method, we require that the target report will have a prompt condition as part of its query filters; this prompt functions as the landing area of the value being passed from the master report.

Getting ready

We need to create a hyperlink between the revenue-per-country report to the orders-per-country report, which uses a country prompt.

The reasons why you should create the hyperlink are as follows:

▸ The two reports are based on different universes

▸ Each report deals with a different level of data (summarized and detailed)

So, by implementing this feature, we will be able to not only analyze the sales data, but also switch and extend the analysis to the order details data.

How to do it...

As we discussed in the previous recipe, we will repeat the same steps of creating the hyperlink, the only difference will be that this time, we will mark the **Country** column and turn its values into dynamic hyperlink passable parameters using the **Add Document Link** feature, as shown in the following screenshot:

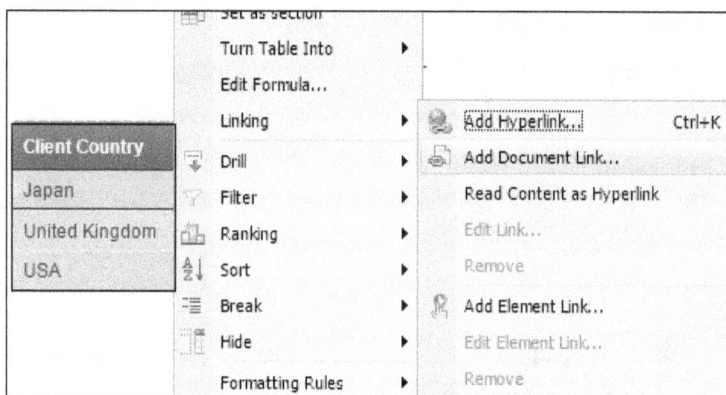

We will choose the orders-per-country report from its location and explore the **Create Hyperlink** options. Initially, all four links are unchecked.

- **Use complete URL path to create hyperlink**: This option adds the complete server name and port number to the URL and enables us to access the report from external sources and embed the link in any web application

- **Refresh on open**: This option is suited to situations where we link to a report, and we need it to refresh as soon as it opens

- **Link to document instance**: We can connect the report's latest instance; this option is great if we need to connect our report to an already scheduled report and not the main report

- **Target area within the document**: This is possible by choosing the option to connect to a specific report tab instead of the entire report

After setting these options, we can define which prompt we will use in order to pass our values. Usually, if we need to pass several different column values, then we need to build appropriate prompts in the report we need to link to. In our example, we are using one **Country** prompt so that we can see the prompt option under the **Document prompts**.

If we have several prompts, we can choose to use all of them or just part of them, depending on which values we need them to pass.

Have a look at the following list of features:

- **Document format**: Using this, we can set the format of the linked report to default (Web Intelligence), HTML, PDF, MS Excel, and MS Word

- **Target window**: Using this, the linked report can be opened in the current window or in a new window

- **Tooltip**: Using this, we can add guiding text that will pop up near the cursor when the mouse is pointed at it and will give us extra direction

The **Link to document** window is shown in the following screenshot:

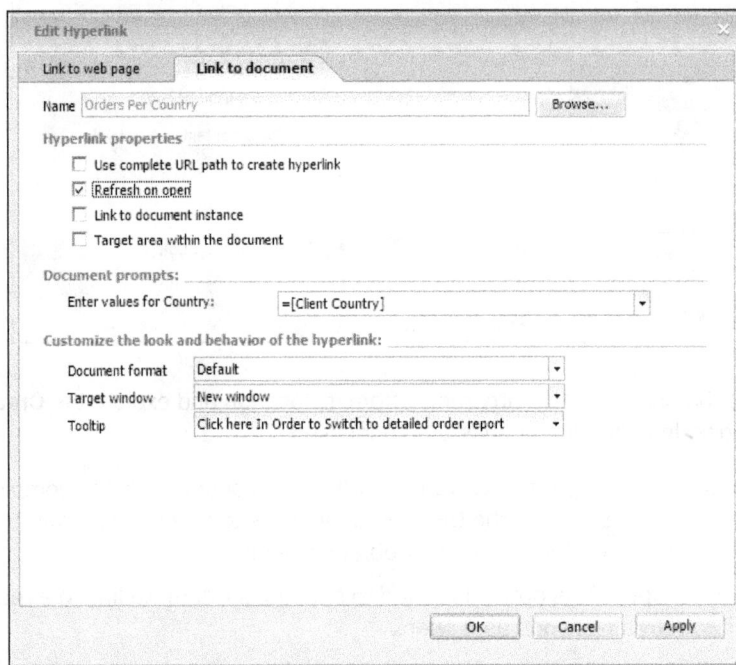

After adjusting the **Hyperlink** option, we will click on **OK**, and move back to the report; the country values will now be seen as links, as shown in the following screenshot:

After clicking on the country value **Japan**, it will be passed into the orders-per-country report and display only Japan's data, as shown in the following screenshot:

Report 1

Country	Order Id	Order Date	Required Date	Shipped Date	Number of Orders
Japan	17	1/18/05	1/31/05	1/18/05	1
Japan	18	1/13/05	1/26/05	1/13/05	1
Japan	19	1/16/05	1/29/05	1/16/05	1
Japan	44	1/15/05	1/28/05	1/15/05	1
Japan	45	1/19/05	2/1/05	1/19/05	1
Japan	70	12/31/04	1/13/05	12/31/04	1
Japan	71	1/6/05	1/19/05	1/6/05	1

How it works...

The hyperlink can be created using the **Add Document Link** wizard, which is a URL builder that can access reports in the SAP BusinessObjects repository. Once we set the appropriate options, we will be able to access reports, embed the links in other web applications, or connect reports directly by passing parameters between them.

Linking to a web page

We can also use the **Add Document Link** option to connect to web pages, web portals, and useful external intranet or Internet pages that can extend and complement the report data.

For example, we can connect our report to a CRM web application and pass a value from the report, such as item ID, and search for this item in our organizational web portal or get additional online data originated from a financial site showing the latest trade rates.

> The **Hyperlink** option is available only if the view mode of Web Intelligence in the preferences is set to **Rich Internet Application**.

Getting ready

We will turn the **Country** column objects to a parameter we can pass into a web page search engine specializing in a country's health information.

How to do it...

Perform the following steps:

1. By right-clicking on the **Country** column, we will navigate to the right-click menu, choose **Linking**, and then choose **Add Hyperlink...**, as shown in the following screenshot:

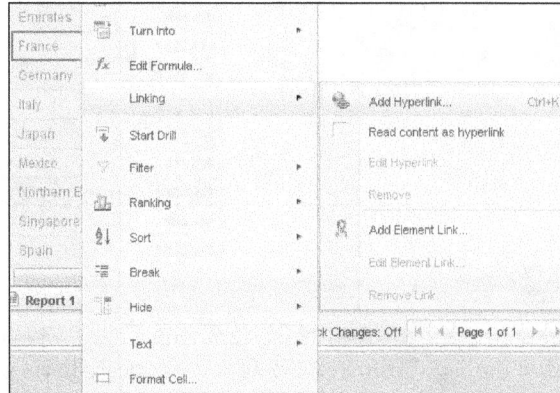

2. After choosing this option, the **Hyperlinks** window will appear. We will copy the web page URL that included the search value and paste it into the **Parse** area. In this URL, we searched for the country France as you can see the value appearing in `http://www.unicef.org/search/search.php?q=France&type=Main`.

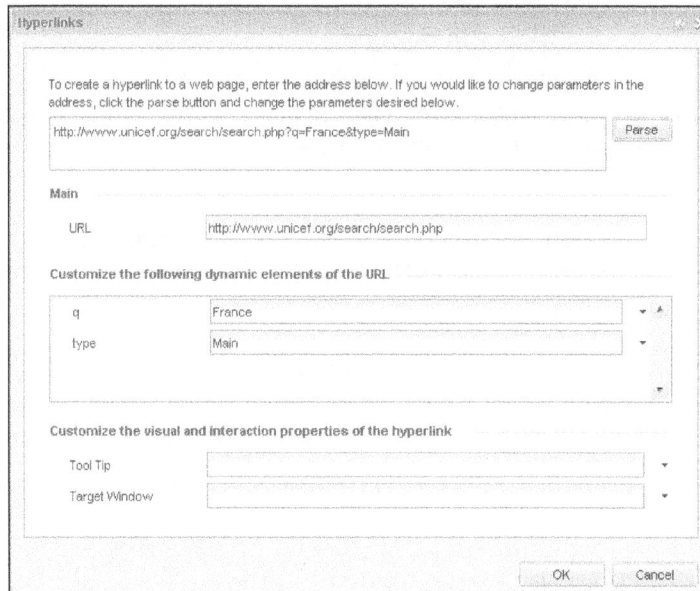

3. As soon as the URL is copied, we will be able to fill in the additional parameters. In the middle of the **Hyperlinks** window, we will edit the **Customize the following dynamic elements of the URL** area.

4. After clicking on the arrow icon, we will be able to choose the **Country** dimension object rather than a static value that was returned by the URL, as shown in the following screenshot:

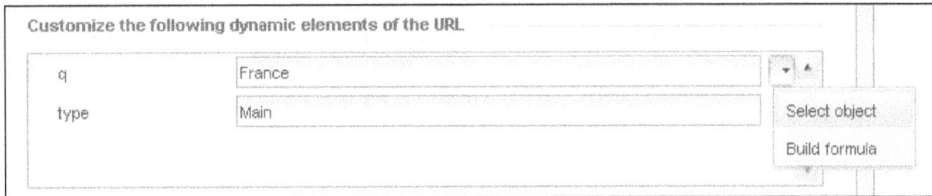

5. After choosing the **Select object** option, we will be able to choose the **Country** dimension, as shown in the following screenshot:

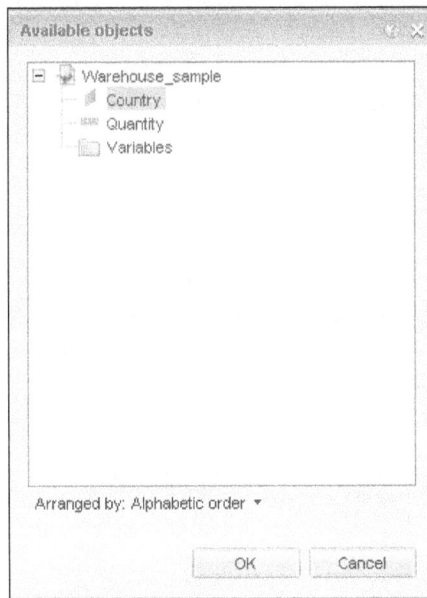

6. Now, it is set as our parameter, so we can pass any of the country values to this web page address. What we are actually doing here is turning the country values list into a dynamic parameter list that will be transferred into the search link by using the custom element **q**, which appears first in the **Customize the following dynamic elements of the URL** area, as shown in the following screenshot:

Customize the following dynamic elements of the URL

q	=[Country]	▼ ▲
type	Main	▼
		▼

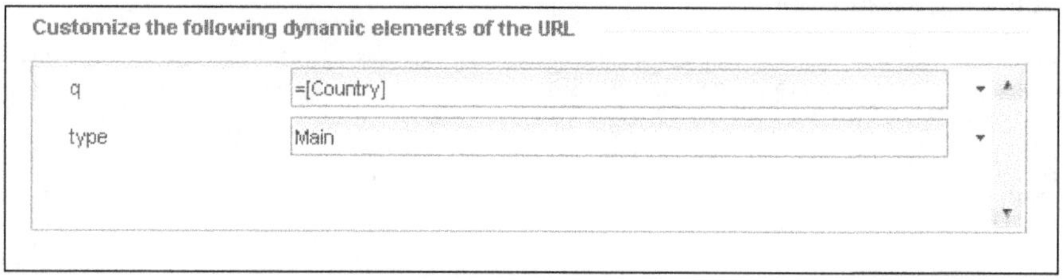

7. We will also adjust the way the hyperlink will open by setting the **Customize the visual and interaction properties of the hyperlink** section and setting the first **Target Window** parameter to **New Window**. So, the hyperlink will be open in a new web browser tab to ensure we can interact with the report and the web page, as shown in the following screenshot:

Customize the visual and interaction properties of the hyperlink

| Tool Tip | | ▼ |
| Target Window | New Window | ▼ |

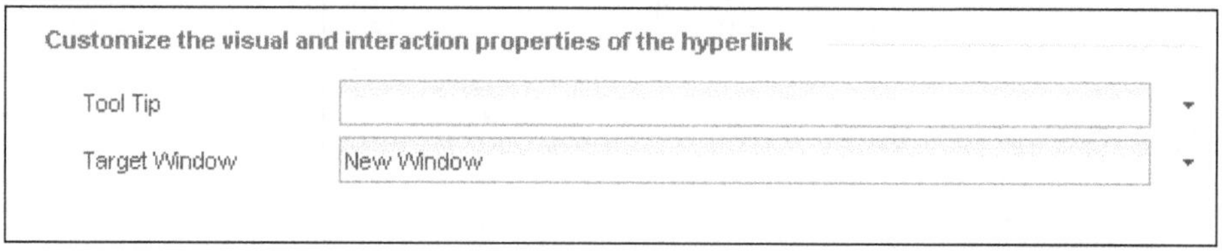

8. Now, our hyperlink is ready, and we will be able to pass any value to the web page search engine. We will pass the **UK** country value, as shown in the following screenshot:

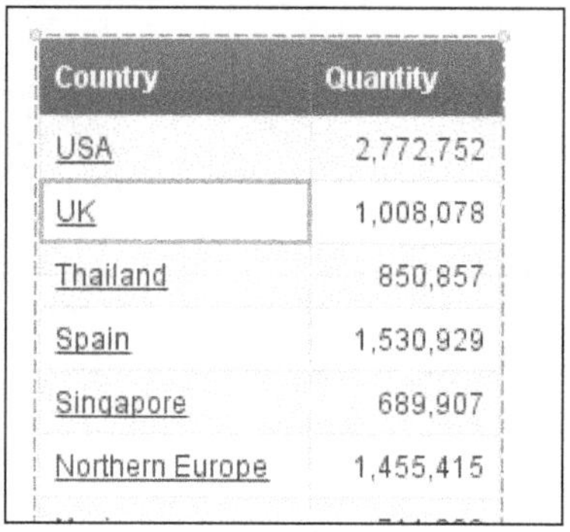

Country	Quantity
USA	2,772,752
UK	1,008,078
Thailand	850,857
Spain	1,530,929
Singapore	689,907
Northern Europe	1,455,415

9. Finally, we get the following result:

How it works...

The hyperlink enables us to connect to web pages by recognizing the URL structure and converting it to an editable-wizard-based feature. We can adjust the URL structure without any URL coding prerequisites.

The hyperlink can be used to pass values from our reports to web pages and by doing so, extend our data collaboration and connectivity.

See also

▶ The hyperlink can also be used in order to connect to other reports in the BI launch pad; for more information refer to the *Creating and editing hyperlinks manually* recipe

Creating and editing hyperlinks manually

Creating links can be also done manually. This type of option requires prior knowledge of OpenDocument programming and contains lots of advanced options that require an understanding of how to use this method.

In this recipe, we will provide basic guidelines on how to use OpenDocument, but in order to master it, further learning and understanding will still be required.

For the full OpenDocument guide you can download the official SAP OpenDocument PDF from `https://help.sap.com/businessobject/product_guides/boexir4/en/xi4_opendocument_en.pdf`.

Getting ready

We will use the **Add Hyperlink** option again in our report and add the appropriate parameters to it in order to connect it to another report.

In order to connect to a specific report, the most basic syntax would be `http://<servername>:<port>/BOE/OpenDocument/opendoc/openDocument.jsp?iDocID=`.

The OpenDocument is a URL in which we can encode a set of parameters that can enable us to use a specific report in the repository in a way just as we have seen when we used the **Hyperlinks** wizard.

One of the most important parameters when creating an OpenDocument is idocID. This parameter enables us to access a specific report in the repository, and it's important as it refers to the unique ID of the report.

How to do it...

Perform the following steps:

1. First, we will get the document ID. Upon right-clicking on the report name and navigating to the properties option, we will be able to get the report ID, as shown in the following screenshot:

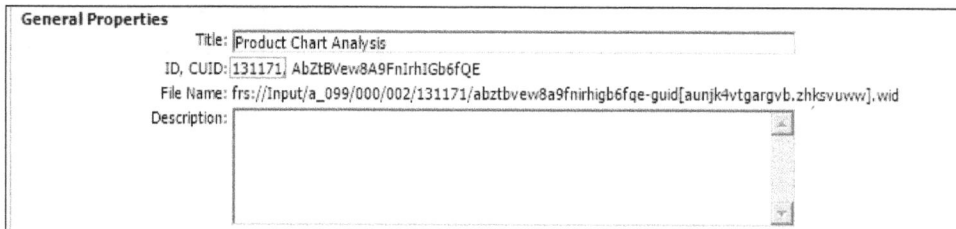

General Properties

Title:	Product Chart Analysis
ID, CUID:	131171 AbZtBVew8A9FnIrhIGb6fQE
File Name:	frs://Input/a_099/000/002/131171/abztbvew8a9fnirhigb6fqe-guid[aunjk4vtgargvb.zhksvuvw].wid
Description:	

2. The document ID is **131171**, and we will be able to use it in our link. We will navigate to the hyperlink menu and paste the `http://thebobaba.blogspot.com:8080/BOE/OpenDocument/opendoc/openDocument.jsp?iDocID=131171` link.

3. After pasting the URL, the **Hyperlinks** wizard will recognize the URL parameters.

4. We will be able to change the DocID here along with adjusting the tooltip and the target window (current or new).

5. We will add two more parameters to our hyperlink that will extend its efficiency:

   - **srefresh**: This is a parameter that determines whether the report will refresh as soon as its opens. This parameter can get the values Y/N (Y = yes for refresh on open and N = no refresh on open).

   - **sOutputFormat**: This indicates in which format the report will be opened. This parameter can get the H (HTML), P (PDF), E (Microsoft Excel (97-2003)— Crystal Reports only) and W (Rich Text Format (RTF)—Crystal Reports only).

6. We will add these two parameters to our URL: `http://thebobaba.blogspot.com:8080/BOE/OpenDocument/opendoc/openDocument.jsp?iDocID=131171&srefresh=Y&sOutputFormat=P`.

7. After pasting this link into the hyperlink we will see that the parameters we added are also edited using the hyperlink editor, as shown in the following screenshot:

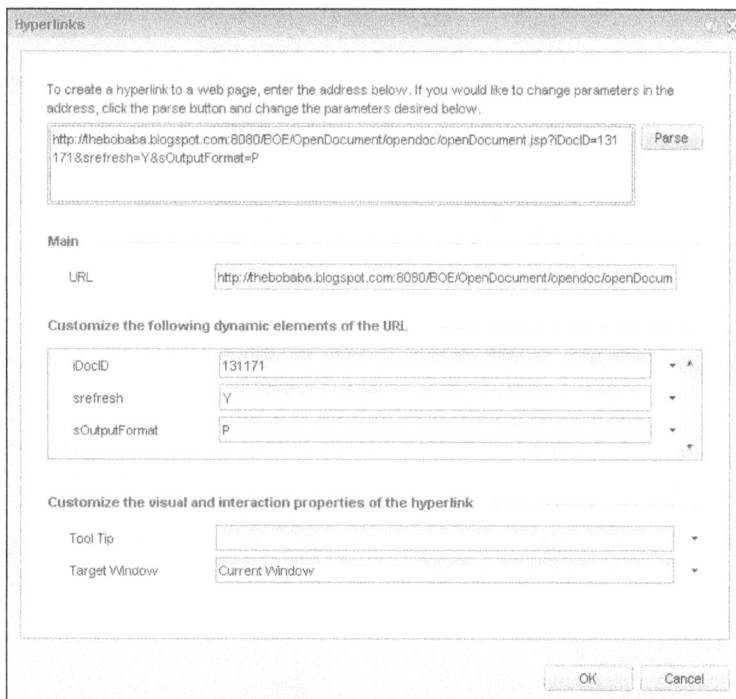

8. By clicking on this link, we will switch to a refreshed version of the report displayed in a PDF format.

9. We will edit our URL, so it will access a specific report tab directly—the **Revenue** tab. This parameter is called **sReportName**. By default, the URL accesses the first tab, so we will change the URL accordingly, but we also have to drop the output format as external formats are not supported with this parameter (`http://thebobaba.blogspot.com:8080/BOE/OpenDocument/opendoc/openDocument.jsp?iDocID=131171&srefresh=Y&sReportName=Revenue`).

10. Upon clicking on the link the **Revenue** tab will be opened directly, as shown in the following screenshot:

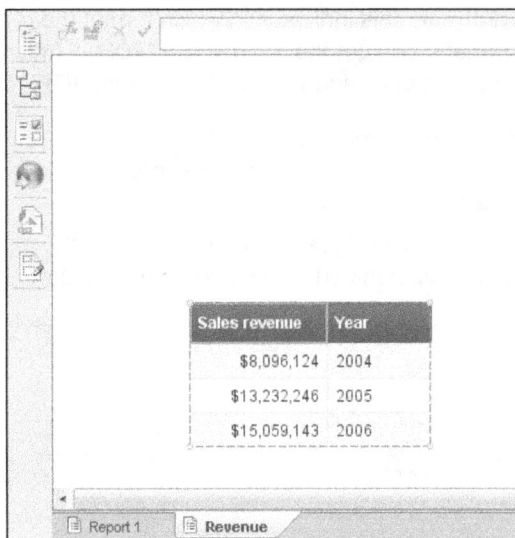

How it works...

The OpenDocument method is a light programming method that enables us to extend the URL options.

As mentioned earlier, there are many more parameters that can be used in OpenDocument, but in order to use them properly, knowledge and understanding of how the OpenDocument feature works is required. On the other hand, we can encode the URL pretty easily, but this method is certainly not a method the common business user will use, and it is more suited for BI developers or experienced Web Intelligence developers.

See also

▶ If you are already familiar with the OpenDocument method in version 3.1, the following SAP document will help you to get a better understanding about the changes added in the new version: SAP BI4 (`http://scn.sap.com/docs/DOC-30154` and `http://scn.sap.com/docs/DOC-30154`)

11
Using Drill

In this chapter, we will cover the following recipes:

- ▸ Using the scope of analysis
- ▸ Using a query drill
- ▸ Using the drill formula

Introduction

What could be the simplest way to define what a drill is?

Drilling is a method that enables us to switch from an aggregative data display to a more detailed level of data, while keeping the data in the same context.

A straightforward answer for what keeps the data in the same context would be: the use of the relevant data hierarchy and determining whether it is a time, geographical, or product hierarchy. The hierarchy can also be costumed, and as long as the business user explores the data in a drill path that makes sense to him or her, it's only a matter of defining it.

For example, a business analyst would like to understand why the sales were higher in a particular year than another year's sales. Is it because a particular product was sold? Or as it because a certain sale campaign was operated successfully?

A team manager analyzes the overall time report and verifies that there were no working hour exceptions, but when he drills to the employee level, he notices that some team members did exceed their working hours. So, how did the hours turn out to be okay overall? This is because some of the team members worked fewer hours than the minimum hour limit.

A drill is carried out to get a "why" answer and not a "how much" answer.

As we saw in the previous chapters, there are several ways to perform an analysis; to use a drill is to use a path of analysis, predecided or on the fly, which could take us down or up the data elevator.

In this chapter, we will demonstrate how to use the drill option in various ways in order to implement it in our reports.

Using the scope of analysis

Our drill paths are based on the universe structure.

Usually, the universe designer defines drill hierarchies that can be used for analysis according to the business user's requirements.

These hierarchies can either be ordered by the object order in the universe folders or by a custom order that can create a structure of objects oriented from different classes in the universe; for example, a costume drill hierarchy can be to switch from the product category to the customer ID. In a more traditional hierarchy, we will explore the items that belong to that product category, such as the category, subcategory, and product name.

We already learned about the basic drill mode and the scope of analysis in *Chapter 2, Creating New Queries*, so we will be adjusting our drill mode into a custom drill mode in order to expand the use of the universe hierarchy structure.

Classical hierarchies are the time, geographical, and organizational structures; they are demonstrated in the following figure:

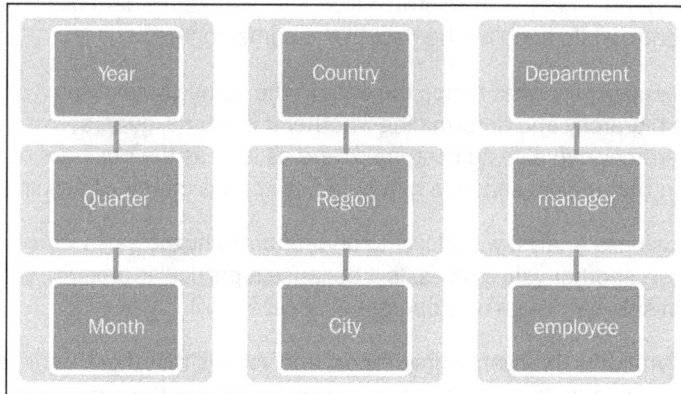

Getting ready

We will add the **Lines** dimension object to the same query based on the **eFashion** demo universe that we used in *Chapter 2, Creating New Queries*, and the scope level will change the drill mode into the custom mode as we are using dimensions with costumed hierarchy levels and not just dimensions that are three levels down, which is an in-built option in the drop-down list of the scope level.

Note that there are three more dimensions in addition to **Year**: **Quarter**, **Month**, and **Week**. Under **State**, we can see the **City** and **Store name** objects, and the **Lines** dimension has no dimension attached to it as we haven't picked it in the result objects but rather dragged it directly to the **Scope of analysis** pane, as shown in the following screenshot:

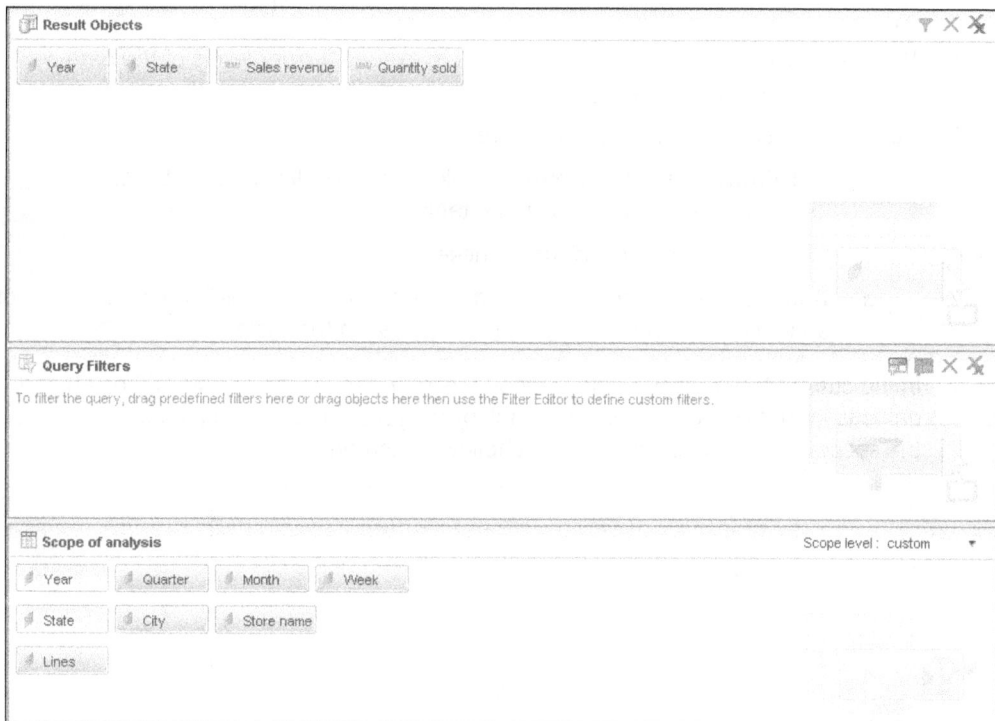

How to do it...

Let's perform the following steps:

1. In order to start drilling, we can either right-click on the result table and choose the **Start Drill** option, or we can navigate to the **Analysis** toolbar under the **Interact** tab and click on the **Drill** icon, as shown in the following screenshot:

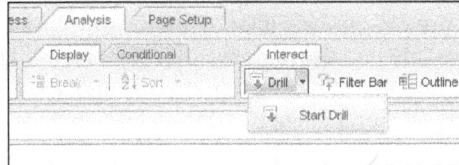

2. After performing this action, we will be able to explore further levels of the data we defined in the **Query Panel**.

3. We can basically drill into three main directions:

   ❏ **Drill down**: This will perform a one-level-down drill according to the dimension object we mark in the table

   ❏ **Drill up to**: This will perform a one-level-up drill

   ❏ **Drill by**: This will use any of the dimension objects we defined in the scope of analysis and that currently aren't displayed in the table

4. In the current table, we will right-click on the **Year** dimension, and we will be able to drill one level down to the quarter or drill by the rest of the dimensions we defined in the scope of analysis, as shown in the following screenshot:

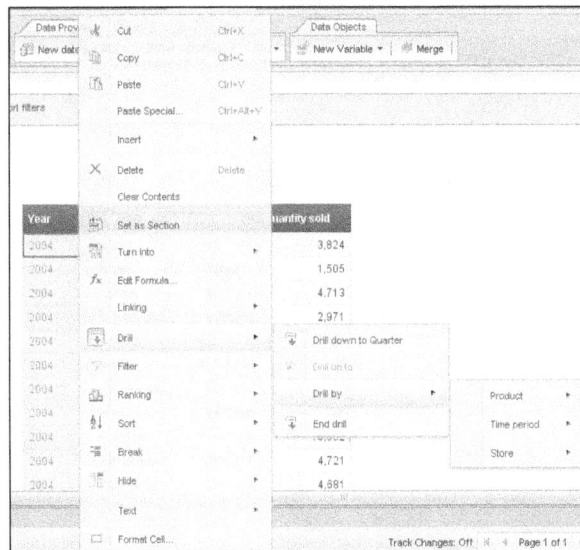

5. By picking the first option of the **Drill down to Quarter** option, we will drill down accordingly, and the **Year** dimension will turn into an interactive filter so we can explore each year's data. Also, we will start drilling each dimension and display a **Drill up** icon in the dimension column header, which will enable us to go back up by one step:

This is basically the entire concept of drill, a way to get to a detailed level of data, further exploring the data while the upper dimension, the year, can still affect the lower level of the data.

6. After performing the first step of the drill, we will be able to go down or climb up in the same dimension hierarchy, depending on our position in the drill ladder. This is the main reason why a hierarchy should be defined in the universe—for better and easier navigation:

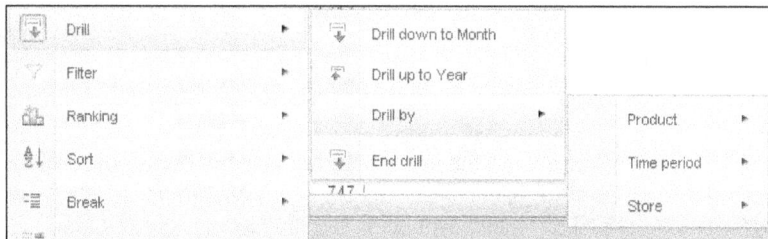

7. Note that when we mark the **Quarter** column, we can drill down further to the **Month** dimension as it is the next dimension in the universe hierarchy or drill back up to **Year** as it's the first dimension in the time hierarchy. We can also take the **Drill by** option, which will display all of the hierarchies (**Product**, **Time period**, and **Store**) and enable us to use the rest of the dimensions.

8. We will continue our drill first by marking the **State** column and choosing the **Drill by** option and then picking **Lines** from the **Product** hierarchy:

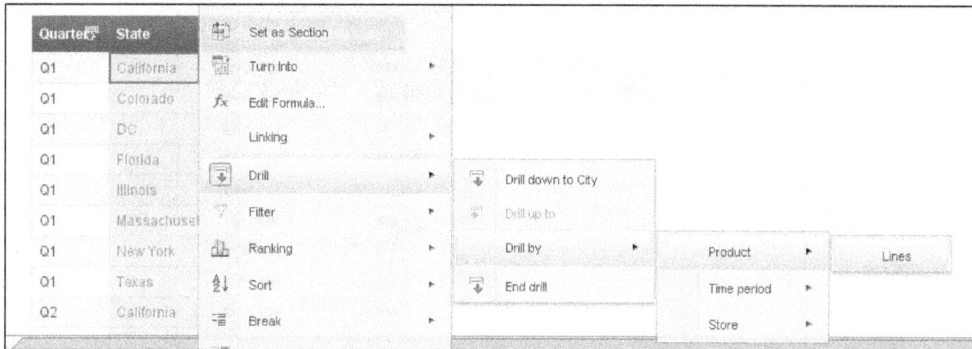

This will result in the **Lines** dimension being placed instead of the **State** column, which will turn into an additional drop-down list filter above the table:

Quarter	Lines	Sales revenue	Quantity sold
Q1	Accessories	$219,766	1,546
Q1	City Skirts	$2,634	15
Q1	City Trousers	$3,006	24
Q1	Dresses	$23,357	197
Q1	Jackets	$13,802	98
Q1	Leather	$3,089	19
Q1	Outerwear	$8,612	85

9. We can also drill by marking a measure column, and the option that will be displayed will be the hierarchy dimensions we used. So in our current state, since we are set on the **Quarter** time level and since **Month** is the next level and the **Lines** dimension has no additional dimension in the report, we will get **Month** as the next suggested drill down option when marking one of the measures:

> A drill can be performed on several tables in the report, and on charts as well. Since the entire report is a drill report, whatever table or chart we drag-and-drop into it will be affected from the **Drill** toolbar dimensions.

Note that when we are defining which dimension objects we require in the scope of analysis, we use a single query and a single refresh action to fetch the data; whatever drill actions we perform afterwards, we execute at the report level.

Now, depending on the data volume and database structure, this scenario could be called the best practice since we won't require an extra refresh of the query. This can be very meaningful when the query takes the same amount of time to retrieve the results.

As always, this will not be the case every time we work with the drill, and in cases where we are required to drill to another dimension in the hierarchy that we haven't defined in the scope of analysis yet, we will be prompted to do so.

In our report, we drill down to the **Category** dimension that we haven't defined in the scope of analysis; therefore, when we hover over the **Lines** dimension, we see the message, **Drill down to Category (new query)**, as shown in the following screenshot.

This drill step will still result in the same way we saw earlier in the **Drill down only** option. It will cost us a refresh of the query (the out of scope dimension requires a new refresh in order to display itself).

So, we usually aim to use the drill in a single retrieve and not refresh the report for every new dimension that we need to explore.

How it works...

The drill enables us to work in a step-by-step manner, retrieving the drill dimensions as well but not displaying them in the report in a common simple table, but instead "hiding" them in the **Available Objects** list and using them according to the user drill direction (up, down, or through).

> A drill can be performed only on dimension objects, which is one of the aspects that we need to consider when setting their qualification in the universe.

Using a query drill

In general, the more dimensions and data we bring, the bigger the report gets, and the fetch time could get longer as well. The performance is of course a subject to changes as we are using in-memory and Big Data databases nowadays that can boost the performance of the queries.

When we are dealing with a drill, we need to take into consideration the performance and data volume and consider whether the extra dimension we require to drill through will result in another long refresh.

In order to optimize the drill performance in some cases, we can use the query drill option.

This option will "push" each value that we use in the drill filter bar into the query structure. For example, if we pick the month number **10** in the drill filter, then the query will add a filter based on this value, as shown in the following screenshot:

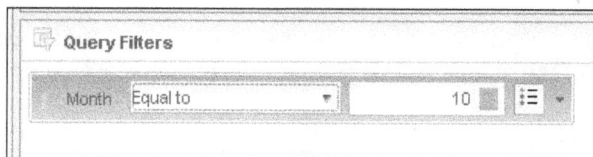

This method has two factors that need to be considered:

 ▸ We can basically optimize the query performance by limiting the results. This option will work best when we already have the aggregative results calculated at the database level.

 ▸ We can increase the number of refreshes (refresh per value) and cause long refresh times for the query.

In short, the use of the query drill depends on the query performance, the database performance, the user requirement, and the query type.

Getting ready

We will set the option by navigating to the **Properties** tab and then selecting the **Document** option. In the **Options** area, we need to check the **Use query drill** option, as shown in the following screenshot:

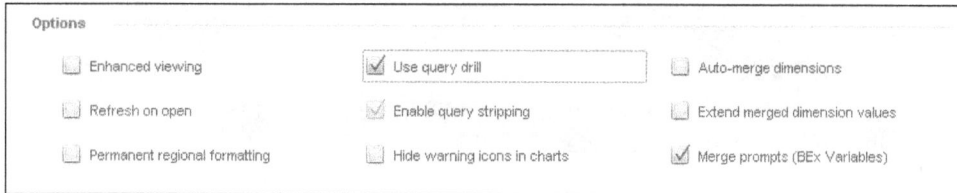

Options

☐ Enhanced viewing	☑ Use query drill	☐ Auto-merge dimensions
☐ Refresh on open	☑ Enable query stripping	☐ Extend merged dimension values
☐ Permanent regional formatting	☐ Hide warning icons in charts	☑ Merge prompts (BEx Variables)

How to do it...

We click on the **State** dimension object in our table and choose the **California** value. The query will drill accordingly by the value that we picked, but if we check the query structure, we will notice that a state filter that uses the equal operator with the **California** value has been added to it. We will choose another value from another dimension, such as the first month of the year, and one more filter will be added to the query and return a smaller amount of rows to the report.

Using the query drill is the process of eliminating the amount of rows fetched to the report one at a time while drilling. This method, as mentioned, has its advantages and disadvantages.

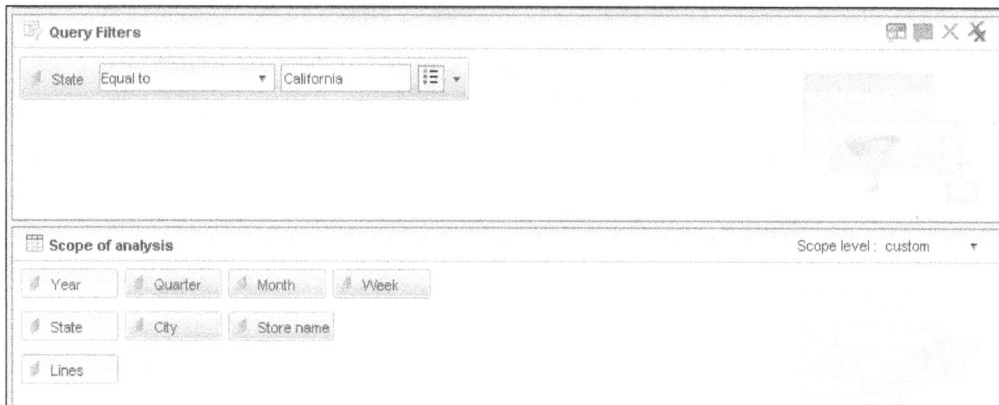

Query Filters

State	Equal to	▼	California	⋮☰ ▼

Scope of analysis   Scope level : custom ▼

Year	Quarter	Month	Week
State	City	Store name	
Lines			

> The **Use query drill** option needs to be set prior to the scope of analysis being set in the **Query Panel**.

Using the drill formula

If we want to keep track of the drill-filtered values and display the data in a more preventative way, or in cases where we want to print the results, we need to add a title that will display the drill values.

Getting ready

We will insert the drill filter values into the report title using the `DrillFilters` formula located in the document functions folder.

How to do it...

Let's perform the following steps:

1. We need to mark the title cell, switch to the formula editor, and choose the `DrillFilters` formula, as shown in the following screenshot:

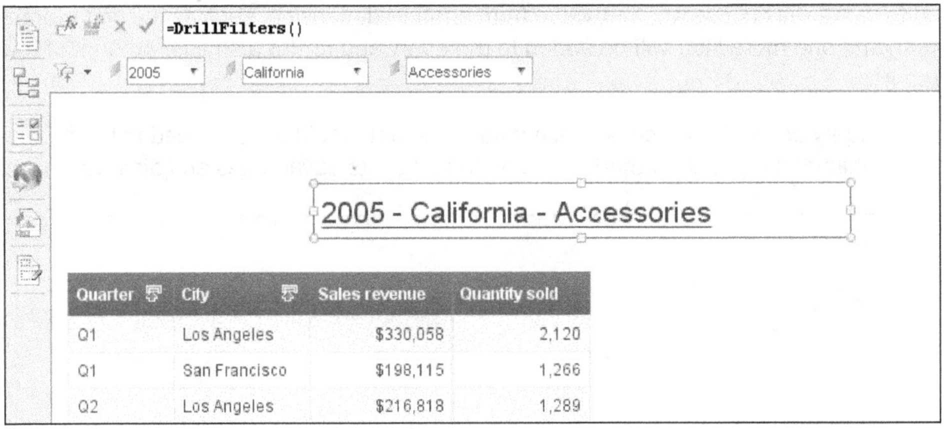

2. The content of the title will change according to the values picked in the drill filters, so it's very easy to keep track of the changing values, and if we are going to print the report, we need to be very clear about what the context of the displayed data is.

> When document hierarchies are defined properly in the universe, when we use them for a drill in our reports, the dimensions that turn into filter drop-down lists will behave in a cascading way when filtering together several dimensions, which means that if we have country and region drill filters and pick a certain country in the first drill filter drop-down list, then we will see the country's region in the second drill filter drop-down list.

See also

▸   For more drill options, refer to *Chapter 14, Web Intelligence Rich Client*

12
Scheduling Reports

In this chapter, we will cover the following recipes:

- ▶ Scheduling a report
- ▶ Working with instance history
- ▶ Publications
- ▶ Advanced publication options

Introduction

One of the most significant and most useful features in a BI environment is the ability to share and distribute data across the organization's business users.

As we have seen so far, the main purpose of data is when it's pulled out from the database and displayed or shared across the organization's business users.

Getting the data into the right hands at the right time is probably the difference between a good and a bad business decision that can affect the entire business process.

Many business departments, managers, employees, and team leaders are dependent on their reports, which are the basis for their ongoing tasks; important for decision making; and useful for tracking, analyzing, and evaluating the business activity.

Scheduling reports is a very convenient and straightforward way to perform automation on reports that don't require manual activation or an automation distribution to a specific or several business users.

There are several advantages of using scheduling:

- ▸ Automated distribution of reports to various destinations such as e-mail, a file folder, or a BI inbox

- ▸ The report can run even when the business user isn't online; when we are dealing with large data volumes and the report generation runs for a long time, we can schedule them to run when we are offline and get the results without any undesired waiting

- ▸ Distributing reports outside the organization to external users, for example, the business customers that require getting their billing information on the first day of every new month

- ▸ Distribute the report to business users who need to consume the data in an Excel, PDF, or CSV text format; in that sense, they are not Web Intelligence users, but data consumers

- ▸ Reports load balance better on the BI systems as we can schedule reports to run when the system isn't fully loaded with business users who are running many reports at the same time

- ▸ Create a smart report trigger, which will ensure the report will run only if there is relevant data or a specific database process that has finished populating the relevant tables with updated data

In this chapter, we will cover how to create a scheduled report, distribute it, and monitor and edit the schedule task.

Scheduling a report

This recipe will cover the creation of scheduled reports.

Getting ready

We want to schedule the **Daily Sales** report for the sales team and want to send the results to their e-mails and in Excel file format.

How to do it...

Right-click on the **Daily Sales** report, choose the **Schedule** tab, and navigate to the scheduling options as shown in the following screenshot:

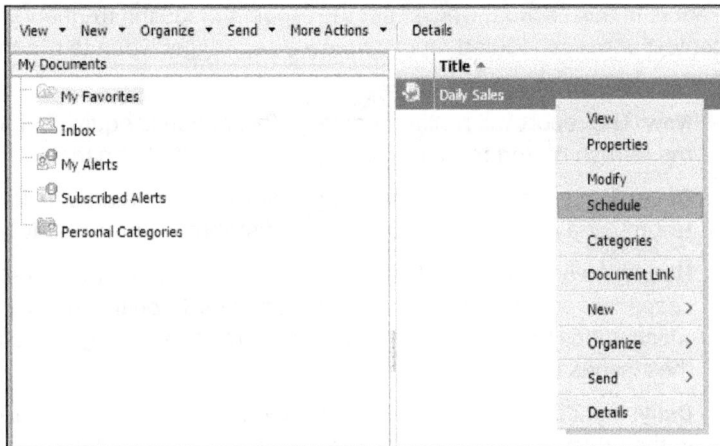

In the **Schedule** window, we will find the following categories we need to configure in order to create the scheduled report:

- **Instance Title**: When the report is being scheduled, we can give it a meaningful name too. So, if a scheduled report has several versions distinguished by the recurrence or a query filter, we might as well mention it in the instance name. This will be helpful when we have a look at the instance list of the report and will help us know which report ran successfully or failed and edit it accordingly.

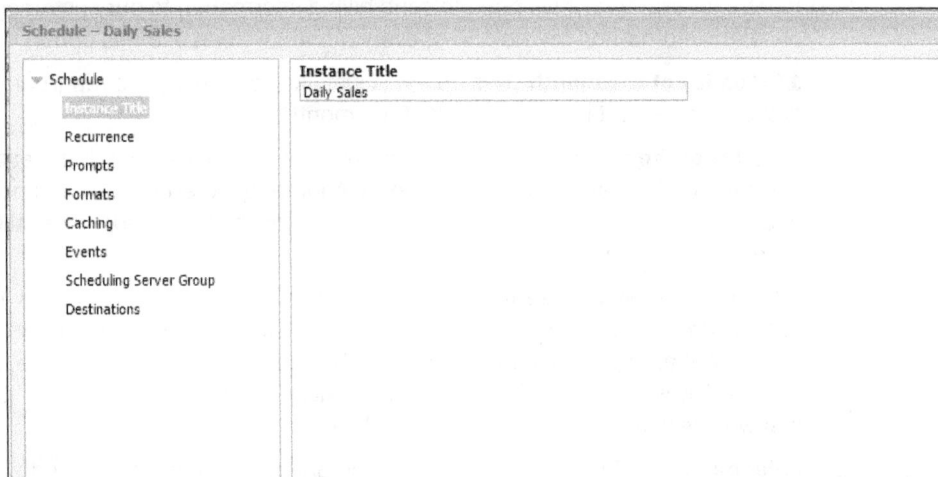

▸ **Recurrence**: In this section, we can set the report scheduling frequency. This is the main context of the scheduled report; here we can trigger when to run the report as follows:

- ❑ **Now**: The report will run immediately. This option is equivalent to clicking on the refresh button from the query panel or the report panel.

- ❑ **Once**: A single one-time scheduling—relevant for one-time tasks or for testing, or a report that requires to be distributed immediately.

- ❑ **Hourly**: An hour interval, for reports that run against a live database that keeps on updating. You can find this kind of scheduling in a call center, which needs to check how many customers called and got a solution to their issues every hour.

- ❑ **Daily**: Most of the reports are scheduled to run every day and then are sent to their relevant audience. We can also set the days' interval and define that the daily report will run every *n* days.

- ❑ **Weekly**: This report will be scheduled every week. Here, we can pick the specific days that the report will be run, which is better than the **Daily** option since Saturday and Sunday are usually non-working days and business users aren't waiting for the triggered data to be sent to them in those specific days.

- ❑ **Monthly**: This report can be scheduled to run every *n* months, for example, every three months.

- ❑ **Nth day of the month**: We can set the report to run on a specific day of each month, for example, if we need to send billing information to our customers or salary information on the 15th of every month, we can use this option

- ❑ **1st Monday of the month**: This option is just like scheduling the report on the first day of the first business week of the month.

- ❑ **Last day of the month**: This is useful for reports that need to fetch the entire current month's data for monthly reports. Another good example would be a budget report, where we want to estimate how much of our budget we still haven't used before the next month starts.

- ❑ **X day of Nth week of the month**: We can customize the schedule time to a specific day in a specific week of the month. This option is configured for events that are specific to an organization's style of working, for example, a specific day when the billing process has reached completion, a specific day that we check if a payment was received, and so on.

- ❑ **Calendar**: Calendars can be created by the SAP BI4 administrators and basically include a customized time schedule for the reports. The calendar can include only days that are relevant for the report scheduling and exclude irrelevant days such as holidays, Saturdays, and Sundays.

After the recurrence type has been picked, we will have to adjust the time range for the scheduled report. This is simply setting the validity of the report, and setting for how long the report will be scheduled.

The basic recommendation is to set the time range to one or two years unless you are planning to use the schedule for more than that, as shown in the following screenshot:

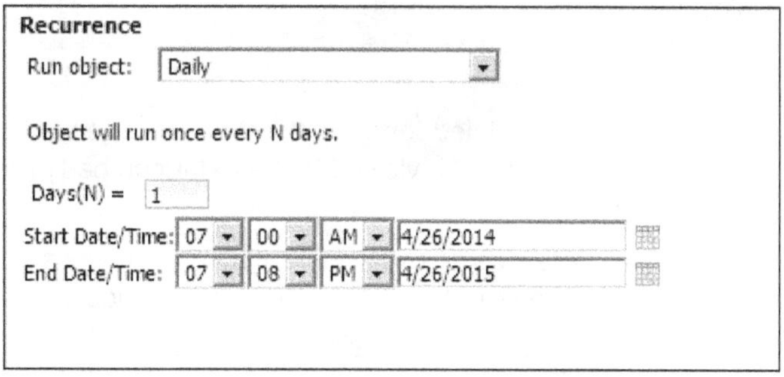

> ▶ **Prompts**: If the report uses prompts, we will be able to adjust them according to our required query prompt filter. Click on the **Modify** button and the prompt window will appear; we will be able to adjust the reports, as shown in the following screenshot:

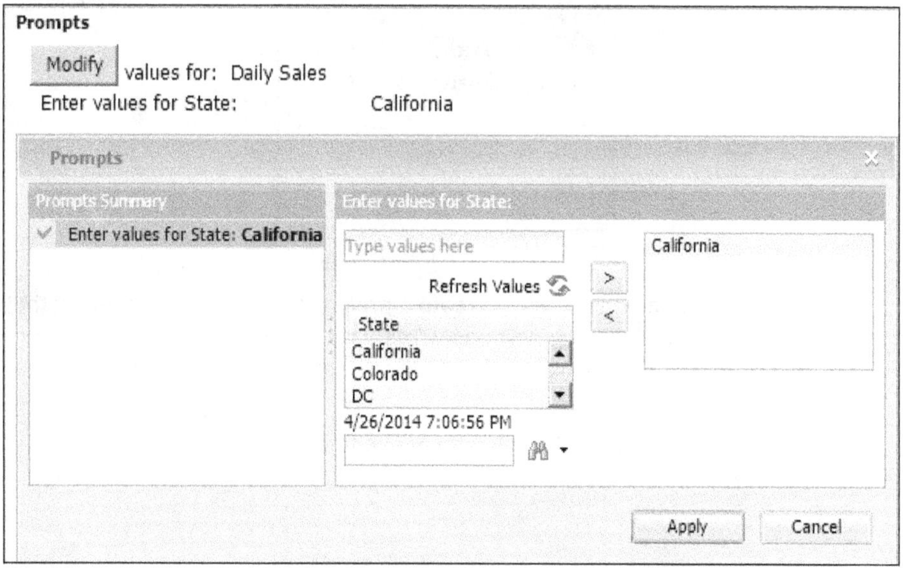

One of the most common problems with scheduled reports is that the reports use date prompts, which are good for daily refresh tasks. However, when these reports are scheduled, they need to be adjusted as date prompts are useless when the same report needs to retrieve the current week data.

There is a method in order to avoid report duplication (one for the daily refresh and another one for the scheduled version); for further reading, please refer to `http://thebobaba.blogspot.com/2013/09/default-dynamic-time-value.html`.

▶ **Formats**: We can send a scheduled report in the Web Intelligence format, which means the report can only be viewed in the BI launch pad or through Web Intelligence Rich Client.

The other standard formats include Excel, PDF, and CSV, which can be configured for external consumption of the report (through e-mail or file folder), as shown:

Formats

Output Format

☑ Web Intelligence
☐ Microsoft Excel
☐ Adobe Acrobat
☐ Comma Separated Values(CSV)

▶ **Cashing**: This option enables us to create a preloaded version of the report that works with Web Intelligence reports only. The data is converted to an HTML, Excel, or PDF cache version. This option is suited for complex reports, multireports, and variable reports.

The report data is stored in the selected cache format and is converted into a Web Intelligence report when it's being viewed.

▸ **Events**: These are trigger objects that are created by the SAP BI administrator and enable us to schedule the report after an event has occurred. The scheduled report can be triggered that way by creating a dependency in the event.

For example, we might want to run our **Daily Sales** report only when the relevant tables in the database have been updated.

Events can be used by simply picking the relevant event from the event list, as shown in the following screenshot:

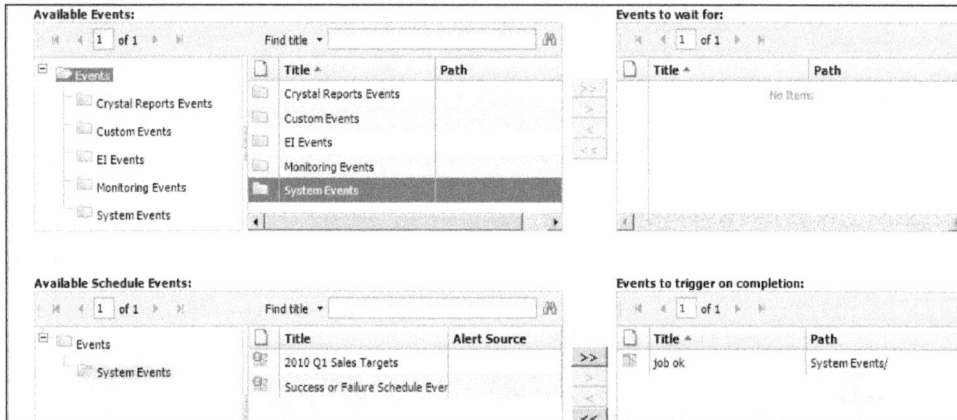

▸ **Scheduling server group**: This option enables us to choose which server will process your scheduled instance. If you are scheduling a very large report that can take a long time to run, the SAP BI administrator can direct the instance to be processed in another server that is more suited to process big requests.

▸ **Destinations**: Here, we can set the destination of the report and to whom it will be sent.

When we first open the drop-down destination list, we will see several options such as **Default Enterprise Location** (which is usually the report location in the repository), **BI Inbox**, **Email**, **FTP Server**, or a file system.

For each destination, it's necessary that we know its credentials (location and a valid user who can access the FTP server of the file folder)

We will pick the **E-mail** option from the drop-down list as shown in the following screenshot:

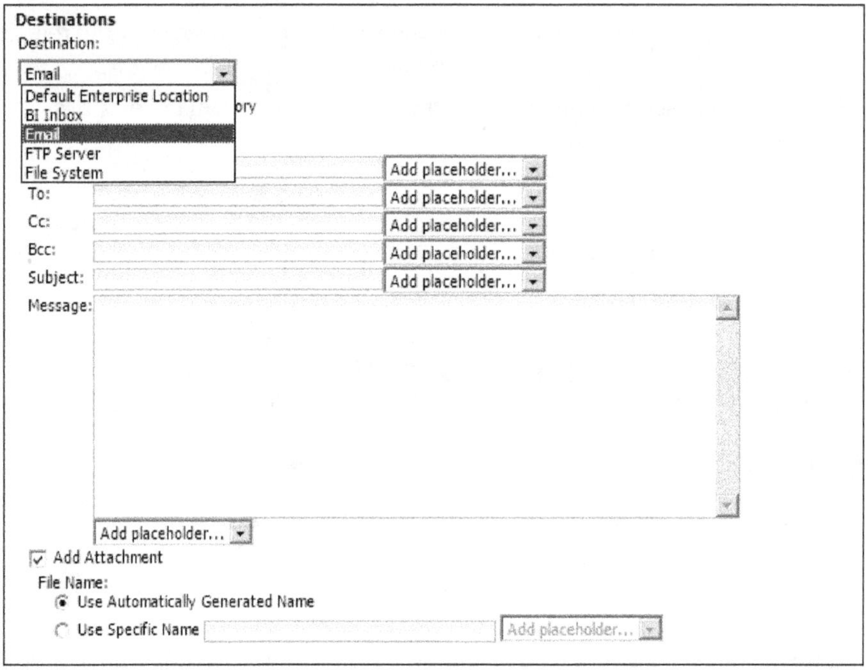

Now we need to fill in the rest of the relevant inputs for the scheduling.

We will fill in the **From** and **To** fields. We can use a dummy e-mail address in the **From** field that will be valid as long as it's using a real domain that is defined in the central management console.

We can also fill **Subject** and **Message** with relevant information using the placeholders from the **Add placeholder** drop-down list.

These placeholders are built-in fields representing useful data such as the following:

- **Title**: This is the instance title that is filled in the first section of the schedule to be placed; the placeholder representing the title is **%SI_NAME%**.

- **ID**: This represents the unique ID of the report using the **%SI_ID%** placeholder.

- **Owner**: This represents the owner of the report using the **%SI_OWNER%** placeholder.

- **DateTime**: This represents the date and time at which the instance actually started to be processed by the **%SI_STARTTIME%** placeholder.

- ▶ **Add Attachment**: This is another important option located under the **Message** box; this option should be checked if we want the file to be received as an attachment in the e-mail. Here, it's recommended to use the title placeholder again with the additional placeholder **%EXT%**.

After filling all the relevant fields and using the appropriate placeholders, our report will be ready for scheduling as shown in the following screenshot:

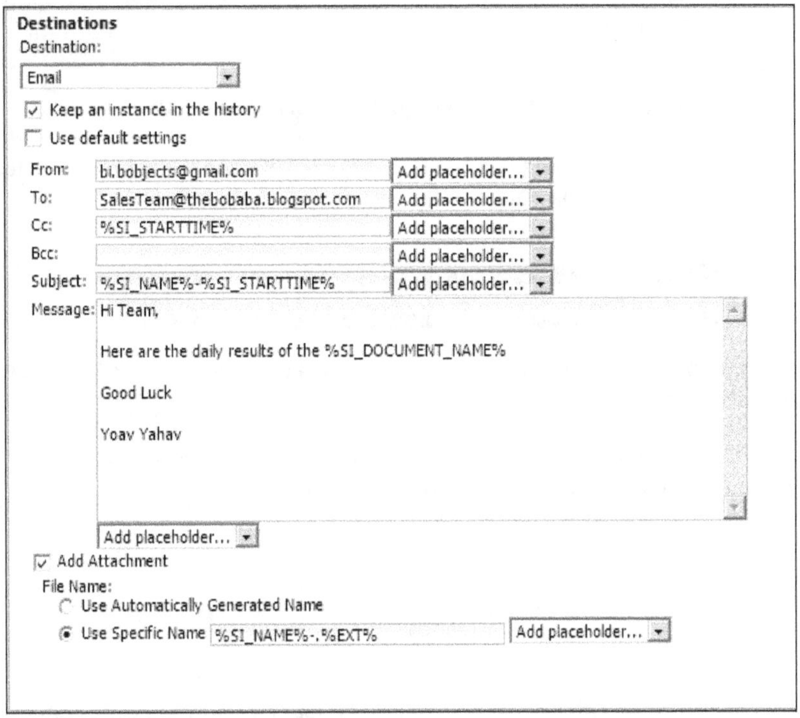

Our report is set to go. We will hit the **Schedule** button and will be able to track the schedule status in the **History** window.

> We can also use separators between placeholders and make a better display in the message box or in any other part in the e-mail area; the basic syntax will be `%placeholder1% - %placeholder%`.

How it works...

A scheduled report is simply an automated task that can reoccur in almost any time interval we choose.

Each schedule uses format, destination, and recurrence as its main definitions.

Once we schedule a report, we can distribute it very easily and make the relevant business user get the latest data on time.

> It's also recommended to consult your SAP BI administrator in order to know when it would be best to schedule your report and perhaps get some better solutions for long, data-heavy reports. A very common scenario is to schedule the reports after the data warehouse has been updated.

Working with instance history

After we set our report to be scheduled, we would also like to check that it has been sent or check its current status.

In the **Instance** column next to the report info, we will be able to see the number of times the report has been scheduled, which is the number of instances.

Getting ready

Right-click on the report from its location (folder or private folder) to navigate to two main options:

▸ **View Latest Instance**: This will take us to the last result of the scheduled report
▸ **History**: By selecting this option, we will switch to the history view of the scheduled report

How to do it...

After selecting the **History** option, we will be directed to the history of the report, as shown in the following screenshot.

Here, we can perform several actions such as viewing, deleting, rescheduling, and pausing the scheduled instance:

The instance statuses can be **Success** for a successful scheduled instance, **Failed** for a schedule that has failed to be delivered, and **Pending**, which is the status for a report that is waiting to start. Another status would be **Recurring**, which marks reports that run in one of the intervals we can set in the **Recurrence** category.

Instances with the recurrence status can also be paused, which means that if we have a recurring instance that we need to suspend for a while, then we don't have to delete it. This option is also useful when we need to make modifications to the original report that the schedule instance is based on and we want to suspend it till we get the new approved version.

The **Pause**, **Run Now**, and **Reschedule** options are available by right-clicking on the instance or through the main menu located under the **Instance Time** toolbar:

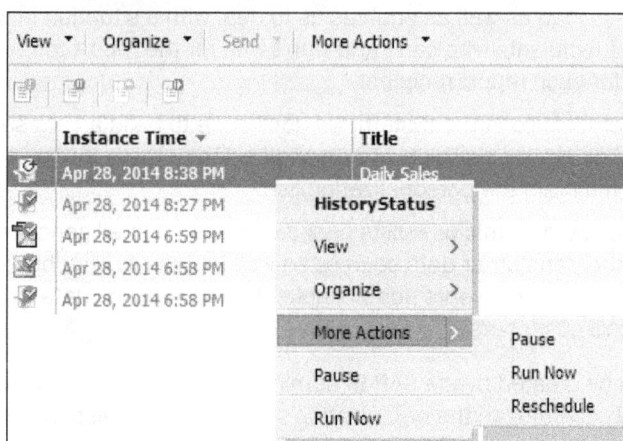

How it works...

The **History** panel can be seen as the control center of the scheduled report, enabling us to easily make modifications in an existing scheduled report and watch its status.

Working with the instance history will save us time and trouble trying to figure out if a report was sent successfully and or if a specific instance has failed as well as address a most important task: editing an existing scheduled report instance.

Publications

Publications are an advanced type of scheduling that enable us to distribute one or more reports to several destinations and in multiple formats.

The publications' unique quality is that it can schedule a report to run just one time and then distribute its data to different users but deliver to each user only the relevant data they need.

This is achieved by using **personalization**. Personalization is the process of filtering the data in the scheduled report according to its recipients and then distributing the report results accordingly.

For example, let's say we need to schedule and distribute the **Revenue per Store** report so that each store manager will get only his or her relevant data.

The report will run and retrieve all stores' data; however, before the data is distributed, personalization will take effect and distribute the data accordingly.

In this way, we have several advantages:

> ▶ The report runs just one time. Running the report just once reduces the server and database load as well as enables us to deal with a situation in which we have hundreds of recipients who can't and won't wait for the report to run each time separately for each report recipient.

> ▶ From the perspective of the system, we don't have to build a data security structure but can rather use the flexibility of personalization at the publication level although it needs to maintain the personalization list.

> ▶ We can also use dynamic user lists based on the Web Intelligence report, Crystal Reports and other data sources as well in order to distribute the data to non-organizational recipients (for example, distribute billing data to an organization's customers).

Personalization can be created by the SAP BI administrator using the **Central Management Console** (**CMC**) and according to the organization's audience and distribution requirements, personalization can be built to enable dynamic delivery of the data.

Getting ready

We will create a publication that will distribute the **Revenue per Store** report which is based on the **eFashion** universe. This report contains the **Store Name**, **Name of Manager**, and **Sales revenue** result objects and will be delivered to the store managers by using personalization. Each store manager will get only their data; for example, **Larry** will only get the **e-Fashion Austin** data as shown in the following screenshot:

We will also distribute each report tab in a different format: the **Manager Data** tab will be exported to an Excel file and the **Pie Chart** report tab to PDF format.

How to do it...

Perform the following steps:

1. Through the **Documents** tab in the main BI launch pad screen, we will navigate to the **BI launch pad** toolbar and under **New**, choose the **Publication** option as shown in the following screenshot:

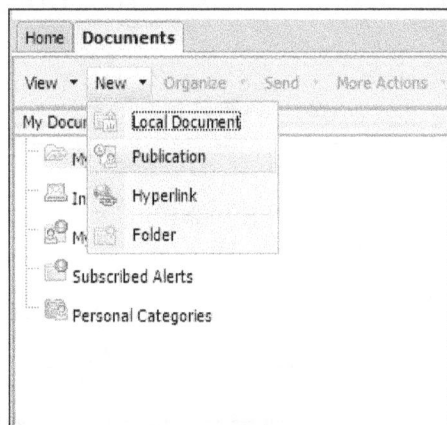

2. In the next screen, we will name the publication `Revenue Per store Publication`. We can also enter a description and supply keywords, which will be good for searching objects in the repository:

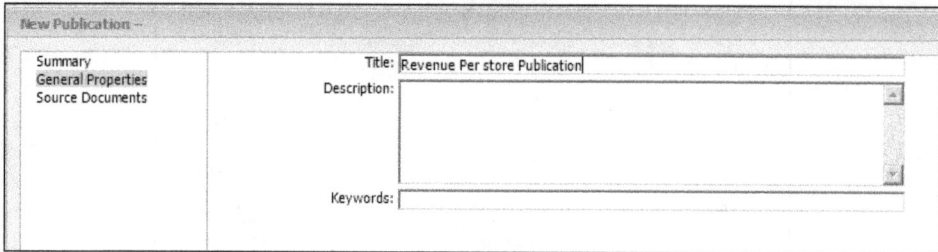

3. In the **Source Documents** options, we will click on the **Add** button:

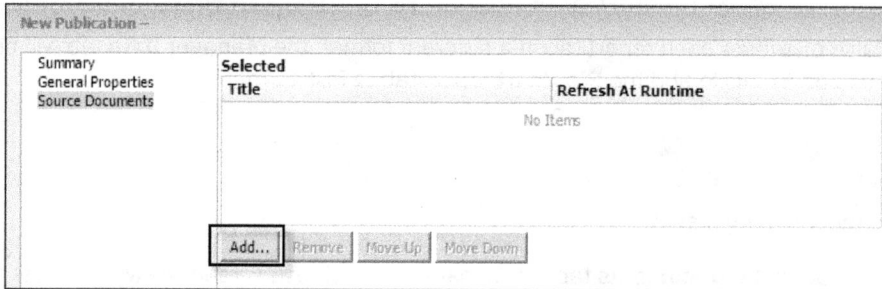

4. Then, we will navigate through the folder structure to the report we are going to schedule, which is the **Revenue Per Store** located in the **Favorites** private folder:

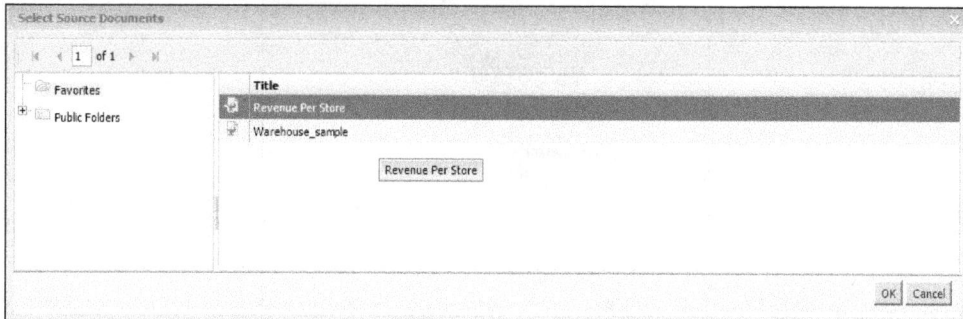

5. The report will be added and we will be able to view the publication options, which are organized by categories that we will go through in the publication creation process.

6. First, we will choose the group we need to deliver the report to from the **Enterprise Recipients** category. This category contains all the registered SAP BI4 users that the report can be sent to directly via their accounts. Here, we will choose the **Store Managers** group and add it to the **Selected** list located at the top-right side of the screen, as shown in the following screenshot:

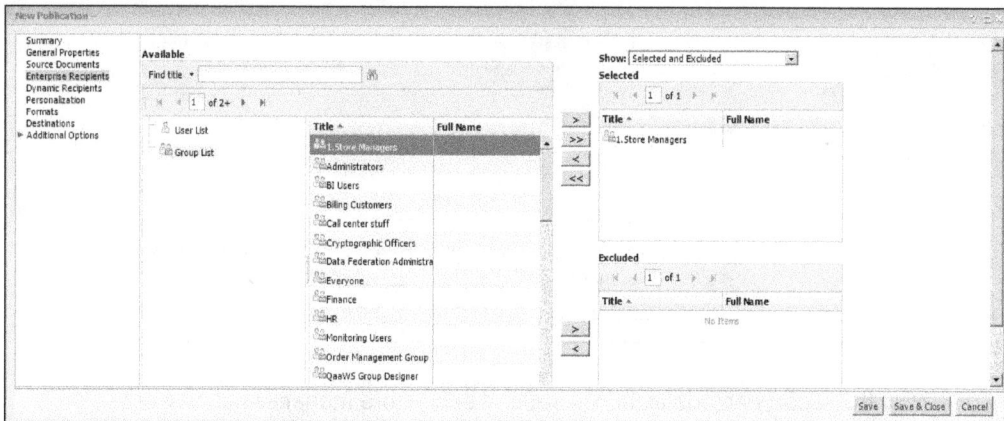

> There is also an **Excluded** list located under the **Selected** list. This option can be useful when we need to send the report to a group of users but exclude some of them.

The **Dynamic Recipients** option that is located under **Enterprise Recipients** is not relevant for this publication practice but holds a very powerful option: distributing the report to external recipients that are not registered BI users.

In this way, we can deliver data outside the organization to customers, coworkers, or subcontractors. One can imagine the usefulness of this functionality for an organization that needs to send a personal invoice on the first day of every month.

In general, **Dynamic Recipients** is a list that holds the recipient name and e-mail address and can be a text file, Excel file, data that originated in a universe, or in any other data source Web Intelligence or Crystal Reports can consume.

These reports simply compare a common identity in the real data report (for example, customer name) to the **Dynamic Recipients** report that holds the customer name as well and its e-mail.

7. Next, we will choose **Personalization**, which as we said is the match between users and their filtered values and is created in the CMC. Here, we will choose the **Store Name** object report field under **Local Profiles** from among the query's possible dimensions. These objects will filter the store values in the report according to the **Sales Mangers** profile that we will pick from **Enterprise Recipient Mapping**:

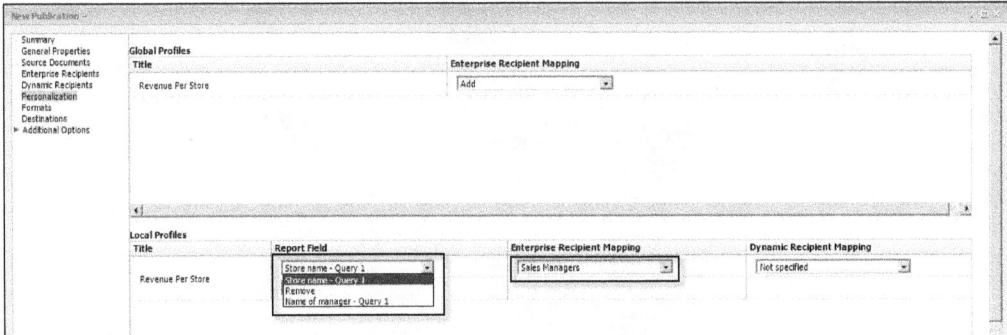

Now the report personalization is set and each store manager will only get data according to the match between the store name values and the profile store managers.

8. Next, in **Format**, we will use another of the publication's unique capabilities and set the format of each report tab to another export extension. The **Manager Data** report tab will be delivered as an Excel file, as shown in the following screenshot:

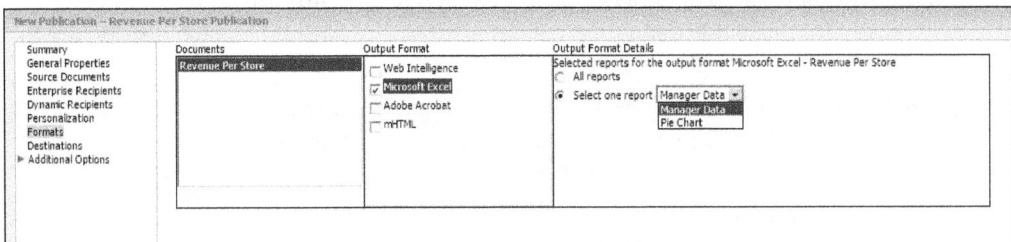

The **Pie Chart** report tab output format will be **Adobe Acrobat**:

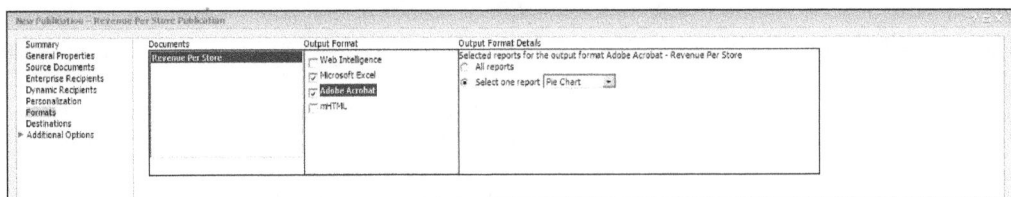

9. In the **Destinations** category, we will choose the **BI Inbox** option. Note that we can choose several destinations as well as the **Zip** option, which is recommended for several documents that need to be delivered in a ZIP file:

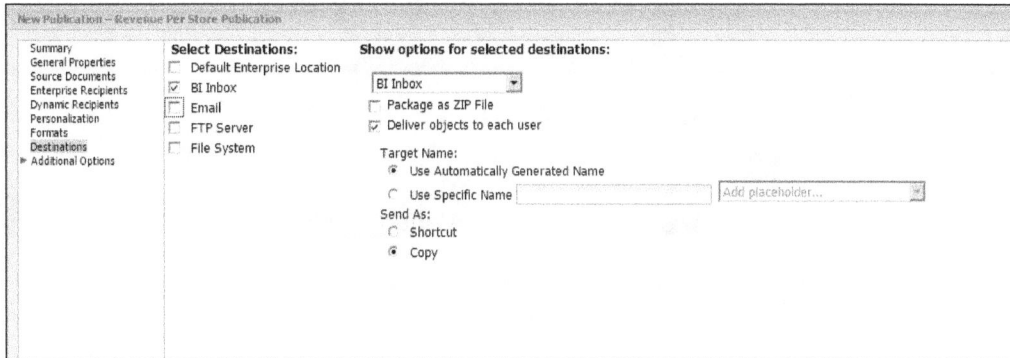

10. Under **Additional Options**, we will choose the category of **Recurrence** that we chose when scheduling. Here, we will pick the **Now** option:

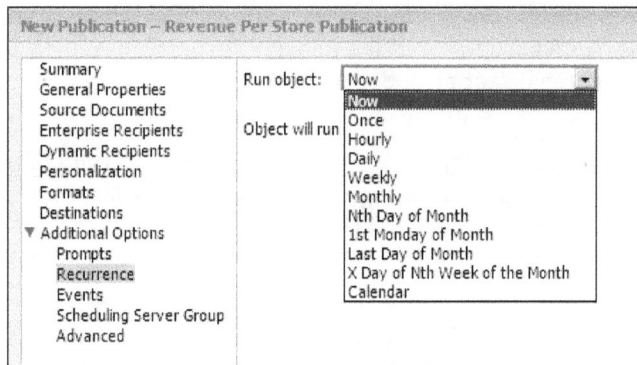

11. Now we will log in to the BI launch pad using a **Barrett** account. We will navigate to its inbox and see that the publications have been delivered, as shown:

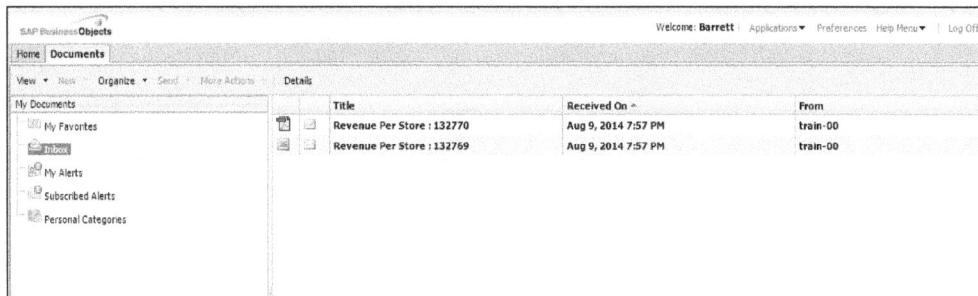

12. If we open the Excel output of the report, we will see that only Barrett's data has been filtered and sent to him:

How it works...

Publications are one of the best practices the BI team can apply to its data audiences and data consumers. The **Personalization** option is simply the universe field mapping for a user or a group.

If we take a deep dive for a second into the CMC under profiles, we will see that the profile Sales manager is a combination of **Profile Targets** and **Profile Values**.

Profile Targets is simply the universe object we need to compare in our report, as shown:

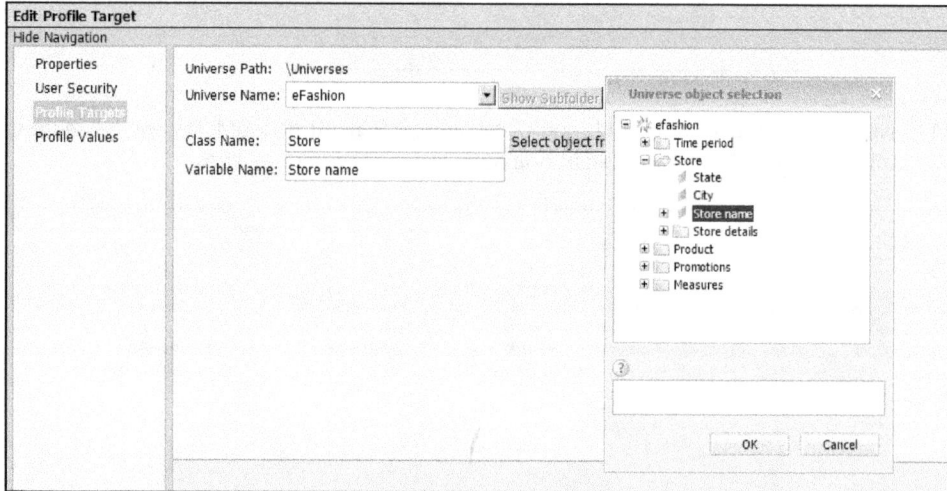

Additionally, **Profile Values** is the mapping and filtering of the object values to a user or a group:

	Type	User/Group	Full Name	Value Type	Profile Value(s)
□		Anderson		Filter	In List[e-Fashion New York Magnolia]
□		Barrett		Filter	In List[e-Fashion Washington Tolbooth]
□		Bennett		Filter	In List[e-Fashion Colorado Springs]
□		Larry		Filter	In List[e-Fashion Austin]
□		Leonard		Filter	In List[e-Fashion Dallas]
□		Mark		Filter	In List[e-Fashion Boston Newbury]
□		Michelle		Filter	In List[e-Fashion Houston Leighton]

Profile Values: Sales Managers — Hide Navigation / Properties / User Security / Profile Targets / Add Remove Refresh

This is what makes the publication use this profile or personal data distribution.

There's more...

Our book does not cover how to create profiles in the CMC. In order to accomplish such tasks, it's recommended to get advice from SAP BI4 administrators.

Advanced publication options

There are some advanced options as well when we create a publication located under the **Additional Options** category.

Getting ready

We want to explore the advanced options and to understand their importance.

How to do it...

We will navigate to the **Advanced** option located under **Additional Options**:

New Publication –

Summary
General Properties
Source Documents
Enterprise Recipients
Dynamic Recipients
Personalization
Formats
Destinations
▼ Additional Options
  Prompts
  Recurrence
  Events
  Scheduling Server Group
  Advanced

Profile Resolution:
⦿ Do not merge (distinct profiles from multiple parent user groups result in separate documents)
○ Merge (distinct profiles from multiple parent user groups apply to the same document)

Personalization:
☐ Display users who have no personalization applied

Report Bursting Method:
⦿ One database fetch for all recipients (recommended for minimizing the number of database queries)
○ One database fetch per recipient (recommended when using row level security within Universes or Business Views)

Here, I'll discuss the options in the **Report Bursting Method**:

> ▸ **One database fetch for all recipients**: This option should be used when we need to run the report once and then, using the profile, deliver it to its recipients. This option reduces database hits as the report runs only once and it's also configured to users that don't have row-level security (security at the database level).
>
> Using this scenario will usually output the report to Excel, PDF, or any other supported output format; otherwise, if we are publishing the report as a Web Intelligence report, then users can access the report filter and remove it as personalization is nothing more than a report filter.

> ▸ **One database fetch per recipient**: The data in a document will be refreshed for every recipient (if we have one hundred users, the report will be run one hundred times). This option uses the SAP BO user credentials to refresh the report and breaks it into multiple fetches.
>
> This option is recommended when the report returns large data volumes and the query needs to be run separately and in order to enforce security in the Web Intelligence report as well.

13
Working with BI Workspaces

In this chapter, we will cover the following recipes:

- ▸ Creating BI workspaces
- ▸ Working with report parts

Introduction

BI workspaces are centralized content areas that are capable of displaying multiple items from our SAP BI environment, such as **Crystal Reports**, **Analysis Edition** for OLAP, **Web Intelligence** documents, and **Dashboards** with agnostic content such as static text, HTML, or web pages external to the BI platform.

While reports are accessed mainly by navigating through folders, a BI workspace can be seen as our BI cockpit or main dashboard that displays just the most important items, such as our last scheduled reports, a sales chart from a specific report, or even data such as Web Intelligence reports or a Dashboard Design presentation from several different BI applications.

The BI workspaces are created by a simple drag-and-drop technique and can display various built-in modules, such as web pages, a report part, a public folder, or specific reports that the business users interact with and need to focus on during work.

We can create many kinds of workspaces, but we can distinguish between the following two main types of workspaces:

- ▶ **Content workspaces**: These provide easy access to preferred folders and reports and shortcuts to the most recent reports or last refreshed reports, as shown in the following screenshot. Here, we can see a workspace that is combined from three subareas. On the left-hand side we can see reports that were sent to our inbox, in the middle we can see the public folder content, and on the right-hand side we can see our recently viewed documents.

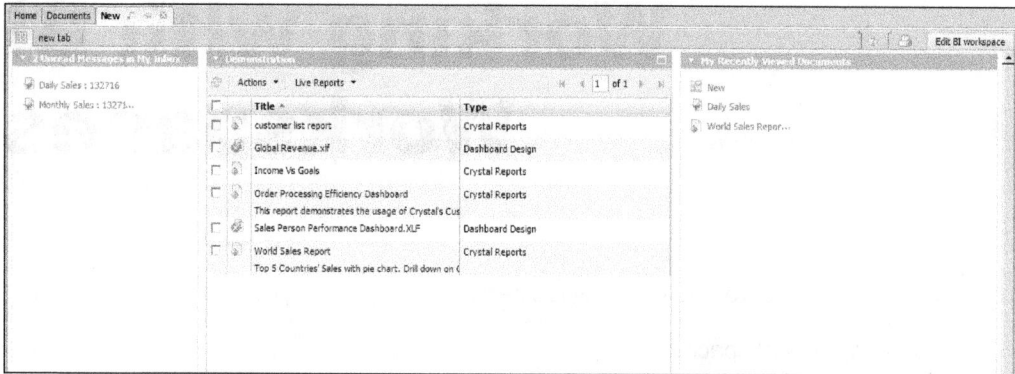

- ▶ **Report and application workspaces**: These are used to display actual data from reports, dashboards, and any BI application, enabling us to centralize the most important data on one screen, even if it's based in different applications and databases, as shown in the following screenshot:

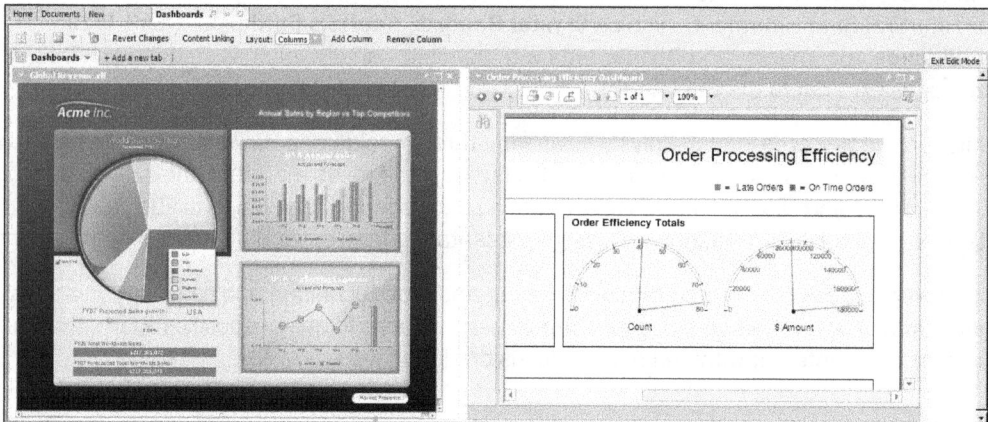

Here, we can see data originating from two different SAP BI applications. On the left-hand side we can see a dashboard that was created in the dashboard design application and on the right-hand side we can see the Crystal Report gauges. In this chapter, we will learn how to create workspaces, work with module libraries, and edit existing workspaces.

Creating BI workspaces

It is possible to create a BI workspace through the **Applications** menu:

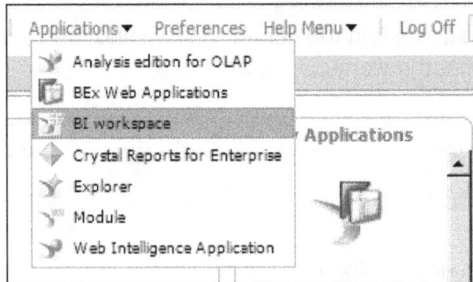

Getting ready

In the BI workspace screen, there are several main parts. The entire idea, in a nutshell, is to select the modules required and drag them into the empty workspace area:

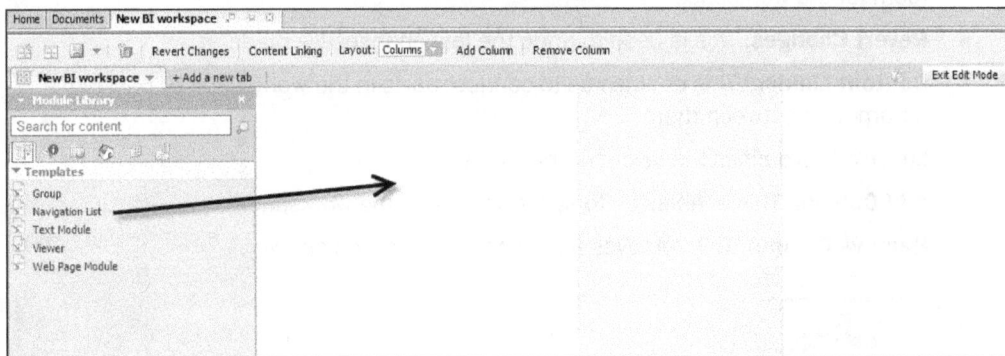

On the left-hand side of the screen, we can find the main **Module Library**, which is divided into the following main module subjects:

- **Templates**: This contains the basic template frames, such as **Viewer** (good for data display based on reports), **Navigation List**, **Text Module**, and **Web Page Module**

- **BI Launch Pad Modules**: This contains the main report custom folders, such as My Recently Run Documents, My Recently Viewed Documents, My Alerts, and My Applications (most of them already exist in the BI launch pad main welcome window)

- **Public modules**: This is a shortcut to the reports and objects that are located in the public folders

- ▸ **Private modules**: This contains shortcuts to the user's private folders and reports
- ▸ **BI workspaces**: This displays the already built BI workspaces
- ▸ **Document Explorer**: This enables us to display specific reports and enables custom navigation to preferred public or private folders

At the top of the workspace screen, in the center, we can find the workspace toolbar, which enables us to edit and format the workspaces we create:

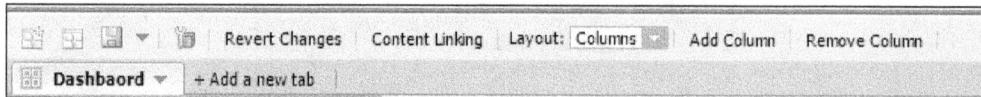

The workspace toolbar contains the following functions:

- ▸ **New**: This creates a new workspace
- ▸ **Open**: This opens an existing workspace
- ▸ **Save**: This saves the workspace
- ▸ **Hide Module Library**: This hides the module library; it is useful when we require more room for the workspace
- ▸ **Revert Changes**: This is used to undo the last changes we made
- ▸ **Content Linking**: This enables us to connect parts in the workspace by passing parameters between them
- ▸ **Layout**: This defines the layout of the workspace
- ▸ **Add Column**: This enables us to add a column to the workspace
- ▸ **Remove Column**: This removes a column from the workspace

How to do it...

We'll perform the following steps:

1. We create a new workspace that will include our last viewed documents and a shortcut to our private folder reports. First, we adjust the workspace area and choose the **Template** option from **Layout**:

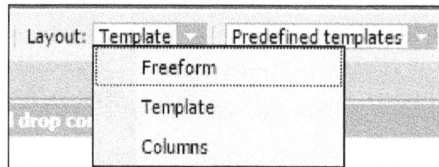

2. From the **Predefined templates** drop-down list, we choose the **2 Columns** option:

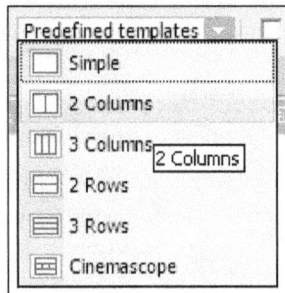

3. From the **BI Launch Pad Modules** library, we pick the **My Recently Viewed Documents** module and drag it into the workspace area. As soon as we drag the module, a view to our recently viewed documents appears in the workspace area:

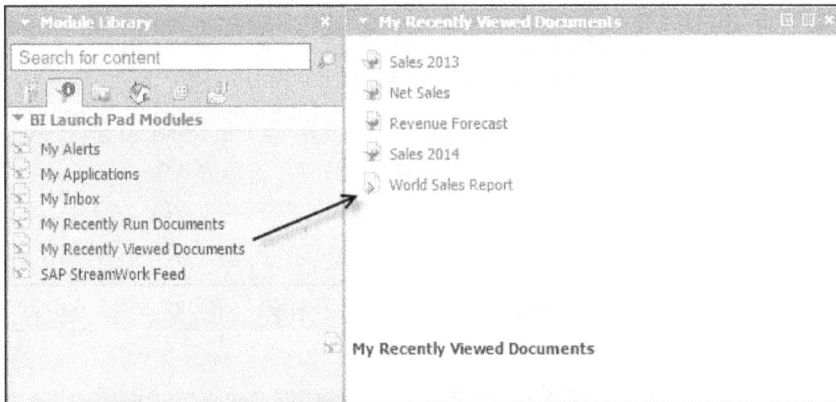

4. We switch to the **Document Explorer** library, choose the **Root Folder** module located under the **Personal Lists**, and drag it into the second column. After we drop the module, a view to our personal folder appears:

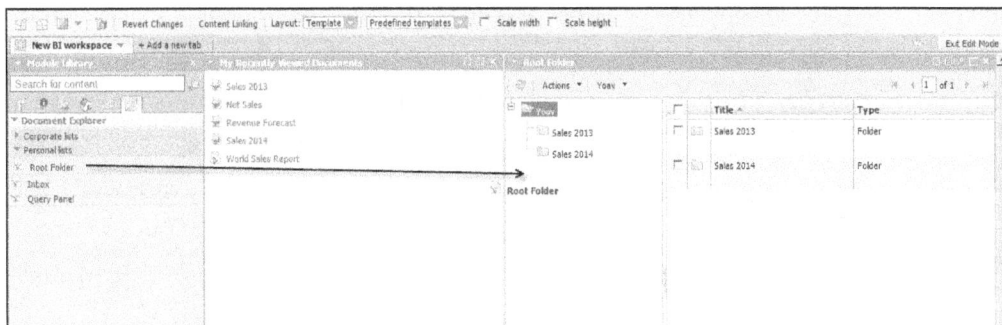

5. We save the workspace using the **Save** button under our main personal folder.

6. Through the BI launch pad **General** preferences, we set our new workspace as our home page by simply selecting it as our new start page:

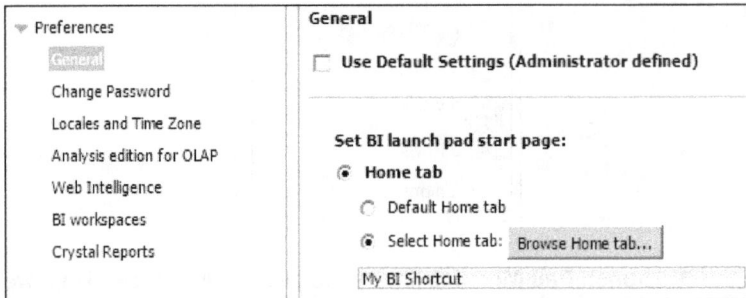

```
▼ Preferences                    General

  General                        ☐  Use Default Settings (Administrator defined)

  Change Password
                                    Set BI launch pad start page:
  Locales and Time Zone
  Analysis edition for OLAP        ◉  Home tab
  Web Intelligence                    ○  Default Home tab
  BI workspaces
  Crystal Reports                     ◉  Select Home tab:  Browse Home tab...

                                    My BI Shortcut
```

How it works...

A workspace is an intuitive design environment that enables us to create BI content frames that improve our way of working and the accessibility to our workspace.

Using the simple drag-and-drop feature, we can access the main module library and create different kinds of workspaces that will unify our scope of business work.

There's more...

We can also add tabs to the workspace and print the workspace view or just a part of it using the print preview and new tab options.

Working with report parts

As we mentioned in the introduction, there are mainly two types of workspaces. In this section, we will demonstrate how to create a report data workspace.

Along with the option to connect to a report, we can actually create a view to a specific report part: a table or a chart that is displayed in one of the report tabs.

This feature is very flexible as we can focus on just the report part we are interested in instead of using the entire report, and on the other hand, we don't need to create another report that will fit exactly to our workspace requirements either.

Getting ready

We will create a workspace that will display two different charts from different reports and data sources, centralizing and unifying them in one workspace.

How to do it...

Perform the following steps:

1. We first create a two-column workspace and drag the **Sales Analysis** report from the **Sales** folder in the **Public Modules** library into the first column:

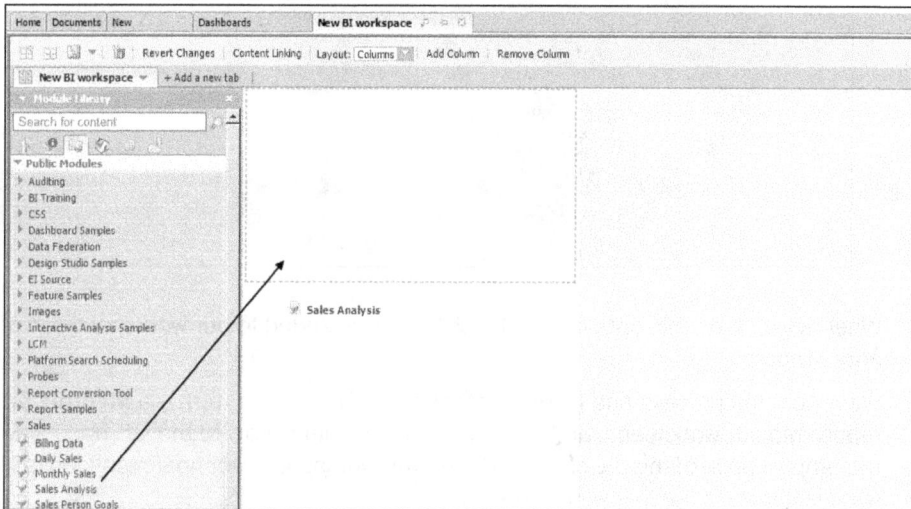

2. As soon as the report is open, we are able to navigate to one of the report tabs and pick the chart located in one of them:

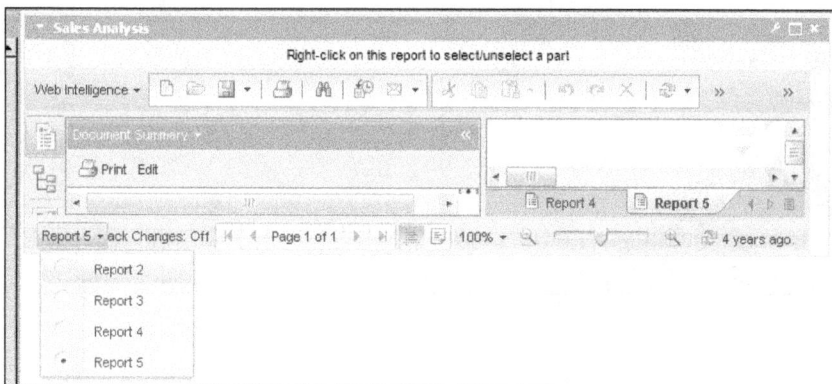

3. Then, we right-click on the chart that we want to insert into our workspace. Next, the **Select this report part** option appears, as shown in the following screenshot:

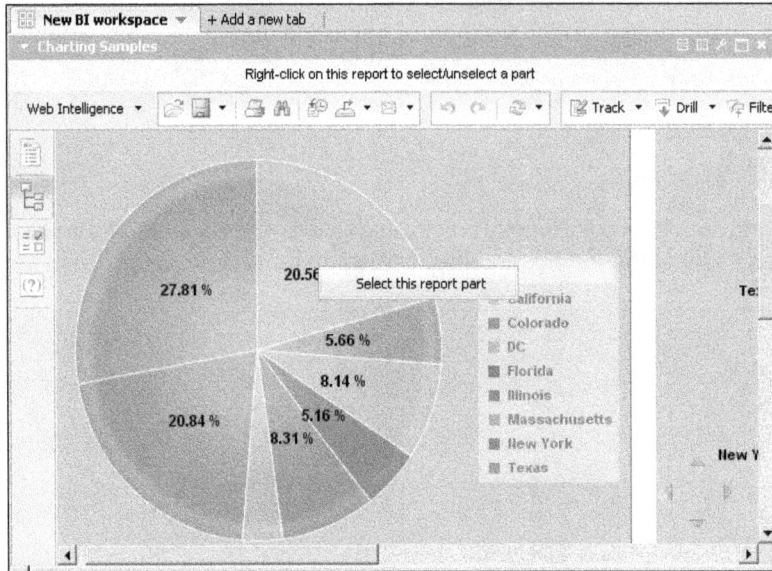

4. When we click on this option, just the chart part is added to our workspace out of the entire report.

5. We repeat the process and insert another part of the report from the **Monthly Sales** report into our workspace, and this time, we add a line chart to the left-hand side of the empty space of the pie chart and save the workspace. Our final result looks like what is shown in the following screenshot:

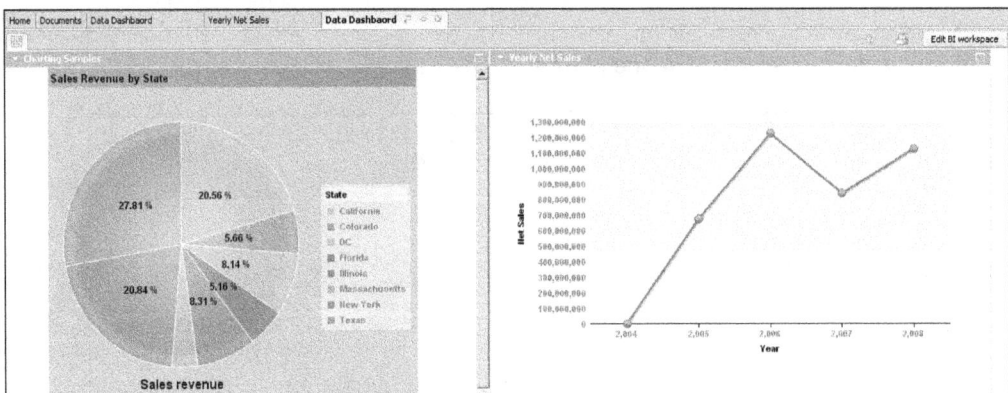

Now, we can actually view data from different reports on the same page without needing to build them in the same report or to use the entire report.

How it works...

As we did with the module library, by dragging our preferred content into the workspace, we can access an existing report in the repository, whether it's a private or public folder, and display a specific part. The original report definitions will affect the data that is displayed in our workspace; a good practice would be to set the report definition to refresh once it is open so that as soon as we open our workspace, the data in it is refreshed as well.

There's more...

Another good practice to keep the data in the workspace updated as well as ensure that it is less time consuming in terms of the refresh task is to connect to a scheduled report's latest instance so that we have the latest and greatest data available in our BI environment.

This can be done using the **Viewer** module, which is located under the **Templates** category. Once it's picked, we will be able to navigate to the required report and set the **Latest Instance** option on the **Viewer** screen:

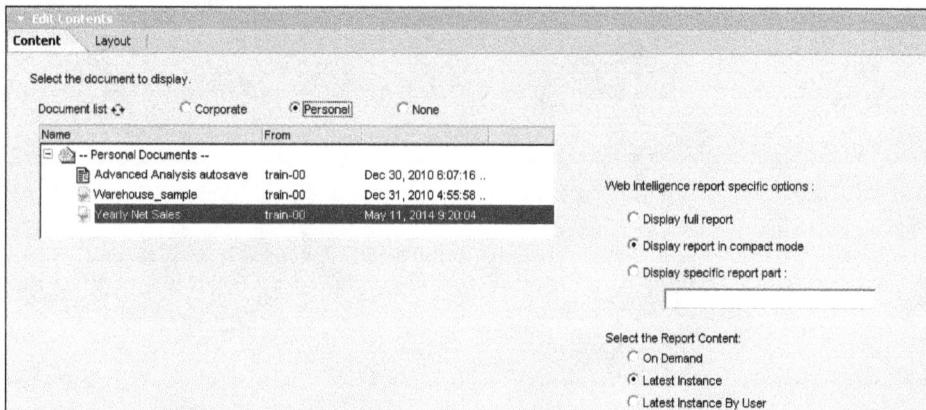

As a best practice, it's recommended that we use visual components and parts that can fit in one workspace in the workspace's aggregative data as we want to maintain the dashboard sense of it.

Also, in most of the workspaces I build, I try not to pass more than four elements in one workspace as more than this will overload the workspace with elements.

14
Web Intelligence Rich Client

In this chapter, we will cover the following recipes:

- ► Working with Web Intelligence Rich Client
- ► Working with local data providers
- ► Adjusting options

Introduction

Web Intelligence Rich Client is a software installed on the user's machine and has similar abilities to Web Intelligence with some additional capabilities and with some differences in the way it is used.

The Web Rich Client is a part of the set of SAP BI Client Tools that can be installed locally on most of the Windows operating systems.

The main distinctive feature about the Rich Client is that we can still access our reports without the necessity to access the SAP BI server.

The Rich Client will not improve the query running time, but in terms of performing analysis and formatting functions, the performance can be different since the client is dependent on the user machine's resources.

Whenever I find users working with Rich Client, they are usually one of the following types of users:

- ▸ BI team members
- ▸ Power users
- ▸ Business analysts

The rule for working with Rich Client is that most of the users don't require it, especially in the latest versions of SAP BI4 where the set of features is almost the same. It is mainly a matter of different working mode.

Another point to take in consideration is that not all the organizations are prepared or are willing to work with the SAP BI web environment.

Although it is a rare case since the entire IT environment is stepping into the era of the Web, we can still find places that are working mainly with Rich Client, for many reasons, some are certainly technical.

If we want to summarize the main difference between Web Rich Client and the Web Intelligence, the following are the differences:

Feature	Web Rich Client	Web Intelligence and BI launch pad
Working offline	Yes	No
Server timeout	No	Yes
Memory resources	The user local machine	The SAP BI4 server
The login method	Can work with no repository authentication	Only works with one of the repository authentication methods (Enterprise, AD, LDAP, and SAP)
Scheduling	No	Yes, through the BI launch pad report menu
Target audience	BI team members, as they can progress with less dependencies in the server shut-down times	Business users, report consumers, analysts
Saving the reports	Can be saved locally or in a shared file server	Only in the repository

Feature	Web Rich Client	Web Intelligence and BI launch pad
Disadvantages	Since the reports can be opened and saved locally, there is a chance that they won't be synched with the updated version of the report in the repository that is maintained by the BI team and report developers	Reports stay in sync with the updated version of the report
Report linking	Only by writing the report URL manually in the Add Hyperlink	The add report link feature can be used with no URL code writing

In this chapter, we will cover how to work with the Web Intelligence Rich Client, how to work with local files, and how to create queries based on local data providers.

Working with Web Intelligence Rich Client

The Rich Client can save the reports on local or network folders in a `.wid` extension format, which is the file extension for Web Intelligence report files. These files have the same sense as Office files and they can be saved, deleted, attached, copied, and maintained in local or network drives.

Getting ready

In order to access Web Intelligence Rich Client, we either use a desktop shortcut if we have created one or navigate to the **Start** menu and then under the **Programs** folder, open the main **SAP Business Intelligence** folder. Now, launch SAP Business Objects BI platform client tools and the Web Intelligence Rich Client from the subfolder.

How to do it...

After launching the Rich Client, the main window will appear, divided into two main panes: creating a new document based on any one of the available data sources or simply opening a local report (the right-hand side pane), as shown in the following screenshot:

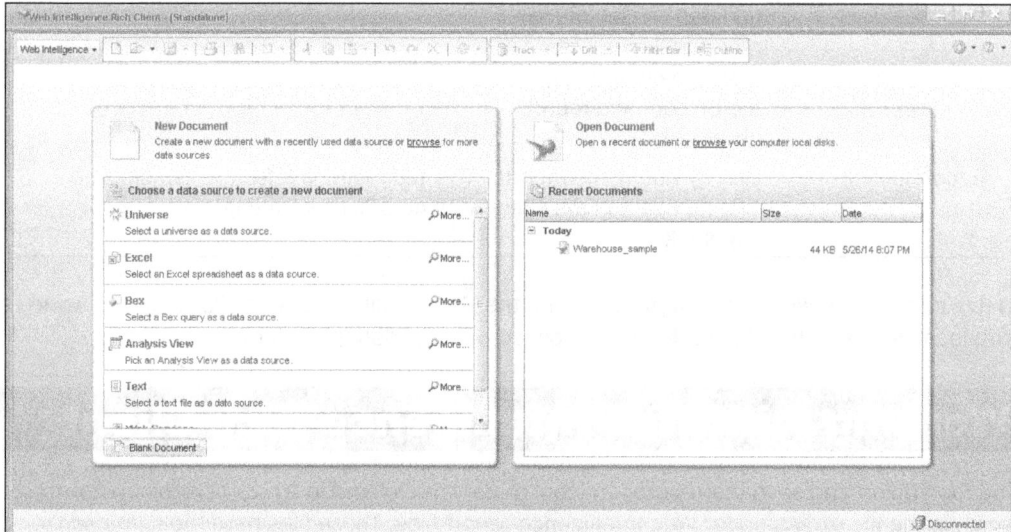

We can also open a report by using the **Open** icon. In the next screen, we will be able to open a report from the repository—**My Enterprise** (we can see the same folder structure and access it through the BI launch pad) or from a local folder.

We will open a local document that doesn't require accessing the repository.

By clicking on the report name or using the **Open** button, the **User Identification** window will pop up, as shown in the following screenshot, and we will be required to choose in what way we want to access the report: by connecting to the repository or by using standalone mode.

The standalone mode doesn't require any SAP BO server and it is mostly suited to cases where we don't have a repository or we need to develop reports based on the local data providers such as Excel or text files or reports that are stored locally on our computer.

The offline mode is most suited for enabling business users to keep their work on an existing report although the server may be unavailable but still using the user's security definitions.

Offline mode requires at least one successful online login to enable the offline mode since the first successful online login downloads the security definitions that will later enable us to access reports in offline mode.

Once we check the offline mode radio button located under the login form window, we will be able to access the Rich Client in offline mode.

Our security rights will still be applied to the local reports that we will open but no export or import of new reports will be available.

A very common example would be a business user using his laptop from his home with no direct network access to the repository, but he will still be able to work on his report locally and continue analyzing the data in it.

Once we open a report, we can apply the entire functionality we already explored in our previous chapters to it and work in the same mode of reporting and analysis. The interface is the same, so there is no need to learn a new BI tool.

When we save a report, we can either save it directly to the repository or locally to our computer as a .wid file; the second option only exists in the Rich Client mode.

These options are **Save As...** for the local file folder and **Save to Enterprise** for uploading a file to the repository to a private or public folder, as shown in the following screenshot:

When choosing the **Save As** option, we will get some additional saving options located at the right-middle part of the save document panel. I'll mention just the ones you can find only in the Web Rich Client:

▸ **Save for all users**: This option is used when we need to transfer the report across different repositories and in order that the report will be recognized in another repository and we will be able to open it; this option has to be set. This option reminds a bit of the windows file security option when a file is coming from another computer and can be blocked unless we remove the block property. For example, we need to transfer a specific report manually from the development to the QA SAP BI environment.

▸ **Remove document security**: The report can be opened by any user even if its initial security was assigned only to a specific group in the CMC. This option can be useful when we need to share the report with users or groups from the same repository, but with security, that doesn't permit them to view the report.

The following screenshot shows the two options:

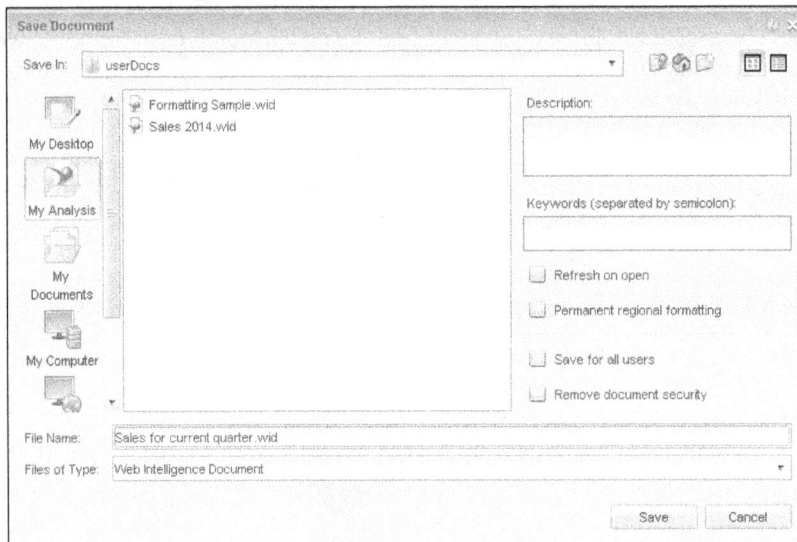

How it works...

As we saw, the Rich Client is pretty straightforward. It contains all the functionality that we use in Web Intelligence but behaves differently in terms of working mode possibilities and local save options.

There's more...

In the **Save As** window, we can also export the report to external files by clicking on the **My Desktop** option. This is one of the most important capabilities in Web Rich Client as well as in Web Intelligence in exporting the data to an external format such as an Excel, PDF or txt file.

While most of the reporting and analysis should be made in the Web Intelligence environment, we can't avoid working with the Excel file or exporting the data to PDF format as some functionality requires to be performed in other ways.

Exporting the data to external formats can be caused for the following reasons:

> ▸ The data consumer requires a static format such as PDF that can be sent to external users and non-SAP BI users and for presentation and reporting uses

> ▸ We require to transfer data to a business partner in a way he can analyze and apply functionality to such as an Excel file

> ▸ We have a target audience in our organization which are Excel experts and they require the Excel unique functionality such as statistical functions as well as formatting the results in a custom look and feel for their departmental requirements

Working with local data providers

One of the greatest options Web Intelligence Rich Client holds is the ability to work with local data providers such as Excel and text files regardless of whether we have the SAP BI server environment. This option of using Excel can be also found in the latest version of SAP BI4 (from SP2), but it's extremely useful as we actually work locally with local files.

This option is great when we require analyzing or using external data sources that are not stored in our main database or data warehouse.

We have already demonstrated in *Chapter 8, Merging Data*, that we can use local and external data providers as well; the main difference in our next example would be that we will be using a local text file in offline mode without actually connecting to the repository.

Getting ready

We want to analyze our local text file containing sales figures of sales persons; this data will be transformed into a Web Intelligence document to be shared with the rest of the sales team members.

How to do it...

In the left-hand side new document panel, we will choose the **Text** option as our data source. In the next dialog box, we will be able to browse the text file:

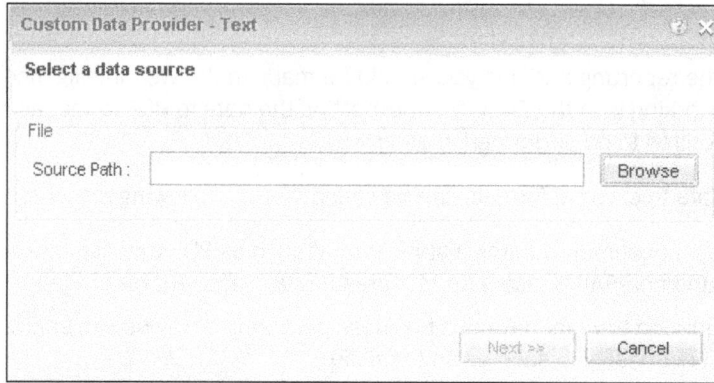

Now, we will actually choose the file located under the My Documents folder, the data-set text file, and import its data to our new Web Intelligence report:

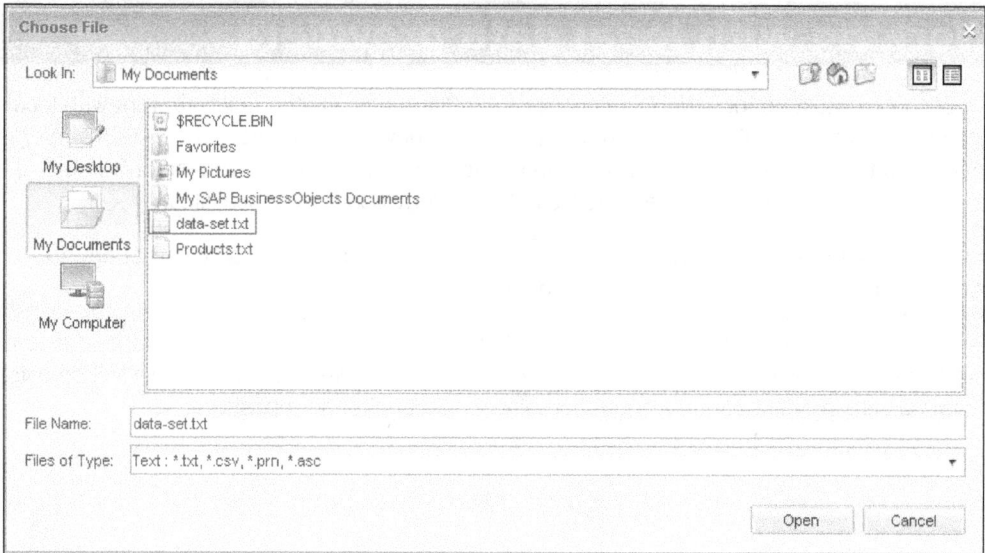

On the next screen, we can adjust and define the data parameters; similar to Excel when importing a text file, we can define the text delimiter and the type of data separator. Also, if we need to support a specific character set and locale, we can adjust the locale, character set, and date format located at the bottom right-hand side of the dialog box:

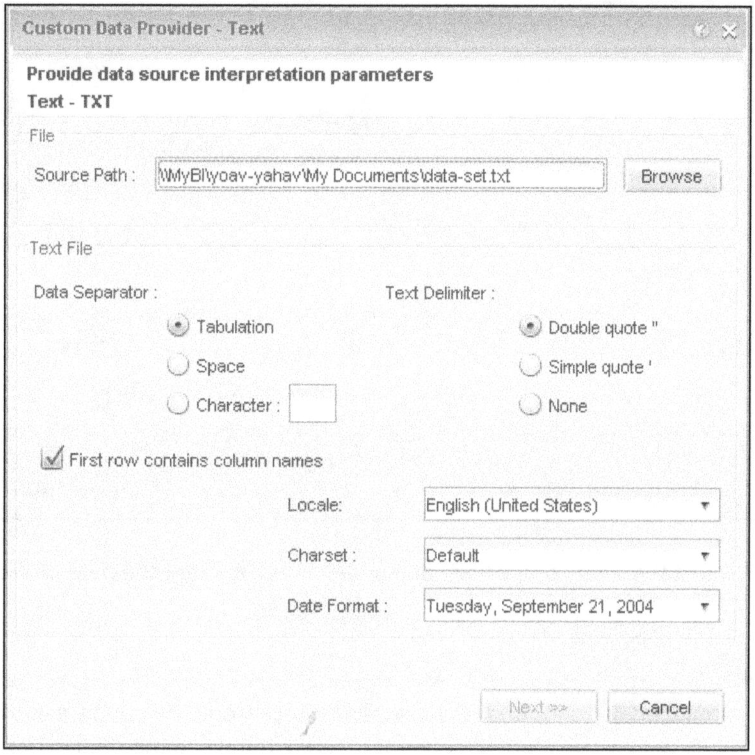

Notice that the **First row contains column names** option is checked by default if the data holds column names as well.

By clicking on **Next**, we will import the file content directly to the **Query Panel** and the report will be ready to be executed:

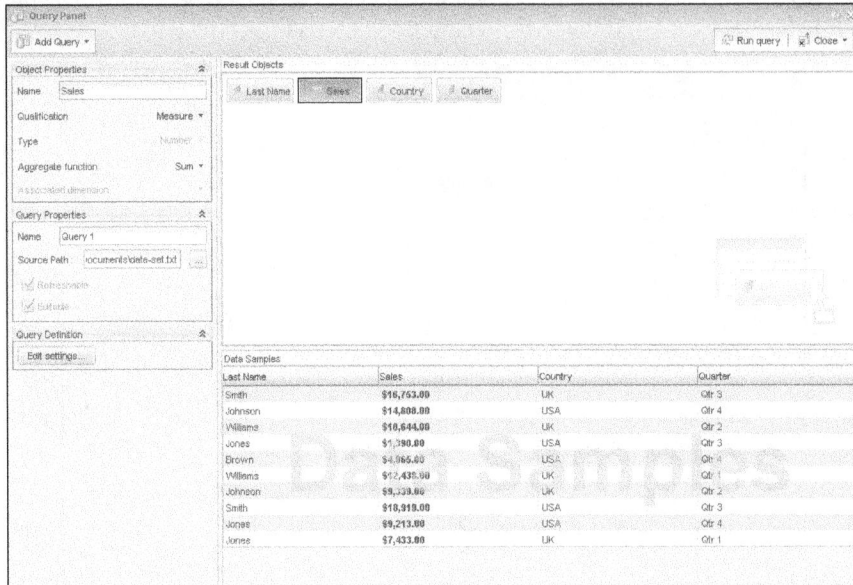

Here, we can adjust the query properties, object definition, and get the data preview as well.

How it works...

Once the file is mapped, we can run the query, the text file would be our data source that can be dynamic as well, which means if the data stored in the file, the data in the report will change accordingly after each refresh, as shown:

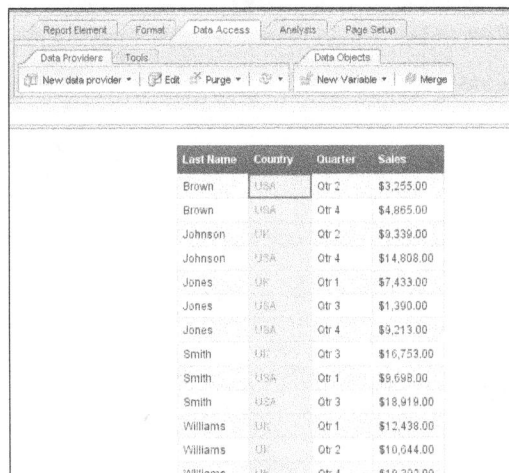

There's more...

In order to make the text file data accessible and refreshable for the rest of the business users, the file must be located in a common network drive (UNC naming convention, which is the folder path format that starts with `:\\Folder\\file`) so that all of the users have reading rights to that folder.

See also

▸ For further reading on how to adjust and define the query if we are using local data providers, see the *Merging data from different data sources* recipe in *Chapter 8, Merging Data*

Adjusting options

We can also set the preferences of the Web Intelligence Rich Client and fit them to our location, time zone, and use some advanced settings such as drill and proxy options.

Getting ready

Through the top-right corner, we will click on the **Tools** button and navigate to **Options...**, as shown in the following screenshot:

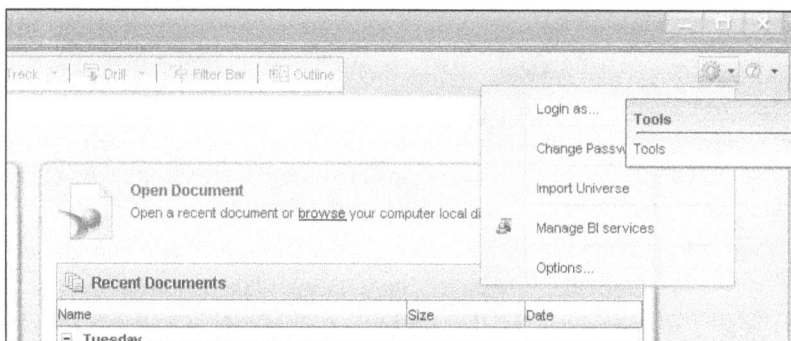

In the **Options** dialog box, we can find five preference categories that we can adjust and edit according to our requirements:

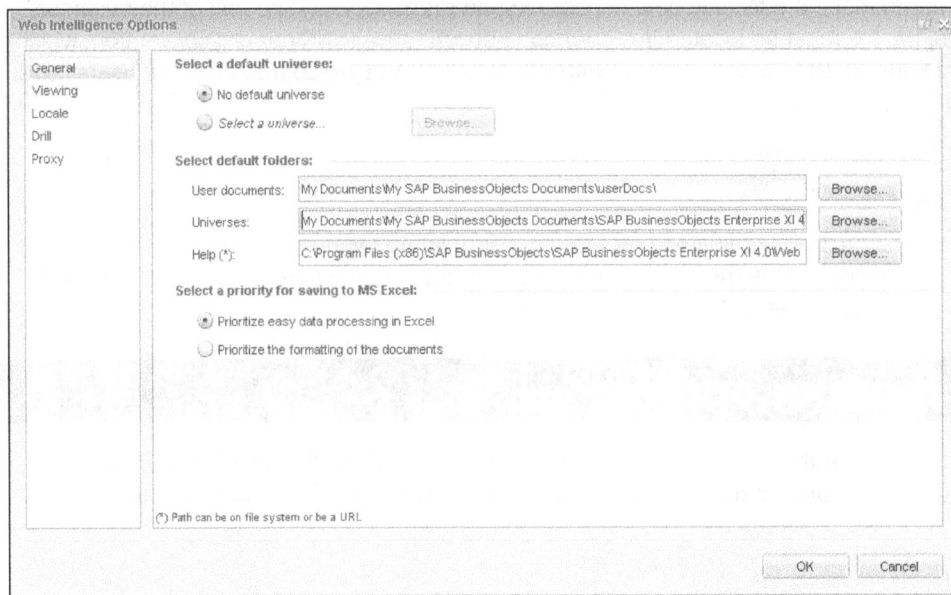

How to do it...

Let's explore the first option:

- ▶ **General**: Here, we can define a default universe and set the default folder location for our report documents, universes, and the help guide. When working in offline mode, our universe security rights as well as our general security rights are still taken into consideration and the fact that universes are stored locally enable us to continue working with the reports and create, edit, and refresh them.

- ▶ **Viewing**: The viewing preferences is an option I hardly ever use and it enables us to define the grid option in the background of the report along with the grid spacing. Although we have the align feature, when working with grid you can locate them easier.

- ▶ **Locale**: We can adjust the product and the view locales as well. The product locale can certainly be useful if we need to view menu items and the text on the buttons and toolbars in our locale. The view locale is very important when we need the data in our reports to be displayed properly such as date format or the number format. We can also set the document locale definitions to use the document definitions or our local definitions defined in the Web Rich Client. This option requires restarting Web Intelligence and closing and reopening the specific report we have applied our locale to so that the changes will take effect.

- ▶ **Drill**: Here, we can find some advanced and extended options of the drill:

  - ❏ **Start Drill session**: This defines whether the drill will start on the existing report or on an the report tab duplication.

  - ❏ **Prompt when drill requires additional data option**: If we need to drill further using an object that was not fetched in the first time the query ran, then we will be prompted so that if the query takes a long time to run, we can choose and understand the consequences of that action before it's taken.

  - ❏ **Synchronize drill on report blocks**: If we have several tables and/or charts that we require to perform drill on all of them, then this option will enable us to respond to common cases such as a table and a chart both being drilled simultaneously.

  - ❏ **Hide drill toolbar on start-up**: If we don't need the **Drill** toolbar to appear along with the drill filtered values in the table, we can hide this toolbar that is usually very effective and important when performing a drill; so we can say this is a less useful option for drill.

- ▶ **Proxy**: This is an advanced and a more rare option fitted to cases when we use URLs and web images in our reports. The proxy definitions can be found in the Internet browser definitions or can be supplied from our system or SAP BusinessObjects administrator.

See also

- ▶ For further reading on how to use the drill, refer to *Chapter 11, Using Drill*

Index

[PACKT] enterprise

PUBLISHING

professional expertise distilled

Thank you for buying
SAP BusinessObjects
Reporting Cookbook

About Packt Publishing

Packt, pronounced 'packed', published its first book "*Mastering phpMyAdmin for Effective MySQL Management*" in April 2004 and subsequently continued to specialize in publishing highly focused books on specific technologies and solutions.

Our books and publications share the experiences of your fellow IT professionals in adapting and customizing today's systems, applications, and frameworks. Our solution-based books give you the knowledge and power to customize the software and technologies you're using to get the job done. Packt books are more specific and less general than the IT books you have seen in the past. Our unique business model allows us to bring you more focused information, giving you more of what you need to know, and less of what you don't.

Packt is a modern, yet unique publishing company, which focuses on producing quality, cutting-edge books for communities of developers, administrators, and newbies alike. For more information, please visit our website: www.PacktPub.com.

About Packt Enterprise

In 2010, Packt launched two new brands, Packt Enterprise and Packt Open Source, in order to continue its focus on specialization. This book is part of the Packt Enterprise brand, home to books published on enterprise software – software created by major vendors, including (but not limited to) IBM, Microsoft and Oracle, often for use in other corporations. Its titles will offer information relevant to a range of users of this software, including administrators, developers, architects, and end users.

Writing for Packt

We welcome all inquiries from people who are interested in authoring. Book proposals should be sent to author@packtpub.com. If your book idea is still at an early stage and you would like to discuss it first before writing a formal book proposal, contact us; one of our commissioning editors will get in touch with you.

We're not just looking for published authors; if you have strong technical skills but no writing experience, our experienced editors can help you develop a writing career, or simply get some additional reward for your expertise.

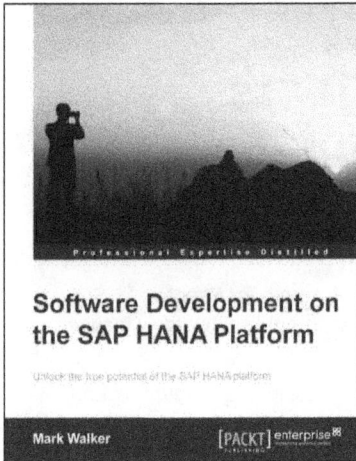

Software Development on the SAP HANA Platform

ISBN: 978-1-84968-940-3   Paperback: 328 pages

Unlock the true potential of the SAP HANA platform

1. Learn SAP HANA from an expert.

2. Go from installation and setup to running your own processes in a matter of hours.

3. Cover all the advanced implementations of SAP HANA to help you truly become a HANA master.

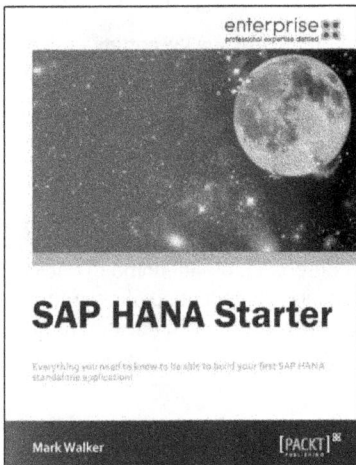

Instant SAP HANA Starter

ISBN: 978-1-84968-868-0   Paperback: 66 pages

Everything you need to know to be able to build your first SAP HANA standalone application!

1. Learn something new in an Instant! A short, fast, focused guide delivering immediate results.

2. Understand key principles behind SAP HANA.

3. Discover the main features of the SAP HANA Studio for application design.

4. Create a reporting application on the SAP HANA platform.

5. Visualize your reporting data in Microsoft Excel.

Please check **www.PacktPub.com** for information on our titles

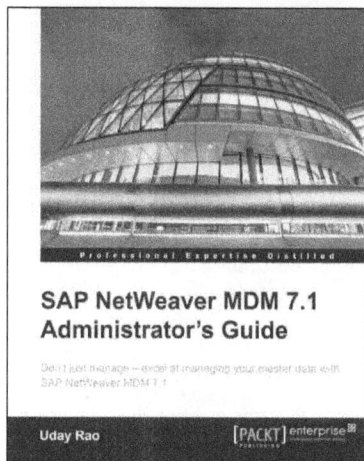

SAP NetWeaver MDM 7.1 Administrator's Guide

ISBN: 978-1-84968-214-5   Paperback: 336 pages

Don't just manage – excel at managing your master data with SAP NetWeaver MDM 7.1

1. Written in an easy-to-follow manner, and in simple language.

2. Step-by-step procedures that take you from basic to advanced administration of SAP MDM in no time.

3. Learn various techniques for effectively managing master data using SAP MDM 7.1 with illustrative screenshots.

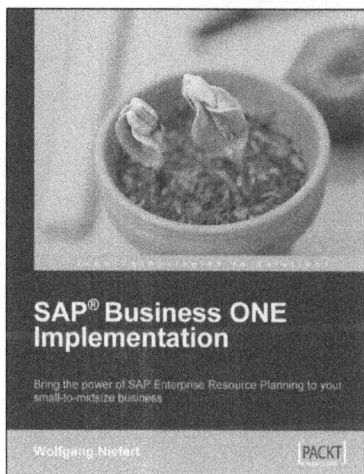

SAP NetWeaver MDM 7.1 Administrator's Guide

Don't just manage – excel at managing your master data with SAP NetWeaver MDM 7.1

Uday Rao   [PACKT] enterprise

SAP® Business ONE Implementation

ISBN: 978-1-84719-638-5   Paperback: 320 pages

Bring the power of SAP Enterprise Resource Planning to your small-to-midsize business

1. Get SAP B1 up and running quickly, optimize your business, inventory, and manage your warehouse.

2. Understand how to run reports and take advantage of real-time information.

3. Complete an express implementation from start to finish.

4. Real-world examples with step-by-step explanations.

SAP® Business ONE Implementation

Bring the power of SAP Enterprise Resource Planning to your small-to-midsize business

Wolfgang Niefert   PACKT

Please check **www.PacktPub.com** for information on our titles